SECESSION AS AN INTERNATIONAL PHENOMENON

SECESSION AS AN INTERNATIONAL PHENOMENON

From America's Civil War

to Contemporary Separatist Movements

EDITED BY

DON H. DOYLE

The University of Georgia Press
Athens and London

© 2010 by the University of Georgia Press
Athens, Georgia 30602
www.ugapress.org
All rights reserved
Designed by Walton Harris
Set in 10/14 Minion Pro by Graphic Composition, Inc.
Printed digitally in the United States of America

Library of Congress Cataloging-in-Publication Data
Secession as an international phenomenon : from America's Civil War to contemporary separatist
movements / edited by Don H. Doyle.

    p. cm.

  Includes bibliographical references and index

  ISBN-13: 978-0-8203-3008-2 (hardcover : alk. paper)

  ISBN-10: 0-8203-3008-6 (hardcover : alk. paper)

  ISBN-13: 978-0-8203-3712-8 (pbk. : alk. paper)

  ISBN-10: 0-8203-3712-9 (pbk. : alk. paper)

  1. Separatist movements—History. 2. Secession—History. 3. Secession—Southern States.
4. Nationalism—History. 5. World politics—19th century. 6. World politics—20th century.
7. World politics—21st century. I. Doyle, Don Harrison, 1946–

  D359.7.S43 2010

  341.26—dc22

2010009553

British Library Cataloging-in-Publication Data available

CONTENTS

ACKNOWLEDGMENTS

I am very grateful to a multitude of institutions and individuals for bringing to fruition what had begun as a dream a few years ago. This project was generously supported by the University of South Carolina, which became my new academic home in 2004. It began with vital seed money from a grant by the Office of the Provost, Research and Productive Scholar Grant program. Two chairs of the Department of History, Pat Maney and Lacy Ford, have been extraordinarily cooperative in allowing me occasional release time from teaching to pursue this project. The Walker Institute of International and Area Studies provided a home for the Association for Research on Ethnicity and Nationalism in the Americas (ARENA), and Gordon Smith, the Walker Institute's director, and Maria Anastosiou and Sallie Buice, administrative assistants, have been very helpful with the administration of grants and local arrangements. In addition, I am most grateful for additional financial support from the University of South Carolina's Institute for Southern Studies and its director, Walter Edgar. My former colleague, Karl Gerth, was most helpful in arranging a generous grant from the Taipei Cultural Foundation in support of our conference, and I thank him and the foundation for their support.

A major share of the funding for this project came from the National Endowment for the Humanities. Joel Schwartz and Elizabeth Arndt in NEH's Collaborative Research Division were very helpful to me from start to finish. I am also grateful to the Watson-Brown Foundation and Tad Brown, its president, for their valuable support of this project, particularly for their sponsorship of the authors' workshop that took place at their magnificent facility, the T. R. R. Cobb House in Athens, Georgia. Sam Thomas and his able staff made us feel welcome and kept us well fed during nearly three days of intensive and very productive work.

Nancy Grayson, editor in chief of the University of Georgia Press, has been a stalwart supporter of this project and of ARENA's mission in collaborative, international scholarship. I am grateful to her and the entire staff of the press for the effort they put into producing a fine-quality book of essays.

Thanks also to the graduate students at the University of South Carolina who helped on this project: Ann Tucker, Justin Liles, Josh Burgess, and Michael Woods for all their help with the conference. Thanks to David Prior for his expert work on the index. Above all, thanks goes to Eric Rose who from the outset served as a valuable assistant to this project.

Finally, my sincere thanks to all the authors of this volume, who proved unusually congenial toward one another and sympathetic with the spirit of this project, which was to bring scholars together across academic and national boundaries. They took seriously the task of criticizing one another's essays, worked diligently at revising their essays in response to those criticisms, and, in an achievement that is more than any editor could possibly wish for, they met their deadlines.

Columbia, South Carolina

DON H. DOYLE

Introduction

Union and Secession in the Family of Nations

Secession has left a bloody trail that runs through nearly every part of the globe. The very word "secession" is fraught with contested meaning. The term has been deliberately employed by its proponents to connote peaceful and legitimate withdrawal from an existing state and by its opponents to connote treasonous rebellion interfering with the unity of a state.

"Treason doth never prosper: what's the reason?" James Harrington asked in the 1590s. "Why if it prosper, none dare call it treason." Win a war for independence, and the leaders become founding fathers after whom cities, mountains, and holidays are named; lose the fight, and they might well be branded traitors and rebels and end with their heads on pikes as a warning to others. Rebels and founding fathers seem to be distinguished by their military fortunes rather than by the virtues of their claims to nationhood.

Though the authors of the present volume carry no banners for any particular cause, save that of reason and peace, they are dealing with a subject rarely governed by either. Our goal, nonetheless, is to examine secession as an international phenomenon with a long and complex history and to make some sense of it.

Let's begin with the word "secession," which has its origins in ancient Rome. The Latin term *secessio* referred to the temporary migration of the plebes outside of Rome, an act of peaceful protest intended to coerce the patrician rulers into redressing grievances. It was only in the nineteenth century, once states began defining territory and citizenry with more precision, that secession came to mean a more permanent separation, usually from a nation-state or other political alliance, though it was also used to describe withdrawal from a church or other nonpolitical organization.

It is, of course, the political meaning related to the breakup of nation-states that intrigues us here. When one nation *cedes* territory to another, the former surrenders all claim to the land as well as all jurisdiction over the inhabitants who remain in the ceded territory. When a territory and its inhabitants *secede*, however, they not only withdraw their allegiance to the nation but also—and here is the rub—separate from it, abolish the former government, and set up a new independent state. To put this another way, whereas the seceding Romans migrated temporarily away from the center of power, modern nationalism has the effect of making political borders do the moving.[1]

The modern nation-state, which took form first in Europe and the Americas after the American and French revolutions, is a polity whose borders and citizens are much more precisely demarcated than those of the political entities that preceded it. Government powers to tax or conscript, as well as government services such as schooling the young, delivering mail, building railroads, and the like, grew vastly under the auspices of the modern nation-state. Not least of the products of the modern age of nations have been nationalist ideologies asserting that states embody the collective will of the people. The nationalist premise that "we are a distinctive people" and the conclusion that therefore "we must have a state of our own" opens the door to new, more particular demands by self-identified "peoples" within an existing nation for their own sovereignty. Nationalism and separatism have always been close cousins, both supporting and bedeviling one another.

Nowhere is this more evident than in the history of the United States, the plot of which centers on the victory of one separatist movement and the defeat of another. For reasons I explain below, it is the second event, America's secession crisis and Civil War, that serves as an important historical benchmark for the essays in this volume. The idea of secession as a peaceful, legitimate withdrawal, as opposed to an aggressive act of rebellion and revolution, was crucial to separatists in the American South, who in 1860–61 made deliberate use of the term "secession" to describe what they were about. It was their goal to demonstrate to their own constituents, to the North, and to the world of nations that they were withdrawing peacefully for just cause, duly declared, from a union they had joined earlier with the purpose of creating a new, independent state. The favorite model among southern secessionists was the very nation they were leaving, and the Declaration of Independence became the template for their own declarations of secession.

Their northern opponents were just as determined to brand the South's separatist leaders as rebels defying federal authority and therefore committing high treason. The United States of America was a perpetual union, not, as Francis Lieber put it, "a political picnic to which the invited guest may go and carry his share of the viands or not, as he thinks fit, or the humor may move him."[2] There were no legitimate grounds for secession under the Constitution, Unionists insisted. No nation, they argued further, and certainly not a democratic republic, could operate if it was constantly threatened by the possibility of groups seceding anytime they did not like the outcome of an election or some act of legislation.

The American secession crisis, along with many others around the world over the next century and a half, would be decided not by debate or law but by force of arms. Underlying the recent discussion of secession—particularly among philosophers, political theorists, and legal scholars—has been an understandable desire to take the question off the battlefields and put it onto the negotiating tables. Political boundaries might be redrawn according to reason, ethical evaluation of claims, and a process of deliberation guided by international law rather than with blood and bullets. This new approach to secession, which emerged in the 1990s, refers to it as "political divorce" and urges us to rethink our old assumptions about permanent unions. Peaceful secession might provide a rational means of ending irreconcilable differences that come to light in "marriages" that were arranged by imperial rulers or forced by circumstances that have changed over time. Today's separatist turmoil in parts of Africa, Asia, Eastern Europe, and the Middle East, as we learn from the essays that follow, very often stems from ethnic and religious conflict within states established by imperial edict rather than popular will. The hope is that we might allow for amicable political divorce that does not require opposing parties to prove fault and win their case through costly, violent battles that often leave open wounds and deep scars.

This endeavor to normalize secession and subject it to the rule of law is neither naïve nor implausible, but it does go up against a long, gruesome history of warfare and terrorist violence. Nations and empires have not readily given up their claims on territory, people, and resources, and separatist movements over time have been grittily determined in their purpose and have proven hostile to compromise or appeasement.

The current approach to the breakup of nations as something normal and negotiable has been informed by a new understanding of the origins of nations and nationalism. Since the 1980s we have come to view the nation-state as a modern invention rather than as the natural product of essentialist human identities with deep historical roots in the territory. Nations are "imagined communities" based on "invented traditions," according to current interpretation.[3] Modern nations typically identify their origin in a struggle to liberate their people from unjust—often foreign—rule and to unify their territory and people under the banner of a single national community. Nationalist narratives usually cast the creation of the nation-state as the predestined culmination of a historic struggle for independence and unity. Once the foundation myth is rooted in history and memory, nations typically promote as given the idea that they are fixed, permanent entities. Any challenge to a nation's sovereignty and unity, either from within or without, is immediately seen as a hostile threat to its historic right to exist.

Still, even if these historical narratives used to justify nationhood are invented, it is difficult to imagine any nation-state presenting itself as a transient, temporary arrangement that it intends to dissolve in the future. Nor are we prepared to countenance a world order based on treaties, constitutions, currencies, and the like that are represented as being impermanent and subject to revision. One of the main functions of nationalism is to project a future of solidarity and sovereignty without end.

Of course, history has upset these presumptions of national perpetuity time and again. When we look back over the long and bloody history of separatist rebellions and civil wars, we realize that those imagined destinies of eternal unity were, as often as not, fantasies and that the unions formed out of those rebellions were doomed to fragmentation. Some nation-states break up because of deep, smoldering differences of language or religion or competition over natural resources within their borders. Many others come apart over what may seem in retrospect to be more transient, even accidental, conflicts of interests, policies, and leadership. Political divorce has rarely been predicted out loud at the wedding, and even more rarely has it been amicable; but by now it has certainly become commonplace if not altogether normal.

Indeed, today's family of nations owes its membership as often to divorce as to perpetual union. About half of the 192 (and counting) members of the UN can be said to have originated in breakaway states. And most of the 51 charter members of the UN in 1945 came into existence through imperial or national fragmentation. As this book goes to press, there are signs that the political divorce rate is rising.[4]

In the 1990s, after the Cold War had come to an end, dozens of separatist movements, suddenly and contagiously it seemed, burst forth on the world scene. Some called for autonomy and multiculturalism within the nation, while others argued that separate nationhood was the only remedy for their oppression. The collapse of the former Soviet Union spurred an understandable impulse among satellite nations to regain a measure of independence and at the same time encouraged long-suppressed ethnic minorities within states to embrace what Michael Ignatieff described as a particularly virulent form of "new nationalism" in the post-Soviet era.[5] Similar ethnic, religious, and postimperial tensions erupted in many of younger nations of Asia and Africa where the disintegration of European empires had left behind postcolonial independent states but not always well-integrated national communities.

Less predictable was the contagion of separatist movements within economically advanced Western nations. The Scots and Welsh in Great Britain, the Basque and Catalans in Spain, the Northern League in Italy, and the Québécois in Canada were among the more prominent examples from scattered Western democracies, but there were dozens more small separatist movements in nearly every corner of the world calling for some form of autonomy or independence. Some national governments responded with conciliatory offers of multicultural autonomy and devolution of powers to minorities within the nation. But for every rebellion that was peacefully resolved there were many others that were met by force.

I remember my first real encounter with the new secessionist spirit. It was the spring of 1995 in Italy, where I was happily serving as a Fulbright professor teaching American history to students in Genoa. The Northern League (Lega Nord), a northern Italian separatist movement, and its bellicose leader, Umberto Bossi, had suddenly gained visibility, and the news was full of Bossi's denunciations of the South and calls for the secession of northern Italy. While I was teaching the history of America's own secession crisis, my Italian students were very curious about why, if there was such hostility in the North toward the South, the North decided to engage in bloody and violent war to keep the nation whole? Their questions started me thinking about separatism, secession, and nationalism as international phenomena.

My interest has been intensified by my fascination with the American South; it is both the subject of my historical research and the place I have lived about half my life. When I moved to the University of South Carolina in 2004, I immediately began laying plans for this project, for few places in the world offer a more stimulating vantage point from which to consider secession. Not only did South Carolina lead the parade of eleven states out of the United States in 1860; it was also among the thirteen colonies that seceded from the British Empire in 1776.

The American Civil War occupies a central place in this book, and not simply because it was the first and bloodiest war over secession in its time. America's Civil War gave the world an alarming preview of both the possibility for national disintegration and the astonishing compulsion of modern nations to resist fragmentation.

Our book began at a conference in Charleston, South Carolina, in December 2007. It took place not far from where South Carolina politicians met in December 1860 amid great jubilation to declare their intention to withdraw from the United States of America. We met in a hotel that occupies the original building of the Citadel. In April 1861, the cadets of this military academy fired on the *Star of the West*, the Union ship sent to resupply Fort Sumter, which guarded Charleston Harbor. In front of the hotel, a statue of John C. Calhoun, the prophet of southern secession, looms high above Marion Square.

Our group took a boat ride out to Fort Sumter on the last afternoon of the conference. As the sun set, we listened to Richard Hatcher, a National Park Service historian, give a riveting account of the day the Civil War began. It had been on a similar day in April 1861 that the citizens of Charleston had gathered on rooftops to witness the beginning of a long and horrendous civil war. They cheered and paraded; no one understood what was coming, but these events set off the deadliest conflict over secession in modern history. More than six hundred thousand men died in the American Civil War, about 2 percent of the total population, which relative to the size of the U.S. population today would amount to six million casualties. It was the bloodiest conflict between the Napoleonic Wars and World War I, at least in the Western world (China's Taiping Rebellion dwarfs all other wars in carnage). For a century, until the 1960s when Biafra tried to separate from Nigeria in a horrific bloodbath that cost over a million lives, the American Civil War stood as history's most deadly war over secession. How many lives have been lost in conflicts over the separation of peoples and territories is difficult to determine, but suffice it to say that separatism has been among the leading causes of warfare in our times. This book and its authors have no collective position on the right to secede, but a grave sense of the human cost involved in the making and unmaking of modern nation-states runs through all the essays.

So it was that Charleston, South Carolina, became the unlikely scene of a gathering of amiable academics on a mission to bring reason and impassioned historical perspective to the inflammatory subject of secession. Our goal was to bring scholars with different approaches and specialized knowledge together, to foster conversation and learning across what are often formidable academic boundaries. The conversation that took place in Charleston, and in a subsequent workshop in Athens, Georgia, was lively, probing, and often critical but always in the spirit of the collaborative enterprise we had joined. Indeed, it was remarkable that a group of academics devoted to the study of irreconcilable hatred, distrust, and violence could be so congenial with one another.

This book came out of a project sponsored by ARENA, the Association for Research on Ethnicity and Nationalism in the Americas, a network of scholars founded in 2002 by a group of historians from the United States, Latin America, and Europe who shared an interest in the forces that unite and divide nations, especially but not exclusively in the Americas. Our first project produced a book of essays titled *Nationalism in the New World*, coedited by myself and Marco Pamplona and published by University of Georgia Press in 2006. It aimed at "Americanizing the conversation on nationalism," by which we meant to bring the Western Hemisphere to bear on a heavily European concern. The present volume is conceived in the same spirit; it seeks to expand the conversation on one particular aspect of nationalism, separatism and secession, and to situate the American experience within an enlarged historical and international framework.

Most of us who have contributed to the present volume specialize in one slice of geographic space or one moment of historical time, and we often pay too little attention to the broader significance of our particular area of human experience. Historians typically take one national case study at a time, closely heeding historical context and causation, but they are often skeptical when it comes to broad generalizations and theory. Social scientists, in contrast, seek to categorize the varied historical episodes of secession and use them to build theories capable of explaining the nature of separatism and secession in the present day. Philosophers, as Christopher Wellman puckishly told us, operate in a "fact-free world" and care less about explaining the actual world than they do about examining the ethical principles underlying human behavior. Legal scholars, in turn, are most interested in matters of fact and law, in the constitutional principles that govern societies, and in the international laws that govern relations between nations.

During the 1990s, as secessionist movements were appearing all over the globe, it was philosophers who took up the ethics of secession, while legal scholars and political theorists considered how constitutions and international law ought to cope with secession in the modern world. Philosopher Allen Buchanan's 1991 book, *Secession: The Morality of Political Divorce from Fort Sumter to Lithuania and Quebec*, sought to define the ethical grounds of secession; more than any other book, this set the course of the new debate over secession. As philosophers worked toward developing a normative theory for the morality of secession, legal scholars debated how international and constitutional law might accommodate legitimate claims to independence. The main thrust of the new conversation on secession has been to detach the question of the right to secede from the passions of nationalism and force of armed might. What are the ethical foundations of claims to national division or unity? What is the moral basis of the right to secession? On what moral grounds can a nation deny secession? And how should constitutions and international law accommodate these competing rights?[6]

One response to these questions supports what is known as just cause theory, which argues that the nation-state has an obligation to protect basic human rights and that any group denied those rights has a justifiable right to secede. This is a historic tradition that goes back to the American Revolution and, before then, to Enlightenment ideas concerning natural rights, government as a social contract that protects those rights, and the ultimate right to revolution should government fail to protect the rights of its citizens. In what was arguably the first modern declaration of secession, Thomas Jefferson noted that "governments long established should not be changed for light and transient causes." He set forth evidence of a "long train of abuses and usurpations" as well as a history of protests and petitions for redress, all to no avail, leaving the thirteen colonies with no recourse except to declare their independence. At the heart of the American Declaration of Independence was the basic assumption that grievances must be both numerous and long endured in order to legitimate a drastic measure like separation. Independence was a remedy of last resort to the prolonged abuse of basic human rights. Thus, the American Declaration of Independence advanced the classic just cause theory of the right to secede, and it was for this reason that it became a widely adopted model for other nations aspiring to independence.[7]

Another principle of secession known as choice theory insists on it as a fundamental right of any group, however defined, but without requiring a long history of injustice under the existing government. In practice, few separatist movements declare their intent to secede as a matter of whim, but many assert a preference for self-rule for its own sake, or they may claim separation is essential to avoid future injustice at the hands of the existing state. The southern Confederates came close to advocating this principle of secession as choice, for they argued first that they had a basic constitutional right to withdraw from the Union, that it was a voluntary compact into which they entered under terms that subsequently were breached. To their constitutional argument for the right to secede by choice they added grievances from the past, but they more often pointed to the future to justify secession.

At our conference in Charleston, Charles Lesser of the South Carolina Department of Archives and History displayed one of the few original prints of South Carolina's 1860 *Declaration of the Immediate Causes Which Induce and Justify the Secession of South Carolina from the Federal Union*. It was the first of several such declarations issued by several of the southern states, and it demands special attention because of its precedence and influence. It is especially interesting because it borrows both the language and logic of the 1776 declaration to support the fundamental right of the state to secede from the Union. Hence, it notes that "whenever any 'form of government becomes destructive of the ends for which it was established, it is the right of the people to alter or abolish it, and to institute a new government.'" The South Carolina declaration set forth a number of justifications for its action and provided historical evidence of violations of its rights as a member state in the Union. It amounted to a legal brief for breach of contract. That is, certain conditions provided for in the Constitution under which South Carolina agreed in 1788 to enter the Union had been violated in recent years, it claimed. All the grievances listed revolved around the threat to slavery. First among these was that fourteen northern states had refused to uphold the provision for returning fugitive slaves to their owners. The declaration went on to complain that these states have "denounced as sinful the institution of slavery." "For twenty-five years this agitation has been steadily increasing, until it has now secured to its aid the power of the common Government," and now the nonslaveholding states have elected to the presidency a man "whose opinions and purposes are hostile to slavery." The rest of the document shifts into future tense, predicting "a war on slavery" and the loss of self-government and self-protection. "All hope of remedy is rendered vain," the declaration concludes.[8]

The South Carolina declaration departed in at least two significant ways from the 1776 model: instead of dwelling on past grievances for justification, it *anticipated* injustice at the hands of an administration not yet in power, and all the state's grievances had to do with the right to perpetuate human slavery. Here again, the American Civil War provides a useful touchstone for our broader consideration of secession, for it returns us to the role of morality at the core of the debate over the right to secession and the right to deny secession. Other nations have long evaluated the moral and legal claims of groups claiming independence. Seceding nations usually depend on the recognition and aid of others in their struggle to exist, and while the material interests of other national powers in the outcome of a secession struggle were always vital to their support or lack thereof, the justification for independence was also crucial. Qualms about the morality of slavery were instrumental in the failure of the southern Confederacy to win international support, but not until Lincoln finally linked the Union cause to that of emancipation and undermined what had been significant international sympathy for the seceding states up to that point.[9]

Beyond the moral and legal questions about the right to secede are several vexing issues related to the impact of fragmentation on the larger world of nations. Even if we accept the principle of a people's right to secede based on just cause or choice, there are practical complications that accompany secession arising from the untidy diversity of human society, which rarely produces homogeneous peoples, let alone like-minded populations, within clearly defined territories. What happens to those individuals or groups within the seceding territory who, for whatever reason, do not want to be ruled by their neighbors? Shall they go the way of British loyalists during the American Revolution who fled to Canada? Or, worse, shall they be subject to the kind of ethnic cleansing, genocide, or repression we have seen in far too many recent examples of national fragmentation? If separation is the best or only real solution to injustice, we also must ask where does it all end?

One secession advocacy web site, Secession.net, promises to sustain "a worldwide Secession Network promoting the Right to Secede." Most of the world's wars and violence, it proposes, result from the simple fact that "at least 5,000 racial, ethnic, linguistic and cultural groups are lumped together into only 189 [now 192] nation states."[10] Five thousand sovereign states, each with their own passports, armies, treaties, trade regulations, and social policies: the implications are daunting to contemplate. There is another question that begs for an answer: do we really want a world of territorially homogeneous populations demarcated by their own nation-states, each "people" fixed in their proper place? Living among neighbors all alike sounds terribly boring, and it would require a static population that is hard to imagine amid the mass migration in today's world. No doubt, this imagined world is preferable to one full of angry minorities bombing one another's homes.

To those who propose secession as a universal solution, we must also ask whether a world of internally homogeneous and perhaps internally harmonious nations that were hostile to one another would produce a more peaceful world in the end. As Abraham Lincoln argued in 1861, secession does not really solve domestic disputes; it only makes them international: "A husband and wife may be divorced and go out of the presence and beyond the reach of each other, but the different parts of our country can not do this. They can not but remain face to face, and intercourse, either amicable or hostile, must continue between them." Lincoln anticipated political divorce as a metaphor for secession, and in doing so he prompted a frightening vision of a world of a thousand squabbling nations divorced from one another politically but still cohabitating territorially.

Our conference in Charleston and the essays in this book were not intended to produce a coherent response to the questions that surround secession. Our goal instead was to commence a fruitful conversation across boundaries of specialization, bringing together philosophers, historians, political theorists, and lawyers. We learned from each other, and though each essay takes its own approach to a specific topic, at some level each addresses the common concerns that motivated our project from the beginning.

The book opens with four broad treatments of the subject, which happen to represent the main disciplinary perspectives we brought together. Christopher Wellman offers a cogent review of the morality of secession that tells us how philosophers became interested in secession as a contemporary problem crying out for thoughtful theoretical discussion. He lays out the different theories on the right to secession and sets forth a defense of his own position, which is that secession ought to be a primary right or choice of any people so long as they do not compromise the fundamental obligation of the state to perform requisite political functions, the chief one of which is to protect human rights.

David Armitage answers this philosophical argument for a more rational and peaceful basis for secession with a stark reminder of the violent historical relationship between secession and civil war. Examining the two major separatist events in U.S. history, Armitage reveals how contested the very words "secession" and "civil war" were in the 1860s as well as during the American Revolution, which he describes as the "first American Civil War." The spread of nationalism, the incorporation of most of the earth's population within nation-states, Armitage argues, has at once stimulated secessionist movements and strengthened the will of existing states to suppress them. The essays by Wellman and Armitage introduce us to a basic tension reverberating through the entire discussion of secession between a minority's right to a state of its own and the existing nation's obligation to protect what is good for everyone within its borders.

The American secession crisis began with both sides invoking what may seem like a narrow language of legal rights before they started appealing to more lofty ideas about moral purpose and national destiny. In "Lincoln, the Constitution, and Secession," Peter Radan brings his legal knowledge to bear on Abraham Lincoln's case against secession. Lincoln was a sharp country lawyer with a good mind for legal argument, and he rested his case against secession on the lack of consent (in both the Union and the seceding states) and the absence of any moral cause for revolutionary secession. Radan cross-examines Lincoln's arguments and then reviews his case in light of contemporary law on the right to secede. Lincoln might have been glad not to have had to present his case to any formal court of international law, certainly not with Peter Radan as his adversary, for it comes up short in Radan's careful evaluation. This presents an interesting example of how the contemporary understanding of normative secession theory may challenge our accepted version of the past.

Margaret Moore has been among the leading voices in the recent debate over secession and the ethical basis of national boundaries. In her essay, "Ethics of Secession and Political Mobilization in Quebec," she makes use of the very interesting case of Canada and the separatist movement in Quebec to reexamine current theories on the right to secede. In this essay she succinctly lays out four leading theories in the current discussion of secession, which she refers to as the statist, just cause, choice, and collective autonomy theories, and at the same time uses these to evaluate the case for a separate Quebec.

Following these first four essays dealing broadly with the philosophy, history, and legal and political dimensions of the secession debate, part 2 of our volume turns to the American South and the violent resistance to its effort to secede. We pay particular attention to this moment in the history of secession for the same reason so many separatists and unionists have for the past century and a half: this was a crisis of great significance owing to its magnitude, its historical precedence as the modern world's first major conflict over secession, and its grave lessons on the human costs of separatism and union.

We venture into the psychology of separatism in Charles Dew's revealing microstudy of one South Carolina politician's turn from moderation to secession and the role that racial fears played in his thinking. Past events played an important role in Congressman Ashmore's radical move, but it was his anticipation of the breakdown of white supremacy following the election of the antislavery Republicans in 1860 that drove him toward secession.

Robert Bonner's essay, "Proslavery Calculations and the Value of Southern Disunion," examines the evolution of thought among southern slaveholders who questioned the material benefit of membership in the Union. Theirs was not an impulsive and irrational reaction to an election in 1860 but instead a long, deliberate process that led them to conclude that their regional interests outweighed loyalty to the Union. What southern secessionists did not and could not calculate was the unknown cost of war and the devastating price of defeat.

Susan-Mary Grant's essay analyzes the North's calculation of the value of the Union. Grant borrows the title of a widely read Civil War pamphlet to ask how a democratic nation carries out a civil war. Her essay questions what is now a taken-for-granted assumption: that the Union would fight a sustained war at great sacrifice over four years in order to preserve what had hitherto been an abstract concept of nationhood. We see in this remarkable study an expansion of nationalism as a response to separatism.

Confederates were busy expounding their own nationalism, as the next two essays portray. Paul Quigley's essay on "Secessionists in an Age of Secession" opens with the observation that we are not the first to consider secession as an international phenomenon. Confederates sought to situate their cause among the celebrated champions of national independence, especially those in Europe, that were struggling to throw off the yoke of tyranny and achieve independence. The effort to align the Confederate cause with liberal European nationalist movements presented complications at home, but the breakaway states hoped it would work to secure recognition and support abroad.

In addition to European liberal ideas of self-government and opposition to tyranny, a powerful strain of romanticism informed nineteenth-century nationalism as well. Frank Towers explores the southern affinity for romanticism and antimodernism and shows how this stream of nationalist ideology became incorporated into a defense of southern separatism.

For all the carnage of the American Civil War, separatist conflict was comparatively rare, and even more rarely successful among the new nations that
emerged in the Americas. But there were exceptional zones of turbulence on
the borders of cultural divides between Spanish America and Anglo-America
(the tension between French and Anglo-American cultures in Quebec and on
the fractious border between Portuguese and Spanish populations in the Rio del
Plata region of South America are also exceptions to the general rule). The next
two essays deal with less well-known separatist agitation in the Gulf of Mexico.
Mexico stands out among the newly independent nations of the Americas for
its fragmentation, losing the Central American Republics in 1824, Texas in 1836,
and all of northern Mexico in the war with the United States in 1848. The Texas
rebellion remains the only popular separatist movement in the Western Hemisphere that succeeded. But as Andrés Reséndez shows in his essay, the Texas
case was one of numerous separatist events that might have redrawn the map of
nations and empires in the entire Gulf of Mexico region. Terry Rugeley focuses
closely on one of the more notable separatist struggles in this region, that of the
Yucatán peninsula, which threatened to break off from Mexico between the Texas
revolt in 1835–36 and the end of the U.S.-Mexican War in 1848. The Yucatecan
rebellions illustrate the dynamics of a separatist movement whose differences
with the central state are confounded by divisions among its own members,
differences that, in the end, undermined the group's drive for independence.

The remaining essays in the book deal largely with recent separatist activities in Europe, the Middle East, and Africa. These regions all deserve far more
attention than space allows in this volume, but the several contributions we
have demonstrate that separatism and secession are international phenomena
that cut across all cultures, erupt in episodes of unpredictable intensity, and
seem to spread with contagious fury no matter what the peculiar ethnic and
historical circumstances are that give rise to these movements.

Bruno Coppieters reviews the myriad separatist movements that have
emerged in Europe in recent years, coinciding paradoxically with the integration of European countries under the auspices of the European Union. As we
learn, separatist movements often see the European Union as a protector of
local autonomy, not a threat to it.

Aleksandar Pavković takes up recent cases in four very different settings:
Slovenia, Kosovo, Chechnya, and Biafra. He returns us to the moral questions
about the ethics of secession (and the denial of the right to secede) with which
this book begins, particularly to the issues David Armitage raises in his discus-

sion of the historic connection between secession and civil war. Pavković asks the simple question whether violence and coercion are ever justified in the making or breaking of nation-states.

Paul Kubicek focuses on a region that has seen a lot of separatist activity in recent times: the former Soviet Union. He turns to a close examination of the logic of separatism within two states that formed after the fall of the Soviet empire: Moldava and Ukraine. Instead of seeing the fragmentation in this region as the natural result of long pent-up ethnonationalist desires among the population at large, Kubicek emphasizes the role of politics and political elites in setting the course toward separatism. He argues that political elites felt their voices went unheard in the former Soviet Union and appealed to secession as a means of redressing their lack of influence.

Stefan Zahlmann brings an interesting perspective to our discussion and returns us to the American South as an enduring international reference for secession. His subject is reunification and the memory of reconciliation in autobiographies by American southerners and East Germans. Though the historical situations of the two are vastly different, there are nevertheless strong grounds for comparison with respect to secession, and the relation between the American South and East Germany is a common theme in recent German thought. This essay focuses as no others in this volume do on the painful process of reunification.

Peter Sluglett takes up the Kurdish people, whose population extends into several nation-states, including Iraq, which is the main subject of his essay. Though Kurdistan has gained a certain level of autonomy, there is ongoing debate over various solutions to its current problems as an autonomous region within Iraq. Kurdistan has been much in the news of late, and it has provoked discussion about partition as a means of controlling ethnic and sectarian conflict within Iraq.

Africa may be the region most torn by separatist violence on the planet. Raphael Chijioke Njoku's essay surveys the postcolonial world in which African colonies became independent states after World War II but not unified national communities. The result has been ethnic, religious, and political conflict that groups have often sought to resolve through secession.

In Alan Wachman's essay on China we learn that the People's Republic of China has frequently invoked Abraham Lincoln in opposing Taiwan's desire for independence. Wachman takes issue with China's interpretation of Lincoln and the American situation, noting that politicians and states often attempt to use history to their own advantage. Wachman's essay demonstrates perfectly the underlying premises of this volume, that each instance of secession, whatever the particular circumstances that divide a country, may be understood as part of a much broader historical and international phenomenon that has shaped the modern era. Both the justifications for secession and the logic of resistance to it borrow from a common language of nationalism and separatism that has become embedded in the way we view the world of nations and their parts. The China-Taiwan story also returns us to one of the main purposes of this volume, which is to situate the American experience with secession and civil war within a broad international and historical context. For better and for worse, the American experience instead of being exceptional has often forecast the experience of other nations.

Notes

1. *Oxford English Dictionary*, "Secession," online edition, http://dictionary.oed.com.pallas2.tcl.sc.edu/entrance.dtl, accessed Oct. 4, 2009.

2. Francis Lieber, *What Is Our Constitution—League, Pact, or Government? Two Lectures on the Constitution of the United States . . . To Which is Appended an Address on Secession* (New York: Columbia College, 1861), 45.

3. Benedict Anderson, *Imagined Communities: Reflections on the Origin and Spread of Nationalism* (London: Verso, 1983); Eric Hobsbawm and Terence Ranger, eds., *The Invention of Tradition* (Cambridge: Cambridge University Press, 1983); Eric Hobsbawm, *Nations and Nationalism since 1780: Programme, Myth, and Reality* (Cambridge: Cambridge University Press, 1990).

4. These and other data on secession are nicely summarized in "Secession and Civil War," David Armitage's contribution to the present volume.

5. Michael Ignatieff, *Blood and Belonging: Journeys into the New Nationalism* (New York: Farrar, Straus and Giroux, 1995).

6. Allen Buchanan, "Secession," *Stanford Encyclopedia of Philosophy*, 2007, http://plato.stanford.edu/entries/secession, accessed May 12, 2009.

7. David Armitage, *The Declaration of Independence: A Global History* (Cambridge, Mass: Harvard University Press, 2007).

8. Charles H. Lesser, *Relic of the Lost Cause: The Story of South Carolina's Ordinance of Secession* (Columbia: South Carolina Department of Archives and History, 1996).

9. Howard Jones, *Abraham Lincoln and a New Birth of Freedom: The Union and Slavery in the Diplomacy of the Civil War* (Lincoln: University of Nebraska Press, 1999).

10. Secession.net, http://secession.net, accessed May 12, 2009.

PART 1

The Problem of Secession

CHRISTOPHER WELLMAN

The Morality of Secession

To say that philosophers did not write about the morality of secession until the 1990s is only a slight exaggeration. Considerable work had been done on the related subject of revolution, of course, and the social unrest of the 1960s provoked a great deal of thinking about civil disobedience, but the paucity of viable secessionist movements on the geopolitical landscape resulted in almost no one studying the morality of state breaking. This changed dramatically with the end of the Cold War, however, when the dissolution of the Soviet Union exposed the lack of theoretical work on secession as an embarrassing lacuna in political theory. Allen Buchanan did more than anyone else to fill this void with his landmark 1991 book, *Secession: The Morality of Political Divorce from Fort Sumter to Lithuania and Quebec.*[1] Buchanan has subsequently expanded on and revised his views, and the literature within political philosophy on this subject is largely a reaction to his seminal work. This essay provides an overview of the morality of secession before engaging with some of Buchanan's most recent work on this subject. In particular, after defending a relatively permissive right to secede, I argue that Buchanan has overestimated the case against reforming international law to allow for primary rights to secede.

SECESSION AND SELF-DETERMINATION

There are some notable exceptions, to be sure, but most political theorists who comment on state breaking belong to either of two camps, which we might label "statist" and "nationalist." Statists deny that there can be any unilateral rights to secede grounded in self-determination because secession necessarily involves taking territory from an existing state, and legitimate states enjoy a privileged position of moral dominion over their territory. The crucial point to appreciate, according to the statist, is that secessionist contests are conflicts over territory, so one cannot posit a secessionist right without thereby implying that the state has no right to retain its territorial boundaries.

Now, most people are willing to concede that a state may *forfeit* a portion of its territory if it treats its citizens sufficiently unjustly, but statists are quick to point out that this implies only a *remedial* right to secede, a secondary right to escape injustice. If a group had a right to secede grounded in self-determination, on the other hand, then (like a spouse in a jurisdiction that allows no-fault divorce) it would not need to suffer any abuse in order to have a right to secede. And if a group has been in no way treated unjustly, then it is hard to see how the state could have forfeited its sovereignty over any of its territory. Thus, statists conclude that since (1) legitimate states are morally entitled to their territory and (2) states retain this claim unless their citizens become the victims of injustice, there can be no primary right to secede grounded in self-determination. There can at most be a remedial right to secede in order to escape injustice.

Nationalists tend to differ from statists not only because they place more of a premium on group self-determination but also because they deny that states retain a valid claim to their territorial integrity as long as they do not act unjustly. There is a great deal of diversity among those I bundle under the label of "nationalists," of course, but many emphasize both that (1) a nation's health directly affects its members' welfare and that (2) political self-determination allows nations to bolster their health. Thus, nationalists have a special interest in group self-determination because they believe that individuals are best positioned to pursue rewarding projects and develop meaningful interpersonal relationships within the context of a healthy culture, and, they argue, a nation's chances of supplying such a healthy cultural context depend largely on its being free to order its own affairs.

In response to statists who insist that national groups have no right to demand that their self-determination be cashed out in the currency of their own sovereign nation-state, nationalists often point out not only that territorial boundaries are human constructions that can be redrawn but that they owe their current configuration to a series of violent conquests and morally dubious treaties. And if one agrees both that political states can be geographically realigned and that existing countries typically have no unimpeachable historical claim to the particular pieces of land they occupy, one is unlikely to regard the statist argument as insuperable. In the end, then, nationalists tend to be among the most enthusiastic about state breaking because they view existing political boundaries as negotiable, and they believe that giving each nation its own state makes for healthier nations, which, in turn, better positions these nations' members to lead rewarding lives.

Although I am sympathetic to the observations that motivate statists and nationalists, my views are importantly distinct from both. In particular, while I join the nationalists in valuing political self-determination, I agree with the statists that territory is the crucial issue. And because secessionist conflicts are essentially contests over who is entitled to exercise political jurisdiction over a portion of territory, it seems clear that we cannot have a principled and systematic theory of secession without first uncovering what justifies the existing state's claim to its territory. Explaining a state's dominion over its territory is a core project in political philosophy that has generated a variety of accounts. My own view, very roughly, is that political states are justified in coercing their constituents because peace and security are possible only when we all follow a single set of rules, and the only way for one set of rules to gain unanimous allegiance is if it is non-consensually imposed on all those who are territorially contiguous. To put this another way, states are functionally justified just in case they perform the requisite political function of adequately protecting the human rights of their constituents. Rogue and failed states have no claim to their territory, then, because the former are unwilling and the latter are unable to perform that function.

Insofar as my view helps explain why a legitimate state has a moral claim to its territory, statists are apt to applaud it. It is important to notice, though, that while my view suggests why a legitimate state's right to its territory would trump the claims of *external* parties, it does not similarly explain why the state's claim should take priority over all of those *within* its territory. So self-determination explains why Canadians, for example, need not defer to the United States when deciding how to govern Canada, but Canada as a whole cannot similarly invoke self-determination in a dispute with an internal province like Quebec. Imagine that Canada is engaged in two conflicts, one with the United States, who threatens to forcibly annex it, and another with Quebec, who wants to secede. On my view, because Canada is able and willing to perform the requisite political function of protecting its citizens' human rights, it can invoke self-determination to ground its claim that it ought not to be unilaterally annexed by the United States. In other words, if the United States forcibly annexed Canada, this would violate Canada's right to political self-determination. Canada cannot simply appeal to self-determination to justify denying Quebec's bid for political divorce, however, because most of Canada is external to Quebec, and thus Canada's ordering of Quebec's affairs would obviously not amount to *self*-determination.

This is not to say that Canada necessarily has no claim to the territory in Quebec; the point is merely that whatever claim it has vis-à-vis Quebec cannot be grounded in self-determination. In my view, a state can rightfully impose itself on a separatist territory if and only if this imposition is required to secure the benefits of political society, that is, if it is necessary to the state's performance of requisite political functions. Thus, whether or not Quebec has a unilateral right to secede depends on whether Quebec would be able to secure the benefits of political society on its own. Were Quebec able and willing to do so (and if the remainder state of Canada would also be left politically viable), then Canada's political coercion over Quebec would not be necessary, and thus Canada as a whole would not be justified in forcibly denying Quebec's right to political self-determination.

To emphasize: the right to political self-determination is not absolute, but a group's right to secede is ordinarily outweighed only if the separatist group is either unable or unwilling to procure the benefits afforded by political society. Thus, while statists are right that a legitimate state has a claim to its territory, they are wrong to suppose that this claim necessarily prevails over all others. As the preceding analysis indicates, a legitimate state can invoke self-determination to justify its territorial sovereignty over all *external* parties, but such a state must equally recognize the rights to self-determination of politically viable groups *within* its territory.

It is not difficult to see why a nationalist would welcome my response to statism. Because I question the statist's contention that legitimate states need only avoid injustice in order to retain an absolute right to territorial integrity, my view supports the nationalist's claim that nations may have a primary right to secede even from perfectly legitimate states. In particular, my account maintains that if a separatist nation can perform the requisite political functions, the existing state has no justification for its nonconsensual coercion. In other words, when a nation is sufficiently large, wealthy, politically organized, and territorially contiguous, it can secede and thereby enhance its national self-determination without jeopardizing political stability. But, while all of this is true, it is important to recognize that even if politically viable nations have a right to secede, those nations lacking the necessary political capabilities will not have a legitimate claim to independence, which suggests that a nation's cultural self-determination cannot ground a claim to independence. If this is so, then there is a sense in which a group's cultural status is beside the point; the crucial variable will be the separatists' ability to govern the contested territory in a safe and just manner. Of course, it may well be that most separatist groups are in fact motivated by nationalist aspirations, but those nations whose claims are legitimate will be justified by political capabilities, not their cultural attributes.

As should now be clear, my position is ultimately importantly distinct from both the statist's and the nationalist's. It diverges from statism in denying that legitimate states have an absolute right to retain their territorial boundaries as long as they do not treat their constituents unjustly, and it differs from the nationalist view by singling out a separatist group's political capacity (rather than its cultural characteristics) as the key feature that would accord it a primary right to secede. In the end, then, I recommend that a state restrict political liberty in a manner analogous to the way it limits the liberty to drive a car. Because many people would be harmed if there were no legal restrictions on who could drive, states legitimately limit drivers based on age, health, and competence. In similar fashion, a state may initially restrict the right to secede to groups of a specific size and then further require that interested parties demonstrate their ability and willingness to govern in a capable and just manner. This is a principled and systematic theory of secession that appropriately values self-determination without implausibly denying the crucial benefits of political stability.

It is important to recognize that if I am right about group self-determination grounding a primary right to secede, there is no reason to suppose that political divisions must occur neatly along the lines of existing administrative units. If a majority of Texans sought to form their own country, for instance, their territory would not need to be limited to the state of Texas. As Margaret Moore explains:

> In many cases, national minorities are correct to point out that administrative boundaries frequently have no moral basis themselves, or that they were often drawn in accordance with a moral or political conception that is irrelevant in the current political situation, or drawn by the central state in order to facilitate assimilation of the minority or its control by the dominant group. It is therefore hard to see why these boundaries should be cast in stone, as the only unit in which self-determination can take place.[2]

Extending Moore's point, I would add that a separatist group also need not be contained within only one host state. Thus, not only might a mere portion of Texas secede from the United States; a contiguous portion of Mexico might secede along with the separatist Texans. Admittedly, there may be cases in which secession should occur along administrative lines (when, for example, there are considerable political advantages to keeping the borders intact or when— as with General Lee and his affection for the state of Virginia—there happens to be substantial and widespread personal identification with the subfederal unit), but one key objective must be to create boundaries that are as responsive as possible to the preferences of constituents. Ensuring that the new states are politically viable will inevitably force us to shape the secessionist territory in a way that includes some unionists and excludes some separatists, but our goal should be for the states to include as many separatists and as few unionists as possible.

Theorists have traditionally shied away from this approach for fear that it is at best messy and at worst utterly confused. Critics delight in quoting W. Ivor Jennings's clever response: "On the surface it [self-determination] seemed reasonable: let the people decide. It was in fact ridiculous because the people cannot decide until somebody decides who are the people."[3] As Charles Beitz notes, however, there is no reason to think the problem is intractable: "One advantage of the view that the right of self-determination is derived from freedom of association is that it supplies a straightforward solution to this problem: the people should decide who the people are."[4] Harry Beran offers a blueprint for how this might be accomplished:

> If the issue of changing political borders arises in a polity, there is usually disagreement as to whether a change should be made. At the time of the breakup of the former Yugoslavia there was a majority in favour of secession from Yugoslavia in Croatia; but in the portion of Croatia known as Krajina, inhabited mostly by Serbs, there was a majority against secession. The reiterated use of the majority principle seems to be the only method of resolving such conflicts that is consistent with the voluntary association principle. According to this method, a separatist movement can call for a referendum, within a territory specified by it, to determine whether there should be a change in this territory's political status, e.g. whether it should secede from its state. If there is a majority in the territory as a whole for secession, then the territory's people may exercise its right of self-determination and secede. But there may be people within this territory who do not wish to be part of the newly independent state. They could show, by majority vote within their territory, that this is so, and then become independent in turn, or remain within the state from which the others wish to secede. This use of the majority prin-

ciple may be continued until it is applied to a single community (i.e. a community which is not composed of a number of communities) to determine its political status.[5]

As long as one takes care not to divide political states into units that are subsequently incapable of performing the requisite political functions, Beran's suggestion ought to work.

Many critics of secession fasten on the fact that even if every effort is made to draw the new territorial lines in a manner that maximally excludes those who oppose secession, there will inevitably be a minority of people (which, in theory, could be as high as 49 percent) who are forced against their will into a new state. It is tempting to conclude that this makes the secession unjust; after all, surely people have a right not to be deprived of citizenship by a vote of others, no matter whether remaining part of the existing state would put them in peril or not. I disagree that people have a right not to be deprived of citizenship. As long as political states remain territorially rather than consensually defined (as they must if they are to perform satisfactorily the functions that justify their coercive presence), then it will simply not be possible for everyone to enjoy complete discretion regarding their citizenship. The best that we can reasonably hope for, therefore, is the more modest goal of giving citizens the maximal say in drawing political borders consistent with maintaining viable, territorially defined states. The way to do this is to allow all and only those secessions that leave the separatists and the divorced party politically viable. What is more, those who protest that this would allow a majority to place a minority in a dispreferred political situation would do well to note that prohibiting political self-determination allows a *minority* to force a *majority* to remain in a dispreferred political arrangement. Indeed, whereas my position admittedly could allow 51 percent of the population to force an unhappy 49 percent into a new state, denying the right to secede would allow 1 percent to force an unhappy 99 percent to remain in their current state. Thus, the concern that we exercise maximal control over our citizenship actually *motivates*, rather than *undermines*, the case for secessionist rights.

Of course, one might object to my expression "dispreferred political arrangement." The key, this critic suggests, is not merely that one would prefer a different arrangement; the real problem with secession is that it forces a minority of people to *change* their political affiliation. This objection is misguided, however, because if it were impermissible to change people's political arrangement without unanimous consent, then mergers like that between East and West Germany would be permitted only if every last citizen in both independent states unanimously agreed to the union. Clearly, this is too strict a requirement.

At this point one might suggest that, unlike secessions, political mergers are permissible in the absence of unanimity because they *add* to the territory over which one's federal government presides, whereas state breaking *restricts* one's government's area of jurisdiction. This qualification helps, but limiting changes in political arrangements to mergers is still too restrictive because it would also prohibit mutual divisions. What if 90 percent of the Norwegians *and* 90 percent of the Swedes had favored political divorce, for instance? (We do not know what the Swedish population thought of the division, but in an August 1905 referendum, 368,392 Norwegians voted to end the union, and only 184 voted against secession.) Or imagine that the vast majority of Germans later decided that the merger was a mistake and 90 percent of them voted to divide once again into East and West Germany. Would we object to either of these divisions on the grounds that a small minority would be forced to belong to smaller states? Presumably not. And if a minority does not have a right to block either political mergers or mutual divisions, it is not clear why it should be given veto power over unilateral divisions.

Here it is worth responding to the increasingly common suggestion that decisions regarding secession should not be reached via only a simple majority in a single plebiscite. Because political divorce is such a momentous step, it is argued, secession should be allowed only after some sort of supermajority has voted in favor of secession in a series of plebiscites spanning a period of several years. After all, what if a simple majority of merely 51 percent votes to secede and then everyone later regrets it?

In principle, it is not clear that a simple majority vote on a single plebiscite should not be taken as decisive. I do not deny that the decision to secede is a grave one, but presumably its gravity would inhibit people from recklessly or nonchalantly voting in favor of division. Moreover, bearing in mind that the existing government typically has (and uses) extensive tools of propaganda to inspire affection for and loyalty to the state, it seems that people would be more likely to err on the side of union than division. Finally, just as we worry about dragging a reluctant minority along in a frivolous or otherwise ill-conceived political divorce, we should equally be concerned not to force an unhappy majority to stay in an unfortunate union. Thus, in principle at least, it is far from obvious that there would be anything unjust or even necessarily unwise about allowing a simple majority to sanction a political divorce on the basis of a single plebiscite.

In practice, on the other hand, I have no strong objections to designing institutional safeguards to ensure that unilateral secession occurs only when a clear majority demonstrates an informed and enduring preference for political independence. Indeed, inspired by analogous considerations, many municipalities require a waiting period before a couple can get married or divorced, and these regulations do not seem intolerable limitations of individual liberty. I should add, though, that I am much more comfortable requiring a majority vote over a series of elections than insisting on a supermajority. Because it will typically take years for an emerging sovereign state to assume its role, there is nothing wrong with intermittently confirming that the majority's preference for separation is an enduring one, especially since it is not unthinkable that a group's passion for independence might wane as it increasingly becomes aware of the real-world problems it must negotiate en route to establishing a sovereign state. I am downright unenthusiastic, on the other hand, about requiring a supermajority to approve the political divorce. It is not uncommon for governments to require supermajority votes over matters where stability is paramount (the U.S. Constitution cannot be amended with a simple majority, for instance), but we must always remember that it is undemocratic to allow a minority to dictate how the majority must live.

Certainly there are features of governments that should not be changed without good reason, but presumably it should be up to the people to decide both what those features are and what constitute good reasons for changing them. Thus, I eschew the requirement of a supermajority in favor of other measures to ensure stability (like a series of votes over time) that seem more in keeping with majority rule. As a result, I am attracted to David Copp's proposal for incorporating secessionist rights into law.

Copp recommends that the International Court of Justice be called on to adjudicate secessionist conflicts in essentially the same manner in which it presides over conflicts between sovereign states.[6] He suggests that any separatist group should be permitted to petition the court. When such a group approached the court, its first task would be to determine if the group had a right to secede. (Copp and I have slightly different accounts of the primary right to secede, but on my view this would require the court to determine if both the separatists and the remainder state would emerge able and willing to perform the requisite political functions.) If the court judged the group to be the type of party that might have a right to unilateral exit, it would then oversee a plebiscite in the proposed secessionist territory to ensure that a majority did indeed desire independence. Assuming that a majority in fact favored separation, the court would then oversee the political divorce settlement to ensure that, as in marital divorce, both the separatists and the rump state were given a fair share of the collective debts and assets. The court would subsequently oversee a second plebiscite "to determine whether the group still want[ed] to secede, given the negotiated terms, and to determine whether it [did] in fact have a stable desire to form a state."[7] If the majority's preference for divorce had remained constant, then the parent state could make one last appeal to the court (arguing, perhaps, "that the secessionist group did not intend in good faith to abide by the settlement").[8] If this final appeal failed (or was not made), then the court would oversee the separation, ensuring that the secessionists and the rump state both honored the separation agreement and generally respected each other's rights. Copp suggests that at this stage "the right of a secessionist society not to be interfered with in forming a state is of a piece with the right any state has not to be interfered with in governing its territory. So these rights of secessionist societies are essentially the same rights that international law now accords to states, and they would have the same legal force as existing rights of existing states."[9]

SECESSION AND INTERNATIONAL LAW

It is tempting to suppose that the preceding arguments illustrate the necessity of reforming the international legal system in something like the manner Copp recommends. After all, if there is a moral right to secede, then international law should protect this right. This inference is too quick, however, because the fact that A has a moral right to X does not necessarily imply that we should *institutionally protect* A's moral right to X. Using an analogy with euthanasia, Allen Buchanan nicely explains this point:

> It may not be difficult to describe a particular hypothetical case in which a physician would be morally justified in actively terminating the life of a hopelessly ill, incompetent patient whose quality of life is extremely poor. And one may be able to formulate the conditions C, D, and E, that make this case one in which active termination of life is morally justified.

But it is quite a different matter to show that it would be morally justifiable for physicians to apply the rule "Whenever conditions C, D, and E obtain, they may actively terminate life." Whether it would be a moral improvement or a moral disaster for physicians to act on the rule the philosopher abstracts from a particular favored case will depend upon a number of factors that are conspicuously absent from the description of that particular case. For instance, one must take into account the overall character of the institutions within which the physicians work and in particular whether reimbursement schemes or other features of the institutional framework create incentives that generate an unacceptable risk that physicians would exercise this authority wrongly. The more general problem is this: even if it is possible by calm reflection on a hypothetical case to formulate conditions under which a certain action would be morally justified, the real world agents who are supposed to follow a rule that is abstracted from the hypothetical case may not reliably identify those conditions and perform the action only when they obtain.[10]

What Buchanan's insight demonstrates is that *even if I have argued flawlessly to this point*, it would be premature to derive conclusions regarding international law without first considering the potential consequences of altering the international legal system. In fact, because my analysis to this point has been *ideal* and *noninstitutional*, we must evaluate both the transition from noninstitutional to institutional analysis and the difference between ideal and nonideal theory before making any recommendations about existing international law.

Buchanan's argument regarding euthanasia should make the distinction between institutional and noninstitutional analysis relatively clear. One's analysis is satisfactorily institutional only if one considers the likely consequences of designing the relevant institutions in certain ways, and one's analysis is noninstitutional if one considers only a single case in isolation. My analysis thus far has been noninstitutional.

As for the second distinction, let us say that one's theory is ideal just in case one assumes that moral agents will generally be constrained by the dictates of morality. Buchanan distinguishes ideal from nonideal theory as follows: "Ideal theory sets the ultimate moral targets, articulating the principles that a just society or a just international order would satisfy, on the assumption that there will be full compliance with these principles. Nonideal theory provides principled guidance for how to cope with the problems of noncompliance and how we are to move closer toward full compliance with the principles of ideal theory."[11] Because I have yet to consider how the various parties should respond if international actors fail to respect the value of political self-determination, my analysis to this point has been ideal.

Finally, notice that because we are considering whether *existing* international law ought to be changed (as opposed to considering what *ideal* international laws would be), we are drawing on *ideal, noninstitutional* analysis to shed light on a *nonideal, institutional* question. There is nothing wrong with making these transitions, but Buchanan is right to caution against rushing from arguments regarding ideal, noninstitutional theory to unwarranted conclusions regarding existing international law.

It is important to recognize, however, that none of the above means that our preceding analysis is irrelevant to the question of international law. On the contrary, if my defense of secession grounded in self-determination is compelling, it creates at least a *presumptive* case for reforming international law. This presumptive case might be defeated by considerations of how institutional changes could affect (potentially noncompliant) actors, but there is no reason why my arguments in favor of the moral right to unilateral secession do not supply an ideal that international law, other things being equal, should approximate. To appreciate this point, consider again the analogous debate regarding euthanasia.

If one can establish via sound ideal, noninstitutional reasoning that there is a moral right to physician-assisted euthanasia whenever conditions C, D, and E obtain, then this establishes a presumption in favor of legally allowing euthanasia in these circumstances. Buchanan is right that we cannot automatically infer that these acts of euthanasia should be legally permitted, because without doing the appropriate nonideal institutional analysis, one cannot be sure that these laws would not have unintended (but nonetheless morally relevant) consequences. But there is nothing in Buchanan's observation that should lead us to deny that our initial analysis of euthanasia supplies an ideal that should be legally approximated to whatever extent is possible without creating negative consequences. After all, there are a variety of considerations relevant to designing the best laws, but surely a chief factor must be the moral rights of those subject to the laws. In short, even if moral rights are not *all* that should be considered when designing governing institutions, certainly they are an important part thereof. And just as the moral right to physician-assisted euthanasia provides (admittedly defeasible) moral reasons in favor of creating domestic laws that permit euthanasia, so too the moral right to unilateral secession provides (defeasible) moral reasons in favor of securing international legal rights to political divorce. In sum, while the arguments in support of primary rights to secede may not create a *conclusive* case in favor of revising international criminal law, they certainly supply *presumptive* reasons for doing so. Thus, we must now review the case *against* creating international legal rights to secession to determine if it outweighs the arguments already supplied on behalf of these rights.

Buchanan has advanced the most compelling arguments against creating international legal rights to unilateral secession. Whatever might be said in favor of secessionist rights considered in an institutional vacuum, he insists that international law should *not* protect primary rights to secede in the fashion I have been proposing. Buchanan is not against all rights to political divorce (indeed, he seeks to *expand* the list of grievances that can accord a group an international legal right to secede), but he is emphatically opposed to creating any international legal right to secede in the absence of injustice. At the heart of Buchanan's argument are concerns about the types of incentives international laws can create. He argues in favor of remedial rights to secede because of the beneficial incentives institutionally protecting these rights will establish, and he argues against primary rights because of the "perverse" incentives that would be created by international laws designed to protect them. To appreciate Buchanan's argument, let us review the incentives he supposes would be attached to the various possible international laws on secession.

First consider why Buchanan thinks the remedial right only theory of secession "gets the incentives right." He writes: "On the one hand, states that protect basic human rights and honor autonomy agreements are immune to legally sanctioned unilateral secession and entitled to international support for maintaining the full extent of their territorial integrity. On the other hand, if, as the theory prescribes, international law recognizes a unilateral right to secede as a remedy for serious and persisting injustices, states will have an incentive to act more justly."[12] In other words, if international law recognizes rights to secede *only* in cases of injustice, then political leaders will be motivated to govern justly because they know both that (1) doing so will lead the international community to support the state in any potential secessionist conflict and (2) sufficient injustices would lead the international community to support the separatists.

As Buchanan explains, the incentive structure would be altogether different if the international legal system also respected primary rights to secede.

> If state leaders know that unilateral secession will be considered a right under international law for any group that can muster a majority in favor of it in any portion of their state, they will not be receptive to proposals for decentralization. They will view decentralization as a first step toward secession, because creation of internal political units will provide the basis for future secessions by plebiscite.
>
> International recognition of a plebiscitary unilateral right to secede would also create perverse incentives regarding both immigration and economic development. States that did not wish to risk losing part of their territory (which includes virtually all of them) would have a strong reason for limiting immigration (or internal migration) that might result in the formation of a pro-secession majority in a portion of the state's territory. And to deter secession by existing internal political units, the state might even seek to prevent them from becoming sufficiently developed to be economically viable. (The Soviet Union's policy of dispersing major industries among the Republics was very likely motivated at least in part by precisely this consideration.)[13]

Thus, not only would a part of the incentive to govern justly be lost (since being a just state no longer insulates one from the threat of secession); institutionally protecting primary rights to secede would also discourage decentralization, open immigration, and freedom of migration because each of these policies potentially nurtures separatism. In brief, there seems every reason to think that institutionally protecting only remedial rights to secede would create positive incentives, while protecting primary rights would eliminate helpful incentives and create additional detrimental ones.

Because political leaders are loath to lose territory and because they have unparalleled power to promote or destroy peace and justice, Buchanan is right to call attention to these relatively neglected considerations. Moreover, I think Buchanan accurately describes the kind of incentives that could be attached to laws protecting remedial and primary rights to secede. For several reasons, however, I doubt that these considerations are sufficiently weighty to defeat the presumptive case created by the moral right to secede.

To begin, there are at least two reasons to think that the "perverse" incentives Buchanan highlights are not that strong. First of all, the negative incentives to which Buchanan refers already exist, so the operative question is to what extent they would be magnified by the international community's support of a primary right to secede. I say this because (as Buchanan's reference to the former Soviet Union illustrates), even in the absence of any international legal right to secede, countries all too often disempower minority groups in an effort to preempt potential independence movements. Thus, if political leaders already have reason to avoid desirable policies like decentralization, then we have reason to avoid creating international laws that protect primary rights to secede only if we know that such laws would *substantially strengthen* these incentives. But this is an empirical matter—it is one thing to speculate about the *kind* of incentive a law might create, but it is another thing altogether to guess the *amount* an existing incentive would be increased by this same law.

Secondly, historical evidence indicates that in many cases separatist sentiment is pacified, rather than enflamed, when minority groups are given additional political powers. As John McGarry explains:

> While states are often reluctant to decentralize, for fear it will promote secession, there is evidence that timely and genuine decentralization achieves exactly the opposite effect. While Francoist centralization coincided with a significant increase in support for Basque separatism, the granting of autonomy to Basques in 1979 resulted in support for independence dropping from 36 per cent to 12 per cent. The long-time existence of the Canadian and Swiss federations also shows that extensive decentralization is consistent with state unity.[14]

On reflection, McGarry's observation is commonsensical; after all, it would be crazy *not* to think that many formerly middle-of-the-road Chechens may have become ardent separatists precisely because of Moscow's brutal campaign to quell the secessionist movement. Thus, leaders with some sense of what actually fuels separatist fires will recognize that *no matter what stand the international legal system takes on rights to political divorce*, they have no incentive to avoid decentralization.

Another factor to bear in mind is that the reasons *against* institutionally protecting primary rights to secede must be balanced against the considerations *in favor of* legally securing these rights. For instance, arming minority groups with an effective right to secede gives these groups political leverage, and this leverage in turn provides the central government with incentives not to mistreat these minority groups. In addition, secessionist movements are likely to emerge whether or not the international legal system condones them, so instituting something like Copp's proposal would be beneficial insofar as it would allow us to bring "secessionist problems to the International Court where the issues could be decided in a peaceful and orderly manner."[15] As Michael Freeman observes, "The restrictive interpretation of the right to self-determination does not inhibit claims to self-determination, but it does inhibit their peaceful and just resolution, since it denies their legitimacy."[16]

In light of the above, it appears that even if Buchanan is right that international laws protecting primary rights to secede could generate some perverse incentives, it is not at all clear how much weight to give this consideration. The fact that some of these incentives will exist whether or not the international legal system protects primary rights and that there would also be some *positive* side effects of institutionally recognizing these moral rights makes it questionable whether Buchanan's concerns are decisive. However, because moral rights hang in the balance, there are two things about which we can be confident: that the burden of proof to establish the empirical fact of the matter lies squarely on the shoulders of those who would *restrict* these moral rights and that it would not be sufficient to show that there is merely a slight advantage in favor of restricting these rights. To appreciate each of these points, consider how we might have reasoned in the United States ninety years ago when deliberating about giving women the legal right to vote. Against such a proposition, one might have suggested that enacting a law granting all literate women the right to vote would have created a perverse incentive for men to keep women illiterate. Such an incentive is certainly relevant, but given that women have a moral right to vote, women should not be denied this legal right unless we have compelling evidence both that (1) the marginal effect of this incentive would often be decisive and (2) the resulting harm would be substantial. Similarly, if there are groups that have primary moral rights to secede, we should legally protect these rights unless those who advocate legal restrictions can offer compelling evidence that sufficient harms would ensue.

To review: while my arguments in defense of secession grounded in self-determination do not by themselves conclusively demonstrate that we should design international laws protecting primary rights to secede, they do create a presumption in favor of doing so. This presumptive case is vulnerable to defeat by competing considerations, but the burden of proof is on those who would restrict political self-determination, and this burden has not yet been met.

I have argued that separatists may have a right to secede as long as they and their rump state are both able and willing to perform the requisite political functions. Although statists recoil from the conclusion that a group may be entitled to secede from a perfectly legitimate state, and nationalists will object that I underestimate the importance of the distinctive cultural characteristics of separatist groups, it strikes me that a group's rights to political self-determination should hinge principally on its political capacities. And because existing states are not the only entities able to perform the requisite political functions, some nonstate entities may qualify for political self-determination. It is important to recognize, however, that I am emphatically *not* a fan of state breaking. Just as one might defend the right to no-fault divorce without believing that more people should separate, I defend the right to secede despite having no interest in the proliferation of small, more homogenous states in the world. In the end, then, my attitude toward secession mirrors that of Serbia's president, Boris Tadic, who responded to Montenegro's recent vote to secede in the following fashion: "I supported the preservation of a joint state, but as a democratic president of a democratic republic, I recognize the expression of the free will of the Montenegrin citizens."[17]

Notes

This essay draws on previous work, especially my book, *A Theory of Secession* (New York: Cambridge University Press, 2005). I have benefited enormously in writing this paper from discussions at two excellent conferences organized by Don Doyle. In particular, I am grateful to Bruno Coppieters for his insightful written comments.

1. Allen Buchanan, *Secession: The Morality of Political Divorce from Fort Sumter to Lithuania and Quebec* (Boulder, Colo.: Westview Press, 1991).

2. Margaret Moore, *The Ethics of Nationalism* (Oxford: Oxford University Press, 2001), 159.

3. W. Ivor Jennings, *The Approach to Self-Government* (Cambridge: Cambridge University Press, 1956), 56.

4. Charles R. Beitz, *Political Theory and International Relations* (Princeton: Princeton University Press, 1979), 106.

5. Harry Beran, "A Democratic Theory of Political Self-Determination for a New World Order," in *Theories of Secession*, ed. Percy Lehning (London: Routledge, 1998), 38–39.

6. David Copp, "International Law and Morality in the Theory of Secession," *The Journal of Ethics* 2, no. 3 (1998): 219–45.

7. Copp, "International Law and Morality in the Theory of Secession," 234.

8. Copp, "International Law and Morality in the Theory of Secession," 235.

9. Copp, "International Law and Morality in the Theory of Secession," 235.

10. Allen Buchanan, *Justice, Legitimacy, and Self-Determination* (Oxford: Oxford University Press, 2004), 22–23.

11. Buchanan, *Justice, Legitimacy, and Self-Determination*, 55.

12. Buchanan, *Justice, Legitimacy, and Self-Determination*, 370.

13. Buchanan, *Justice, Legitimacy, and Self-Determination*, 377–78.

14. John McGarry, "'Orphans of Secession': National Pluralism in Secessionist Regions and Post-Secession States," in *National Self-Determination and Secession*, ed. Margaret Moore (Oxford: Oxford University Press, 1998), 225–26.

15. Copp, "International Law and Morality in the Theory of Secession," 243.

16. Michael Freeman, "The Priority of Function Over Structure: A New Approach to Secession," in *Theories of Secession*, 15.

17. Tadic's statement was reported in *AP Online*, May 23, 2006.

DAVID ARMITAGE

Secession and Civil War

For the past two centuries, state breaking has been the primary method of state making around the world. More than half the states currently represented at the UN emerged from the wreckage of colonial empires, the collapse of multinational federations, or the fission of existing states. The rate of state birth accelerated in the decades after the Second World War; the incidence of state death, whether through conquest, occupation, confederation, or dissolution, declined in the same period.[1]

Whenever a new state is recognized as legitimately occupying territory formerly claimed by another state, a process of secession can be said to have reached its successful conclusion.[2] Where once 51 states had been (in 1945), 192 would be (by 2010). This near quadrupling of the number of acknowledged states seemingly vindicates the principle of self-determination and indicates the international community's endorsement of secession as the major means by which to achieve independence. Yet in the last sixty years there have been more attempted secessions than there have been accessions to the UN. Moreover, at least until the past decade, only a minority of these secessions were peaceful.

Violence has been secession's most frequent companion. In this chapter, I want to examine secession's relationship with perhaps the oldest, often the most destructive, and in the past half century certainly the most prevalent form of collective violence: civil war. At first blush, the link between secession and civil war would seem to be quite straightforward. A group within a state, exasperated by what it sees as the suppression of its right to self-determination, asserts that right as a claim to independent statehood. In response, the existing state maintains its right to territorial integrity and authority over all its inhabitants by forcibly resisting that claim with coercive violence. Secession—the attempt to create a new state—thereby leads to civil war—armed conflict within an established state. Examples from the United States in 1861 to Yugoslavia in 1991 confirm this correlation. Although there have been some peaceful secessions—

for example, Norway's from Sweden in 1905, Iceland's from Denmark in 1944, Singapore's from the Malaysian Federation in 1965, Montenegro's from Serbia in 2006, and (so far) Kosovo's, also from Serbia, in 2008—they are exceptions: "Until the 1990s violence and violent conflict was a feature characterizing most secessions and attempts at secession."[3] And the kind of conflict secession was most likely to produce was internal, or civil, war.

The logic of history is seemingly as impeccable as it is implacable: secession causes civil war, just as civil war was until recently the most likely outcome of attempted secession. The most comprehensive recent macrohistorical account of warfare around the world counts 484 separate wars between 1816 and 2001; 296 of those were civil wars, of which 109 were fought with the goal of creating a new state rather than taking control of an existing one. Secessionist conflicts thus comprise more than a fifth of all wars in the past two centuries and account for a substantial minority of the civil wars in this period. Many of these secessionist civil wars have accompanied "the two institutional transformations that have shaped the landscape of the modern world," that is, imperial expansion and the process of state creation, especially as a product of decolonization. The onset of such wars also "show[s] a dramatic peak immediately before nation-state formation," while "the odds of civil war onset are more than five times higher in the first two years after independence than in the other post-independence years."[4]

These findings appear to show a direct correlation between secession and civil war, and not just a causal one (secession leads to civil war) but also a circumstantial one (secession and civil war are more likely to occur together during the process of nation-state formation, especially in a context of anti-imperial decolonization). Yet they can also be taken to prove that the correlation between secession and civil war, however strong, is strictly contingent. Nonetheless, until recently, most definitions of secession implied that violence and resistance would necessarily be part of the process. This reflected the assumptions that the rulers of states would be likely to protect their territorial integrity by force and that they would be justified in doing so. As the Commission of Rapporteurs in the Åland Islands case affirmed in 1921: "To concede to minorities, either of language or religion, or to any fractions of a population the right of withdrawing from the community to which they belong, because it is their wish or good pleasure, would be to destroy order and stability within States and to inaugurate anarchy in international life; it would be to uphold a theory incompatible with the very idea of the State as a territorial and political unity."[5]

Subsequent definitions of secession were not quite so explicit about its prima facie injustice, but they continued to assume the likelihood of violence. For example, James Crawford defined secession classically as "the creation of a State *by the use or threat of force* without the consent of the former sovereign."[6] And even when it has not been assumed that the existing state would use force, it has at least been taken for granted that the state would resist. In this vein, the editor of a major recent collection of essays on secession and international law defined secession as "the creation of a new independent entity through the separation of part of the territory and population of an existing State, *without the consent of the latter*."[7]

These definitions of secession commit two logical errors by assuming that violence must be an element of it. First, they beg the question of whether secession must be achieved by "the use or threat of force" and thereby build a contestable conclusion into their basic premises. And second, they confuse a part for the whole by assuming that nonconsensual secession can stand for all forms of it. Consensual secessions have been rarer historically than unilateral secessions, but to conclude from this that unilateral secession is the model is to mistake an empirical inference for a normative description.[8] To address these problems, some students of secession have recently proposed more inclusive definitions: for example, "withdrawal from a state or society through the constitution of a new sovereign and independent state," "the separation of a part of the territory of an existing state to form an independent state," or "the creation of a new state upon territory previously forming part of, or being a colonial entity of, an existing state."[9] These definitions have the virtue of being compatible with both consensual and unilateral secessions. They also do not prejudge whether host states will resist separation or whether secessionists will demand force to accomplish their aim of independence.

Definitions of civil war have been fraught and embattled no less than those of secession. As the author of the best recent survey of the social science literature on the subject has noted, "Civil war . . . is a phenomenon prone to serious semantic confusion, even contestation." And this confusion and contestation are not just a concern for scholars: "The description of a conflict as a civil war carries symbolic and political weight since the term can confer or deny legitimacy to a warring party."[10] That term can also determine the policy and strategy of external actors.

A good case in point is the heated discussion in 2006–7 over whether or not to call the internal violence in Iraq a civil war. Two British journalists, John

Keegan and Bartle Bull, who opposed using the label, argued that for any conflict to be termed a "civil war," "the violence must be 'civil,' it must be 'war,' and
its aim must be either the exercise or the acquisition of national authority": that
is, it has to be fought by organized bodies of combatants drawn from a single
national population who use force either to grasp or to retain political authority within their national territory. They counted only five wars in modern world
history that fit these stringent criteria: the English Civil War (1642–49), the
American Civil War (1861–65), the Russian Civil War (1918–21), the Spanish
Civil War (1936–39), and the Lebanese Civil War (1975–90). Iraq did not, according to Keegan and Bull, qualify (their reasons were perhaps more political
than strictly taxonomical).[11] Using these yardsticks, the relationship between
secession and civil war would appear to be utterly contingent because historically unique, as only the American Civil War among these five conflicts could
be described, even in part, as secessionist.

A very different assessment of the numbers of civil wars has emerged in light
of the conventional definition used by political scientists. This stipulates that
there must be "sustained military combat, primarily internal, resulting in at least
1000 battle-field deaths per year, pitting central government forces against an
insurgent force capable of . . . inflict[ing] upon the government forces at least
5 percent of the fatalities the insurgents sustain."[12] When used to debunk both
the social science metrics and their applicability to the ongoing violence in the
country, that definition produced a total of *seven* civil wars in Iraq since 1945.[13]
The same definition is also the basis for a generally accepted global total of nearly
150 civil wars between 1945 and 1999—a number spectacularly different from
the 1 civil war (in Lebanon) in the same period and from the grand total of 5 civil
wars in 350 years of world history that Keegan and Bull's definition yields.[14] This
radical divergence should remind us how sensitive data can be to definitions
and how much is at stake in defining "civil war" as well as "secession."

All such definitions are the product of history. And because they are contextual, arising from debate and dissension, they also conflict. For example, the
U.S. Army's 1990 *Field Manual for Military Operations in Low Intensity Conflict* defined civil war in this way: "A war between factions of the same country;
there are five criteria for international recognition of this status: the contestants
must control territory, have a functioning government, enjoy some foreign recognition, have identifiable regular armed forces, and engage in major military
operations."[15] Apart from a glaring tautology—that "international recognition"
depends on "some foreign recognition"—it is notable that this definition could

both exclude and include secessionist conflict from its purview. The first part of the definition—"a war between factions of the same country"—adopts the perspective of the host state from which a portion that has seceded still remains under the authority of the sovereign. This would be the view of the Federal government of the United States toward the Confederacy in 1861 or, to take a more recent example, the attitude of the Russian Federation toward separatists in Chechnya. However, criteria such as control of territory, possession of a functioning government, foreign recognition, and the undertaking of major operations by identifiable armed forces enumerate many of the marks of a people engaged—and engaged somewhat successfully—in a process of secession. As we will see, this definition is itself a product of the American Civil War. That conflict was fought at least in part over definitions of both secession and civil war. Any conclusions derived from it about how these two forms of state breaking might be related would necessarily be somewhat peculiar and rife with their own enduringly contentious legacies.

The American Civil War is the locus classicus for the relationship between secession and civil war, as many of the chapters in this volume confirm.[16] The most enduring articulation of that reciprocity during that conflict itself came from Abraham Lincoln. In his address to Congress on July 4, 1861, Lincoln argued that the Confederate attack on Fort Sumter three months earlier had starkly presented not just to the United States but "to the whole family of man the question, whether a constitutional republic, or a democracy—a government of the people, by the same people—can or cannot maintain its territorial integrity against its own domestic foes." He stated that the Confederate States had posed the issue baldly as one of secession or civil war, "immediate dissolution, or blood." Yet Lincoln rejected his enemies' description of their action as secession; he mocked "the seceded States, so called" and dismantled their argument that "secession is *consistent* with the Constitution—is *lawful* and *peaceful*" with a reductio ad absurdum. Even if it were agreed that secession was constitutional, he went on, then logically the Confederate States should retain a right of secession in their own constitution, even at the cost of self-destruction: "The principle [of secession] itself is one of disintegration, and upon which no government can possibly endure."[17]

Secession would also be the casus belli Lincoln invoked in his speech at the dedication of the cemetery at Gettysburg on November 19, 1863. Eighty-seven years earlier, he recalled, "our fathers brought forth on this continent, a new nation, conceived in Liberty, and dedicated to the proposition that all men are created equal." "Now," he continued, in response to a rebellion, "we are engaged in *a great civil war*, testing whether that nation, or any nation so conceived and dedicated, can long endure."[18] Lincoln might not have wished to utter the word "secession," but his Gettysburg Address left no doubt that he saw a great civil war as the morally necessary and politically unavoidable response to the cascading fissiparousness produced by any constitutional recognition of a right of secession.[19]

Lincoln implied that in the American case secession and civil war were joined both sequentially and causally. They were joined sequentially because the so-called secession of South Carolina and the other states of the Deep South had demanded that the Union defend its integrity; its armed response took place within the borders of the United States and led to a domestic, or civil, war. And they were linked causally because without the assertion of a right to secede there would have been no need for formal hostilities: no secession, no civil war. For Lincoln, these connections were hardly accidentally or exclusively American. They could, he thought, be felt by "any nation," any member of "the whole family of man," whose statehood was grounded in its territorial integrity. With the benefit of another 150 years' experience in the proliferation of states, we can hear in Lincoln's words the voice not just of the great emancipator and champion of popular government but also of the defender of indivisible sovereign statehood itself. That voice would often be heard across the course of the twentieth century, as the harbinger of civil war in retaliation for attempted secession.

Lincoln acknowledged that the very term "secession" was almost as challenging to a constitutional order as the act of secession itself. As he reminded Congress in 1861, the withdrawal of the Confederate States from the Union was in fact not a secession; it was a rebellion. This was the view of the executive—that is, the president himself—delivered from the political heart of the Union, and with a unitary theory of the Constitution's perdurability and infrangibility in mind. But, Lincoln argued, he was not alone in distinguishing rebellion from secession: "It might seem, at first thought, to be of little difference whether the present movement at the South be called 'secession' or 'rebellion.' The movers, however, well understood the difference. At the beginning, they knew they could never raise their treason to any respectable magnitude by any name which implies *violation* of law." Accordingly, he went on, they "sugar-coated" rebellion with the argument that secession was compatible with the Constitution and thereby succeeded in "drugging the public mind of their section for more than thirty years."[20]

Lincoln also recognized that secession could be legal only if it was consensual: "No State, upon its own mere motion, can lawfully get out of the Union[;] . . . *resolves* and *ordinances* to that effect are legally void; and . . . acts of violence within any State or States, against the authority of the United States, are insurrectionary or revolutionary, according to circumstances."[21] He was apparently untroubled by what is now the most pressing question in contemporary legal discussions of secession: that is, whether or not international law acknowledges a peremptory norm in favor of the practice.[22] He implicitly assumed that it did not and asserted instead the proposition that it was incompatible with current American constitutionalism. The basis of that constitutional order was the principle "that government of the people, by the people, for the people, shall not perish from the earth," and that principle had to be defended, even at the cost of "a great civil war."[23]

Lincoln's logic of unitary statehood rendered southern "secession" rebellion and the conflict to suppress it a "civil war." Yet, of course, to the supporters of the Confederacy, the conflict was not a civil war in this sense but a war between states: not an *intra*national conflict but an *inter*national one. By May 1861, all sides—northern and southern, American and British—had recognized the existence of a war within the borders of the United States.[24] To call it a *civil* war was, ipso facto, to accept the Unionist interpretation of southern actions as a rebellion against the unity of the nation and to assume that what was at stake was the inviolability of the Constitution as well as the illegitimacy of unilateral secession. To term it "the Civil War" at any time after 1865 was, and still is, to accept the victory of that interpretation and of the principles the Union sought to protect and defend. Yet it was not until January 1907, in a debate on pensions for veterans of the Mexican War and the Civil War, that the United States agreed that the latter conflict should no longer be called the "War of the Rebellion" (the preferred northern name up to that point) or the "War between the States."[25]

It would be as historically futile as it would be morally unacceptable to seek a more neutral term than "the Civil War" for the defining cataclysm of American history. Yet to say that in the American case, secession led to civil war is self-contradictory: if the conflict was a civil war, fought within one state, then the Confederates were rebels; if the Confederacy had seceded, then what ensued was, at least temporarily, a war between states. As one Democratic senator vainly protested in 1907, when arguing for the name "War of Secession": "It was a war to establish the right of secession. . . . The war was in the nature of a rebellion, and to a certain extent it was a civil war, but in the broad sense, in the full sense, it was a war of secession."²⁶ It may be admirably multiperspectival to incorporate both northern and southern, Unionist and Confederate, descriptors by talking about "secession" leading to "civil war," but to do so does risk obscuring important aspects of what was at stake in both secession and civil war during this period.

Contemporaries during the conflict itself struggled with defining and disentangling these terms. The question went to the highest forum in the land in February 1863 when the Supreme Court heard arguments in four cases, collectively known as the Prize Cases, that were appealing decisions from courts in Boston, New York, and Key West. All arose from President Lincoln's order in April 1861 to blockade ports from Chesapeake Bay to the mouth of the Rio Grande on the grounds that the states of the Confederacy had raised "an insurrection against the Government of the United States." The plaintiffs argued that the blockade, and the subsequent use of prize law to distribute the proceeds from four captured ships, applied the laws of war when no war had been declared and hence that such laws could not be operative. The main question before the Supreme Court was, therefore, whether there was a state of war that would justify the president's deployment of the laws of war. Justice Robert Grier, writing for the majority in March 1863, was persuaded by the government's lawyers that there was indeed a war in progress. To call the action of the Confederacy an "insurrection" did not mean it could not also attain the status of a war, nor did the absence of a declaration of war mean the government could not treat them as belligerents: "A civil war always begins by insurrection against the lawful authority of the Government. A civil war is never solemnly declared; it becomes such by its accidents—the number, power, and organization of the persons who originate and carry it on." The president was obligated to face this conflict "in the shape it presented itself, without waiting for Congress to baptize it with a name," but Grier himself did not hesitate to call it the "greatest of civil wars."²⁷

This momentous Supreme Court ruling opened the way for the first formal legal definition of civil war—a definition Grier's decision had assumed but not provided. It appeared in the Union Army's General Orders no. 100, *Instructions for the Government of Armies of the United States in the Field* (April 24, 1863), perhaps better known as the Lieber Code after its main author, the Columbia College law and political science professor Francis Lieber.²⁸ The Union general Henry Halleck commissioned Lieber to produce codified rules for land warfare, which would be the first such formal code for any Western army, and later the basis for the Hague and Geneva conventions. When Lieber sent his initial draft to Halleck in February 1863, the general objected that it lacked one crucial component: a definition of the particular kind of internal conflict in which his army had been engaged for over a year. As he wrote to Lieber, "to be more useful at the present time [the code] should embrace civil war as well as war between states or *distinct* sovereignties."[29]

It was with some anguish that Lieber set to work on defining civil war. This was not just because his three sons were in uniform, two for the Union, one for the Confederacy ("Behold in me the symbol of civil war," he lamented[30]). He also had no legal precedent to hand and soon discovered the semantic confusion surrounding the term of which others complained: "I am writing my 4 sections on civil war and 'invasion,'" he told Halleck in March 1863: "Ticklish work, that!"[31] In 1861, Lieber had attempted to define civil war in a series of lectures at Columbia, in which he called it "the protracted state of active hostility of one portion of a political society against another portion," but this description was evidently too vague and cumbersome to find its way into his formal code.[32]

What, then, was Lieber's definition of civil war? And how did it relate to the question of secession? He distinguished civil war both from "insurrection" and from "rebellion," in ways that reflected the specific political conditions under which he wrote:

> 149. Insurrection is the rising of people in arms against their government, or a portion of it, or against one or more of its laws, or against an officer or officers of the government. It may be confined to mere armed resistance, or it may have greater ends in view.
>
> 150. Civil war is war between two or more portions of a country or state, each contending for the mastery of the whole, and each claiming to be the legitimate government. The term is also sometimes applied to war of rebellion, when the rebellious provinces or portions of the state are contiguous to those containing the seat of government.
>
> 151. The term rebellion is applied to an insurrection of large extent, and is usually a war between the legitimate government of a country and portions or provinces of the same who seek to throw off their allegiance to it and set up a government of their own.[33]

The nature of the hostilities as they had unfolded since 1861 clearly shaped Lieber's distinctions. The difference between "insurrection" and "rebellion" was one of degree, the latter approaching the condition of interstate conflict, or war, if undertaken for "greater ends," such as throwing off allegiance and setting up an independent government, which is what a self-styled secessionist movement such as the Confederacy did.[34]

Lieber's two conceptions of civil war were, respectively, traditional and novel. The first—"war between two or more portions of a country or state, each contending for mastery of the whole"—could be traced back to Republican Rome, where *bellum civile* denoted a war waged between citizens (*cives*) within the bounds of the city whose object was control of the community or *civitas* itself, as in the case of Caesar and Pompey.[35] The second—"sometimes applied to war of rebellion, when the rebellious provinces or portions of the state are contiguous to those containing the seat of government"—was unprecedented. Lieber had made it up out of whole cloth and tailored it to the circumstances of the American conflict, in which the "rebellious provinces" were indeed contiguous with the seat of sovereignty.

According to the classic Roman definition of civil war that Lieber echoed in his code, the American Civil War was not a civil war at all. It may have been fought between two parts of the country, but only one side aimed at mastery or claimed to be the legitimate government of the whole territory. The Confederacy claimed moral continuity with the original rebels of the American Revolution, but such assumed legitimacy did not amount to a claim to authority over the territory in the nonseceding states. By Lieber's own reckoning, the Civil War was thus in fact a rebellion: hence, presumably, the official Union designation of it after the conflict as the War of the Rebellion and the Fourteenth Amendment's reference to "engage[ment] in insurrection or rebellion" as a disqualification for public office.[36] Indeed, the fact that both Lieber and Lincoln generally referred, both publicly and privately, to the conflict as a "civil war," great or otherwise, made something of a mockery of Lieber's attempt at definitional precision.

Lieber had been reflecting on the issues of rebellion, revolution, and, crucially, secession for many years before he drafted his code and was forced to change his mind on his definitions by the pressures of his task of codification. In some early notes from around 1850, he ran through the various terms that could be used to describe different species and degrees of revolution and included among them both "secession" and "civil war."[37] Writing around the same time, he reflected at length on the question of secession, especially in relation to South Carolina, where he was living and teaching at the time as a professor at the University of South Carolina (a post he left for New York in 1857, largely due to his disgust with secessionism). He viewed the prospects of a successful secession dimly: "No peacible [sic] secession is possible . . . theory or no theory, right or no right, the Union will say: We must keep you; we cannot afford one of the south to cave in; the Union *shall* continue."[38] And so, of course, it would transpire a decade later. Success, or the prospect of success, was for him a major criterion for distinguishing the different kinds of collective antistate action: "A State can resist, can rebel and if the rebellion be successful it will be called revolution. But . . . [l]et us call things by their right names. The right of secession is one thing and that of rebellion another."[39] The example he used in this case is the one to which I now turn, as indeed Abraham Lincoln had also done: the American Revolution and, more specifically, the Declaration of Independence. We are accustomed, thanks to Lincoln, to seeing the Civil War as the second American revolution; by briefly considering the question of secession and civil war before 1861, I hope to suggest—in line with contemporaries' own conceptions of the conflict—that the American Revolution was, in fact, both a war of secession and the first American civil war.[40]

The American Revolution presents a causal relation between secession and civil war that is seemingly the reverse of that associated with the American Civil War. What had begun as a fairly conventional provincial tax revolt escalated to the point of punitive police action by the metropolitan government and its colonial agents. In this regard, Lexington and Concord marked the beginning of an imperial civil war, fought within the single political community of the British Empire, that also comprised a series of local civil wars pursued in colonies such as New York and South Carolina between those who would come to be called Loyalists and Patriots. The nationalist historiography of the American Revolution has, of course, long denied that the conflict was a civil war. Only recently has a new generation of Revolutionary historians, most of them writing in the context of British or Atlantic history, restored contemporaries' conceptions of the conflict as a civil war (or wars) with a document of secession—the Declaration of Independence—as its pivotal act.[41]

The American conflict can only be designated a "civil war" if the British Empire as a whole is conceived of as the political community within which the conflict took place. Such a designation also takes seriously the colonists' protestations before the latter months of 1775 that they had no intention of seceding from the empire. This was the message of the Continental Congress's other declaration, the "Declaration . . . Setting Forth the Causes and Necessity of Taking Up Arms" (July 6, 1775), in which its members justified the move to armed resistance and tried to reassure "the minds of our friends and fellow subjects in any part of the empire . . . that we mean not to dissolve that Union which has so long and so happily subsisted between us, and which we sincerely wish to see restored." Their stated aim was "reconciliation on reasonable terms, . . . thereby to relieve the empire from the calamities of civil war."[42] Yet that aim was almost certainly vain, even at the moment the Continental Congress expressed it. Within a month, George III would declare the colonists outside his protection, thereby rendering them outlaws within the boundaries of the British Empire.

Almost from the moment hostilities began between the colonists and representatives of British authority, commentators in Britain called the conflict a civil war, even "the American Civil War."[43] By that designation, they meant that it was (to use Lieber's later definition) "a war between two or more portions of a country or State" and that it fit into a sequence of British civil wars, stretching back (by some definitions, at least) through the Glorious Revolution via the three English civil wars of 1642–45, 1648, and 1650 to the Middle Ages.[44] None of these sets of events involved an act of secession, nor would the American War of Independence until the Continental Congress voted on July 2, 1776, to approve a resolution "that these United Colonies are, and of right ought to be, free and independent States, that they are absolved from all allegiance to the British Crown, and that all political allegiance between them and the State of Great Britain is, and ought to be, totally dissolved."[45] Two days later, on July 4, 1776, the Congress voted to approve a document explaining that act of secession from the British Empire. This was the "Declaration by the United States of America, in General Congress Assembled," better known as the American Declaration of Independence.

The Declaration of Independence was the first formal secession proclamation in world history.[46] It announced to the world that thirteen united states, formerly colonies under the British Crown, had agreed "to dissolve the Political Bands which have connected [one People] with another" and presented facts to a "candid World" to prove that "the United Colonies are, and of Right ought to be, Free and Independent States . . . and that all political Connection between them and the State of Great-Britain, is and ought to be totally dissolved."[47] Congress did not negotiate its declaration of independence with the parent country before promulgating it, nor had it secured guarantees of immediate recognition from any of the other "Powers of the Earth." The declaration was thus not only the first such assertion of independence; it was also the first *unilateral* declaration of independence, and it would not in fact be recognized by a third party until France entered into the Treaty of Amity and Commerce with the United

States in February 1778. It had, of course, avoided the word "secession" in favor of the language of dissolving bands and connections with Great Britain. Yet secession—in the sense of "the creation of a new state," or in this case states, "by the withdrawal of a territory and its population where that territory was previously part of an existing state"—was exactly what it declared.[48]

In the American Revolution, secession was the product of civil war, not its cause. The aim of the Declaration of Independence was to transform British colonies into American states, to change rebels within the British Empire into belligerents outside it, and to turn an imperial civil war into an international conflict between the United Kingdom and the United States. The ultimate success of the declaration in effecting these multiple and concentric transformations marked the beginning of what I have called elsewhere a "contagion of sovereignty."[49] This was the diffusionary process by which statehood, expressed in the language of territorial sovereignty, spread to encompass almost the whole of the earth's surface, barring Antarctica and not counting the states of exception (such as Guantánamo Bay) that states themselves have created. Thanks to that contagion of sovereignty, we all now inhabit a world in which states exercise authority over defined territories and the populations that inhabit them. It has increased the drive toward secession, and yet secession is less likely to succeed because of it. As territorial sovereign statehood became universally diffused in the decades after the Second World War, the drive to secure autonomy through statehood presented an ever-greater threat to the integrity of existing states.

It seems to be one of the few observable regularities of global history since 1776 that a state that has declared its own independence—that has seceded, usually from an empire or multinational confederation—will generally resist any internal threat to its own territorial integrity, even at the cost of civil war. This is the case even when the secessionists invoke the very principles, even the precise language, of the founding movement for secession, as, for example, South Carolina's secession convention did in December 1860 when it adapted the words of the Declaration of Independence for its own purposes: "South Carolina has *resumed* her position among the nations of the world, as a separate and independent State; with full power to levy war, conclude peace, contract alliances, establish commerce, and to do all the other acts and things which independent States may of right do."[50] However, such appeals have generally been more inflammatory than effective. They are almost certain to be resisted, even at the cost of a "great civil war," as they were after 1861. The record of the last sixty years underscores this fact. Between Iceland's separation from Denmark in 1944 and Kosovo's exit from union with Serbia in February 2008, the number of successful secessions during this period amounts to barely fifteen. There have been at least as many attempted secessions, most of which either have been violently suppressed or have precipitated civil war, from Biafra (1967) to Chechnya (1994–96, 1999–2009).[51]

Every attempt at secession raises two radical questions: for what ends is the secession undertaken, and can secession be undertaken unilaterally in pursuit of those ends? Abraham Lincoln debated those questions in 1861, and the answers he gave were distinctly Janus-faced. As he had argued in his First Inaugural, and then reaffirmed before Congress on July 4, 1861, secession could only be undertaken on consensual grounds and to protect the highest ideals. Because the integrity of the democratic state itself was among those ideals, secession could never be justified and must be suppressed. Lincoln's grave words on that occasion became an ambivalent legacy for future secessionists and sovereigns. Was it worth the price of a civil war to achieve secession? Was it inevitable that nationalists would become statists, as two sections of the American population had over the course of the years between 1776 and 1861? And, still more challengingly, could even a peaceful and consensual secession still manage to produce a state that later would risk civil war to maintain its own territorial integrity? The logic of territoriality, which welds nationhood to statehood, would seem to imply as much.

The contemporary options for securing statehood have effectively been narrowed to two. "How do you get a state?" the political scientist James Fearon has asked: "Either by winning control of an already established state or by establishing a new one."[52] Control can be won peacefully, via the ballot box, or aggressively, by rebellion or civil war. Likewise, a new state can be established uncontentiously, by means of a mutual agreement to separate, as in the case of Norway and Sweden or the Czech Republic and Slovakia, or by a well-prepared path to recognition like Montenegro's in 2006 or Kosovo's in 2008. More often, secession cannot be negotiated so successfully and leads to war between states (the likely outcome, for example, if Taiwanese nationalists were to declare independence from mainland China) or war within a state (what might have happened if, say, Serbia had forcibly resisted the independence of the Albanian Kosovars). It is therefore hardly a coincidence that the global frequency of civil war increased in the half century after the Second World War, the period in which the process of state creation reached its height. Nor should it be surprising that civil wars have become less frequent in the past fifteen years as the pace of state making has once again slackened.[53] Just how long the short peace that has followed the long trauma of the late twentieth century's civil wars will last remains to be seen. Neither historians nor political scientists can foretell whether there will be new waves of secessions and civil wars, or if indeed the current dispensation of territorial sovereignty can long endure.

Notes

I am especially grateful to Robert Bonner, Don Doyle, Mikulas Fabry, Tanisha Fazal, Alexander Pavković, and Peter Radan for their generous help and salutary criticism.

1. Tanisha M. Fazal, *State Death: The Politics and Geography of Conquest, Occupation, and Annexation* (Princeton: Princeton University Press, 2007), 19–30.

2. Peter Radan, "Secession: A Word in Search of a Meaning," in *On the Way to Statehood: Secession and Globalisation*, ed. Aleksandar Pavković and Peter Radan (Aldershot, U.K.: Ashgate, 2008), 18–19. On state recognition, see especially Mikulas Fabry, *Recognizing States: International Society and the Establishment of New States since 1776* (Oxford: Oxford University Press, 2010).

3. Aleksandar Pavković with Peter Radan, *Creating New States: Theory and Practice of Secession* (Aldershot, U.K.: Ashgate, 2007), 65. For an extensive discussion of peaceful secessions, see 65–94.

4. Andreas Wimmer and Brian Min, "From Empire to Nation-State: Explaining Wars in the Modern World, 1816–2001," *American Sociological Review* 71, no. 6 (2006): 881; Andreas Wimmer, Lars-Erik Cederman, and Brian Min, "Ethnic Politics and Armed Conflict: A Configurational Analysis of a New Global Data Set," *American Sociological Review* 74, no. 2 (2009): 316–37.

5. *The Åland Islands Question*, League of Nations Doc. B7.21/68/106 (1921), 28, quoted in Andrew Hurrell, "International Law and the Making and Unmaking of Boundaries," in *States, Nations, and Borders: The Ethics of Making Boundaries*, ed. Allen Buchanan and Margaret Moore (Cambridge: Cambridge University Press, 2003), 292.

6. James Crawford, *The Creation of States in International Law*, 2nd ed. (Oxford: Oxford University Press, 2006), 375 (my emphasis).

7. Marcelo G. Kohen, introduction, in *Secession: International Law Perspectives*, ed. Marcelo G. Kohen (Cambridge: Cambridge University Press, 2006), 3 (my emphasis).

8. Allen Buchanan, "The Making and Unmaking of Boundaries: What Liberalism Has to Say," in *States, Nations, and Borders*, 246.

9. Bruno Coppieters, introduction, in *Contextualizing Secession: Normative Studies in Comparative Perspective*, ed. Bruno Coppieters and Richard Sakwa (Oxford: Oxford University Press, 2003), 4; Buchanan, "The Making and Unmaking of Boundaries," 259 n. 17; Radan, "Secession: A Word in Search of a Meaning," 18.

[52] DAVID ARMITAGE

10. Stathis Kalyvas, "Civil Wars," in *The Oxford Handbook of Comparative Politics*, ed. Carles Boix and Susan Stokes (Oxford: Oxford University Press, 2007), 416; cf. Jan Angstrom, "Towards a Typology of Internal Armed Conflict: Synthesising a Decade of Conceptual Turmoil," *Civil Wars* 4, no. 3 (2001): 93–116, and Nicholas Sambanis, "What Is Civil War? Conceptual and Empirical Complexities of an Operational Definition," *Journal of Conflict Resolution* 48, no. 6 (2004): 814–58.

11. John Keegan and Bartle Bull, "What Is a Civil War? Are We Witnessing One in Iraq?" *Prospect*, Dec. 2006, 18–19.

12. Melvin Small and J. David Singer, *Resort to Arms: International and Civil Wars, 1816–1980* (Beverly Hills, Calif.: Sage Publications, 1982), 210–20.

13. David A. Patten, "Is Iraq in a Civil War?" *Middle East Quarterly* 14, no. 3 (2007): 27–32.

14. Errol A. Henderson and J. David Singer, "Civil War in the Post-Colonial World, 1946–92," *Journal of Peace Research* 37, no. 3 (2000): 275–99.

15. FM 100-20, *Military Operations in Low Intensity Conflict*, Dec. 5, 1990, www.global security.org/military/library/policy/army/fm/100-20/10020gl.htm, accessed Jan. 12, 2009.

16. See especially the chapters by Robert Bonner, Charles Dew, Susan-Mary Grant, Paul Quigley, Peter Radan, and Frank Towers in this volume.

17. Abraham Lincoln, "Message to Congress in Special Session," July 4, 1861, in *The Collected Works of Abraham Lincoln*, 11 vols., ed. Roy P. Basler (New Brunswick: Rutgers University Press, 1953–55), 4:426, 435, 436 (Lincoln's emphases).

18. Abraham Lincoln, "Address Delivered at the Dedication of the Cemetery at Gettysburg," Nov. 19, 1863, in Lincoln, *Collected Works*, 7:23 (my emphasis). The Confederate Constitution did not include a right of secession; see Stephen C. Neff, *Justice in Blue and Gray: A Legal History of the Civil War* (Cambridge, Mass.: Harvard University Press, 2010), 14–15.

19. For comprehensive discussions of Lincoln's views on secession, see Christopher Heath Wellman, *A Theory of Secession: The Case for Political Self-Determination* (Cambridge: Cambridge University Press, 2005), 65–96, and Peter Radan, "Lincoln, the Constitution, and Secession," in this volume.

20. Lincoln, "Message to Congress in Special Session," 4:433.

21. Abraham Lincoln, "First Inaugural Address," Mar. 4, 1861, in Lincoln, *Collected Works*, 4:265. Lincoln had originally written "treasonable" in place of "revolutionary" (4:265 n. 16). See also the discussion of Lincoln's views on consensual secession in Radan, "Lincoln, the Constitution, and Secession."

22. On which see, for example, Pavković with Radan, *Creating New States*, 221–40.

23. Lincoln, "Address Delivered at the Dedication of the Cemetery at Gettysburg," 7:23.

24. Quincy Wright, "The American Civil War (1861–65)," in *The International Law of Civil War*, ed. Richard A. Falk (Baltimore: Johns Hopkins Press, 1971), 43; Neff, *Justice in Blue and Gray*, 4–29.

25. *Congressional Record*, Jan. 11, 1907, 944–49, Record Group 94, Office of the Adjutant General, Administrative Precedent File (Frech File), box 16, bundle 58, National Archives, Washington, D.C. On the naming of the war, see E. Merton Coulter, "A Name for the American War of 1861–1865," *Georgia Historical Quarterly* 36, no. 2 (1952): 109–31; Michael P. Musick, "A War by Any Other Name," *Prologue: The Journal of the National Archives* 27, no. 2 (1995): 149; and John M. Coski, "The War Between the Names," *North and South* 8, no. 7 (2006): 62–71.

26. Thomas M. Patterson (D-Colo.), *Congressional Record*, Jan. 11, 1907, 944.

27. The Prize Cases, 67 U.S. 635 (1863); Brian McGinty, *Lincoln and the Court* (Cambridge, Mass.: Harvard University Press, 2008), 118–43; Thomas H. Lee and Michael D. Ramsey, "The Story of the *Prize Cases*: Executive Action and Judicial Review in Wartime," in *Presidential Power Stories*, ed. Christopher H. Schroeder and Curtis A. Bradley (New York: Foundation Press, 2009), 53–92; Neff, *Justice in Blue and Gray*, 24–28.

28. Richard R. Baxter, "The First Modern Codification of the Law of War: Francis Lieber and General Orders No. 100," *The International Review of the Red Cross* 3 (1963), 170–89, 243–50; James F. Childress, "Francis Lieber's Interpretation of the Laws of War: General Orders No. 100 in the Context of His Life and Thought," *American Journal of Jurisprudence* 21 (1976): 34–70; Richard Shelly Hartigan, *Lieber's Code and the Law of War* (Chicago: Precedent Publishing, 1983).

29. Henry Halleck, annotation to Francis Lieber, *A Code for the Government of Armies in the Field, as Authorized by the Laws and Usages of War on Land, Printed as Manuscript for the Board Appointed by the Secretary of War (February 1863)*, 25–[26], 243077, Henry E. Huntington Library, San Marino, Calif. (hereafter HEH).

30. Francis Lieber to George Stillman Hillard, May 11, 1861, Lieber MSS, LI 2308, HEH.

31. Lieber to Halleck, Mar. 4, 1863, Lieber MSS, LI 1778, HEH; cf. Francis Lieber, [*Instructions for the Government of the Armies of the United States, in the Field*] *Section X: Insurrection—Rebellion—Civil War—Foreign Invasion of the United States* [1863], 240460, HEH.

32. Francis Lieber, "Twenty-seven Definitions and Elementary Positions Concerning the Laws and Usages of War," 1861, Lieber MSS, box 2, item 15, Eisenhower Library, Johns Hopkins University, Baltimore, Md.

33. Francis Lieber, *Instructions for the Government of Armies of the United States, in the Field* (New York: D. Van Nostrand, 1863), 34.

34. Stephen C. Neff, *War and the Law of Nations: A General History* (Cambridge: Cambridge University Press, 2005), 256–57; Neff, *Justice in Blue and Gray*, 15–19.

35. Paul Jal, *La guerre civile à Rome: Étude littéraire et morale* (Paris: Presses Universitaires de France, 1963), 19–21; Robert Brown, "The Terms *Bellum Sociale* and *Bellum Ciuile* in the Late Republic," in *Studies in Latin Literature and Roman History*, ed. Carl Deroux (Brussels: Latomus, 2003), 102–20.

36. See, for example, U.S. Department of War, *The War of the Rebellion: A Compilation of the Official Records of the Union and Confederate Armies*, 70 vols. (Washington, D.C.: U.S. Government Printing Office, 1880–91).

37. Francis Lieber, "[Notes on the] English and Ferench [sic] Revolutions," ca. 1850, LI 365, HEH.

38. Francis Lieber, "Some Questions Answered—Secession—The Strength of Armies and Navys, &ca," ca. 1851, LI 369, HEH.

39. Francis Lieber, [Remarks regarding the *Right of Secession*], ca. 1851, LI 368, HEH.

40. Cf. Henry Belcher, *The First American Civil War: First Period, 1775–1778*, 2 vols. (London: Macmillan, 1911).

41. See, for example, John Shy, *A People Numerous and Armed: Reflections on the Military Struggle for American Independence*, rev. ed. (Ann Arbor: University of Michigan Press, 1990), 183–92; Andrew O'Shaughnessy, *An Empire Divided: The American Revolution and the British Caribbean* (Philadelphia: University of Pennsylvania Press, 2000); Brendan Simms, *Three Victories and a Defeat: The Rise and Fall of the First British Empire, 1714–1783* (London: Allen Lane, 2007), 593–600; and Wim Klooster, *Revolutions in the Atlantic World: A Comparative History* (New York: New York University Press, 2009), 11–44.

42. "Declaration . . . Setting Forth the Causes and Necessity of Taking Up Arms," July 6, 1775, in *A Decent Respect to the Opinions of Mankind: Congressional State Papers, 1774–1776*, ed. James H. Hutson (Washington, D.C.: Library of Congress, 1975), 96, 97.

43. See, for example, *Civil War: A Poem, Written in the Year 1775* [n.p.: n.p., n.d. (1776?)], sig. A2ʳ; David Hartley, *Substance of a Speech in Parliament, upon the State of the Nation and the Present Civil War with America* (London: J. Almon, 1776), 19; and John Roebuck, *An Enquiry, Whether the Guilt of the Present Civil War in America, Ought to Be Imputed to Great Britain or America* [n. p., n.d. (1776?)].

44. Cf. Thomas Paine, *Common Sense: Addressed to the Inhabitants of America* (Philadelphia: Robert Bell, 1776), 26. On Britain's sequence of civil wars, see also J. G. A. Pocock, "The Fourth English Civil War: Dissolution, Desertion and Alternative Histories in the Glorious Revolution," *Government and Opposition* 23, no. 2 (1988): 151–66.

45. Richard Henry Lee, "Resolution of Independence," June 7, 1776, in *Journals of the Continental Congress, 1774–1789*, 5 vols., ed. Worthington C. Ford (Washington, D.C.: U.S. Government Printing Office, 1904–6), 5:425–26.

46. David Armitage, *The Declaration of Independence: A Global History* (Cambridge, Mass.: Harvard University Press, 2007).

47. *A Declaration by the Representatives of the United States of America, in General Congress Assembled*, July 4, 1776 (Philadelphia: John Dunlap, 1776), n.p.

48. Pavković with Radan, *Creating New States*, 5.

49. David Armitage, "The Contagion of Sovereignty: Declarations of Independence since 1776," *South African Historical Journal* 52, no. 1 (2005): 1–18; Armitage, *The Declaration of Independence*, 103.

50. "Declaration of the Immediate Causes Which Induce and Justify the Secession of South Carolina from the Federal Union," Dec. 24, 1860, in *Journal of the Convention of the People of South Carolina, Held in 1860, 1861 and 1862* (Columbia, S.C.: R. W. Gibbes, 1862), 461–66 (my emphasis). More generally, see Emory M. Thomas, *The Confederacy as a Revolutionary Experience* (Englewood Cliffs, N.J.: Prentice-Hall, 1971).

51. Pavković with Radan, *Creating New States*, 257–58.

52. James D. Fearon, "Separatist Wars, Partition, and World Order," *Security Studies* 13, no. 4 (2004): 402.

53. Wimmer and Min, "From Empire to Nation-State," 883, 887–88, table 2.

PETER RADAN

Lincoln, the Constitution, and Secession

khil Reed Amar has written that "the legality or illegality of secession was
probably the most serious constitutional question ever to arise in America."[1] In relation to this "most serious constitutional question," Cass Sunstein
has asserted that "no serious scholar or politician now argues that a right to secede exists under American constitutional law."[2] Laurence Tribe cites President
Abraham Lincoln's First Inaugural Address of March 4, 1861, as the "definitive
articulation" of this view of Amar's "most serious constitutional question."[3]

That Lincoln firmly rejected the legality of the secession of the eleven Confederate States is clear. However, Lincoln never claimed that secession from the
Union was impermissible. Lincoln recognized the legitimacy of secession if it
was consensual or pursuant to a morally justified revolution. For Lincoln, the
unilateral secessions of the eleven southern states lacked any legitimacy because
they were not accompanied by either of these two conditions.

This chapter explores these two routes to secession. The first part outlines
and critiques Lincoln's arguments in support of his proposition that consent
was necessary for a constitutionally legal secession. The second details and
evaluates Lincoln's views on revolutionary secession. The third assesses the impact of Lincoln's views against the background of contemporary jurisprudence
on secession in a number of constitutional law decisions from Canada and the
former Yugoslavia as well as in express stipulations in the constitutions of states
such as Ethiopia, St. Kitts and Nevis, and Liechtenstein.

LEGAL SECESSION BY CONSENT

For Lincoln secession was constitutionally legal only if achieved by consent.
This required a state, first, to demonstrate that its population wanted to secede

and, second, to obtain the consent of the union as a whole. It thus followed that unilateral secession was constitutionally illegal.

Lincoln set out his views in his First Inaugural Address and his message to Congress of July 4, 1861. In the former he referred to the right of "the people" to "exercise their *constitutional* right of amending [their constitution]."[4] In his message to Congress, he referred to and rejected the southern states' argument that a state could "withdraw from the Union, without the consent of the Union or of any other State."[5] Later he questioned whether a state could "go off without leave" or "without consent."[6] In opposing secession without consent, Lincoln clearly implied that secession could legally occur with the leave or consent of the Union.

Two issues arise from Lincoln's propositions on consensual secession. The first is the practical question of what constitutes consent. Lincoln does not elaborate in detail on this question. The second, which he more fully analyzes, is the theoretical question of why the consent of a country as a whole is necessary for a constitutionally legal secession. In addressing this issue, Lincoln gives legal and nonlegal reasons. However, in his legal reasoning he reframes the question to ask why unilateral secession of a state is illegal rather than why consent is necessary for a legal secession.

The Meaning of Consent

For Lincoln, consent involves a two-phase process. First, the population of the seceding state must clearly indicate its consent. Such consent legitimates the demand for secession. Second, the country as a whole must also consent to that state's secession. Here consent relates to the effectuation of a legitimate demand for secession.

Lincoln's views regarding the consent of the population of a seceding state are revealed in his comments on the secession declarations of the Confederate States. In his 1861 message to Congress, Lincoln said: "It may well be questioned whether there is, to-day, a majority of the legally-qualified voters of any State, except perhaps South Carolina, in favor of disunion. There is much reason to believe that the Union men are the majority in many, if not every other one, of the so-called seceded States."[7] Lincoln also questioned the legitimacy of elections in Virginia and Tennessee on account of the coercive tactics used by prosecessionists. In making these points, Lincoln was insisting that unless secession had the genuine support of at least the majority of the population of the secessionist state, it would be illegitimate.

For Lincoln, a legitimate demand for secession by the Confederate States could only be legally effectuated if it secured the consent of the United States as a whole. In his First Inaugural Address, Lincoln stipulated that a constitutional amendment was the only means by which such consent could be garnered. Establishing a constitutional amendment would require, first, generating a valid proposal for it and, second, adopting or ratifying it.

As to the first step, article 5 of the Constitution stipulates that a constitutional amendment can be proposed by a resolution passed at a joint session of the two houses of Congress by a two-thirds majority or by a convention that is called for by the legislatures of at least two-thirds of the states. In relation to the second step, article 5 states that the Congress must stipulate that the proposed amendment be adopted either by the legislatures of at least three-quarters of the states or by conventions in at least three-quarters of the states. Article 5 presents almost insurmountable obstacles to any state wishing to secede through constitutionally legal processes.

In his message to Congress, Lincoln suggested a somewhat different form of consent. Although the meaning of Lincoln's reference in this message to the illegality of any secession that does not have "the consent of the Union or of any other State" is not altogether clear, Douglas Sanders is arguably correct when he claims that Lincoln meant that a secession, to be legal, required the consent of "a majority of the populace" as well as of "a majority of the states."[8] This is a procedure at variance with article 5, but it also amounts to an almost insurmountable obstacle to any state wishing to secede.

On the other hand, Amar has suggested that a national referendum alone that endorsed a state's desire to secede would have been accepted by Lincoln. Amar suggests that given Lincoln's commitment to principles of democratic majoritarianism, such a referendum would have carried "great moral weight with those government actors . . . ordinarily involved in the amendment process."[9] In support of Amar's contention, one can refer to the Constitution's preamble, which states: "We the people of the United States . . . do ordain and establish this Constitution." If "the people" are the supreme authority in the United States, then logically "the people" could, through a national referendum, consent to the secession of a state of the Union.

The Necessity for Consent

For Lincoln, the absence of the Union's consent to any secession rendered unilateral secession constitutionally illegal. In stark contrast was the view of the southern states, who argued that unilateral secession was constitutionally valid. The difference between Lincoln and his southern interlocutors on the constitutional legality of secession stemmed from conflicting conceptions of sovereignty in the context of American constitutional law.

The Confederate States' argument rested on the proposition that sovereignty resided with the peoples of the individual states that constituted the Union. Southern spokesmen argued that state popular conventions, which had ratified the Constitution drafted in Philadelphia in 1787, were the fora in which the question of whether states should secede from the Union ought to be decided. The leading exponent of this constitutional theory was John C. Calhoun, who wrote:

> The government is a federal, in contradistinction to a national government—
> a government formed by the States; ordained and established by the States,
> and for the States—without any participation or agency whatever, on the part
> of the people, regarded in the aggregate as forming a nation.... In all its
> parts ... [our system of government] emanated from the same source—the
> people of the several States. The whole, taken together, form a federal com-
> munity—a community composed of States united by a political compact—
> and not a nation composed of individuals united by, what is called, a social
> compact.[10]

Calhoun went on to explain the basis of the right of secession from the Union defined as a "political compact" as follows: "A State, as a party to the constitutional compact, has a right to secede.... This results, necessarily, from the nature of a compact—where the parties to it are sovereign: and, of course, have no higher authority to which to appeal."[11]

In rejecting Calhoun's explanation of the founding of the Union, Lincoln marshaled two distinct arguments. First, Lincoln claimed that a proper understanding of American constitutional history established that it was the Union that preceded and created the states rather than the other way around as Calhoun maintained (the legal historical argument). Second, Lincoln maintained that even if Calhoun's explanation was accepted as correct, it did not follow that unilateral secession was constitutionally legal (the contract argument). Each of Lincoln's arguments needs to be critically evaluated.

The Legal Historical Argument

In his First Inaugural Address, Lincoln asserted that the Union was "perpetual" and preceded the Constitution, the latter's purpose being "*to form a more perfect Union.*"[12] In his message to Congress Lincoln elaborated on this same theme as follows:

> Our States have neither more nor less power than that reserved to them in the Union by the Constitution, no one of them ever having been a State out of the Union. The original ones passed into the Union even before they cast off their British colonial dependence, and the new ones ... only took the designation of States on coming into the Union, while that name was first adopted for the old ones in and by the Declaration of Independence. Therein the "United Colonies" were declared to be "free and independent States"; but even then the object plainly was not to declare their independence of one another or of the Union, but directly the contrary, as their mutual pledge and their mutual action before, at the time, and afterwards abundantly show. The express plighting of faith by each and all of the original thirteen in the Articles of Confederation, two years later, that the Union shall be perpetual is most conclusive. . . . The Union, and not themselves separately, procured their independence and their liberty. By conquest or purchase the Union gave each of them whatever of independence and liberty it has. The Union is older than any of the States, and, in fact, it created them as States. Originally some dependent colonies made the Union, and in turn the Union threw off their old dependence for them and made them States, such as they are.[13]

For Lincoln, the Declaration of Independence, rather than the Constitution, was the Union's most relevant founding document. And the central proposition he made relying on it was that the Union constituted a federation that did not afford its states a right of unilateral secession. This is what Lincoln meant by a perpetual union. The fact that the Constitution, adopted in 1788, did not declare the union thereby established to be perpetual in this sense did not matter, because it predated the Constitution and had acquired the attribute of perpetuity pursuant to the Articles of Confederation and Perpetual Union that came into effect in 1781. That attribute remained fundamental by virtue of the Constitution's provision relating to the formation of a "more perfect" union. The states, being creations of a perpetual union, could not, in the absence of express provisions in the Constitution to that effect, unilaterally secede from it.

However, the documents that Lincoln relied on to establish his argument in fact readily demonstrate its falsity. In his First Inaugural Address, Lincoln specifically referred to the Articles of Association of 1774, the Declaration of Independence of 1776, the Articles of Confederation and Perpetual Union, which were drafted in 1777 and became operative in 1781, and finally to the Preamble to the Constitution.

The Articles of Association did not create any American Union. Nowhere in the text of the document does the word "union" appear. The articles stipulated that the British colonies would "associate" for the limited purpose of seeking, in a coordinated manner, redress of various grievances that they had against Great Britain and that the colonies would "adhere to this association" only until the legislation responsible for these grievances was "repealed."

The divisions and tensions between Great Britain and her colonies escalated in the wake of the Articles of Association, compelling the thirteen colonies to draft the Declaration of Independence, which asserted that they were now "FREE AND INDEPENDENT STATES" and that as such "they [had] full Power to levy War, conclude Peace, contract Alliances, establish Commerce, and to do all other Acts and Things which INDEPENDENT STATES may of right do." This assertion can hardly be said to express the notion that there is a union and no independent states. In fact, to the contrary, article 1 of the Treaty of Paris of 1783, which formally concluded the American War of Independence, witnessed Great Britain's recognition of its former colonies as "Free, Sovereign, and Independent States,"[14] a reality Lincoln ignored in his brief historical account of the emergence and transformation of the union ostensibly established by 1774.

The adoption of the Articles of Confederation and Perpetual Union saw the creation of a "perpetual" union (albeit of a limited scope), since its article 2 stipulated that "each state retains its sovereignty, freedom, and independence." As Amar observes, "Both before and after ratifying the Articles, the people of each state—and not the people of America as a whole—were sovereign."[15] However, when the Articles of Confederation proved to be unworkable and the United States was threatened with international intervention by external powers, delegates of most of the states met at Philadelphia in 1787, in what David Hendrickson has aptly described as "an international conference, conducted . . . among diplomatic plenipotentiaries of the states" to negotiate a peace pact in the form of a "reasoned response to a serious security problem that espied a sequence in which internal division and the intervention of external powers would create the same whirlwind in America that had undone Europe."[16] The peace pact was the draft of a constitution, which, when ratified, would create a new and stronger union to replace the limited union that had been established by the Articles of Confederation.

It must be recalled that although article 13 of the Articles of Confederation referred to a "perpetual" union, it also stipulated that changes to the Articles of Confederation required the unanimous consent of all of the states. However, in making a "more perfect" union, the Constitutional Convention of 1787 felt it necessary to breach that condition. Article 7 of the Constitution stipulated that ratification by nine of the thirteen states would be "sufficient for the establishment of this Constitution between the States so ratifying the same." Article 7 made it clear that the new union was not necessarily going to be constituted by the same states as the old union, and this in fact was a reality, since there was a period of time during which two states remained outside the union established by the Constitution. David Kowalski has aptly observed that the fact that the founders selected the article 7 process for ratification of the Constitution suggests they "did not see the Constitution as a continuation of the Articles, but as a break from them."[17]

On June 21, 1788, New Hampshire became the ninth state to ratify the Constitution, although Virginia and New York also ratified it five days later. The remaining two states of the union established by the Articles of Confederation, North Carolina and Rhode Island, remained outside the new union until November 21, 1789, and May 29, 1790, respectively. Thus, when the new federal government was constituted in March 1789, only eleven states were bound by the Constitution.[18] During this time the right of these states to refuse to ratify the Constitution was not denied and no attempt was made to forcibly coerce them to do so.

From the perspective of the Articles of Confederation, the adoption of the Constitution was an illegal and revolutionary act, a point conceded by James Madison who, in *Federalist No. 40*, justified the abandonment of the Articles of Confederation and the adoption of the draft Constitution on the basis of the right of revolution articulated in the Declaration of Independence.[19] In effect, the eleven states that ratified the Constitution before the new federal structures were established in March 1789 had seceded from the union established by the Articles of Confederation and formed a new union governed by the

Constitution.[20] This is further confirmed by the preamble to the Constitution, which states that the Constitution was adopted to *"form* a more perfect union" (emphasis added) or, as Kenneth Stampp observes, "to create a new and better one."[21]

The references to a "perpetual" union in the Articles of Confederation does not support Lincoln's argument that the union that he was defending in 1861 was perpetual in a way that would make unilateral secession from it unconstitutional. Given that the union of the Articles of Confederation was, in violation of its article 13 provision as to its "perpetuity," terminated by the ratification of the Constitution, article 13's references to a "perpetual" union cannot be appealed to to interpret the Constitution as establishing a union in which unilateral secession was prohibited. As Stampp notes, "The break in historical continuity undermines the case for a perpetual union based upon the country's political condition before 1787. . . . Therefore, a valid case for perpetuity cannot lean on the terms of the Articles [of Confederation] but must demonstrate that it is clearly articulated in the Constitution itself."[22]

It now remains to be determined whether the words "more perfect Union" in the Preamble to the Constitution justify Lincoln's argument that the union created by the Constitution was perpetual in the sense of prohibiting unilateral secession of any state. The conclusion that perpetuity is not a necessary adjunct to perfection is supported both by the standard rules of construction and the historical record.

It is quite clear that difficulties in the functioning of the United States under the Articles of Confederation and threats of international intervention by external powers were the motivation for the convention that met in Philadelphia in 1787.[23] The "more perfect Union" expression in the Preamble to the Constitution referred to making the union more workable from the perspective of government and administration rather than to making it perpetual in the sense Lincoln used the term. Had the framers of the Constitution intended the new union to be perpetual in that sense, it is reasonable to assume they would have used explicit words to that effect, especially given that the word "perpetual" was used in a number of provisions of the Articles of Confederation. But, as Amar has noted "the Preamble did not expressly proclaim that its new, more perfect union would be 'perpetual'—and for good reason: Why borrow a word from the Articles of Confederation that did not quite mean what it said in that document, a word that was being thrust aside by the very act of constitution itself?"[24]

Lincoln's interpretation of the Articles of Association, the Declaration of Independence, the Articles of Confederation, and the Preamble to the Constitution does not support his proposition that the Union preceded the states and that, by implication, no state had the right of unilateral secession from the Union. The union Lincoln was committed to defending in 1861 was not the same union that had existed prior to June 1788 but was rather created by the eleven states that at that time ratified the draft Constitution stitched together in Philadelphia in 1787.

If the above analysis of Lincoln's legal historical argument is accepted as sound, the question then arises as to whether his contract argument supports his proposition that unilateral secession is illegal and unconstitutional.

The Contract Argument

Lincoln, for the sake of argument, was prepared to accept Calhoun's proposition that the Union was a political compact. But Lincoln questioned whether the compact, "as a contract," could "be peaceably unmade, by less than all the parties who made it": "One party to a contract may violate it—break it, so to speak; but does it not require all to lawfully rescind it?"[25] The unstated answer to his question is that all states would need to agree to the secession of any state, and since such consent had not been secured in the case of the Confederate States, their unilateral secessions were illegal.

However, Lincoln's argument is flawed. The agreement of all the parties to a contract to bring it to an end is only necessary when there has been no previous terminating breach or repudiation of the contract. If one party commits such a breach or repudiation, the other party can, by service of a notice of termination, terminate the contract. Thereafter, both parties are discharged from any further performance of the contract.[26] This is the contract law analogy that was relied on by the Confederate States. Thus, South Carolina asserted the right of secession in its declaration of December 24, 1860 in the following terms:

> We maintain that in every compact between two or more parties, the obligation is mutual; that the failure of one of the contracting parties to perform a material part of the agreement, entirely releases the obligation of the other; and that where no arbiter is provided, each party is entitled to his own judgment to determine the fact of failure, with all its consequences.[27]

According to South Carolina, the North's failure "to perform a material part of the agreement" was manifested in its refusal, in various ways, to protect the institution of slavery, especially its failure to effectively enforce fugitive slave laws, as well as "Lincoln's refusal to accept the Supreme Court's resolution of the constitutional issues decided in [*Dred Scott v. Sandford*]."[28]

If these claims by South Carolina were unsustainable, her secession would have been unlawful. In the context of the contract argument, it would have amounted to a terminating breach of contract by South Carolina. This then raises the issue of whether, if contract law analogies were applied, suppression of the secession would have been permitted in such circumstances. In contract law, where there has been a breach of contract, the innocent party may be entitled to a decree of specific performance to force the contract breaker to carry out its obligations. However, this is a discretionary order, which can be refused on various grounds. One such ground relates to contracts of personal service that are not generally enforced, the reason being that it is not appropriate to enforce a personal relationship against the will of one of the parties to it.[29] Translating this principle to the case of an unlawful secession, it can be fairly argued that suppression of the secession would be illegal, since a political compact of states is analogous to a contract of personal service. This was, in effect, the view of President James Buchanan who argued that the secession of the southern states was illegal, but so too was any attempt to use force to prevent them from seceding.[30]

On the other hand, if Lincoln's contract argument is valid, the consequence is that a state is contractually bound to remain part of the United States in perpetuity. This proposition can be questioned on philosophical grounds. Although the people of the states originally ratifying the constitution or of the states that subsequently joined the Union may be said to have been bound to the Union, they could not have similarly bound later generations of citizens of those same states.[31] Further, periodic participation in the structures of the Union in the form of voting is not enough to clearly establish a continuation of the original ratification of or consent to the union established by the Constitution.[32]

One can point to yet another contract law analogy, not mentioned by Lincoln, which also negates Lincoln's arguments against the legality of unilateral secession. In contract law, there is a doctrine called the doctrine of frustration, which states that if, subsequent to its making, a contract becomes "incapable of being performed because the circumstances in which performance is called for would render it a thing radically different from that which was undertaken by the contract," the parties to the contract are automatically discharged or released from any further or future obligations under the contract.[33] One such change of circumstances arises when parties enter into a contract on the basis of a fundamental assumption or condition and there is a subsequent failure of that assumption or condition.[34]

In the context of antebellum America, it was generally agreed that the terms of the ratification of the Constitution were that it remained legally binding for only so long "as constitutional institutions functioned in ways consistent with the original constitutional commitment to bisectionalism."[35] However, with Lincoln's election to the presidency came his commitment to majoritarianism as the means of determining constitutional questions not clearly addressed by explicit constitutional provisions, such as whether slavery was permissible in the unorganized western territories. Lincoln's adherence to majoritarianism is visible in his First Inaugural Address where, after referring to such constitutional questions, he states:

> From questions of this class spring all our constitutional controversies, and we divide upon them into majorities and minorities. If the minority will not acquiesce, the majority must, or the Government must cease. There is no other alternative, for continuing the Government is acquiescence on one side or the other. . . . A majority held in restraint by constitutional checks and limitations, and always changing easily with deliberate changes of popular opinions and sentiments, is the only true sovereign of a free people.[36]

In the words of Mark Graber, Lincoln "incorrectly invoked a constitutional commitment to majority rule when justifying Republican attempts to ban slavery in all territories without any significant Southern support."[37] This "unwillingness to share power . . . 'frustrated' the constitutional contract, providing legal grounds for Southern secession."[38]

If, as has been argued, Lincoln's contract argument is, like his legal historical argument, unsound, then Lincoln did not establish any legal basis for his proposition that unilateral secession from the Union was unconstitutional. Consequentially, he also failed to underpin his proposition that a constitutional secession could only be achieved by consent.

SECESSION AS A REVOLUTIONARY ACT

If, as Lincoln argued, the southern states' attempts at unilateral secession were unconstitutional, then secession could only be legitimized if it was a morally justified revolutionary act. Lincoln's recognition of revolutionary secession is not novel, nor is it surprising given his well-documented devotion to the Declaration of Independence.[39] The Declaration of Independence, which announced the secession of thirteen British colonies in America from Great Britain, asserted that "whenever any form of government becomes destructive . . . it is the right of the people to alter or to abolish it, and to institute new government, laying its foundation on such principles and organizing its powers in such form, as to them shall seem most likely to effect their safety and happiness."

In his First Inaugural Address Lincoln made two references to the revolutionary right of secession—first when he noted that "if, by the mere force of numbers, a majority should deprive a minority of any clearly written constitutional right, it might, in a moral point of view, justify revolution—certainly would, if such right were a vital one" and second when he pointed out that "this country, with its institutions, belongs to the people who inhabit it. Whenever they shall grow weary of the existing government, they can exercise their *constitutional* right of amending it, or their *revolutionary* right to dismember, or overthrow it."[40] These passages demonstrate that for Lincoln revolutionary secession is not a legal right but rather a moral right. In a draft of his message to Congress Lincoln made it clear that this moral right could only be exercised for "a morally justifiable cause."[41]

Confederate spokesmen, such as Jefferson Davis, invoked the Declaration of Independence as the basis of a revolutionary right of secession that legitimated their cause.[42] However, although secession might have been seen as a revolutionary right in 1776, by the time of the Civil War—at least for nationalists such as Lincoln—secession had become taboo.[43] For them, the Confederate States' invocation of the revolutionary right of secession lacked legitimacy because of the absence of any moral justification for secession.

Radical abolitionists such as William Lloyd Garrison argued that the South's defense of slavery rendered the Confederate States' secessions illegitimate.[44] Indeed, the defense of slavery by southern states provided Garrison with a moral justification for his advocacy, during the antebellum period, of the right of secession from the Union by nonslave states in the North. Thus he argued in a speech he made on March 5, 1858, that "we shall be told that [disunion] is equivalent to a dissolution of the Union. Be it so! Give us Disunion with liberty and a good conscience, rather than Union with slavery and moral degradation."[45]

However, the perpetuation of slavery was not, nor could it have been, the basis of Lincoln's argument that the Confederate States lacked a moral justification to secede from the Union. Lincoln's attitudes toward slavery and America's black population have been endlessly debated.[46] What is clear is that at the time of his election to the presidency and through to the outbreak of the Civil War, Lincoln was committed to upholding the policy on which he was elected, namely, preventing the extension of slavery into America's unorganized western territories.

Lincoln's claim that the Confederate States lacked a moral justification for their secession was based on his belief that secession amounted to an attack on America's system of constitutional democracy. Lincoln did not articulate the issue of morality by referring to its absence from the cause of the Confederate States but rather by asserting the moral right of the northern states to suppress the attempt at secession of the eleven southern states. In his message to Congress, Lincoln argued that the hostilities ignited by the Fort Sumter incident had cast the conflict as one of "immediate dissolution" of the Union or "blood":

> This issue embraces more than the fate of these United States. It presents to the whole family of man the question, whether a constitutional republic, or democracy—a Government of the people by the same people—can or cannot maintain its territorial integrity against its own domestic foes. It presents the question, whether discontented individuals, too few in numbers to control administration, according to organic law, in any case, can always, upon the pretenses made in this case, or on any other pretenses, or arbitrarily, without any pretense, break up their Government, and thus practically put an end to free government upon the earth.[47]

One can readily agree with Lincoln's view that revolutionary secession is not a legal right. However, it is difficult to see why this revolutionary right is conditional on there being a morally justifiable basis for its exercise. A revolution either succeeds or fails irrespective of its morality. No other factors are relevant. The success or failure of the revolution is simply a question of fact. As the renowned legal theorist Hans Kelsen has explained (albeit in the slightly different context of a coup d'etat):

> Suppose that a group of individuals attempt to seize power by force. . . . If they succeed, if the old order ceases, and the new order begins to be efficacious, because the individuals whose behavior the new order regulates actually behave, by and large, in conformity with the new order, then this order is considered as a valid order. It is now according to this new order that the actual behavior of individuals is interpreted as legal or illegal. But this means

that a new basic norm is presupposed. It is . . . a norm endowing the revolutionary government with legal authority.[48]

Recognition by other states, especially the state from which secession is attempted, of the claim to independent statehood is often crucial to the success of a revolutionary secession. Although recognition is not necessary to achieve statehood, as the Canadian Supreme Court pointed out in *Reference re: Secession of Quebec* in the context of secession "the viability of a would-be state in the international community depends, as a practical matter, upon recognition by other states."[49] Given the importance of international recognition in relation to the success or failure of any revolutionary claim to secession, it is hardly surprising that Lincoln's major foreign policy goal during the Civil War was to prevent international recognition of the Confederacy. Lincoln was even prepared to risk war with Great Britain over this issue. For the Confederacy, international recognition was the single most important diplomatic goal.[50] Lincoln's strategy succeeded. However, had Great Britain and the rest of Europe recognized the Confederacy it is arguable that the latter's secession from the Union would have succeeded.

LINCOLN'S LEGACY

The essential proposition that emerges from Lincoln's analysis of secession and constitutional law is that the secession of an American state can be legally achieved only with the consent of the population of that state as well as of the United States as a whole. Thus, unilateral secession is unconstitutional, although it may be legitimate pursuant to a revolutionary right of secession, provided it is underpinned by a morally justified cause.

Notwithstanding the deficiencies in Lincoln's reasoning in support of his analysis, his basic proposition has been confirmed subsequently. For example, in the United States, Salmon Chase, chief justice of the Supreme Court of the United States, echoed Lincoln's views and some of his reasoning when, writing for the majority in the 1869 case of *Texas v. White*, he said:

> The Union of the States never was a purely artificial and arbitrary relation. It began among the Colonies, and grew out of common origin, mutual sympathies, kindred principles, similar interests, and geographical relations. It was confirmed and strengthened by the necessities of war, and received definite

form, and character, and sanction from the Articles of Confederation. By these the Union was solemnly declared to "be perpetual." And when these Articles were found to be inadequate to the exigencies of the country, the Constitution was ordained "to form a more perfect Union." It is difficult to convey the idea of indissoluble unity more clearly than by these words. What can be indissoluble if a perpetual Union, made more perfect, is not?

But the perpetuity and indissolubility of the Union, by no means implies the loss of distinct and individual existence, or of the right of self-government by the States. . . . The Constitution, in all its provisions, looks to an indestructible Union, composed of indestructible States.

When, therefore, Texas became one of the United States, she entered into an indissoluble relation. . . . The union between Texas and the other States was as complete, as perpetual, and as indissoluble as the union between the original States. There was no place for reconsideration, or revocation, except through revolution, or through consent of the States.[51]

SECESSION BY CONSENT

In relation to secession by consent, Chase diverges from Lincoln in stating that secession of a state required the consent of "the States," whereas Lincoln referred to the consent of the people. The difference is explained by their differing views on the states. Chase did not subscribe to the nationalist school of constitutional interpretation. Nor was he a member of the rival classic states' rights school. Rather, Chase adhered to a theory of dual federalism in which sovereignty was divided between the national and state governments. Such a theory was inconsistent with the nationalist interpretation of the Constitution as a document that asserted federal supremacy over the states.

Dual federalism theory adherents relied heavily on the Tenth Amendment to the Constitution to underscore the importance of the states in the federal system. This amendment reserves to the states all powers that are not delegated to the federal government. This is what Chase is referring to when he notes the "distinct and individual existence . . . [and] right of self-government by the States."[52]

For Chase the preservation of the states was as much a concern of the Constitution as was the preservation of the national government.[53] It was thus hardly surprising that in *Texas v. White* he declared both the Union and the states to be "indestructible." In the words of Herman Belz, for Chase, the secession of the Confederate States of America was "unconstitutional because its proponents wrongly claimed for individual states a power rightly possessed by the states in union or collectively."[54]

More recently, substantially similar propositions to those propounded by Lincoln have emerged in a string of Constitutional Court decisions in the former Yugoslavia relating to the secessions that occurred there during the early 1990s and, in particular, in the 1998 landmark decision by the Canadian Supreme Court in *Reference re: Secession of Quebec*.[55] Lincoln's views are also consistent with explicit constitutional law provisions relating to secession in Ethiopia, St. Kitts and Nevis, and Liechtenstein.

This recent judicial jurisprudence on secession indicates that the fundamental legitimizing principle that informs the rules of constitutional law regulating the process of secession is that of consent. Secession cannot be legitimate unless there is a manifested willingness on the part of the relevant territorial community of its desire to secede. But such consent is, of itself, insufficient to legitimize secession. The host state must also be willing to allow that territorial community to secede. The focus of recent judicial analysis of secession, in contrast to that of Lincoln's, has been on the question of determining the will of the territorial community to secede. The key mechanism for finding out whether a community desires to secede is the referendum, which was described by the Supreme Court of Canada as "a democratic method of ascertaining the views of the electorate on important political questions."[56]

Although states will differ with respect to the specific details relating to the conduct of a secession referendum such as who calls for the referendum to be held, who is entitled to vote, and what majority vote must be reached for the referendum to be passed, Antonio Cassese is undoubtedly correct when he notes that the holding of a referendum has been "elevated . . . to the status of a basic requirement for the *legitimation of secession*."[57]

Contemporary jurists and legal thinkers appeal to more universal principles than Lincoln did to define what counts as constitutionally legal secession. Whereas the pre–Civil War debate on the legality of secession was rooted in different conceptions of the founding of the United States, such considerations are essentially irrelevant today. Thus, the Canadian Supreme Court anchored its propositions on secession in "four fundamental and organizing principles of the Constitution." These are federalism, democracy, constitutionalism and the rule of law, and respect for minorities.[58] These principles could equally underpin the right of consensual secession in the American context.

REVOLUTIONARY SECESSION

Lincoln's view that revolutionary secession must also be morally justified has its contemporary adherents. Both the late John Rawls and Daniel Farber have argued that the Confederate States' defense of slavery denied them any moral justification to secede.[59]

However, the courts have seen revolutionary secession as simply a matter of fact. When Chase recognized the revolutionary right of secession in *Texas v. White*, he made no mention of it being contingent on some morally justified reason.[60] Similarly, eight years later in *Williams v. Bruffy* the Supreme Court, in discussing the validity of acts "where a portion of the inhabitants of a country have separated themselves from the parent State and established an independent government," wrote that "the validity of its acts, both against the parent State and its citizens or subjects, depends entirely upon its ultimate success. If it fail to establish itself permanently, all such acts perish with it. If it succeed, and become recognized, its acts from the commencement of its existence are upheld as those of an independent nation."[61]

More recently, the Canadian Supreme Court in *Reference re: Secession of Quebec* observed that a constitutionally illegal unilateral secession could, nevertheless, be effective because "the ultimate success of such a secession would be dependent on effective control of a territory and recognition by the international community."[62]

In 1861, although Lincoln recognized that secession could be legal, he argued that the unilateral declarations of independence by the states of the Confederacy were constitutionally illegal because they did not fulfill the requirement of attaining consent, especially the consent of the Union as a whole. Furthermore, he maintained that the absence of a moral justification for secession meant these states could not invoke the revolutionary right of secession embodied in the Declaration of Independence of 1776. However, close scrutiny suggests that the reasoning underpinning these two claims is flawed. The problem with Lincoln's notion that consent is required if a secession is to be legal is that it is grounded in the mistaken belief that the Union's constitutional founding preceded the ratification of the Constitution drafted in Philadelphia in 1787. And the problem with his argument about the right of revolutionary secession is that it is false that such a right could only be exercised for a morally justifiable cause.

Notwithstanding the flaws in his reasoning, his principle of consent forms the core of contemporary constitutional law jurisprudence on secession, as is evidenced in several recent constitutional law cases in a number of jurisdictions, especially Canada. These cases reaffirm Lincoln's insistence that a constitutionally legal secession requires the territorial community seeking independence first to affirmatively demonstrate its desire for independence and second to obtain the consent of the state from which it seeks independence. On this basis it can be fairly said that Lincoln is one of the founding fathers of a right of secession grounded in constitutional law.

Notes

1. Akhil Reed Amar, "An Open Letter to Professors Paulsen and Powell," *Yale Law Review* 115, no. 8 (2005–6): 2105–6.

2. Cass R. Sunstein, "Constitutionalism and Secession," *University of Chicago Law Review* 58, no. 2 (1991): 633.

3. Laurence H. Tribe, *American Constitutional Law*, vol. 1, 3rd ed. (New York: Foundation Press, 2000), 32 n. 3.

4. Abraham Lincoln, "First Inaugural Address," Mar. 4, 1861, in *Abraham Lincoln: His Speeches and Writings*, ed. Roy P. Basler (Cleveland: World Publishing Company, 1946), 586.

5. Abraham Lincoln, "Message to Congress in Special Session," July 4, 1861, in *Abraham Lincoln*, 603.

6. Lincoln, "Message to Congress," 605.

7. Lincoln, "Message to Congress," 606.

8. Douglas G. Smith, "An Analysis of Two Federal Structures: The Articles of Confederation and the Constitution," *San Diego Law Review* 34, no. 1 (1997): 337–38.

9. Akhil Reed Amar, "Abraham Lincoln and the American Union," *University of Illinois Law Review* 5 (2001): 1115.

10. "A Discourse on the Constitution and Government of the United States," 1850, in *Union and Liberty: The Political Philosophy of John C. Calhoun*, ed. Ross M. Lence (Indianapolis, Ind.: Liberty Fund, 1992), 116.

11. "A Discourse on the Constitution and Government of the United States," 212.

12. Lincoln, "First Inaugural Address," 582.

13. Lincoln, "Message to Congress," 603–4.

14. *Definitive Treaty of Peace between Great Britain and the United States*, Sept. 3, 1783, art. 1, in *The Consolidated Treaty Series*, ed. Clive Parry, 213 vols. (Dobbs Ferry, N.Y.: Oceana Publications, [1969]–81), 48:487–98.

15. Akhil Reed Amar, *America's Constitution: A Biography* (New York: Random House, 2005), 26.

16. David C. Hendrickson, *Peace Pact: The Lost World of the American Founding* (Lawrence: University of Kansas Press, 2003), 259; *Gibbons v. Ogden*, 22 U.S. 1, 187 (1824).

17. David Kowalski, "Red State, Blue State, No State? Examining the Existence of a Congressional Power to Remove a State," *University of Detroit Mercy Law Review* 84, no. 3 (2007): 346.

18. In *Owings v. Speed*, 18 U.S. 420, 422 (1820), the Supreme Court held that the Constitution came into effect when the first session of Congress began on March 4, 1789.

19. Federalist No. 40, in Alexander Hamilton, James Madison, and John Jay, *The Federalist, with Letters of "Brutus,"* ed. Terence Ball (Cambridge: Cambridge University Press, 2003), 192–93.

20. Kenneth M. Stampp, "The Concept of a Perpetual Union," *Journal of American History* 65, no. 1 (1978): 7–8.

21. Stampp, "The Concept of a Perpetual Union," 8.

22. Stampp, "The Concept of a Perpetual Union," 9–10.

23. Andrew C. McLaughlin, *A Constitutional History of the United States* (New York: Appleton-Century-Crofts, 1935), 137–47.

24. Amar, *America's Constitution*, 33.

25. Lincoln, "First Inaugural Address," 582.

26. *Heyman v. Darwins Limited* [1942] A.C. 356.

27. "Declaration of the Immediate Causes Which Induce and Justify the Secession of South Carolina from the Federal Union Declaration," Dec. 24, 1860, http://yale.edu/lawweb/avalon/csa/scarsec.htm, accessed Nov. 13, 2007.

28. Michael Stokes Paulsen, "Stare Decisis and Nonjudicial Actors: Lincoln and Judicial Authority," *Notre Dame Law Review* 83, no. 3 (2008): 1271.

29. *Giles v. Morris* [1972] 1 All E.R. 960.

30. "Fourth Annual Message," Dec. 3, 1860, in *The Works of James Buchanan, 1860–1868*, vol. 11, ed. John Bassett Moore (New York: Antiquarian Press, 1960), 10–19.

31. Christopher Heath Wellman, *A Theory of Secession: The Case for Political Self-Determination* (Cambridge: Cambridge University Press, 2005), 80.

32. Mark E. Brandon, *Free in the World: American Slavery and Constitutional Failure* (Princeton: Princeton University Press, 1998), 187–88.

33. *Davis Contractors Ltd. v. Fareham Urban District Council* [1956] A.C. 696, 729.

34. *Krell v. Henry* [1903] 2 K.B. 740.

35. Mark A. Graber, *Dred Scott and the Problem of Constitutional Evil* (Cambridge: Cambridge University Press, 2006), 177, 187–96, 199–200.

36. Lincoln, "First Inaugural Address," 584–85.

37. Graber, *Dred Scott*, 239.

38. Graber, *Dred Scott*, 177.

39. David Armitage, *The Declaration of Independence: A Global History* (Cambridge, Mass.: Harvard University Press, 2007), 96–97.

40. Lincoln, "First Inaugural Address," 584, 586–87.

41. Quoted in Thomas J. Pressly, "Bullets and Ballots: Lincoln and the 'Right of Revolution,'" *American Historical Review* 67, no. 3 (1962): 659.

42. Armitage, *Declaration of Independence*, 128–29.

43. Armitage, *Declaration of Independence*, 142.

44. John L. Thomas, *The Liberator: William Lloyd Garrison* (Boston: Little Brown, 1963), 403–4.

45. Quoted in Mason I. Lowance Jr. *A House Divided: The Antebellum Slavery Debates in America, 1776–1865* (Princeton: Princeton University Press, 2003), 329.

46. The most recent major study on Lincoln's views on slavery is Richard Striner, *Father Abraham: Lincoln's Relentless Struggle to End Slavery* (New York: Oxford University Press, 2006).

47. Lincoln, "Message to Congress," 598.

48. Hans Kelsen, *General Theory of Law and State* (New York: Russell and Russell, 1945), 118.

49. *Reference re: Secession of Quebec* (1998) 161 D.L.R. (4th) 385, 443.

50. John M. Taylor, *William Henry Seward: Lincoln's Right Hand* (New York: HarperCollins, 1991), 177–79.

51. *Texas v. White*, 74 U.S. 700, 724–26 (1869).

52. *Texas v. White*, 725.

53. Herman Belz, "Deep-Conviction Jurisprudence and *Texas v. White*: A Comment on G. Edward White's Historicist Interpretation of Chief Justice Chase," *Northern Kentucky University Law Review* 21, no. 1 (1993): 125–26.

54. Belz, "Deep-Conviction Jurisprudence and *Texas v. White*," 129.

55. The court cases relating to the breakup of Yugoslavia are discussed in Peter Radan, "Secession and Constitutional Law in the Former Yugoslavia," *University of Tasmania Law Review* 20, no. 2 (2001): 181–204.

56. *Reference re: Secession of Quebec*, 424.

57. Antonio Cassese, *Self-Determination of Peoples: A Legal Appraisal* (Cambridge: Cambridge University Press, 1995), 272.

58. *Reference re: Secession of Quebec*, 403.

59. John Rawls, *The Law of Peoples* (Cambridge, Mass.: Harvard University Press, 1999), 38; Daniel Farber, *Lincoln's Constitution* (Chicago: University of Chicago Press, 2003), 101–5.

60. *Texas v. White*, 726.

61. *Williams v. Bruffy*, 96 U.S. 176 (1877), 186.

62. *Reference re: Secession of Quebec*, 449.

MARGARET MOORE

Ethics of Secession and Political Mobilization in Quebec

Most of the normative debate on secession focuses on outlining the central ethical theories of secession, based on theories of state legitimacy, and applying these theories to determine whether and under what conditions these normative theories are satisfied. This sometimes also involves specifying the train of events that would generate conditions permitting secession. This approach is not very useful in understanding either the motivating element of secession or the discourse by nationalists (or secessionists), though it is useful in understanding the arguments of unionists—that is, those who want to keep the state united. It has also been useful in focusing attention both on theories of state legitimacy and on the related question of how we should think about state borders and what makes boundaries legitimate. This chapter examines the dominant normative theories, suggesting the degree to which they are helpful in shaping debate about secession. It argues that proponents of collective self-determination, or secession, tend to assume the justice of their project, based on a general conception of national self-determination (according to which every nation is entitled to be collectively self-determining) and/or a very specific nationalist reading of constitutional history, which suggests the unsatisfactory nature of the current constitutional and/or political order.[1] Unionists, by contrast, often appeal to the more abstract arguments associated with the statist position on secession. Although this dynamic (of contextual reasoning on the part of nationalists and abstract reasoning in defense of the state on the part of unionists) works with respect to Quebec, I also believe that it is more generally applicable.

In order to make this argument, I examine the three dominant theories of secession. The first position, which is antisecession or anti-self-determination, fundamentally opposes any kind of right to secession. A number of commitments can account for this opposition, but liberal individualist and statist/realist ones are typical. I argue that this position is typically held by unionists in the state. The second is the just cause theory, according to which secession is justified if the group in question has suffered egregious and long-standing injustices at the hands of the state. This is essentially Allen Buchanan's view, but it is also continuous with a traditional view of state legitimacy as rooted in deeper justice considerations. The third is the so-called choice theory associated with David Copp, Harry Beran, and Daniel Philpott. They take a permissive stance on the right of secession that is grounded in considerations of individual autonomy. I argue that this theory is wrongheaded because the collective autonomy of a group cannot be *derived* from individual autonomy and that in many cases, including Quebec, its recursive implications mean that it is problematic to deploy (even rhetorically).

There is also a group of theorists who advance national self-determination theories, which justify secession or self-determination of national communities. On this view, the right to national self-determination is typically rooted in a value that nations are said to have, and secession is viewed as an extension of that right.[2] I do not directly consider this view here, because proponents of secession do not argue for the objective moral value associated with their (or similar) communities, but they do presuppose such objective value to the extent that they treat the national community as obviously beneficial and as entitled to various forms of collective self-determination.

These various theories about secession all do some work, but they are too universal to have much explanatory merit. What is more significant here is a certain quite specific constitutional story about the nature of the Canadian federation and the disjuncture between that story and the current reality. I discuss this story in the last part of this essay, suggesting that nationalist claims parallel claims by indigenous peoples, some of which are rooted in specific promises or treaties or understandings rather than in a universal theory of justice, legitimacy, or autonomy. In the case of Quebec, the central normative argument in favor of collective self-determination refers to a contextually specific constitutional narrative that (1) presupposes that Quebec is entitled to be collectively self-determining and (2) shows the inadequacy of the current constitutional arrangement in accommodating this collective self-determination.

THE STATIST VIEW

The statist claim that secession of any part of the state is unjustified can take a number of forms, but I examine only three. One argument depends on a realist view of the international order. On this account, the state system is crucial to the achievement of peace and stability, borders are crucial to the maintenance of the system, and secessionist movements are fundamentally destructive and destabilizing, which leads to the conclusion that secession should not be allowed.[3]

This fairly nonnormative account of secession, though, presupposes exactly what is at issue: that the group in question does not have a right to secede in the first place. To see that this is an assumption of the argument, rather than its conclusion, we need only reflect on the nature of rights momentarily: part of what it means to have a right is that one has a right to do wrong (or the wrong thing), and we can accept that people have rights—for example, the right to divorce their partner—even if acting on them would be destructive to and destabilizing for the other people affected. That is, the mere fact that there can be harmed or negatively affected third parties does not mean there is no right, although the question of the impact on third parties is a relevant moral consideration.

A second, more worked-out account of the statist position tells a democratic story of the transformation, through a defining constitutional moment, of the various peoples into a single people and of creation of a government (or federal government, in federal systems) that is expressive of the common will of the whole people, conceived as a unity. In the modern world, self-government takes on a territorial form: it tends to operate over a geographical domain and to conceive of all people within that domain as equal citizens. Territory refers not to property or even land but to a geographical area or domain of legal and political rules. It is implicit in the notion of popular sovereignty that the territory of the state stands in a special relationship to the people as a whole and that the people exercise sovereignty within that jurisdiction. On this understanding of territorial jurisdiction, territory is conceived as in some sense belonging to all the people and benefiting all the people.[4] This account of the relationship between the territory of the state and popular sovereignty suggests that the federal government is an agent of the people as a whole and so implies a fairly statist view of political boundaries.

Although this view does have democratic credentials, the problem is that there are no doubt equally democratic arguments that could be made to the effect that the subunits or provinces are self-determining. Canada is what is called a "coming-together federation"; the various colonies of Britain and Quebec, which had been conquered by Britain prior to making the decision to join with three other English-speaking British colonies, merged create the country of Canada. If they had the democratic power to enter into the union, so the argument goes, they have the democratic power to exit, too. At a minimum, it is part of the Quebec nationalist story about Canadian constitution making that the country was founded by two peoples—English and French—and that both peoples have to be present or represented as equal partners in the constitutional order that they create for it to be legitimate. (Note, however, that the original inhabitants are excluded from this constitutional narrative.) On this understanding, dominant in Quebec and shared by many in English Canada too, Canada comprises two founding nations, or equal races, in the old eighteenth-century meaning of the word "race" as "civilization." This "two nation" understanding of Canada is a fundamental principle of the federation and was the basis on which upper and lower (English and French) Canada joined together. Thus although the statist argument has a democratic story, it might be that the terms of the creation of the union suggest residual rights for its constituent elements. These elements might likewise be democratically organized and represent a legitimate democratic "voice."

A third statist, or antisecessionist, argument associates states with a number of moral goods—the achievement of peace and stability, the rule of law, the protection of individual rights—and argues that secession from such a legitimate political order is unjustified. On this view, the basic justification of the state also gives it its legitimacy, and so by its lights, whether the state has democratic legitimacy cannot ever be in question. This is an argument against secession, but since it assumes that there might be states that fail to procure the requisite moral goods, it also shades into the just cause theory of secession. But there are moral goods that are so basic that they would be hard *not* to be achieved by any functioning political order; if those goods have not been achieved, then, on this account, such entities cannot be counted as functioning states. So, depending on how high the threshold is for justifying the state (and so rendering it legitimate), this version of the statist argument can overlap with the just cause theory of secession.

In the Canadian case, there are a number of people who hold this statist view. They are typically referred to as "Charter Canadians." There was a slogan that was popular in the 1990s (before the 1995 Quebec referendum on secession), "My Canada includes Quebec," that seemed on the face of it to be tolerant and inclusive but that had a darker side in that it rejected the legitimacy of any change in the territorial boundaries of Canada and so rejected the claims of Quebec nationalists to self-determination rights. This hard-line statist argument is no longer dominant among Canadian politicians, and there have been efforts to set out the conditions under which secession would be warranted (through the Clarity Act, which sets out the terms under which Canada would negotiate with Quebec, following a positive vote on secession).[5] The Clarity Act was justified on the grounds that Canada should not go blindfolded into another secession crisis but should have rules and principles in place to manage that process. Inasmuch as it countenances the idea of secession, however, it definitely runs counter to a strict statist, or antisecessionist, view (even if the rules might in practice prevent secession).

JUST CAUSE THEORY OF SECESSION

Just cause theories, among which the best known is Buchanan's, typically argue that groups that have suffered certain kinds of injustices at the hands of the state have a right to secede.[6] Different just cause theories focus on different kinds of injustices. Some point to prior occupation and seizure of territory and some to serious violations of human rights, including genocide. Others view discriminatory injustice as sufficient to legitimize secession.[7] One advantage of this type of theory is that it suggests a strong internal connection between the right to resist tyranny and the collective right to self-determination, or secession, and in so doing grounds the ethics of secession within the generally accepted framework of human rights and a generally accepted theory of state legitimacy.

A superficial grasp of the way this theory works might suggest that it not only has the advantage of being continuous with credible and generally accepted conceptions of justice, human rights, and state legitimacy but that it is relatively easy to apply. It should require only a backward-looking assessment of the policies and practices of the state and the veracity of claims made by the would-be secessionist group concerning violations of human rights. Of course, no one would deny that there are contentious cases. The facts may be unclear or contested, and there may be no reliable, independent witness to ascertain which narrative of events is true. But this is not a philosophical objection to just cause theory, since the same is true of criminal trials in which wrongdoing is alleged.

However, there may be other, more challenging, obstacles, such as disagreements about what justice requires, especially in the realm of fairly fine-grained theories of distributive justice. Buchanan argues that unfair distributive arrangements should be counted as giving just cause (to secede) to a group. But this argument immediately runs up against the problem that there is no agreement on which particular theory of distributive justice we should accept (e.g., Dworkinian equality of resources vs. Rawlsian original position theories vs. Nozickian proceduralism). To address this problem, we could agree not to "count" grievances that are based on particular, contested, fine-grained theories of distributive justice as violations of justice. We could focus instead only on those egregious violations of human rights—those commonly thought to protect fundamental human interests, such as the right not to be tortured or the right not to be unjustly killed—that are generally accepted as deeply troubling both in the philosophical literature and by the international legal order.[8]

Just cause theory would give the green light to secessionist groups that have suffered serious injustices. If we accept this understanding of just cause theory, we are able to distinguish clearly, at least at the theoretical level, between the theory proper and the applications of it. No doubt, of course, there remain difficulties in *applying* the theory. One problem is connected to the fact that groups that have suffered most at the hands of a dictator, and so have a moral right to secede, often have no mechanism to enforce that right. The repressive state disallows it and indeed uses the "threat" of secession as a ground for further repression. Another problem is that if, as is likely, there is no constitutional procedure in place to bring secession under the rule of law, the act of insurrection on the part of secessionists will push the remainder state to take measures designed to dampen it. Insurgents are well aware of this and will often engage in actions they know will lead to repression of their community (by the state), which they can then appeal to both to help mobilize their group behind the secession and to seek the recognition of the international community, which is typically horrified by the brutal and repressive policies enacted by the state.[9] But these are not serious philosophical problems: they only suggest that it is not always easy to constitutionalize rights or get people to agree to particular rights.

This theory is, however, much more restrictive than it first appears. It is restrictive in the obvious sense that it limits secessions to groups that have been victimized or discriminated against, but it sets the bar even higher by requiring that the injustice be the result of deep state structures rather than simply of the actions of an illegitimate government. To see this, we must return to the structure of the argument and the connection between the justice-based argument and the theory of state legitimacy. In his book *Secession*, Buchanan argues that the desires and claims of the secessionists have to be weighed against the claims of the state, which, if it is a just state, is the "trustee for the people, conceived as an intergenerational community."[10] The just state, therefore, has an obligation to protect all (existing and future) citizens' legitimate interests in the political and territorial community. In Buchanan's view, secession is permissible only when the state forfeits its claim to being a legitimate trustee by failing to fulfill its justice-based obligations. Here it is clear where the just cause argument dovetails with the statist argument described above.

Interestingly, the structure of this argument is such that it doesn't require that the would-be secessionist group itself be the victim; rather, it requires only that the state that is being dismembered is the perpetrator of injustice. The state's claim to a right to territorial integrity, then, does not need to be weighed against the desires of the secessionists, and this is so even if the would-be secessionists are a different group from the victimized group.

Since the crucial issue is whether the state has perpetrated, or is perpetrating, acts of injustice, the question then becomes what distinguishes a state from a particular governing regime. In *Justice, Legitimacy and Self-Determination*, Buchanan elaborates on this distinction, defining a "state" as an "enduring structure of basic institutions for wielding political power, where this structure includes roles to be filled by members of the government."[11] The "government" can be thought of as the human agency by which the institutional resources of the state are employed. If the state is illegitimate, its government is illegitimate. But if the government is illegitimate, it does not follow that the state is illegitimate.

If unjust acts are committed by a particular government, then the logic of the analysis is that they can be rectified by a change in government. We are then in the realm of revolution, as John Locke argued in 1681. Buchanan argues that remedying the flaws of an illegitimate state involves more than a change of character in the government: it requires profound constitutional changes that transform the state itself. An example of such a profound constitutional change is secession. And of course secession is justified if the state is illegitimate, because by definition the state does not deserve the rights (to territorial integrity) that it has had conferred on it by the international community if it is illegitimate.

The conditions that have to be met to qualify as an "unjust state" are quite stringent, and this makes the just cause theory of secession very restrictive. Indeed, Buchanan cites only two examples of unjust states: apartheid South Africa and the antebellum South of the United States.[12] And in the end, just cause theory might be interesting philosophically, and it certainly challenges our thinking about when a state is unjust and when a regime is unjust, but it is not very applicable to the case of Quebec. This is because Quebec nationalists, or even Quebec sovereigntists, don't make just cause arguments (or, if they do, their conception of justice presupposes strong nationalist rights of self-determination, which means the national self-determination account is more appropriate to their case, since that account is crucial to deriving the rights in question). In the past, Quebec in part based its right to sovereignty (or secession) on a claim of unjust treatment, but this is no longer so.

The reason why Quebec does not rely on a just cause theory is because the Canadian state cannot plausibly be seen as running roughshod over the human rights of Canadian citizens and certainly not over Canada's Quebec citizens (or to the extent that it can be, so too can all other states). In many recent discussions in political theory, the notion of "structural injustice" is employed to suggest that some groups were historically marginalized and disenfranchised or powerless and that these groups are still subject to discrimination and oppression. This is the tenor of much recent normative work in the United States following in the Iris Marion Young tradition of analyzing group-specific rights. But although there have been times when Quebec "lost" arguments (even over significant matters)—as in the 1982 patriation of the constitution—and nationalists have claimed a certain amount of unjust treatment, it would be an exaggeration to claim that Quebec's experience has largely been one of marginalization and powerlessness. Indeed, within the Canadian federation, Quebec is relatively powerful: it enjoys fairly strong autonomy over areas of jurisdiction that are quite important (the provinces control health, education, roads, natural resources, and so on). And in the federal order of government, Quebec is strongly represented politically: four of the last seven prime ministers of Canada held seats in the Parliament from Quebec (Trudeau, Chretien, Mulroney, and Martin). In fact, given voting patterns, the truth is that it's extremely difficult to form a national government without significant Quebec representation. Historically, elections have been determined by the large votes of the two central Canadian provinces—Quebec and Ontario—and Montreal and Toronto have historically been the two dominant cities in Canada.

INDIVIDUAL AUTONOMY OR CHOICE THEORIES OF SECESSION

Individual autonomy arguments, sometimes referred to as choice theories of secession, as advanced by David Copp, Harry Beran, and Daniel Philpott typically require that a territorially concentrated majority express a desire to secede in a referendum or plebiscite for the secession to be legitimate and do not require that the seceding group demonstrate that it is the victim of injustice at the hands of the state or the majority (remainder) group on the territory.[13] Typically, those who adopt this line of argument view the right to self-determination, including a right to secession, as being based on the right of political association. The right of political association is then grounded in a deeper argument about the value of individual autonomy. This type of theory typically requires that both the seceding unit and the remainder units are capable of performing the function of states, that the areas be territorially contiguous and viable (Beran), and that the groups are territorially concentrated and are as likely to be protective of human rights as the state from which they are leaving (Philpott). Although individual autonomy theories represent a philosophically rich argument based on liberal conceptions of consent and political legitimacy, they do not make a good fit with the situation in Quebec.

One ambiguity in the choice theory of secession is the relationship between territory and democratic will. There is a very complex relationship between self-determination, geographical space, and citizenship. In part this complexity may derive from the simple fact that humans are physical beings. They occupy space and have to exist somewhere, and proximate location is a basic condition of the requirement that there be shared institutional rules for self-government. The modern state, then, has a very strong territorial dimension in the sense that its jurisdictional domain is defined geographically. As Burke Hendrix writes: "At times states appear to rule particular territories first, and citizens only incidentally—being born within a state's territory usually makes one legally a citizen, unless some clear and obvious commitment to another state prevents this."[14] Moreover, states usually claim the right to conscript citizens to defend their territories, even when those territories were themselves acquired through force and fraud (most of the United States) or are virtually uninhabited (much of Greenland). This leads Hendrix to speculate whether mere geographical control translates into authority over persons or whether it's the other way around, that control over persons leads to control over territory.

If we think that democratic will determines the boundaries of the state, then we will conclude that this theory would justify a referendum in areas of Quebec that seek secession, and it is probable, based on the empirical evidence that, in a nationally charged situation, all parts of Quebec would vote "yes" except the area adjacent to Ottawa, which has many federal government jobs, and the island of Montreal itself. Of course, it's hard to predict exactly how votes would be configured, since the very knowledge that voting would determine boundaries might affect it.[15] But, if we assume fairly constant voting behavior (an admittedly strong assumption but perhaps not unjustified in light of the idea that there are areas that are Parti Québécois (PQ) strongholds and Liberal Party strongholds, which can translate into sovereigntist and federal constitutional positions), then it seems that it might be consistent with secessions from secessions. At least, the very same democratic argument that may be said to justify the secession of Quebec from Canada could apply to smaller subunits within Quebec.

On the other hand, there are also reasons to think that democratic choice does not determine territory but rather that territory operates as a fairly arbitrary, but historically contingent, area or geographical domain that defines the area of self-government. This seems to be the view implicit in the Badinter Arbitration Committee's decision (even if it was motivated mainly by international relations concerns about the "stability of frontiers"), which was based on a territorial view of the legitimacy of republican borders. That is to say, the (belated) response of the UN and EU, in particular, was to recognize the self-determination of peoples, defined in territorial terms, as members of specific republics but not as national groups. Federations could disintegrate along the lines of their constituent units, but there was to be no reconsideration of borders, "no secession from secessions." And this view suggests the perhaps untenable, or at least not yet theoretically worked out, position that territories primarily determine peoples rather than the other way round.

In the Canadian context, there is almost no political support in the Quebec nationalist community for an individual autonomy or democratic will argument, at least if this is understood as making democratic will determinative of boundaries themselves. This is not least because it threatens to dismember Canada and then dismember Quebec after it, leaving it a nonviable unit. While the 1995 referendum lost by a very narrow margin (less than 1 percent of votes), the Francophone heartland of Quebec voted more than 60% in favor of self-determination and Anglophones voted more than 90% against it. If Canada adopted a democratic choice approach to secession, then assuming a referendum that passed with similar voting patterns, it would have the unenviable result of ripping Montreal from the heart of Quebec. Of course, some of the theories would avoid this result on fairly utilitarian grounds, requiring contiguity of territory, but Quebec nationalists would be unlikely to consider such a result as legitimate. Statists or unionists might invoke the idea of secession from secession as a kind of threat about the likely effects of these sorts of demands.

COLLECTIVE AUTONOMY IN CONTEXT

This brings us to the collective autonomy (or national self-determination) argument, which, like the individual autonomy arguments of Beran, Copp, and Philpott, would support a democratic vote in the self-determining area, although not a statewide vote throughout the overholding region. This is justified in terms of the collective autonomy of the nation or people: this autonomy gives them the prerogative to decide as a group whom to associate with, and it would be violated by a statewide vote. Indeed, most accounts of national identity that have a strong subjectivist element (that is, in which part of the prerequisite for being classified as a nation is a generally shared sense of identity as a member of a group that aspires to be collectively self-governing) will have the same results as the individual autonomy argument.[16] However, a democratic vote is not always required on this argument: many proponents of national self-determination rely on "tests" of shared national identity or political community, such as markers of national mobilizations—electing national parties, lobbying or organizing along national lines, possibly a majority vote in a referendum on secession, especially if there are indications of a persistent desire for a self-determining political community.

There are a number of different justificatory arguments for national self-determination, but most suggest that nations are moral communities and that the bonds of membership and shared identity that co-nations feel have ethical value.[17] Institutional recognition is important to members' sense of identity and gives expression to their political aspirations. In some versions of the argument, emphasis is put on the instrumental value that these bonds have in undergirding a democratic community and its redistributive practices.[18] The different versions of this argument emphasize different goods that collective autonomy (or collective self-determination) realizes—goods that suggest a prima facie case for valuing collective autonomy. The value that resides in national communities or that is promoted by a shared national identity is itself based on the value that these communities have for individuals. National communities are not the only repositories of value, however—there are many components of human flourishing. Therefore, almost all arguments that take this form tend to argue in favor of balancing the good being realized (collective autonomy) with other competing goods, such as the likelihood that the resulting state will realize justice, support democratic governance, and secure peace. Of course, as noted above, the recognition of such groups as legitimate will depend on, first, agreement by other countries that they represent national political communities, and, second, their fulfilling their obligation to promote the claimed moral values.

These arguments are not made in this abstract form in the Quebec case to justify collective self-determination, but they are presupposed in the sense that nationalists assume that collective self-determination is a good thing and that Quebec has a right, an entitlement, to be collectively self-determining. However, this sort of argument is not sufficiently contextual to make the case for secession. Even if we feel confident that Quebec represents a national political community of the appropriate kind and that it embodies the moral values outlined above, a contextual assessment of the balance of goods realized against losses is crucial to the moral judgment as to whether secession is justified. This is so because the moral good involved in secession is collective autonomy (or collective self-determination) and it can take different institutional forms, including nonsecessionist ones. And if collective self-determination is a value, which I think it is, and it can be realized in a number of institutional forms, then why (or when) is secession the most appropriate one? This question is important since secession may be more disruptive to the international community and to the national identities of millions of people in the remainder state than simple constitutional changes, and it may involve more rigorous duties (or assigning more people to duties) than other forms of self-determination.

The argument for Quebec's collective self-determination is often made by reference to the Canadian constitutional arrangement, and specifically, to a contextually specific historic narrative to the effect that Canada was initially conceived as a union of two founding peoples, that this was the basis of the original "contract" between the four colonies (of Britain), and that not only has this not been upheld but in some cases has been violated. There is also a related argument that it has been particularly difficult to make changes to the Canadian federation to accommodate the different identities and preferences of its citizens.

With respect to the first point, the patriation of the Canadian constitution over the objections of then–Quebec premier René Lévesque and subsequently the Quebec National Assembly made it clear that Quebec was not, as Quebec had conceived, one of two equal founding partners. Quebec could be outmaneuvered and outvoted, and indeed major constitutional change, including a charter of rights, could be made legal in the country without their consent. The legality of this was determined prior to the patriation of the constitution in 1982 by the Supreme Court decision in the Quebec Veto Reference case, in which the Supreme Court ruled that the federal government could petition the British Parliament to pass the Canada Act 1982 (which was essentially the British act necessary to patriate the constitution) as long as it had a substantial measure of provincial consent and as long as the new constitution would apply to all provinces regardless. This was a serious blow to the Quebec vision of the basis of the Canadian constitution. After the legal decision, the federal government proceeded to adopt the 1982 Constitution Act, including the Charter of Rights and Freedoms, thereby demonstrating that constitutional change affecting the powers of Quebec could be effected without Quebec's assent.

Moreover, the Canadian constitution has proved remarkably resistant to amendment, updating, and change. After 1982, there was a sense in Quebec that the Canadian constitution lacked legitimacy, and when Prime Minister Mulroney came to power, from a Quebec seat, he attempted to rectify that. At the time that he began this political process, sovereignty was essentially a "dead issue." The PQ had secured power in the 1981 provincial election with a strong majority, on a campaign that was based on good governance rather than on the national question. Indeed, the PQ explicitly placed it on the back burner, observing that who should govern the province should be separated from the sovereignty question and that the latter would be subject to a separate referendum. But under Prime Minister Mulroney, a round of negotiations led to the Meech Lake Accord in June 1987, which revealed the difficulty of changing the Canadian constitution and increased the frustrations of Quebec sovereigntists. The Meech Lake round (named after a resort in Quebec at Lac Meech where it was negotiated) was designed to gain the province of Quebec's support for the constitution. Although it wasn't required for the constitution to be legal, the lack of ratification from Quebec was thought by many (including Quebec nationalists) to impugn the legitimacy of the Canadian federation.

The Meech Lake Agreement had five principal components: (1) it recognized the province of Quebec as a distinct society (and it was a recognition that would inform all later constitutional readings/decisions); (2) it gave a constitutional veto to Quebec, which is what the province has sought as consistent with its vision of Canada as having two founding peoples; (3) it increased provincial powers with respect to immigration; (4) it had an opt-out clause from federal programs (with financial compensation) that would enable provinces to increase their powers/ jurisdictional authority; and (5) it authorized provincial input in appointing Supreme Court judges.[19] Because the accord would have changed the constitution's amending formula (giving Quebec a veto) and because it also would have changed the composition of the Supreme Court, it needed to gain unanimous consent of all provincial and federal legislatures within three years to become law. This is a very demanding requirement for constitutional change, and thus it is instructive that, even when the signs were extremely propitious, and there was a general mood of goodwill and Canadian harmony, it couldn't be achieved.

At this point, it is worth recounting briefly how despite auspicious indications, constitutional change was not forthcoming. As noted, then–prime minister Brian Mulroney managed to get the support of the federal government and to get the two main opposition parties as well as all ten provinces to agree to the substance of the Meech Lake Accord. According to the amending formula, the accord had to be ratified by all ten provinces within three years. However, Newfoundland premier Clyde Wells was very unhappy with the deal and with the special status it gave Quebec. He said that he opposed it, but—in what was widely interpreted as a jab at Quebec's position with respect to the 1982 patriation of the constitution—he also said that he did not think that one province should hold up the constitution. Although he disagreed with the accord, he said that Newfoundland would ratify it if all other provinces and the federal government did so too.

But then there was a change of government in Manitoba that led to delays and ultimately to the accord failing to be ratified by the three-year deadline. Under the rules of the Manitoba legislature, any extension of the deadline for ratifying the constitution required unanimity. Unanimity was thwarted, however, because one member of the provincial legislature, Elijah Harper, who was an aboriginal member of the provincial parliament, stood up every time that the vote was taken and, holding an eagle feather, said that he did not think Quebec's needs should be put before the needs of Canada's aboriginal peoples. Having failed to be ratified by the three-year deadline in Manitoba, the accord was also not ratified by Newfoundland. The accord was dead.

Subsequently, there was another round of constitutional negotiations—the Charlottetown Accord—that was more inclusive than the Meech Lake Accord but that nevertheless failed.[20] The Charlottetown Accord not only addressed the situation of Quebec in the constitution but also that of Canada's aboriginal people as well as other perceived deficiencies.[21] Further, in response to criticisms of the backdoor "consociational" nature of the previous round of constitutional negotiations, ratification was to proceed by a national referendum (and in addition several provinces also had legislation for their own provincial referendum). The referendum requirement made ratification of this constitutional amendment even more difficult—referendums commonly fail because voters not only compare what's being proposed in the referendum to the status quo but also to other perceived alternatives. Moreover, there was more to disagree with: many nonaboriginal Canadians were opposed to additional rights for Canada's native people, or they were in favor of making concessions to Quebec but not in favor of certain decentralizing tendencies embodied in the Charlottetown Accord.[22]

It would seem, then, that constitutions come in many kinds. Two, however, are common. First, there are ones that stipulate very broad rights or entitlements or claims that can be interpreted differently; these sorts of constitutions often have pretty strict amendment formulas but can be revised by judicial interpretations and decisions. Second, there are constitutions that have more precise wording, which leaves less up to the courts, but that also have relatively less demanding amending formulas. The Canadian constitution is, I would argue, the worst kind of hybrid of these two. Its wording is very tight, particularly in parts dealing with language rights and so on, but at the same time its requirements for amendment are stringent. This makes it hard for federalists to argue that the constitution can be responsive to Quebec's needs and demands and is one of the contextually specific dimensions of the secession problem— the failure to deal with Quebec nationalism within the terms of the current constitution.

I have argued that dominant nationalist leaders in Quebec do not typically appeal to the central justificatory arguments in the ethics of secession, at least not directly and not in the abstract form that they take in the literature on state legitimacy. In part, this is because these arguments bear on the legitimacy of states in general rather than on the specific difficulties the national community has with the encompassing state. The normative arguments for forms of collective self-determination typically focus on quite specific features of the constitutional arrangement and its limitations from the point of view of the national community, and so the statist argument deployed by antisecessionists does not answer its claims. It is possible, however, that national communities that are subject to egregious human rights abuses would appeal directly to the illegitimacy of their state and hence to the arguments typically deployed by theorists who make the case for the ethics of secession.

Notes

I am grateful to Don Doyle for inviting me to give this paper and to the Social Sciences and Humanities Research Council of Canada for a research grant in support of this project.

1. I do want to emphasize, however, the normative dimension of my argument. I do not discuss, as a comparative political scientist might, the conditions under which a secession is likely to be successful. In fact, I think that normative arguments are one thing and empirical examinations of successful secessions quite another. My own view, not really tested but that I have often stated without being contradicted, is that a comparative examination of the likelihood of successful secession suggests that it is most likely to occur when there is a breakdown at the center. In the period between 1900 and 1945, there were only two secessions: the 1905 secession of Norway from Sweden and the 1921 secession of Ireland from the United Kingdom. In the period between 1945 and 1990, there was only one case of successful secession: Bangladesh. Since 1990, however, the instances of secession have proliferated: Croatia, Slovenia, Bosnia, Macedonia, Slovakia, Czech Republic, Russia, Ukraine, Turkmenistan, Kazakhstan, Kyrgyzstan, Belarus, Latvia, Estonia, Lithuania, Armenia, Georgia, Moldova, Azerbaijan, Uzbekistan, Eritrea, and East Timor. In not a single case since the 1990s was the secession opposed by the central government. The Soviet Union and Yugoslavia shattered into many pieces, but it is possible to claim that in both cases there was no central government, or core state, to resist the secession. So it seems that weakness in the center (or lack of interest in holding the state together) is a crucial requirement for a successful secession, and whether or not that is present is not determined by the normative evaluation of the case, or if it is, it is so only in the attenuated sense that when a permissive, normative view of secession becomes sufficiently hegemonic, it might lead political elites to acquiesce in the secession of a part of the state.

2. Arguments along these lines have been put forward by Kai Neilsen, "Liberal Nationalism and Secession" in *National Self-Determination and Secession*, ed. Margaret Moore (Oxford: Oxford University Press, 1998), 103–33; David Miller, *On Nationality* (Oxford: Oxford University Press, 1995); and Margaret Moore, *Ethics of Nationalism* (Oxford: Oxford University Press, 2001).

3. This argument was deployed by Steve Saideman in oral comments at a Liberty Fund conference on secession in New Hampshire, Apr. 3–6, 2007.

4. The relationship described here between self-determination and territory does not apply only in secession. Such a relationship also obtains in a straightforward way in a unitary state: the state exercises its authority over a geographical domain, or territory, its rules apply to all people within its territory, and, in a democratic state, all citizens relate to one another from a position of political equality, making collectively binding decisions over their collective life together. However, the exercise of political authority

across territories is not usually an all-or-nothing matter. Boundaries between states are not the only determining factor as far as political control goes—in federal states, subunits have jurisdictional authority over some areas of life (for example, in Canada education and health are the domain of the province), while other areas fall under the authority of the central government. But political power can also take a territorial form and raise issues regarding control of territorial and natural resources. Control over natural resources also rears its head in federal states, where the typical model is that the federal (or central) unit has control over natural resources and the subunits do not; but there are also countries—such as Canada, or Iraq under its new constitution—where the subunits have significant control over natural resources.

5. The terms are, essentially, that there should be a clear majority on a clear question. The "clear question" requirement is based on a debate during the October 30, 1995, referendum on sovereignty. The salient part of the 1995 referendum question asked "Do you agree that Quebec should become sovereign, after having made a formal offer to Canada for a new economic and political partnership? YES or NO." This formulation was problematic not only because it introduced strategic decision making in the place of decision making based on first-order preferences—that is, voters might end up voting "yes" to increase Quebec's bargaining power vis-à-vis the rest of Canada, even though their first preference was to remain in Canada with a more fair constitutional dispensation—but also because there was a great deal of confusion about what being "sovereign" actually involved. Polls in Quebec indicated that many people were in favor of Quebec being "sovereign" but not in favor of Quebec becoming a "sovereign country," and federalists in the Quebec legislature argued (unsuccessfully) for the latter formulation in the referendum question.

6. Allen Buchanan, *Secession: The Morality of Political Divorce from Fort Sumter to Lithuania and Quebec* (Boulder, Colo.: Westview Press, 1991).

7. In his elaboration (and defense) of just cause theory, Wayne Norman cites five kinds of injuries to a group that are considered to give just cause: "(1) that it has been the victim of systematic discrimination or exploitation, and that this situation will not end as long as the group remains in the state; (2) that the group and its territory were illegally incorporated into the state within recent-enough memory; (3) that the group has a valid claim to the territory it wants to withdraw from the state; (4) that the group's culture is imperiled unless it gains access to all of the powers of a sovereign state; (5) that the group finds its constitutional rights grossly or systematically ignored by the central government or the supreme court" ("Ethics of Secession as the Regulation of Secessionist Politics," in *National Self-Determination and Secession*, ed. Margaret Moore [Oxford: Oxford University Press, 1998], 34–61).

8. These rights are also embodied in the major international human rights conventions, such as the Universal Declaration of Human Rights, the International Covenant

on Civil and Political Rights, and the International Covenant on Social, Cultural and Economic Rights (all of which, in fact, protect more rights than what I have listed). The decision to focus on egregious violations doesn't need to be regarded as a purely pragmatic one. The gravity of the situation, or the remedy sought, might necessitate a greater degree of determinacy both about the justice violation and the consequences attached to rectifying it. See Allen Buchanan, "Human Rights and the Legitimacy of the International Legal Order," *Legal Theory* 14, no. 1 (2008):39–70.

9. That an international law of secession might compel states to adopt even harsher repressive measures is often invoked as a reason for not establishing such a law. It is not clear, however, that that objection would apply in the case of constitutionalizing a domestic right of secession, since such a right of secession tends to be based on a plebiscitary kind of framework (choice theory). Thanks to Bruno Coppetiers for pointing this out.

10. Buchanan, *Secession*, 109.

11. Allen Buchanan, *Justice, Legitimacy, and Self-Determination: Moral Foundations for International Law* (Oxford: Oxford University Press, 2004), 281–83. Here Buchanan is principally concerned with the issue of legitimacy as it applies to state recognition policy (recognitional legitimacy), but the question of who should be the object of recognition (with all the rights and obligations that that entails) is another way of posing the question of the legitimacy of secession.

12. Buchanan, *Justice, Legitimacy and Self-Determination*, 282–83.

13. Daniel Philpott, "In Defence of Self-Determination," *Ethics* 105, no. 2 (1995): 357–72; Harry Beran, "A Liberal Theory of Secession," *Political Studies* 32, no. 1 (1984): 21–31; David Copp, "International Law and Morality in the Theory of Secession," *Journal of Ethics* 2, no. 3 (1998): 1–26.

14. Burke A. Hendrix, *Ownership, Authority, and Self-Determination* (University Park: Penn State University Press, 2008), 3–4.

15. We should perhaps not assume, however, that the voters would have that knowledge. In both referendums in Quebec, critics have alleged that it wasn't clear exactly what the population was voting for. In the first Quebec referendum, held under the leadership of then-premier René Lévesque, the vote was on the right to negotiate with the federal government for "sovereignty association." This is not the same as secession, especially since the promise was that any move to sovereignty would go back for a second referendum.

16. This subjectivist component is argued for by Ernst Renan in his famous definition of the nation. "Nationhood", he wrote, is a "spiritual principle" comprising two elements, "a rich heritage of memories" and "actual agreement, the desire to live together" ("What Is a Nation?" in *Modern Political Doctrines*, ed. Alfred Zimmern [London: Oxford University Press, 1939], 203). Many others also emphasize the subjective component as a necessary condition for national belonging. See Yael Tamir, "The Enigma of Nationalism," *World Politics* 47, no. 3 (1995): 418–49, who argues that the category "nation," like

"friends" and "lovers," is a community that is distinguished by the perceptions and feelings of agents. Among the five elements that make a nation, David Miller argues that the first is that it be "constituted by shared beliefs and mutual commitments" (*On Nationality* [Oxford: Oxford University Press, 1995], 27). Margaret Moore, *The Ethics of Nationalism* (Oxford: Oxford University Press, 2001), argues that subjective identification is a necessary (though perhaps not sufficient) condition for shared nationality.

17. See Miller, *On Nationality*; Moore, *Ethics of Nationalism*; Avishai Margalit and Joseph Raz, "National Self-Determination," *Journal of Philosophy* 87, no. 9 (1990): 439–61; and Tom Hurka, "The Justification of National Partiality," in *The Morality of Nationalism*, ed. Robert McKim and Jeff McMahan (New York: Oxford University Press, 1997), 139–57.

18. Miller, *On Nationality*; Moore, *Ethics of Nationalism*, chap. 4.

19. For a complete text of the Meech Lake Accord, see http://solon.org/Constitutions/Canada/English/Proposals/MeechLake.html, accessed Dec. 14, 2009.

20. For the full text of the Charlottetown Accord, see http://solon.org/Constitutions/Canada/English/Proposals/Proposal.english.txt. See also "Constitutional Activity from Patriation to Charlottetown (1980–1992)," Depository Services Program, http://dsp-psd .pwgsc.gc.ca/Collection-R/LoPBdP/BP/bp406-e.htm, accessed Dec. 14, 2009.

21. In fact, although it is not central to my argument, the Charlottetown Accord attempted to remedy all the deficiencies of the Constitution and to bring in a wider number of stakeholders. It addressed some of the centralizing dimensions (especially by making the declaratory power in section 92 (10) subject to provincial consent), it required the federal government to enter into negotiations with the provinces to "harmonize" the policies in telecommunications, labor development and training, industrial development, and immigration, and it gave the provinces exclusive control over mining and forestry. It also constitutionally entrenched the Supreme Court, allowed for an elected upper house (Senate) in which each province would be represented equally, and ensured that, no matter the demographic weight of Quebec (it has a declining birth rate), it would never have less than one-quarter of the seats in the House of Commons. See the report of the Centre for Constitutional Studies, http://law.ualberta.ca/centres/ccs/uploads/PointsofViewNo3 .pdf, accessed Dec. 14, 2009.

22. Indeed, I would argue—although this takes me far from the themes of this chapter—that this new political (not legal) requirement of a referendum by province makes constitutional change almost impossible. As evidence, consider the situation of Australia, where there have been three failed rounds of constitutional change, all falling through at the referendum stage, in part because it seems that people reject the proposal both because it goes too far and because it doesn't go far enough. This mechanism does not seem to lead people to engage in simple pairwise comparisons.

PART 2

The Case of the American South

CHARLES B. DEW

Lincoln, the Collapse of Deep South Moderation, and the Triumph of Secession

A South Carolina Congressman's Moment of Truth

Among the complex sequence of events that led to the American Civil War, none was more important than the secession of South Carolina. On December 20, 1860, less than two months after the election of Abraham Lincoln as president, delegates to the South Carolina convention voted unanimously to sever all ties with the Union. South Carolina's action was the trigger for a disunion movement that swept across the Deep South in the opening months of 1861. By February 1, six more states—Georgia, Florida, Alabama, Mississippi, Louisiana, and Texas—had joined the secessionist tide. By early April, the stage had been set for the explosive confrontation at Fort Sumter that began the bloodiest war in American history.

Thousands of documents, both public and private, have survived from this era, offering insight into the secessionist mindset in South Carolina and the lower South on the eve of the Civil War. Nothing I have read, however, is more revealing than a single letter written the day before Lincoln's election by John Ashmore, a moderate first-term congressman from the South Carolina Upcountry. Ashmore's four-page reply to friend and fellow Democrat Horatio King of Washington, D.C., dated Monday, November 5, 1860, is the clearest and most compelling statement of the secessionist persuasion that I have encountered during all the years I have been trying to understand the coming of the

Civil War. That letter and the political journey of the man who wrote it are the subjects of this chapter.

Unlike many of South Carolina's antebellum political leaders, John Durant Ashmore came into the world with neither wealth nor high social standing behind him. Born in the Upcountry district of Greenville in 1819, Ashmore lost his father at the age of thirteen and, as he wrote later, "was thrown on my own resources without education or money." He was a bright, hard-working young man, however, and he learned enough on his own to begin moving up in the world. After his father's death, he moved to central South Carolina, where he served as a clerk for a Sumter merchant. He became a teacher in a country school at age eighteen and stayed in that position for three years. His next step was to spend another three years reading law, but he soon abandoned the legal profession for what he referred to as "the quiet independence of a farmer's life." Ashmore prospered as a cotton farmer, acquiring land and slaves in the Sumter District, and he soon became a leader in local affairs. As was often the case in the Old South, militia service became a stepping stone to a political career. Ashmore was elected to three terms in the South Carolina legislature beginning in 1848 and then served two terms as comptroller-general of the state from 1853 to 1857.[1]

Ashmore's success came at a cost. His residence in swampy Sumter District led to his contracting malaria, and after several severe attacks, he decided to move back to his native Upcountry. He purchased a farm in Anderson District, and in January 1855 he left the Sumter area for good.[2]

During these years, Ashmore also married and began raising a family. By 1860, he and his wife, Mary, had six children, two boys and four girls. The 1860 census also revealed that he owned twelve slaves—two adult men, two adult women, and eight children. Ashmore told the census taker in Anderson that he owned real estate valued at $8,500 and a personal estate (this figure included the value of his slaves) worth $29,500.[3] John D. Ashmore had come a long way from the indigent youth who had set out on his own at thirteen.

Ashmore's political views in the late 1850s placed him squarely in the mainstream of his Upcountry constituents. This mountainous area of western South Carolina was primarily a region of small- and medium-sized farms, and the local yeomen took great pride in their independent views. The Democratic Party dominated the Upcountry, and two men, Benjamin F. Perry and James L. Orr, dominated the Upcountry Democratic Party.

Perry was a prominent lawyer and the editor of the Greenville *Patriot and*

Mountaineer, one of the leading newspapers in the region, and he and Orr, a longtime member of Congress, were the principal proponents of what became known as the national Democratic movement in South Carolina. Both Perry and Orr were strong supporters of the Union, and they argued that the rights of the slaveholding South could best be defended by southerners fully participating in the affairs of the Democratic Party at the national level: by attending presidential nominating conventions, helping the party organize Congress, and supporting the Democratic administrations of Franklin Pierce and James Buchanan. The national Democrats maintained that a sympathetic government in Washington was the strongest bulwark against northern aggression. As long as a party supportive of southern interests was in power, slaveholders would have nothing to fear.[4]

When Ashmore was asked to give a succinct summary of his political views in 1859, he responded with words that clearly reflected his embrace of the Perry-Orr philosophy. "I belong to the States Rights Jeffersonian School of Politics— am as much opposed to the ultraism of the South, as I am to the aggressive fanaticism of the North," he wrote. Ashmore added that he had "never given a vote but for the Democratic Party."[5]

Ashmore's moderate Upcountry politics cut against the grain of the radical forces elsewhere in South Carolina. The states' rights Democrats, as they were known, had supported the nullification movement in the 1830s and had looked to John C. Calhoun for leadership until his death in 1850. During the last antebellum decade, the Charleston *Mercury*, edited by Robert Barnwell Rhett Jr., carried the radical states' rights banner; it advocated nonparticipation in corrupt national political organizations and offered a hard-edged defense of "southern rights." Those "rights" included secession by individual states—"separate state secession," it was called—if antislavery forces in the North threatened the South's political, social, and economic order. The radicals also favored the expansion of slavery into the western territories and called for the reopening of the African slave trade.[6]

Most of the state's congressmen during the 1850s came from the radical ranks, men like Laurence M. Keitt, Milledge L. Bonham, and John McQueen. Orr, who served in the House of Representatives from 1848 to 1858 and was elected Speaker in 1857, was the principal spokesman for South Carolina's national Democrats in Washington. Orr's decision not to seek reelection in 1858 created a vacancy in the state's congressional delegation that Ashmore moved swiftly to try to fill.

Ashmore's first step was to seek the support of Benjamin F. Perry. "I have had such demonstrations made to me from various sections of the Congressional District that I am strongly inclined to enter the field myself," Ashmore wrote Perry on January 7, 1858. "I feel perfectly satisfied that with your support my election would be almost certain," he added. Ashmore felt no need to explain his political views in detail to Perry; the two men agreed on practically everything. But Ashmore took pains to point out that other potential candidates were inclined to "identify themselves . . . with the ultraism of other sections of the state." The radicals had tried in 1851 to get South Carolina to secede in the wake of the tumultuous events surrounding the Compromise of 1850, and Ashmore wanted no one of that stripe representing the district in Congress. Men like Ashmore had carried the day against Rhett and his allies back then by insisting on "cooperation" among the slaveholding states as a precursor to any separate secessionist move by South Carolina, and he was determined to stand on the same ground in 1858.[7]

Ashmore's commitment was, first and foremost, to "moderation," as he told Perry a week later. "There has been for years, from other sections of this state, an influence at work to put men in position in this Congressional District, who when they obtain it, are from the strength of that position to Revolutionize the political feelings of our people," Ashmore continued. "I will not yield the field to men of this cast, who have done the state no service, and who have no claims upon the people of the District."[8]

Although Ashmore had not felt it necessary to outline his political views to Perry, for his part, Perry seems to have wanted a fuller statement of Ashmore's views before committing himself, and his newspaper, to his candidacy. Ashmore was relatively young—he was only thirty-eight years old in January 1858—and he had been residing in the district for a scant three years. Perry had questions, particularly, it appears, about Ashmore's commitment to Unionism, so Ashmore sought to answer those concerns in a long letter to the Greenville editor dated January 30, 1858.

"In becoming a candidate for Congress I shall pursue the policy you indicate from a firm conviction throughout my whole life that Disunion is the direst calamity that can befall the people (both North and South)," Ashmore wrote. "I regard disunion as the *derrier resort*," he went on. "I believe the right of secession correct in the abstract, but *inseperable* [sic] from Revolution." He promised to be unyielding on the subject of party loyalty: "I endorse Mr. Buchanan's Administration in toto, at all points and on all subjects, and shall continue to identify myself with the great Democratic party of the Union—the only constitutional party in it." Ashmore pledged his "firm determination . . . to avoid all extremes, all ultraism, that leads or tends towards *isolation* and to use any influence I may be possessed of . . . to discountenance extreme factions of the Rhett and Keitt school and tread as nearly as I can (should I be elected) in the footsteps of Orr." He added that he would "look to yourself and Col. Orr on all occasions for counsel and advice." In closing, Ashmore expressed his determination to hold to his moderate course so as to do no harm to the South, but he would certainly defend his native region should necessity require him to do so. Moderation, in short, meant avoiding trouble if at all possible, but it did not mean the abandonment of southern rights.[9]

Ashmore received Perry's support, and despite the fact that he was a relative newcomer to the district and was challenged by two other Democratic candidates, his prospects looked good. "If Ashmore continues temperate I presume he will be elected," Orr wrote Perry in late May.[10]

Ashmore did remain temperate, and he was elected, by a sizable margin, in November 1858. It was, in many ways, a stunning victory for the young man. He would now be moving onto a much more elevated and demanding political stage, and he wanted as many friends in high places as he could get. Perry and Orr would be there to counsel him, of course, but Ashmore also sought the support and advice of another prominent South Carolina moderate, U.S. senator James H. Hammond.

"I have long desired to meet you, especially since you have become a Senator, that I might have the benefit by your conversation & counsel in regard to affairs of State," Ashmore wrote Hammond on November 9, 1858. The newly elected congressman had been particularly impressed by a recent speech Hammond had given at Barnwell Court House. Hammond's Barnwell Address, as this speech was soon labeled, had attracted national attention and had caught Ashmore's eye as well.[11]

In that address, Hammond had expressed his view that "the great body of the Southern people do not seek disunion." He insisted that, in the end, northerners would pull back from a confrontation with the South because "the sense of danger and the love of cotton and tobacco would . . . in every crisis, override their love of negros [sic]." Southerners should seek strength through internal unity and external cooperation with "faithful allies in the free States," which meant, of course, northern Democrats. In closing, Hammond had offered a final piece of advice and made a personal pledge as well. "If the South has any desire to remain in the Union, and control it, she, as her safety requires . . . must conciliate her northern allies," he said. "But if she determines . . . to throw off her northern friends and dissolve this Union, I need scarcely say that I shall, without hesitation, go with her fully and faithfully."[12]

Ashmore was effusive in his praise of Hammond's Barnwell Address. It "shows the stamp of the true leader, wise statesman, and fearless & independent Senator," he wrote.[13] The speech outlined exactly the course of action that a South Carolina national Democrat like Ashmore would want to follow once he took his seat in Congress: strong support of the party and the Union coupled with an equally strong defense of southern rights.

The problem for Ashmore was that the Democratic Party was coming apart at the seams in 1858. The genesis of this division was a bitter split between President Buchanan and Senator Stephen A. Douglas of Illinois over the issue of slavery in the territories. The principal bone of contention was Kansas. Douglas favored a policy of letting the settlers themselves decide the future of slavery there by a free and fair vote—"popular sovereignty," Douglas called it. Buchanan, under intense pressure from the southern wing of the party, supported a proslavery constitution that had been drafted in Lecompton, Kansas, following a clearly fraudulent election to choose convention delegates. The dispute between Buchanan and Douglas came to a head when the two men met in the president's office in December 1857. Buchanan demanded that the senator support administration policy on Kansas as a matter of party loyalty. Douglas refused. The result was a deeply divided Democratic Party and a serious blow to Douglas's aspirations to secure the Democratic nomination for president in 1860 and to carry a united party into the November election.[14]

What Ashmore saw as Douglas's apostasy on Kansas was too much for the new congressman to swallow. "Is it true that Douglas will not allow his name to be used for the Presidency in 1860?" he asked Senator Hammond in a moment of wishful thinking early in 1859. "I hope so, for I should be very unwilling to see him receive the nomination & so would the State at large in my judgement." Ashmore added that Douglas "was my favorite until his tergiversation on the Lecompton constitution showed his utter want of sincerity & fair dealing with the rights of the South."[15]

Ashmore was obviously well aware of the fragile state of his own party, and this situation was potentially disastrous because of the growing menace of Republican politics. In 1858, the Republican Party was not far removed from its birth, yet it was maturing all too rapidly into a threatening adult. Organized in response to the passage of Senator Douglas's Kansas-Nebraska Act and the repeal of the Missouri Compromise in 1854, the Republicans preached the gospel of "free soil"—the territories should be off limits to slavery and a haven for free white men. "Free soil, free labor, free men" encapsulated the Republican political philosophy, and the young party made unprecedented gains throughout much of the North in the late 1850s.[16] For men like Ashmore, the Republicans represented the emergence of a hostile, openly sectional political organization that threatened all that the South held dear. Even though Republican leaders insisted that they had no abolitionist designs on slavery where it already existed, southerners did not believe them. They refused to accept that Republicans were sincere in their insistence that their only interest was in keeping the territories free from slavery. In the view of most white southerners, a territorial ban was nothing more than a stalking horse for the Republicans' true purpose: the emancipation of the South's four million slaves. As his subsequent actions would show, Ashmore clearly believed that "Republicanism" and "abolitionism" were interchangeable words. If this party managed to ascend to power, his moderation and his Unionism would be put to the ultimate test.

When Ashmore took his seat in Congress in December 1859, the country was still reeling from the impact of John Brown's raid. Brown had led a band of abolitionists in an assault on the federal arsenal and armory at Harper's Ferry, Virginia, on October 16 in an effort to spark a slave insurrection. He and his surviving men were captured after a two-day standoff, and Brown was swiftly tried and convicted of treason in a Virginia court. His hanging took place on December 2, 1859.

Tension between North and South spilled over onto the floor of the House of Representatives. A bitter sectional battle over the election of the Speaker ensued, and Ashmore feared for the fate of the country as "disunion sentiment" gripped both houses of Congress. "If disunion is upon us Virginia must bring it & then our position is a clear one," he wrote Perry on December 15. "The tone of the Northern men & Northern presses is against us [in] every way," he added, and he believed that if this hostile attitude continued, "our glorious government must soon end." Ashmore had not yet surrendered to despair, however, as the last sentence of his letter revealed: "Still I am not without hope."[17]

Ashmore did what he could to encourage that hope. On March 1, 1860, he delivered his first and, as it turned out, his only major speech in Congress. In brief remarks made a month earlier, he had told the House that he was "not a southern fire-eater," but he also wanted the members to know that he was "a southern-rights man from the crown of my head to the sole of my foot" and that he would "yield to no man in my fixed purpose and unalterable determination to sustain those rights."[18] This same effort to hold to the middle of the road, to seek common ground between North and South, informed his March 1 address.

Ashmore began his speech by castigating both "southern ultraists" and "northern Abolitionists" for their "maddened fanaticism," but he warned the House that the Union could be preserved only if men of goodwill in the North could "arrest the mad onslaught made upon the rights and institutions of the South." The other precondition for the survival of the government was the North-South unity in the upcoming election that Hammond had called for: "Planting ourselves under the standard of the great Democratic party of the South, we will make one more effort to bear into the presidential chair a fair exponent of the Constitution in the person of a man, whoever he may be, whom the delegates in convention from the South and from the true Democracy of the North shall present to us." But if northern attacks continued and the Democratic Party divided, the consequences would be dire indeed. In language that foreshadowed the words he would use on the eve of Lincoln's election, Ashmore outlined what was ultimately at stake in the sectional struggle. "The hardy farmer or mountaineer, who has been accustomed to the use of the ax, the hoe, the plow, and, more important still, the rifle, grasps it yet the more firmly in his hand when he is told that it is the object of the North to turn loose a hungry horde of free negroes upon him, who, he well knows, without the guardianship of a master, are too lazy to work, but not too proud to steal," he warned. "But more than all, he knows that the honor of his wife and daughter would hardly be safe an hour if these slaves, totally unfit for self-government, were turned loose upon his community."[19]

Less than three months later, in May 1860, Ashmore's political world came crashing down around him. A group of fifty southern delegates to the Democratic national convention, including most of the South Carolina delegation, walked out of the meeting in Charleston after failing to secure a platform plank guaranteeing positive federal protection for slavery in the territories. From his vantage point in Washington, Ashmore saw disaster looming. "We are in a sad state of confusion and uncertainty here in consequence of the breaking up of the Democracy in the Charleston Convention, which was most ill-timed and inconsiderate," he wrote his brother Henry on May 13. The southern "dissenters" in the convention were "rashly hurrying on events," he lamented. "We are but one step from anarchy and Revolution and totally unprepared for it."[20]

In a long, despairing letter to Perry, written on the same day he wrote his brother, Ashmore took his forebodings one step further. "It is in my judgement utterly impossible to preserve the Constitution & the Union if the Republicans succeed," he told Perry. "It would degrade & disgrace the South beyond all measure to live under the control & dominion of this corrupt & aggressive party."

In closing, he repeated the same point he had made to his brother: "We are but one step from anarchy & revolution now."[21]

The subsequent emergence of two Democratic candidates—Stephen A. Douglas nominated by the northern wing of the party, John C. Breckinridge by the southern wing—virtually guaranteed a Republican victory in November. That party's ticket—Abraham Lincoln of Illinois for president, Hannibal Hamlin of Maine for vice president—seemed unstoppable, Ashmore wrote Hammond in July 1860. But he refused to endorse precipitous action by his native state. "I shall take strong ground against the Republicans & advocate dissolution rather than live under their rule, but will not specify time or event when the final blow is to be struck, but advise preparation & harmony of action in order to meet the emergency," he told Hammond. "I shall antagonise [i.e., oppose] every thing that tends to the seperate [sic] Secession of S.C. & . . . placing her in the head or van of the movement," he continued. "But as I have no hopes whatever of [Democratic] success & believe that Lincoln & Hamlin will be elected I go for preparation first & dissolution afterwards on the first favorable opportunity."[22]

Ashmore's language here is important. Although he was talking about "dissolution" of the Union, he was also acknowledging that he had not abandoned his moderate stance, that he was, in the political nomenclature of the time, still a "cooperationist." In the South in 1860, "cooperation" meant, as he said, strong opposition to the radical immediate secessionists and an insistence on "cooperation" with other slave states before taking such a revolutionary and potentially explosive step as disunion. This cooperation could take several forms. It could mean a joint slave-state conference like the Nashville convention of 1850. It could mean a unified presentation of southern grievances to the North prior to any effort to secede. It could mean secession en masse if those grievances were not redressed. But, above all, "cooperation" meant steadfast opposition to South Carolina fire-eaters like Rhett, Keitt, Bonham, and McQueen; it meant giving joint deliberation a chance; it meant delay. In the heated political climate of the summer of 1860, "cooperation" was about as far as a South Carolina politician could go in opposing radical, straight-out secessionism.

In the midst of this tumultuous political season, Ashmore had received word in Washington that one of his four daughters living at home in Anderson had fallen ill. This message prompted him to leave at once for South Carolina, although the seriousness of her illness had not been conveyed to him. When he reached Anderson, he learned the worst. "I arrived 27 hours after her death & only in time to accompany her remains to their last resting place," he wrote

Hammond on July 10. "It was a sad return & a hard blow. She was the best tempered, sweetest & loveliest of all my children . . . with a face as bright & beautiful as the morning."[23] For Ashmore, this tragedy provided a poignant personal backdrop to the political events that lay just ahead of him.

Later that summer, Ashmore did exactly what he had earlier told Hammond he would do. He crisscrossed his Upcountry district calling for "preparation" for a Republican electoral victory in November and for "resistance" should that dire calamity occur. "He thought the discussion of separate secession" was "premature at this time," reported the Edgefield *Advertiser* on September 26. Ashmore "went for cooperation" among the southern states as a prelude to secession, but "sooner than see slavery abolished, which would be the result if we acquiesced in the Black Republican policy, he would unfurl the banner of the Palmetto State and rally under her folds every man he could—would make a last struggle, if need be, to sustain the institution which was the life-blood and heart of our social system."[24] In the summer and early fall of 1860, the shifting sands of Deep South politics offered scant footing to a moderate like Ashmore, but he was still seeking some sort of traction on that shrinking middle ground.

Then came Lincoln's victory. Even before election day, however, it was clear that he would win. In October, Republican triumphs in state elections in Pennsylvania, Ohio, and Indiana provided unmistakable evidence of what was looming just over the horizon. For John D. Ashmore, the ultimate moment of truth had finally arrived. From his home in Anderson, he announced his irrevocable conversion to southern radicalism and explained why he felt compelled to abandon the political philosophy of a lifetime. Ashmore's extraordinary statement, written on Monday, November 5—the day before the election—was prompted by an earnest plea from a northern friend asking Ashmore to stand fast for the Union. Horatio King, a high official in the Post Office Department and a longtime political operative in Washington, had written on October 29 begging Ashmore to do everything he could to try to slow down the secessionist tidal wave threatening to engulf the lower South. King, a Maine native (and Hannibal Hamlin's one-time newspaper partner in that state), was a Democratic Party stalwart who had been part of the Washington establishment since the Jacksonian era. He was appalled by the disunionist rhetoric coming from the Deep South as the presidential election neared, and he tried to persuade his southern Democratic friends to return to their senses.[25] Ashmore's November 5 letter was penned in response to King's anxious appeal.

"On my entree into Congress it was as a Constitutional Union loving man,"

Ashmore wrote. "From the days of my childhood I have loved the Union.— during youth and manhood I still loved it," he went on. "For more than 20 years I have worn the commission of my state & during all that time from sincere love & honest hope of the Union I have spoken & urged conservative doctrines on my people & taught patience, liberality and forbearance." But along with the love of Union, his ancestors had "also handed down to me certain rights & institutions which are now, and have been consistently, persistently & systematically assailed since my earliest recollection." Nothing less than a series of intolerable outrages had been committed on the South: "Treason, insurrection, & murder has been perpetrated upon quiet unoffending fellow citizens because they have defended & sustained these rights & institutions." Over the course of the year, Ashmore had become convinced "for the *first time* that they can no longer be preserved in *this* Union." Under these circumstances, "disunion" was "the only remedy," and he had conveyed his views to his constituents. The stakes could not be higher, Ashmore clearly believed, and King's request to support the national government moved the South Carolina congressman not at all. Ashmore's stinging reply, offered with "all candor & respect," obviously came from the depths of his being:

> If Lincoln be elected as I have no doubt he will be, & the South submits to his inauguration, then are they in my judgement cowards and traitors to their own rights, unworthy of any other condition than that which awaits them,— inferiors, provincialists and subjects. If by my individual act I could pull down the pillars of the Republic & plunge it ten thousand fathoms deep into the ocean rather would I do it than see my section submit to Black Republican rule for one day or one hour. The booming of 100,000 cannon & the slaughter of an hundred Waterloo's would be music to my ear & gladness to my sight rather than see S.C. the victim of Lincoln, Seward, Sumner, Wilson, Lovejoy, Helper et id omne genus.

Ashmore acknowledged that he had undergone a conversion to radicalism, but he emphasized that he had good and ample reason for doing so: "Men like myself who for a lifetime have fought the extreme ultraism of the South, & the mad fanaticism of the North will not permit Abe Lincoln's banner inscribed with 'higher law,' 'negro equality,' 'irrepressible conflict' and 'final emancipation' to wave over us."

Ashmore saw with remarkable prescience the importance federal military installations in the South would play in the coming crisis. Forts were something tangible, bricks and mortar, manned by troops, and they had the potential to transform the political struggle over the constitutionality of secession into a test of arms. In no more time than it would take an artilleryman to jerk a lanyard, the forts could turn an abstraction into a concrete and bloody reality. Ashmore assured King that his countrymen had "*Three hundred thousand swords . . . now* ready to leap from their scabbards in support of a Southern Confederacy. Fort Moultrie will be in the hands of the South on the morning on the 4th day of March next," he continued. "Every fort South of it will share the same fate a few days after Secession is proclaimed."

It was at this point in his letter that Ashmore cut to the core of the secession persuasion. The reason for his transformation from moderate Unionist to secessionist firebrand lay in his absolute conviction that Republican-sponsored emancipation would plunge the South into a racial nightmare:

> Our women & children are ready & eager for the conflict & would kick us out of our own homes if we basely & tamely yield again. Our young girls,— Daughters—from 12 to 15 years of age are entreating us,—their Fathers,—to train them in the use of firearms and daggers.—Think you Sir, that it is their fears [that] prompt the demand? No! By the God of Heaven, it is the blood of their Fathers that is burning in their veins. We *will arm them*, & if dire necessity drives us to thus expose them, *we will carry them to the battlefield with us.* Better for them that they encounter the horrors and chances of war, than endure "negro equality," "final emancipation" & its logical results "amalgamation." We are ready for the issue.[26]

So there it was: "amalgamation." In the end, it came down to this, what Thomas Jefferson in 1785 had called "staining the blood" of the white race.[27] Ashmore, like so many white southern males of his generation, was absolutely convinced that the fate of white southern womanhood was hanging in the balance in the wake of Lincoln's election. Reason flew out the window under these circumstances. Who could flinch when the stakes were so high? Who would sacrifice his honor and his manhood to help preserve a national government headed by a "Black Republican" abolitionist? These questions answered themselves in the Deep South in 1860.

Explaining this psychosexual fear is the ultimate challenge for southern historians, it seems to me, and no one, to my knowledge, has done so. All I know is that it was there, in the marrow of their bones, and they launched the region on the tides of war in large part because of it. These fears proved to be remarkably long lived. I heard virtually the same thing said when I was a boy growing up in the South in the 1940s and 1950s. Integrate the swimming pools, the town library, the transit system, and especially the public schools, and the destruction of white southern civilization would inevitably follow, the adults all around me said. The end of this road to perdition was always the same: the sexual breaching of the color line. Miscegenation, it was called in the middle of the twentieth century. Ashmore used a different word—amalgamation—but the gut fear was the same. He and his generation in the Deep South destroyed a political union rather than live under a leader who, they were convinced, would visit such horrors on their land and their people.

In 1860, every issue separating the North and South was negotiable except one: slavery. Slavery was many things, of course. It was a highly profitable labor system—slave men, women, and children were worth billions of dollars in 1860—and the institution was a means by which five million southern whites could exert social control over four million southern blacks.

Nothing, however, was more important than preventing what a writer for a Texas Methodist weekly in 1860 called the "designs of the abolitionists" to force the "fair daughters [of the South] into the embrace of buck negroes for wives."[28] Alabama's Leroy P. Walker, subsequently the first Confederate secretary of war, predicted in December 1860 that in the absence of secession, "the sacred purity of our daughters" would be sacrificed on the altar of Republican abolitionism.[29] Judge William L. Harris of Mississippi told the Georgia legislature later that same month that Republicans demanded "equality between the white and negro races[;] . . . equality in the right of suffrage, . . . equality in the social circle, equality in the rights of matrimony."[30] Another Mississippian, Senator Albert Gallatin Brown, told his constituents in October 1860 that Republican-led abolition meant that "the negro . . . shall share the white man's bed, and the white man his—that his son shall marry the white man's daughter, and the white man's daughter his son."[31] Stephen F. Hale, Alabama's secession commissioner to Kentucky, wrote in December 1860 that "the election of Mr. Lincoln" was "an open declaration of war" on the South, "consigning her citizens to assassinations and her wives and daughters to pollution and violation to gratify the lust of half-civilized Africans."[32] Henry L. Benning of Georgia, speaking before the Virginia convention in March 1861, forecast a string of apocalyptic disasters for the South under Republican-led emancipation. Race war would "break out everywhere like hidden fire from the earth," he said, "and as for our women, the horrors of their state we cannot contemplate in imagination."[33] In words that provided an eerie echo of Jefferson's 1785 reference to "staining the blood" of

the white race, a secessionist delegate to the Louisiana State Convention predicted in January 1861 that Lincoln's inauguration would inevitably be followed
by emancipation and the "corruption of the American blood."[34]

John D. Ashmore knew exactly what these men were talking about. Lincoln
was at heart an abolitionist—of that almost all white southerners were sure.
His party, the "Black Republican Party," as they insisted on calling it, was abolitionist to the core—of that they were equally sure. Put the man and his party
in power, and the fate of the South was sealed: emancipation, racial equality,
race war, amalgamation. Ashmore's transformation from moderate Unionist to
radical secessionist was driven by such convictions, and in this he mirrored the
driving force behind secession in South Carolina and all across the lower South
in the aftermath of Lincoln's election. His fears, shared by countless others in
the Deep South, shredded the moderate position that might have at least slowed
the secessionist juggernaut in the cotton states. If such a slowdown had occurred, if the moderates had been able to buy some precious time in late 1860
and early 1861, the subsequent refusal of the upper South to embrace immediate secession might have had more consequence. Instead, South Carolina's pell-
mell rush to secede in November and December served as the catalyst for the
triumph of disunion all across the Deep South in January and February 1861.
The stage was thus set for the April crisis at Fort Sumter and the onset of the
bloodiest conflict in American history.

The fears that Ashmore gave voice to in his November 1860 letter lay at the
very heart of secession. In the end, those fears let slip the dogs of war on the nation Ashmore had once loved so dearly.

APPENDIX

Letter of J. D. Ashmore to Horatio King, Washington, D.C.

Anderson, S.C.
Nov. 5, 1860

My Dear Sir. —
On my return home yesterday from a visit to a portion of my Congressional District I found yours of the 29th Ult., on my table. Accept my thanks
first, for your kind expressions of personal regard & friendship. They are re-
ciprocated. Of all the Employees of Government & high functionaries, on my
Debut in Washington you were the most kind, considerate & cordial. Would

I could say as much for some others whom I have neither friendship nor even respect. In the second place I thank you for the permanent appointment of my friend Moses whom you will find faithful, honest, industrious & grateful. Having proven his competency there is nothing to apprehend in his case hereafter.

To the latter part of your letter I reply frankly. On my entree into Congress it was as a Constitutional Union loving man. From the days of my childhood I have loved the Union.—during youth and manhood I still loved it. For more than 20 years I have worn the commission of my state & during all that time from sincere love & honest hope of the Union I have spoken & urged conservative doctrines on my people & taught patience, liberality and forbearance. It was the doctrine handed down to me by my two Grandfathers & all their race whose blood & toil aided to secure American Liberty. With these inculcations they also handed down to me certain rights & institutions which are now, and have been consistently, persistently & systematically assailed since my earliest recollection. Treason, insurrection & murder has been perpetrated upon quiet unoffending fellow citizens because they have defended & sustained these rights & institutions. The events of the last 12 months have satisfied me for the *first time* that they can no longer be preserved in *this* Union. Hence, since my return from Washington I have boldly proclaimed disunion as the only remedy. It is this you deprecate in me, my neighbor, friend & predecessor Col. Orr & beg us to look to the conservation of the Union in the event of Lincolns election, rather than to its dissolution. I cannot answer for Col. Orr & here let me say that my position was taken without consultation with or reference to his views. He keeps his own counsel & gives no one the benefit of it, except as he promulg[at]es it to the public. For myself I have this to reply in all candour & respect for you personally. If Lincoln be elected as I have no doubt he will be, & the South submits to his inauguration, then are they in my judgement cowards & traitors to their own rights, unworthy of any other condition than that which awaits them,—inferiors, provincialists & subjects. If by my individual act I could pull down the pillars of the Republic & plunge it ten thousand fathoms deep into the ocean rather would I do it than see my section submit to Black Republican rule for one day or one hour. The booming of 100,000 cannon & the slaughter of an hundred Waterloo's would be music to my ear & gladness to my sight rather than see S.C. the victim of Lincoln, Seward, Sumner, Wilson, Lovejoy, Helper et id omne genus. You will call this extravagant. Be it so.

A few more weeks will prove whether we know our rights, & knowing dare maintain them. *Lincoln will never be the President of 33 Confederated States.* Men like myself who for a lifetime have fought the extreme ultraism of the South, & the mad fanaticism of the North will not permit Abe Lincoln's banner inscribed with "higher law," "negro equality," "irrepressible conflict" and "final emancipation" to wave over us. We have & do deserve a better & a more glorious destiny. Let Mr. Buchanan consider well his position, (if he would accept my advice I would give it to him most fully & unreservedly) & if he is a wise man he will send privately an request to the S.C. Legislature & to other Southern States politely *requesting* that Secession shall not be enforced until the last day of *his* term of office. Any attempt, or display of force on his part will meet the same consequences that it will meet from Lincoln. For Mr. Buchanans sake, I would save him, who has been true to the Constitution & the South these terrible consequences & delay action until he would be free of responsibility. *Three hundred thousand swords* are *now* ready to leap from their scabbards in support of a Southern Confederacy. Fort Moultrie will be in the hands of the South on the morning of the 4th day of March next. Every fort South of it will share the same fate in a few days after Secession is proclaimed. Our women & children are ready & eager for the conflict & would kick us out of our own homes if we basely & tamely yield again. Our young girls,—Daughters—from 12 to 15 years of age are entreating us,—their Fathers,—to train them in the use of fire arms & daggers.—Think you Sir, that it is their fears [that] prompt the demand? No! By the God of Heaven, it is the blood of their Fathers that is burning in their veins. We *will arm them*, & if dire necessity drives us to thus expose them, *we will carry them to the battle field with us.* Better for them that they encounter the horrors & chances of war, than endure "negro equality," "final emancipation" & its logical results "amalgamation." We are ready for the issue. Before this reaches you the fate of this great Republic is sealed if Lincoln be elected. N.Y. alone can save it. With the earnest hope that she may do so & save the country the direst calamity the world ever saw

I am My Dear Sir
most truly & sincerely your friend
J. D. Ashmore

P.S. I shall be glad to hear from you at all times.—I fear my letter is hardly readible [sic], having been the victim or subject, rather, of neuralgia for the last four months to such an extent that my nerves are so shattered my hand is exceedingly tremulous. — Am happy to say I am now improving greatly.

Yrs &c

J. D. A.

Source: Horatio King Papers, Manuscript Division, Library of Congress, Washington, D.C.

Notes

1. J. D. Ashmore, autobiographical statement, [1859], John D. Ashmore Papers, South Caroliniana Library, University of South Carolina, Columbia, S.C.

2. J. D. Ashmore, autobiographical statement.

3. Eighth Census of the United States, 1860, manuscript Population Schedules, manuscript Slave Schedules, National Archives Microfilm Publication M653, rolls 1212, 1229.

4. Lillian A. Kibler, *Benjamin F. Perry, South Carolina Unionist* (Durham: Duke University Press, 1946); Roger P. Leemhuis, *James L. Orr and the Sectional Conflict* (Washington, D.C.: University Press of America, 1979); Laura A. White, "The National Democrats in South Carolina, 1852 to 1860," *South Atlantic Quarterly* 28, no. 4 (1929), 370–89.

5. Ashmore, autobiographical statement.

6. Harold S. Schultz, *Nationalism and Sectionalism in South Carolina, 1852–1860* (Durham: Duke University Press, 1950); Manisha Sinha, *The Counterrevolution of Slavery: Politics and Ideology in Antebellum South Carolina* (Chapel Hill: University of North Carolina Press, 2000).

7. J. D. Ashmore to Benjamin F. Perry, Jan. 7, 1858, Benjamin F. Perry Papers, Alabama Department of Archives and History, Montgomery, Ala.

8. Ashmore to Perry, Jan. 14, 1858, Perry Papers.

9. Ashmore to Perry, Jan. 30, 1858, Perry Papers.

10. James L. Orr to Perry, May 25, 1858, Perry Papers.

11. J. D. Ashmore to James H. Hammond, Nov. 9, 1858, James H. Hammond Papers, Manuscript Division, Library of Congress, Washington, D.C.

12. *Charleston (S.C.) Daily Courier*, Nov. 3, 1858.

13. Ashmore to Hammond, Nov. 9, 1858, Hammond Papers.

14. Kenneth M. Stampp, *America in 1857: A Nation on the Brink* (New York: Oxford University Press, 1990), 292–93.

15. Ashmore to Hammond, Jan. 16, 1859, Hammond Papers.

16. Eric Foner, *Free Soil, Free Labor, Free Men: The Ideology of the Republican Party before the Civil War* (New York: Oxford University Press, 1970).

17. Ashmore to Perry, Dec. 15, 1858, Perry Papers.

18. *Congressional Globe*, Jan. 31, 1860, 646.

19. *Congressional Globe*, Mar. 1–2, 1860, 959–62.

20. J. D. Ashmore to Henry Ashmore, May 13, 1860, in "Letters Dealing with the Secession Movement in South Carolina," ed. Rosser H. Taylor, *Bulletin of Furman University*, n.s., 16, no. 4 (1934), 8–9.

21. Ashmore to Perry, May 13, 1860, Perry Papers.

22. Ashmore to Hammond, July 10, 1860, Hammond Papers.

23. Ashmore to Hammond, July 10, 1860, Hammond Papers.

24. *Edgefield (S.C.) Advertiser*, Sept. 26, 1860. See also *Anderson (S.C.) Intelligencer*, Aug. 28, Oct. 4, Nov. 1, 1860.

25. Allen Johnson et al., eds., *Dictionary of American Biography*, 20 vols. (New York, 1928–96), 10:391–92; Horatio King, *Turning on the Light: A Dispassionate Survey of President Buchanan's Administration, from 1860 to Its Close* (Philadelphia: J. B. Lippincott, 1895), 87–88.

26. J. D. Ashmore to Horatio King, Nov. 5, 1860, Horatio King Papers. The full text of Ashmore's letter appears at the end of this essay.

27. Thomas Jefferson, *Notes on the State of Virginia* (1785; rpt., New York: Harper and Row, 1964), 139.

28. R. S. Finley of Rusk, Tex., Aug. 30, 1860, to the *Texas Christian Advocate*, quoted in Ollinger Crenshaw, *The Slave States in the Presidential Election of 1860* (Baltimore: Johns Hopkins Press, 1945), 96. See also Donald E. Reynolds, *Texas Terror: The Slave Insurrection Panic of 1860 and the Secession of the Lower South* (Baton Rouge: Louisiana State University Press, 2007), 97.

29. *Montgomery (Ala.) Weekly Mail*, Dec. 14, 1860.

30. *Address of Hon. W. L. Harris, Commissioner from the State of Mississippi, Delivered before the General Assembly of the State of Georgia, on Monday, Dec. 17th, 1860* (Milledgeville, Ga., 1860), 4.

31. Quoted in Percy Lee Rainwater, *Mississippi: Storm Center of Secession 1856–1861* (Baton Rouge, La.: O. Claitor, 1938), 149–50.

32. S. F. Hale to Beriah Magoffin, Dec. 27, 1860, in *The War of the Rebellion: A Compilation of the Official Records of the Union and Confederate Armies*, 128 vols. (Washington, D.C., 1880–1902), ser. 4, 1:8.

33. George H. Reese, ed., *Proceedings of the Virginia State Convention of 1861*, 4 vols. (Richmond: Virginia State Library, 1965), 1:66.

34. Preamble, Alcibiade DeBlanc, Jan. 24, 1861, *Proceedings of the Louisiana State Convention (in English and French) Together with the Ordinances Passed by Said Convention . . .* (New Orleans: J. O. Nixon, 1861), 9.

ROBERT E. BONNER

Proslavery Calculations and the Value of Southern Disunion

Early in 1859, as the upstart Republican Party consolidated its electoral base across the North, Alfred Iverson of Georgia offered fellow U.S. senators an enticing vision of the southern future. "Sir, there is one path of safety for the institution of slavery in the South," he explained, forecasting how the secession of the cotton states should be the first step towards a new proslavery Confederacy. Iverson confidently predicted how this new alliance would contain within itself "elements of more political power, national prosperity, social security, and individual happiness, than any nation of ancient or modern times." Speaking on behalf of a "large and growing party," Iverson acknowledged that "scarcely a voice could be heard in all the South calculating the value of the Union" prior to 1850. Times had since changed, however, and "now their name is legion."[1]

Iverson's growing throng of prosecession calculators, coolly forecasting the disruption of one federation and the formation of another, contrasts with prevailing notions of a more frenzied process of southern disunion. Most accounts focus on "fire-eating" agitators who whipped up crowds with passionate harangues on the hustings and in the radical press. As other chapters in this volume demonstrate, a number of powerful arguments for proslavery separatism did follow William Yancey's injunction to "stir the Southern heart." Over the course of the antebellum period, proponents of disunion regularly appealed more to the brain stem than to the cortex, whether they compared their own circumstances to European examples of nationalist humiliation (as Paul Quigley explores), propounded an intoxicating form of antimodern nostalgia (as Frank Tower sketches), or stirred deeply rooted psychosexual anxieties (as Charles Dew notes). In retrospect, southern secession can be seen as a model in its stark emotionalism, anticipating the similarly heated cases of "political divorce" in our own day.[2]

Yet no less an agitator than William Yancey himself recognized a corresponding need to "instruct the Southern mind" and to establish through a dispassionate survey of facts and figures how slavery would benefit from the Union's dismemberment. Neither Yancey nor Iverson did much of this calculating work themselves. They instead relied on those pamphleteers who in blending reams of statistics with a survey of broad geopolitical developments sought primarily to convince and assure rather than to foment or inspire. Their case for the efficacy of disunion was by no means self-evident, given that the slave regime had greatly prospered in a union over the course of the preceding six decades. Since the framing of the "compound republic" in the late 1780s, American masters had accumulated an enormous concentration of cotton-based wealth at the same time that slave regimes elsewhere were toppled by an emancipation process hemispheric in its extent. Lincoln's election sparked enough alarm among proslavery southerners to convince a critical mass to withdraw from an arrangement that had worked remarkably well up to that point. Profound fears bolstered this newfound willingness to embrace radical action late in 1860. But comparatively sober voices within the separatist camp also played a role in having already calmly established that even greater opportunities lay on the horizon.[3]

This chapter addresses a select number of those who presented separatism as an intrinsic good prior to Lincoln's election and who took a utilitarian approach to it, generating a set of miscalculations about the fate of slavery after secession. Only the broadest outlines of this persuasion and of its consequences can be sketched in a single essay. For that reason, my account focuses on those figures who raised the profile of a proslavery calculating tradition during the 1820s before it turns to those who most completely perfected this approach during the early 1850s. Rather than delve into the statistical dimensions of such computations, I pay more attention to how the most methodical disunionists attended to secession as an international phenomenon. To be persuasive, proslavery separatists had to explain how precisely secession would rearrange that mixture of geopolitical threats and opportunities they had experienced within the Union. Separatists of the 1850s were more inclined than their predecessors to attend to the continental and global contexts, and they were more likely as a result to frame their vision in such a way that it became an ironic echo of the Union's spread-eagle imperialism. Their vision of expansionism anticipated the ethical concerns that prevailed during the early 1860s, when civil war prompted the first extended debate over the morality of secession. As critics at the time pointed out, Confederate withdrawal was not simply a means of preserving slavery or escaping a quasi-colonial form of economic subordination. Separatist visions had by 1860 become more ambitious than that, featuring the imperial propagation of a messianic form of bondage.

Three decades before Alfred Iverson's address, a more celebrated Senate speech condemned the impiety of Deep South efforts to "calculate the value of the Union." In one of his most influential addresses, Daniel Webster of Massachusetts noted the tendency of South Carolina radicals to "speak of the Union in terms of indifference" and thus to reduce what ought to be a sacrosanct political partnership into "a mere question of present and temporary expediency" and "a mere matter of profit and loss." Most in Webster's audience recognized his reference as a thinly veiled attack on the English-born utilitarian Dr. Thomas Cooper, then serving as the "nullifying" president of South Carolina College. In the summer of 1827, Cooper had gained notoriety by rousing a Columbia audience to be "up and doing" in computing whether it was still "worth our while to continue this union of states, where the north demand to be our masters and we are required to be their tributaries." Setting aside his earlier concerns about antislavery political action, Cooper complained how "we of the South hold our plantations under this system, as serfs and operatives of the north, subject to the orders, and laboring for the benefit of the master minds of Massachusetts, the lords of the spinning jenny, and peers of the power loom!" The cotton South's increasingly degraded economic position presented masters the stark choice of either "submission or separation."[4]

If Cooper's "Value of the Union" speech was hardly the first expression of proslavery calculation, it nonetheless gained infamy by eliciting counterattacks from Webster and others. If Cooper had made his speech a few years earlier, if he had been a less divisive figure, or if he had not later joined a heated political struggle, his basic proposition would have sparked far less controversy. From the original drafting of the Constitution in 1787 up through the first quarter of the nineteenth century, proslavery politicians had understood their region's loyalty to a federal union as contingent on that government's effectiveness in insulating bound labor from outside threats and in mitigating the dangers of internal insurrection. Like most American citizens, they considered the United States a provisional form, to be judged according to its benefits. In 1825, Cooper's mentor Thomas Jefferson had clarified this logic when he reasoned that states' rights constituencies should only "separate from our companions" when it had became clear that "the sole alternatives left, are the dissolution of our union with them, or submission to a government without limitation of powers." "Between these two evils when we must make a choice, there can be no hesitation," Jefferson insisted, adding that to live momentarily with the injustices of an unequal union should be only "a temporary yielding to the lesser evil—until their accumulation shall overweigh that of separation."[5]

As Jefferson's balancing test implies, Daniel Webster's case for an "absolute" federal alliance was more novel than Cooper's calculations about the Union's conditional status. The forward-looking patriotism of the 1820s and 1830s produced an opening, however, for new conceptions of a "perpetual" union that would inform policies of presidents Andrew Jackson and Abraham Lincoln in suppressing separatist threats with armed federal force. Broad support for federal "coercion" against disunionism coincided with a discrediting of Deep South "calculations" as the wily machinations of slavocratic separatists. Cooper was a prime target of such efforts, even if his own idiosyncrasies make it hard to pigeonhole him as simply the "father of secession." His pioneering use of advanced quantifying techniques against the transatlantic slave trade during the 1790s, his willingness to be imprisoned as a Jeffersonian martyr of free speech in 1800, and his outspoken religious skepticism, which led to his removal as president of South Carolina College, all demonstrate how Cooper was sui generis within the Deep South. In remaining a "learned, ingenious, scientific and talented madcap" (as John Adams famously had described him), Cooper continued to speak more for himself than for Carolina as a whole.[6]

Cooper departed from the Deep South pattern most strikingly by infusing greater passion into his antitariff writings than into his comparatively temperate defenses of slavery and white supremacy. 1823 saw him, for instance, working in a lawyerly fashion through the issue of "Colored marriages" (a topic that in other hands would have been far more incendiary) while reserving his hottest rhetoric for recently enacted tariffs. Those who embraced the "protective policy" (which Cooper considered "one of the most entangling and extensive evils of the old governments of Europe") disgraced America by suggesting a republican incapacity to follow the supposed scientific truths of laissez-faire political economy. In a more self-interested vein, Cooper focused on how the hostile action of the U.S. government endangered $32 million in southern plantation exports by inviting Great Britain to turn to the East Indies for rice, to Brazil for cotton, and to Crimea for tobacco. Fostering manufactures at the expense of slave-grown produce seemed thus "calculated to lay desolate our Southern States—to annihilate their staple article—and to deprive them in fact of the means of subsistence." "What worse could you do by openly declaring war against the Carolinas and Georgia?" Cooper asked. "Is not this war in disguise?" The South, he maintained, was being threatened "NOT WITH TAXATION, BUT DESTRUCTION."[7]

Cooper's fury at the tariff touched a nerve among anxious Carolinians who feared congressional designs to "manage our household affairs, to drive our children and our servants from the plough to the spinning jenny and our [produce] to the mountains rather than the sea shores for a market." Because they had their suspicions regarding the territorial aspirations of the North, cotton producers of the 1820s largely shared Cooper's preference for overseas markets over internal ones.[8] This export orientation bolstered their appreciation for how stormy the Atlantic world remained even after the conclusion of the Napoleonic Wars in the 1810s. The tumultuous decade of the 1820s saw the dissolution of Spanish authority and fragmentation around the Gulf of Mexico (both preconditions for the separatism that Andrés Reséndez explores in his contribution to this volume), the unification of Haiti under Jean-Pierre Boyer, and proposals for a pan-American alliance, which sparked the Panama Conference of 1824. This complex mixture of splits and unions intensified the perception of geopolitical flux that had arisen during the Missouri crisis of 1820. The bitter congressional battle over Missouri's admission as a slave state not only stoked hostility between "North" and "South," but hastened consideration of more sweeping geopolitical alterations. John C. Calhoun tacitly admitted that Carolina might be forced to leave the Union and become a de facto economic satellite of Great Britain; others foresaw how Missouri might become the nucleus of a new western confederacy and thus draw the entire Mississippi Valley outside the orbit of Washington, D.C. Visions of fragmentation and reorganization proceeded along several axes, and with these came a quickening of considerations about how such changes might or might not provide a more secure basis for southern slavery than the cis-Mississippi federal Union had furnished.[9]

Such geopolitical dynamics received scant attention from Cooper, who said little about what would happen after Carolina seceded. Unlike Jefferson (who saw evils in fragmenting disunion as well as in centralization), Cooper concluded that an independent Carolina republic would ipso facto enhance slave-produced exports. He neglected what in today's economic parlance would be called "dynamic scoring," which would have forced him to acknowledge that at the same time that secession would remove federal burdens it would also inflict unforeseen harm on slave-owning South Carolinians daring enough to reconfigure their relationship to the rest of a tumultuous world. Cooper assumed that independence would simply foster free commerce and failed to consider other possible less salutary consequences of disunion, which might disrupt the viability of the regime.

Over the months that followed Cooper's injunction to "calculate the value" of a Union led by protariff forces, the publicist Robert Turnbull broached at least a few of these geopolitical contingencies. *The Crisis*, which Turnbull completed late in 1827, moved from a critique of the tariff to an even more withering assault on efforts of the American Colonization Society (or, as Turnbull put it, the "insurrection" society) to secure congressional funding. Such an initiative, which would use national monies to relocate black Americans to the new African colony of Liberia, taught southern slaves to "regard Congress as uncontroulable in its authority over the State" and worked to convince them that "their future destiny belongs not to South Carolina, but to Congress." Fearing that southern slaves, no less than southern masters, might begin to calculate their future stake in the American federation, Turnbull adamantly affirmed that he was "not so silly, or so sentimental, as to regard union above all price." "On the contrary," he believed that "the price we have already paid for union, is more than a fair and a sound price for the commodity" and insisted that "were the bargain to be made over again, I would not give as much." Like Cooper, Turnbull thus discounted the past advantages of a viable American state and the relative stability enjoyed by the Deep South amid the revolutions incited by the de facto secession of the Haitian "black republic" from the French Empire. "Give me disunion," Turnbull could thus blithely declare, over the "hydra" of an African colonization scheme that would disrupt the "peace of the Southern States."[10]

Turnbull gave at least cursory consideration of what might follow a dissolution of the current federal partnership. "Make me a colonist," he announced, suggesting that the exposed situation of Deep South masters required them to gravitate toward a viable expression of imperial power, even if in doing so masters relinquished their stake in republican independence. Unlike Calhoun and others who coupled Carolina independence with a new alliance with Great Britain, Turnbull had little interest in resuming links with this most powerful of the Atlantic empires. He was acutely aware that the British Parliament since 1823 had expressed a growing willingness to intervene in Caribbean colonial slavery; a partnership with the British would thus move Carolina "from the frying pan into the fire." Making Carolina into a dependent territory of Spain, France, or Holland—to take those three empires that had not yet emulated British "philanthropy"—was in his mind a better alternative. What he would not abide was being a "permanent resident of South-Carolina, with a power on the part of an American Congress, to legislate, directly or indirectly, on the subject of slavery."[11]

Given that Turnbull lived in a political culture that nurtured republicanism as its preeminent ideal, his looking toward the monarchical powers of Europe was a quixotic gesture at best. Formal political dependency of the sort Turnbull suggested would have been rejected by most southern masters (though some would question early in 1865 whether a European protectorate was preferable to Yankee domination).[12] The neocolonial economic dependence that Cooper had invited—and that became the norm for many South American republics— was only slightly more palatable. Distaste for such alternatives helps explain why Cooper, Turnbull, and other radicals of the late 1820s gathered such scant support for their program of unilateral separation from the United States, especially after John C. Calhoun's doctrine of nullification established a way to achieve state sovereignty goals within the Union.[13] Slaveholders were no doubt willing to calculate the value of the Union, just as they consistently had done since the 1790s. But their skeptical attitude toward secession suggests that once such calculations were made, the forty-year-old federal union remained comparatively attractive as a guarantor of Deep South order and prosperity.

As historians from Ulrich Phillips to William Freehling have emphasized, South Carolina contributed more than any other state to the antebellum South's defiantly proslavery politics. This state's penchant for radicalism continued past the prickly 1827 responses to tariffs and African colonization and expressed itself in the Carolina-led nullification movement of the early 1830s, the Carolina-led proslavery polemics of the late 1830s, and the Carolina-led push for immediate disunion of the 1850s.[14] In this respect, a line can be drawn from Cooper's tiny 1820s Columbia circle of straight-out disunionists all the way to James Henry Hammond's 1858 "Cotton is King" manifesto, which became nearly as notorious as Cooper's "Value of the Union" speech. Hammond himself traced a direct lineage when he marveled in 1849 at how much progress had occurred since his mentor Cooper had "shocked the public feeling of both sections" by demanding that the Union's worth be coolly recomputed. With debates over slavery's expansion into new territories upending American politics, Hammond eagerly reported how "scarcely a knot can be fallen in with in the street which is not engaged in discussing the Union—its advantages and disadvantages and probable duration." In this account, Cooper's insistence in the 1820s that masters re-evaluate their federal partnership was the first step in an ongoing tradition. The ghost of the long-dead Cooper seemed to have risen, and his vision of unilateral separation seemed finally ready to carry the day.[15]

There is a risk of making too much of the connections between Cooper-ite calculations of the 1820s and more expansive visions set forth on the eve of Civil War, however. There were at least as many differences as commonalities between the calculations made at either end of this complicated process, which was never the unidimensional "secession movement" so often presented in the scholarly literature. A new, more aggressive variant of the calculating separat-ism of the late antebellum years was the work of a younger generation of more obscure Carolinians, who broke with inherited assumptions about the South's destiny. Mustering far greater statistical detail than previous disunionists had assembled, these ideologues considered secession less as an emergency mea-sure than as the first step toward a proslavery variant of manifest destiny. Slav-ery would not simply be the motor of economic production within transatlan-tic commercial networks but in their reckoning was destined to become the informing spirit of defiantly proslavery New World empire.

Among the most influential exemplars of this new sensibility was Edward B. Bryan, a self-described "obscure individual" who in 1850, at the age of twenty-five, sought to "lay before the public the result of his search after facts" regarding slavery and southern independence. Bryan defended the dry nature of his work by referring to the countless men who "from time to time, hear something, read something, or think something about this wide-spread question" of slavery but did not have "either time or inclination to forsake their daily avocations at the plough or the anvil, the loom or the desk, the store or the counting-room; to pour over musty books and dry discussions in order to find a few historical facts which are interesting and valuable when obtained; but tedious in obtain-ing." It would not be through flashy speech making but by a bookish immersion in numbing detail that Bryan would make a difference. Providing the empirical basis for further arguments thus became his main objective in the early 1850s, which he accomplished through both his own influential pamphlet, titled *The Rightful Remedy*, and his efforts to disseminate the most persuasive arguments others made for dissolving the federal union.[16]

Edward Bryan's modest ambitions as a compiler of facts contrasted with the exuberance he expressed as a calculating prophet of disunion. "Who will un-dertake to estimate the value of our cotton, the value of our slaves?" this West

Point–educated planter asked. What Thomas Cooper had considered a pre-carious cotton interest had entered a takeoff period, which had swelled the ex-port crop of 128 million pounds in 1820 to 1.75 billion pounds by 1860. South-ern prosperity furnished, in Bryan's account, the means by which the South would "ensure commercial independence" and achieve "political power and in-dependence" in the near future. Such wealth assured that "we are identified with all that is majestic in the affairs of the world" and slave-grown cotton, he proclaimed, was nothing less than "the Archimedean lever which can upheave a continent, convulse a world." Slavery's future greatness depended not on for-eign markets or on Atlantic security but on southerners' basic resolve to set aside a misbegotten alliance with an increasingly antislavery North and wield its power on the world stage. In confronting this threat, Bryan defiantly in-sisted: "We know the value of slavery, and we know the value of the Union. We have the bane and the antidote. There is Union and Abolition on one hand, and Disunion and Slavery on the other. Which of the two shall we choose? Reader! we can not tell what you and other men may think, but as for us, give us SLAV-ERY or give us death!"[17]

Bryan's memorable inversion of Patrick Henry's famous quip capped an ava-lanche of precise figures offered over the course of 150 pages. In chapter after fact-crammed chapter, he built on what had become a regional distinction in statistical endeavor pioneered by the Charleston-born editor James De Bow. Accomplishing what Thomas Cooper had called for (but which only De Bow and his protégés would provide), Bryan charted economic growth through ex-ports, tallied population, determined the returns on investments in slave-grown cotton, charted the decline in West Indian property values that followed eman-cipation, worried over the mounting financial expenditures of the federal gov-ernment, and surveyed the mortality of whites and blacks by region and age. He laced such facts and figures with an unapologetic reference to slavery's antiq-uity and to the gains that immediate disunion would produce.

In the midst of a numbing barrage of statistical information, Bryan demon-strated a talent for making more evocative appeals and showed how effective rhetorical flourishes could be in twining hard facts with lofty exhortation. In moving from a lengthy history of slavery and a full-throated defense of the in-stitution (the topic that dominated the first half of his pamphlet) to a sustained brief for secession, he invited readers to "lay open the map of the American continent before you, on the one side, and that of the old world on the other."

This hinting toward the territorial dimension of a future southern empire was the sort of striking gesture likely to rouse those who found the nitty-gritty details to be tedious. Just as Thomas Paine had noted the absurdity of a continent ruled by an island kingdom in his 1776 *Common Sense*, so Bryan rested his case on the proven capacity of slaveholders to project the Cotton Kingdom across a seemingly illimitable expanse of territory. That the slave South occupied an area much larger than seaboard colonies of the 1770s occupied was a testament to its viability. That masters were destined to expand still further promised to make their postsecession polity one of the great powers of human history.[18]

Both Bryan's calculations and his grandiose territorial vistas echoed the picture painted by Muscoe Garnett in his even more widely circulated pamphlet entitled *The Union Past and Future*, which was published some months before Bryan's in 1850. Like Bryan, this twenty-nine-year-old Virginia patrician invoked the interests of slavery in his very first paragraph. Any attack on the "fourteen hundred millions of dollars" in human property was sure to undermine "all of honor and of happiness that civilization and society can give." More skittish about accusations of disloyalty than his South Carolina counterparts, Garnett insisted that "the South loves the equal Union of her forefathers" and was fully devoted to the country's "stars and stripes." Such a profession of patriotism did not blunt his stark declaration that the South would not allow "her stars to be changed into satellites," especially if these were destined to orbit around an antislavery sun. With a congressional crisis brewing over the admission of a free-soil California, slaveholders had "passed the Rubicon" and begun what Garnett prophetically termed an "onward march to EQUALITY OR INDEPENDENCE."[19]

Though Muscoe Garnett did not match Bryan in the number of statistics and calculations he offered, his pamphlet still catalogued plenty of pertinent evidence. Its stated intent was to "count" and to use such computation to instruct fellow masters on "the means of resistance, the relative strength of the opponents, the value of what we must hazard, and the surest ways of preserving the Union in its original equality." Systematizing a still inchoate "southern rights" program, Garnett argued that the South had to "preserve the Union as it was" by demanding "sufficient guarantees for the observance of her rights and her future political equality." Losing absolute political parity with the North (a likely outcome given the prevailing tendencies of immigration and expansion to favor the free states) would require southerners to "dissolve a Union which no longer possesses its original character." Garnett bolstered his argument by pointing to differential rates of growth, the preponderance of southern whites in both the Revolutionary and the Mexican war armies, and even the North's disproportionate gains from the federal pension system. Though these items did not directly relate to any aspect of the slavery controversy, they helped support his claim that southern masters deserved better than they were getting, given all they had expended in blood and treasure. Having made this case, he warned that if not treated better, white southerners would absent themselves from the Union and wreak destruction on the free North.[20]

For all his facts and figures, however, Garnett harbored a basic ambivalence about the computational imperative established by the utilitarian Cooper. Economic appeals to southern self-interest were not, in fact, particularly important to his quantitative analysis of "how the Union works," nor was his main objective to bolster southerners' self-confidence, as had been the case with Bryan. Signaling how Yankees supposedly guided by the bottom line were his main concern, Garnett noted that "when we are considering the value of the Union, it may be as well to calculate what it has been worth in money to the North in its influence on our trade" and how, as a result, "plain, common sense and figures" might become a "mighty stumbling block" to the North's "fine talkers about liberty and human rights." Taking advantage of the tendency of "Northern allies" to "feel the peculiar fitness of such a test as dollars and cents," Garnett devoted nearly a third of his pamphlet to depicting the ruin that disunion and a reconfiguration of the lucrative cotton trade would bring to the parasitic, volatile free society.[21]

Like Bryan, Garnett also opened his map, though rather than sketch southern greatness, he warned of a coming free-state monopoly of the West. His methodical consideration of current and future territories concluded with his prediction that the Union would soon more than double in size, increasing from thirty to sixty-eight states. Waning legislative influence was less important to him than the likelihood that the fourteen slave states then existing would soon be unable to block constitutional amendments. This domino effect could spread from California (whose admission had sparked the 1850 crisis) to Kansas and other free states over the following decade, as a Union steadily coming under the dominion of free-labor interests seemed to pose a long-term challenge to slavery. Given the thriving nature of the international cotton trade, a sectionalizing mode of organizing new states was by this time fraught with far more peril than the sectionalizing mode of economic development that had fueled the tariff disputes of the 1820s. In this calculus, throwing off political bonds would assure southern clout across North America as well as in international markets.

Garnett catered to a southern appetite for national distinction on the world stage in an 1850 summertime oration, when he hailed bondage as a messianic institution with a world-historical significance. Along with other proslavery ideologues, he argued on that occasion how the economic, military, or territorial power of bondage was less important than its ideological implications. After assailing that "loud-mouthed braying of Exeter Hall and the World Conventions" associated with international abolition, Garnett drew attention to "the low undercurrent setting in the opposite direction." Such a tendency toward political reaction "needs but a rallying point, a country where people are not afraid to speak out," Garnett continued. "In this night of human wisdom, when property, and law, and order are tottering to the base, when religion is cold, and philosophy wild, is it rash to believe that this is the chosen land, and ours the chosen people, to stem the torrent?" he asked. "In this ark, may the hope of the human race be sheltered, and hence, when the waters have abated, may the world be repeopled with a new progeny of truth?" Might a proslavery nation fulfill not just human calculations but those of Providence itself?[22]

This new emphasis on territorial preeminence and a proslavery mission produced unforeseen political consequences in the short term. Bryan had called for "the prompt, positive and unqualified secession of each State, independent of the others, in its capacity as sovereign" in his pamphlet, but he assumed that a vaguely coordinated process would thereafter produce a proslavery Confederacy sizeable enough to attain hemispheric hegemony. Yet when state after state declared its willingness to abide by the Compromise of 1850 (and likewise accepted its pairing of California's admission in exchange for a tougher fugitive slave law), fire-eaters in South Carolina faced a dilemma. They could protest California's admission by unilateral withdrawal and thus settle for the sort of territorially restricted slave republic that Cooper and Turnbull had imagined in the 1820s. Or they could bide their time until other plantation states could become radicalized enough to join this effort and lay the groundwork for an extensive slave Confederacy. In these circumstances, "southern nationalism" emerged as an alternative to immediate secession rather than as an impetus to it. Immediate secessionists too impatient to wait for the entire South to be roused to action were thus put on the defensive, suffering a setback comparable to that of the radicals of the 1820s, who had seen the overturning of the "American System" in the 1830s and the corresponding neutralization of the threats posed by tariffs and by African colonization.[23]

By 1852, the first extended secession crisis had thus passed with proslavery radicals internally divided as to whether or not disunion was worth the inward turn that secession on a state-by-state basis would produce. The politics of the 1850s encouraged the outward-looking strategies; as Arthur Bestor has written, it was the quest for "extraterritorial" power in the territories and via the fugitive slave law that formed the leading edge of late antebellum proslavery politics.[24] Not surprisingly, the analyses of Bryan and Garnett continued to resonate in this context, as did other proslavery pleas that considered how a distinctive social order might regenerate the world. In 1855, by which time Garnett had taken to articulating his vision of southern power as a U.S. congressman, *The Union Past and Future* was republished. Bryan's 1850 figures and his cataloguing of the history of slavery worked their way into countless "southern rights" appeals in this same period, though he had by then turned his attention to a radical advocacy of the African slave trade, which he believed was the most important path to southern continental supremacy.[25]

The notion that slaveholders might pursue glory within the Union ended once Lincoln was elected in 1860, when the free-soil Republican Party "seized the sceptre of American empire," as Garnett put it. As the coequal "Union of sections" became a thing of the past, the idea of setting up a new Confederacy in which masters would have full control became far more popular than it earlier had been. A great many slaveholders understood this move as a last-ditch attempt to launch a "pre-emptive counter-revolution" against the incoming Lincoln administration. However, there remained those who learned from the likes of Garnett and Bryan that disunion might have a positive value by providing a path to a glorious slaveholding future.[26]

Of course, emphasizing the benefits rather than the costs of disunion turned out to be a truly stunning mistake on the part of slavery's most stalwart champions. Withdrawing from the United States in the wake of a rare electoral defeat was predictably understood by the northern majority as a defiance of the democratic process. Such a provocation set in motion forces that would rapidly lead to the vindication of Republican Party governance through armed conflict, a process whose most sensational result was the overthrow of bondage that had reached the height of its economic power.

Not all who had painstakingly calculated the benefits of disunion lived to experience the dispiriting course of the Confederate war. As one of those who did, Muscoe Garnett received an especially bracing dose of reality as a Confederate congressman from Virginia's first district. Following his political allies among the Virginia "chivalry," the former fire-eater quickly became a leading critic of the Jefferson Davis administration, finding particular fault in those encroachments on propertied interests made by the war and treasury departments. Unprecedented levels of taxation and impressments of slaves and other valuable resources were enacted with a heavy hand that would have been unimaginable outside the context of military mobilization. Such unforeseen intrusions on slaveholders' authority coincided with a failure of government to perform its basic tasks, which most had taken for granted as long as the Union was intact. Confederate diplomats abroad became supplicants for European aid, assuming a stance that earlier proslavery ambassadors would have rejected as unbearably demeaning to themselves and to the society they represented. Most important of all, the Confederate government failed to halt the combined invasion of Union armies and navies, whose might allowed Federals first to threaten and then to occupy Garnett's Tidewater district and then to upend his mastery of a workforce that in 1860 numbered 128 black slaves.[27]

Separatists had earlier disagreed about the probable military consequences of disunion. Thomas Cooper had privately predicted that by breaking the 1787 pact, his adopted state would be given the opportunity to achieve glory and renown by besting the United States in a military showdown. Like a great many others, Edward Bryan had begged to differ, baldly stating that "this is not a fighting age" and that no more force would be used against secession than that provided by the "pop-guns" that had "grown rusty in the Senate, and can only shoot squibs and tirades across the floor."[28]

The most ironic forecast came from Muscoe Garnett, whose visions of a future war were made with the same geopolitical detail that he had brought to his discussion of multiplying free-soil states in the American West. A successful military invasion following disunion would occupy a central river artery, he wrote, thus dissecting one part of the enemy's territory from the rest. A coordinated prong of troops would then establish another military position that slashed through a vulnerable heartland.[29]

Garnett died of typhoid during his last weeks in office, living only long enough to witness the first part of this scenario take place. It did not happen exactly as he had envisioned. No British forces moved from Canada to control the Hudson Valley. New England continued to remain connected to the rest of the Union. The area between Lake Erie and Pittsburgh never witnessed a fortified line across its expanse. The free states under Republican leadership showed few of the economic, military, or geopolitical vulnerabilities that Garnett had deployed statistics to diagnose. A United States committed to free labor emerged in 1865 as the preeminent force in the hemisphere and would remain a force to be taken seriously not only in the Atlantic but across the entire world.

A radically different fate awaited the slave South once the secessionist gamble was ventured. By the middle of 1863, General U. S. Grant had taken control of the Mississippi and severed the areas of Louisiana, Arkansas, and Texas from all communication with Richmond. Eighteen months later, with Garnett dead and his plantation in Federal hands, Sherman slashed his way through Georgia and the Carolinas, thus effectively trisecting the rebellion. In Washington, the American Congress was at this time considering a Constitutional amendment that, when enacted, would assure that "neither slavery nor involuntary servitude" would "exist within the United States, or any place subject to their jurisdiction."

The blaze of Confederate military glory during this final episode of pro-slavery calculation received most of the attention from defenders of the "Lost Cause." Confederate memorialists would focus an enormous amount of attention on the particulars of campaigns and of military strategies, usually to re-consider what conditions might have helped the armies of Lee and Jackson to achieve victory. There was no Cooper to come in and cut through all these hazy assertions and wishful thoughts to compute instead exactly how secession had, in failing to achieve its stated aim, proved both what the Union had actu-ally been worth and how costly separation had been. Fierce debates over the le-gitimacy of secession precluded similarly searching explorations of whether it had been wise. An obvious fact was thus lost. Whether it was constitutionally or morally permissible, dissolving the Union ranks as a uniquely dramatic in-stance of precipitous action producing very nearly the opposite of what its most forceful proponents had predicted.

Notes

1. Alfred Iverson, speech, *Congressional Globe*, Jan. 6, 1859, 243–44.

2. William Yancey, letter, *New York Times*, July 10, 1858.

3. I develop this point in *Mastering America: Proslavery Nationalists and the Crisis of the Federal Union* (New York: Cambridge University Press, 2009).

4. Herman Belz, ed., *The Webster-Hayne Debate on the Nature of the Union: Selected Documents* (Indianapolis, Ind.: Liberty Fund, 2000), 24; Thomas Cooper, "Value of the Union," July 2, 1827, *Niles' Weekly Register*, Sept. 8, 1827.

5. Paul C. Nagel, *One Nation Indivisible: The Union in American Thought, 1776–1861*

(New York: Oxford University Press, 1964); Kenneth Stampp, "The Concept of a Perpetual Union," *Journal of American History* 65, no. 1 (1978): 5–33; Thomas Jefferson, quoted in *Columbia [S.C.] Telescope*, Sept. 27, 1827.

6. Dumas Malone, *The Public Life of Thomas Cooper, 1783–1839* (New Haven: Yale University Press, 1926).

7. [Thomas Cooper], "Colored Marriages," *Charleston (S.C.) Mercury*, Oct. 29, 1823; Thomas Cooper, *Two Tracts: On the Proposed Alteration of the Tariff, and on Weights and Measures . . .* (Columbia, S.C.: A. E. Miller, 1823).

8. Malone, *The Public Life of Thomas Cooper*; *Columbia (S.C.) Telescope*, Oct. 1, 1827; David Miller, *South by Southwest: Planter Emigration and Identity in the Slave South* (Charlottesville: University of Virginia Press, 2002); Ernest Lander, *Reluctant Imperialists: Calhoun, the South Carolinians, and the Mexican War* (Baton Rouge: Louisiana State University Press, 1979).

9. Robert Forbes, *The Missouri Compromise and Its Aftermath: Slavery and the Meaning of America* (Chapel Hill: University of North Carolina Press, 2007); James E. Lewis, *The American Union and the Problem of Neighborhood: The United States and the Collapse of the Spanish Empire, 1783–1829* (Baton Rouge: Louisiana State University Press, 1998).

10. [Robert J. Turnbull], *The Crisis; or, Essays on the Usurpations of the Federal Government, by Brutus* (Charleston, S.C.: A. E. Miller, 1827), 130–32.

11. Robin Blackburn *The Overthrow of Colonial Slavery, 1776–1848* (London: Verso, 1988).

12. "The Foreign Protectorate," *Augusta (Ga.) Constitutionalist*, Jan. 7, 1865.

13. William W. Freehling, *Prelude to Civil War: The Nullification Controversy in South Carolina, 1816–1836* (New York: Oxford University Press, 1965), 323–27.

14. Ulrich B. Phillips, *The Course of the South to Secession* (New York: Appleton-Century, 1939); William W. Freehling, *The Road to Disunion*, vol. 1 (New York: Oxford University Press, 1990).

15. [James Henry Hammond], "The North and the South," *Southern Quarterly Review* 15, no. 3 (1849): 273.

16. Edward B. Bryan, *The Rightful Remedy: Addressed to the Slaveholders of the South* (Charleston, S.C.: Walker and James, 1850), 3. Bryan's obituary, which appeared in the *Charleston Mercury*, on April 29, 1861, gives biographical details; his chairmanship of the Southern Rights Association Committee on Publications and Correspondence is noted in a bound "Secession Tracts for the People" volume held by the University of North Carolina Rare Books Library.

17. Bryan, *Rightful Remedy*, 69, 147; Brian Schoen, "The Fragile Fabric of Union: The Cotton South, Federal Politics, and the Atlantic World, 1783–1861," (PhD diss., University of Virginia, 2004).

18. Bryan, *Rightful Remedy*, 78.

19. [Muscoe R. H. Garnett], *The Union, Past and Future: How It Works, and How to Save It* (Charleston, S.C.: Walker and James, 1850), 1–3.

20. [Garnett], *The Union, Past and Future*, 5–15; James Mercer Garnett, "Biographical Sketch of Hon. Muscoe Russell Hunter Garnett, of Essex County, Virginia," *William and Mary Quarterly* 18, no. 2 (1909): 17–37.

21. [Garnett], *The Union, Past and Future*, 11–12.

22. Muscoe R. H. Garnett, *Address Delivered before the Society of Alumni of the University of Virginia at Its Annual Meeting, Held in the Rotunda, on the 29th of June, 1850* (Charlottesville, Va.: O. S. Allen, 1850), 35–36.

23. Manisha Sinha, *The Counterrevolution of Slavery: Politics and Ideology in Antebellum South Carolina* (Chapel Hill: University of North Carolina Press, 2000), 95–123.

24. Arthur Bestor, "State Sovereignty and Slavery," *Illinois State Historical Society Journal* 54, no. 2 (1961): 117–80.

25. Muscoe R. H. Garnett, "The South and the Union," *DeBow's Review*, Feb. 1855, 145–54; Sinha, *The Counterrevolution of Slavery*, 125–52.

26. Muscoe R. H. Garnett, *Speech of Hon. M. R. H. Garnett of Virginia on the State of the Union* (Washington, D.C.: McGill and Witherow, 1861), 9, 11; James M. McPherson, *Battle Cry of Freedom: The Civil War Era* (New York: Oxford University Press, 1988), 245–46.

27. Ezra J. Warner, *Biographical Register of the Confederate Congress* (Baton Rouge: Louisiana State University Press, 1975), 97–98; Thomas Alexander, *Anatomy of the Confederate Congress* (Nashville: Vanderbilt University Press, 1972), 366.

28. Freehling, *Prelude to Civil War*, 325; Bryan, *Rightful Remedy*, 132.

29. [Garnett], *The Union Past and Future*, 35–42.

SUSAN-MARY GRANT

"How a Free People Conduct a Long War"

Sustaining Opposition to Secession in the American Civil War

> The *right* of revolution does not exist in all cases where the *power* of revolution is found.
> Joel Parker, *The Right of Secession*, 1861

One of the most widely distributed Union propagandist pamphlets of the American Civil War was Charles Janeway Stillé's *How a Free People Conduct a Long War: A Chapter from English History*. Stillé was born in Philadelphia in 1819; a lawyer before the Civil War, he joined the U.S. Sanitary Commission when war broke out and later published an official account of that body. Following Union general George B. McClellan's costly but indecisive Peninsula Campaign of 1862, Stillé sought to boost flagging Union morale with the publication of a pamphlet that highlighted for the northern public the comparisons between the recent abortive attempt to seize Richmond via the James Peninsula and events on a rather different peninsula, the Iberian, on which the British under Wellington faced Napoleon in a protracted campaign lasting from 1808 to 1814. Disseminated by the Sanitary Commission in 1862 and republished the following year by the Loyal Publication Society of New York and the Union League of Philadelphia, the pamphlet eventually came to have some five hundred thousand copies in print.

Stillé was concerned, as Frank Freidel noted, "with the volatile nature of public opinion in such nations as the United States and Great Britain—overenthusiastic at the beginning of a war, certain of spectacular victory, then over-pessimistic when adversity instead ensued." This was an especially acute problem in a war fought, as the American Civil War was, mainly by volunteer troops. The Civil War was, in several senses, a "people's contest," as Abraham Lincoln famously called it, but for the Union this meant persuading the people to keep fighting; it meant convincing them that the nation as a single nation was worth the sacrifice and that secession was, as Lincoln saw it, not a constitutional right but "the essence of anarchy." Once the Union realized that the battle to bring the South back into the nation would be neither quick nor painless, it became a matter of urgency that the North work out, and fast, just how a free people might conduct a long war.[1]

The northern response to this challenge has frequently taken second place in the literature to an interest in the development of southern, or Confederate, nationalism; historians have been far more interested in why the South seceded and whether by that process a separate nation was created than in why the North sought to prevent secession and how by that process a single nation was sustained. Hindsight is part of the problem here, but historians' fascination with the perceived underdog, the lack of appreciation of the development of a specifically northern nationalism against which southern nationalism developed in the first place, and the sense of the South as a region persistently different from if not at odds with the rest of the United States have all contributed to a large literature on the subject of white southern support for secession and a concomitant dearth of material on northern opposition to it.[2]

The American Civil War was a war of state formation, yet when the war came many of the most influential bodies with respect to propaganda and support were private concerns, not state ones. Northern elite organizations such as the Loyal Publication Society of New York had the self-appointed task of both promulgating their own perspective on American nationalism and interpreting and disseminating the Lincoln administration's position on secession in support of that nationalism: in the denial of secession a nation was finally conceived but not yet born. It would take a military victory to confirm America's "new birth of freedom," and for that, the morale of the people was a crucial component. In successfully meeting the challenge of how to conduct, and win, a long war, the people established beyond doubt the legitimacy of the American federal system as a constitutionally validated perpetual union.

When Kenneth Stampp revisited the concept of a perpetual union nearly thirty years ago, he observed that the debate over secession lacked "the urgency of a still relevant political issue." This volume is a testimony to the revived sense of urgency attending the subject at the start of the twenty-first century. If the United States has had no secession movement with the momentum that the Confederacy acquired between 1861 and 1865, other nations have; even in the United States as "established at Appomattox" the debate is muted, but has never entirely fallen silent.[3] Yet although a great many studies have explored both Union troop motivation and Confederate popular support, our understanding of the conflict, from the Union's perspective, remains hampered by a tendency to separate the broader debate over the legitimacy and the morality of the war that took place in the public, political, and military spheres from the question of its military execution. As Brooks Simpson has stressed, this "bifurcation of inquiry into the political world of the why and the military world of the how" has served only to distort "our understanding of the war by divorcing means from ends. . . . The relationship between why one fights a war and how it is fought," he argues, "offers a way to comprehend how civil and military leaders sought an appropriate method to wage war which took into account both the context in which the war was waged and what they sought to achieve through armed conflict." This bifurcation is reflected in the different questions asked of each side in the conflict. Historians ask why the South lost, on the one hand, and how the North won, on the other.[4] Between the "why" and the "how" lies a virtual no-man's-land of historical engagement as far as the Union is concerned.

A MORE PERFECT UNION?

A great deal of ink has flowed on the vexed subject of the "secession winter" of 1860–61 and on the question of why the war came when it did. Scholars have pored over the various declarations issued by the seceding states in defense of the act of secession, but it's not clear, as Phillip Paludan once pointed out, how far that will get us: "A description of the decision for secession is not," he emphasized, "a description of why the war came. . . . To understand why the war came we must look not at secession but at the Northern response to it." While a South Carolinian like John S. Preston could with confidence declare that "slavery is our king—slavery is our truth—slavery is our Divine Right," and the state of Mississippi could describe itself as "thoroughly identified with the institution of slavery," the various states of the North and West seemed to have no such emotive or centralizing idea they could appeal to to defend the cause of, or make the case for, perpetual union. The Constitution offered no help, being as it was silent on this most crucial point. Yet when the argument against secession was first iterated, it was made on already rehearsed and generally widely understood Constitutional grounds.[5]

Many of the Union's arguments against secession—and the Confederacy's arguments in its favor—were thus already broadly familiar when secession became a reality in 1860–61. The rapidity with which the Constitutional defense of union emerged in the press and in the periodicals of the day was testament to the extent of debate on the subject that had already taken place not just in the years immediately preceding the war but fairly consistently since 1787. South Carolina had not yet left the Union when the *New York Times* offered its opinion that "even if the Union . . . be only a treaty—a compact between the States—it is nevertheless binding upon them all." All states, the paper insisted, "parted with a portion of their sovereignty" when they "agreed to accept a common arbiter." Secession was a misnomer, the *Times* concluded; the actions South Carolina was contemplating were both illegal and insurrectionary. This was an argument reiterated time and again in the press and in the periodicals once secession was a reality. There was a distinct sense indeed that the writers of such "think-pieces" that appeared in the early months of 1861—after South Carolina had garnered the support of several of her sister states but before Fort Sumter had brought matters to a head—were not entirely displeased to have the subject so much in the forefront of public debate once again.[6]

Poet and diplomat James Russell Lowell, writing in February 1861 on the subject of the Union, saw the crisis—his word—as an opportunity for American nationalism: "Rebellion smells no sweeter because it is called Secession," Lowell pronounced, yet only secession, he believed, could arouse in Americans "a sense of national unity, and make them feel that patriotism was anything more than a pleasing sentiment, . . . a feeble reminiscence, rather than a living fact with a direct bearing on the national well-being." Above all, Lowell stressed, America constituted "a unitary and indivisible nation, with a national life to protect, a national power to maintain, and national rights to defend. . . . Our national existence is all that gives value to American citizenship," he asserted, and it should not be dismissed "by a mere quibble of Constitutional interpretation."[7]

The problem for many northerners was that before the Civil War the Constitution allowed for precisely this kind of "quibble," and the debate over which came first—the national eagle or the state egg—had not been resolved by 1860. In defending his right to oppose secession, Lincoln asserted the Union's preeminence over the Constitution, the nation over the state. In his First Inaugural he argued that the Union was formed "by the Articles of Association in 1774[,] . . .

matured and continued by the Declaration of Independence in 1776[,] . . . further matured . . . by the Articles of Confederation of 1778," and finally, in 1787, fixed in a Constitution that sought "to form a more perfect Union." His point was reiterated by Joel Parker, Royall Professor of Law at Harvard, who argued that it was "preposterous to contend that this more perfect Union, established for posterity . . . and thus substituted for the perpetual, indissoluble Union under the Articles, is one which was to exist only at the pleasure of each and every State, and to be dissolved when any State shall assert that it is aggrieved. . . . The Union could not be made 'more perfect' in relation to its endurance," he opined. "It certainly was not intended to be made less perfect in that particular."[8]

The arguments over Constitutional interpretation on the eve of the war were too convoluted, perhaps, to have a widespread and immediate appeal to the populations of the nonseceding states. In any case, for all Americans, as Paludan argued, "'states' rights and sovereignty' was a potent rallying cry whose validity and attraction was not diminished but rather demonstrated by the fact that all sections used it when it suited their purposes." Further, he pointed out, "the trouble with emphasizing the nation when discussing pre–Civil War nationalism is that such an emphasis misconstrues the nature of loyalty and allegiance." Developing this point, Paludan constructed a plausible argument in defense of what Don Doyle has described as "localism as nationalism," specifically in relation to the issue of law and order, which, for Paludan, was the defining feature of Union support on the eve of the war. Americans north and west, he argued, "were seriously concerned with the preservation of the institutions of government that they were a part of, and they linked their experience with that government to the survival of the Union." As A. L. Peabody, professor of Christian morals at Harvard, put it, "our Constitution claims our allegiance because it is law and order."[9]

Paludan's thesis provides a valuable starting point from which to trace the flow of ideas about the nation from the intricate Constitutional interpretations set out by men like Joel Parker to the notions of the population at large and from which to identify how many northerners came to equate their well-being with opposition to secession. Lincoln had set the case out clearly in his First Inaugural: secession was "the essence of anarchy." He developed the point a few months later in his July 4, 1861, address to Congress. "Must a government," he inquired, "of necessity be too strong for the liberties of its own people, or too weak to maintain its own existence?" Lincoln was not the only one asking that question. "Where will the rebellion leave us?" asked one writer in August 1861. "The fundamental idea of the American system is local self-government for local purposes, and national unity for national purposes. Our national Union," the writer stressed, "is synonymous with our national existence," and thus until the Constitutional position on secession was settled, Americans would have "neither a flag nor a country." In short, "chaos" had "come again."[10]

The theme of the nation's return to chaos, a chaos that the Constitution had rescued it from, was also expounded by historian John Lothrop Motley, whose expertise on the subject of republics and their formation had been established via his best-selling study *The Rise of the Dutch Republic* (1856). Motley's analysis of "the causes of the American Civil War" was not initially aimed at Americans, but at the British, whose bemusement at events transpiring across the Atlantic was matched only by their hesitation to get involved. Motley's letter to the London *Times*, disseminated in pamphlet form, offered a nuanced defense of the Constitution as the originator and guarantor of the "*nation*." America was not, Motley asserted, "*a confederacy, not a compact of sovereign States, not a copartnership; it is a commonwealth.*" Following independence, Motley observed, Americans "sank rapidly into a condition of utter impotence, imbecility, anarchy. We had achieved our independence, but we had not constructed a nation." Only via the Constitution had America as a nation been created, and only through the denial of secession could America as a nation be maintained. Secession, argued Motley, is "the return to chaos from which we emerged three quarters of a century since," and whilst the right of revolution was "indisputable," secession was not revolution; it was rebellion.[11]

The task taken up by the northern elites like Motley to construct an alternative definition of revolution, one that denied secession's revolutionary aspects, was explored many years ago now by George Fredrickson and revisited by Peter Dobkin Hall, who argued that the elites saw in the war an "opportunity to bring about the moral revolution in American life, that final fulfillment of the covenant that Americans had made in undertaking the political revolution of the eighteenth century."[12] This became a persistent theme in the propaganda of patriotism that was disseminated throughout the North and West and the armies in the field between 1861 and 1865. Its early incarnation, however, highlights both the threat and the opportunity that secession offered American nationalism in the Civil War era. It also underscores how the North's version of the nation moved beyond the notion that the Constitution was the binding document of the Union and beyond the theme of law and order to construct a more robust version of nationalism that established the grounds for what Lincoln would famously describe at Gettysburg as "a new birth of freedom" for the nation.

THE LIMITS OF LOCALISM

In the spring of 1861, few of the Union's initial volunteers needed intricate con-stitutional arguments to fire their enthusiasm, and the concept of localism as nationalism was reinforced by the manner in which the Union armies were raised. Lincoln's initial call for seventy-five thousand volunteers drew on the militias, but these did not offer a long-term solution. Although the Constitution enabled the president to call the militias out, they fell under state, not federal, control, and even when federal control was achieved, it remained indirect: regi-ments were raised at state level even if they were commanded at the federal one. The basis for the Union's mass volunteer army was laid in May 1861, when Lin-coln called for forty-two thousand volunteers in forty regiments. By the start of July, 208 regiments had been raised, and by the time Congress met on the 4th, over three hundred thousand men had enlisted for the Union. The competition between states and between different constituencies within states to prove their patriotic credentials resulted in the raising of a variety of regiments, some based on social interest such as temperance, others on ethnic ties, and still others on a connection to the revolutions in Europe, as was the case of the Garibaldi Guard (39th New York), the first of the New York three-year regiments, which com-prised an eclectic mix of immigrants who had previously served in the revolu-tionary armies of Europe, some under Giuseppe Garibaldi himself.

This state-based raising of the armies meant that for many northerners the Civil War was very much "a national war fought by local communities," and military morale, in its early stages, was sustained by a combination of volun-tarism and private activism.[13] Civilian morale was another matter, and on the home front there were limits to the efficacy of localism, limits that by late 1862 the Union had reached. Indeed, in the context of maintaining the war effort, law and order as impetus proved something of a double-edged sword, as the cru-cial midterm elections in 1862 revealed. By that point, the Republicans realized that war weariness was taking its toll, and no one was surprised by the marked swing the election produced away from the Republicans. New York lawyer and staunch Republican George Templeton Strong saw quite clearly in late October "that unless we gain decisive success before the November election, this state will range itself against the Administration. If it does, a dishonorable peace and permanent disunion are not unlikely." After the election, he wrote that the out-come of the midterms was, for him, "a national calamity." It was "like a great, sweeping revolution of public sentiment, like a general abandonment of the loyal, generous spirit of patriotism that broke out so nobly and unexpectedly in April, 1861," although he understood that it represented the natural response of a population "suffering from the necessary evils of war and from irritation at our slow progress." Nevertheless, the risk of what Strong termed "national suicide" was a real one if northerners came to regard law and order not as guaranteed by opposition to secession but as in fact threatened by the war.[14]

The danger posed to the Union war effort by political opposition grew as the war progressed. At first, there was little disagreement between the parties on the war aims of the North. The Democratic slogan, "The Constitution as it is, and the Union as it was," had defined the Union cause in 1861, but by 1863, it no longer did. Increasingly, the views of the Republican administration clashed with those of the Democrats over the nature, and purpose, of the war. Lincoln's delivery of the Emancipation Proclamation at the start of the year brought this clash to a head. In its attack on southern "property," the Emancipation Proclamation seemed to clearly deviate from the Constitutional strictures that, many Democrats believed, protected the American republican experiment. That, combined with Lincoln's assumption of an increasing range of war powers, notably the draft, and, above all, the suspension of habeas corpus, left many Democrats concerned. "Conservatism is our only chance of safety," they argued. "Conservatism of our own American institutions[,] . . . [l]iberty of speech, liberty of the press, liberty of the person" was what was at stake.[15] After 1863, the *Chicago Times* abandoned its moderate line on Lincoln, denouncing the Emancipation Proclamation as "the most wicked, atrocious, and revolting deed recorded in the annals of civilization," and a month later the paper was advocating peace at any price. The challenge for the Union was how to counter such charges and, in the face of them, maintain support for the war; it was a challenge that necessitated a move beyond localism.[16]

Confronted by declining numbers of volunteers in late 1862, the Republican administration and private associations in the North and West employed a variety of methods to maintain momentum with respect to the war. On the private front, the foremost tactic was simple encouragement, and Stillé's pamphlet was a prime example of that approach: it was essentially an attempt to reinforce faith in the war by emphatically pointing to the equally slow and apparently ineffective efforts of Wellington during the Peninsular War and highlighting his eventual victory over Napoleon. The few references made to British national power deriving from this campaign were less overt than were the obvious—and slightly strained—attempts to compare Wellington and McClellan. A straightforward attempt to boost morale, Stillé's pamphlet simply advised the Union to hold on, on the grounds that it was always darkest before dawn.

The Lincoln administration utilized a combination of threat and the promise of material gain to fill the ranks. The Enrollment Act of March 1863 established a draft, but it was hardly effective. Historians estimate that some fifty thousand draftees actually served, while twice as many troops were made available by the raising of the African American regiments. Over one hundred thousand substitutes also served (the drafted man could secure the services of a substitute if he had $300). The draft was designed not to raise troops directly but to stimulate volunteering. Each congressional district was assigned a quota, and the assumption, which often proved to be correct, was that a combination of local pride and additional financial bounties offered by the state would encourage men to avoid the draft and volunteer instead. The amounts involved were staggering: Massachusetts, it was estimated, issued $13 million in bounties from public funds alone, and private benefactors contributed even more. Of course, the system was open to abuse by bounty jumpers and corrupt bounty agents, but even the honest individual could earn a significant amount of money—over $800 in Massachusetts and $500 in Jacksonville, Illinois. This was private gain in pursuit of public good. Still, money was not enough to keep the war going; other, less material factors also came into play.[17]

Although many people were uncomfortable with the idea that the war to save the Union had become a war to free the slaves, in fact maintaining the Union war effort required emphasizing just that. This is not to suggest that Lincoln's Emancipation Proclamation was dictated by military necessity alone. Rather it is a fact of war that in the context of an extended conflict, as casualties mount and as the initial enthusiasm for the war diminishes, the justifications invoked at the outset may have to be revisited, perhaps even revised, if the momentum of support for the war is to be sustained. Leading American statesman Daniel Webster demonstrated that he had grasped as much when, during the War of 1812, he argued that "party support is not the kind of support necessary to sustain the country through a long, expensive, and bloody contest. . . . The cause, to be successful, must be upheld by other sentiments, and higher motives. . . . Armies of any magnitude" in the United States, Webster stressed, can "be nothing but the people embodied—and if the object be one for which the people will not embody, there can be no armies."[18]

For democracies in particular, there is a pressing need "to convert wars into crusades," to hold out the promise not merely of maintaining the *status quo ante bellum* but of achieving a higher purpose, such as "a moral crusade, a national rebirth, a spiritual revival, a new world order." In the context of what Peter Parish termed the "calculus of suffering and its justification," the redirection of the war effort toward "a new birth of freedom"—not just for slaves but for the nation as a whole—served to sanctify past sacrifices and legitimate future ones.[19]

The impulse behind this reconfiguration of the Union war effort away from local ambitions and toward national ones did not derive from Lincoln alone. It is important to stress this: secession was opposed in America not only by the executive, nor just by constitutional theorists, but by the mass volunteer armies of the Union, who were supported in their sentiments by their home communities. And such support was not merely familial or social but also ideological. By 1863, as the cost of the war was beginning to weaken the armies, home-front support became more crucial. Further, arguments in support of the war effort that were promulgated both among the armies in the field and the civilian population at home were not simply the views of Lincoln distributed through the rank and file. On the contrary, they came as much from the press, the pulpit, and the pamphlet as they did from the president. In seeking to comprehend, first, how the Union maintained the war effort after 1863 and, second, how it successfully raised the stakes in that war, effectively elevating it into a crusade, this unity of political, religious, and patriotic utterance represents the key.

The case made against secession via the various propagandist pamphlets disseminated across the North after 1863 was, in its initial stages, neither new nor responsive to the changing nature of the war. Several of the most widely distributed documents simply reprinted antebellum debates, revived at this juncture because of their opposition to secession. A case in point was the work of Francis Lieber, German exile and one-time professor of history and political economics at South Carolina College. In 1851, Lieber had publicly denied the right of secession and had made the case for a perpetual union, one deliberately constructed, as he believed America had been, and one "leaving separate what ought to be separated, and yet uniting the whole by a broadcast and equal representation, changing with the changing population, so that we cannot fall into a dire Peloponnesian war[,] . . . that internecine war into which all other confederacies have fallen, and in which they have buried themselves under their own ruins." Further, he warned, "no great institution, and, least of all, a country, has ever broken up or can break up in peace, and without a struggle commensurate to its own magnitude[;] . . . when vehement passion dashes down a noble mirror, no one can hope to gather a dozen well-framed looking-glasses from the ground."

The Union, he asserted, was not "a sort of political picnic to which the invited guest may go and carry his share of the viands or not, as he thinks fit."[20]

Ten years later, by which point Lieber was teaching at Columbia University in New York and the political picnic was in the process of breaking up, he expanded on the subject of secession at the conclusion of his course on the modern state and left his students in no doubt that the Constitution was "a national fundamental law, establishing a complete national government—an organism of national life . . . with living functions; not a string of beads in mere juxtaposition on a slender thread, which may snap at any time and allow the beads to roll in all directions." For Lieber, the "normal type of modern government is the National Polity," but the American variant was nevertheless special, positioned as it was "between Europe and Asia, on a fresh continent." "I see the finger of God in it[;] . . . I believe our destiny to be a high, a great, and a solemn one," he argued.[21] Lieber's analysis of the organic unity of nations may have found a relatively limited audience beyond the academy, but his defense of the perpetuity of the Constitution reached a broader demographic when the Loyal Publication Society, of which he was president, reprinted it in 1863. It was, however, his invocation of America's special destiny that most loudly resonated, as America's secular and religious leaders came, increasingly, to position the Civil War within a "millennial framework."

FAITH AND PROGRESS

Evolving northern arguments in support of the war have been too readily positioned as solely deriving from, if not confined to, a closed intellectual sphere. It was, however, the overlap between the arguments of politicians, the pamphlets, and, above all, the pulpit that got the message from the gentlemen's clubs and drawing rooms of Boston and New York to the population at large and, through them, to the armies in the field. Importantly, after 1863, this confluence produced a marriage of sorts between the "constitutional argument in defense of duly constituted authority" and the more radical abolitionist arguments that had run alongside the appeal to law and order from the beginning; the conflagration was increasingly described not as a war to save the Union but as a war "to defend the principles for which the Union stood—order, democratic liberty and popular institutions" and, even beyond that, as a war to achieve those ends through the eradication of chattel slavery. In this process, the impact of the Protestant churches was crucial, as Parish has argued: "Better able to cope with the question of God's role in the historical process because of the millennial framework within which their ideas were cast," the North's protestant preachers could invoke a version of the war as part of the divine plan, as presaging the second coming, and thereby position America at the heart of that particular religious narrative. Millennialism, as James Moorhead has shown, "provided a major way in which Americans defined their country as a Redeemer Nation," and the Civil War, in this context, could be presented to northern Protestant congregations not only as "an Armageddon of the Republic" but as a world-wide crisis. As Methodist bishop Matthew Simpson put it, "if the world is to be raised to its proper place, I would say with all reverence, God cannot do without America." The fact that Simpson delivered a version of this speech in New York only three days before polling day in the 1864 election was hardly a coincidence in the context of the shift in the representation of the war from defensive campaign to national crusade.[22]

The raising of the stakes for the Union war effort both relied on and yet also moved beyond localism, and this is nowhere more clear than in the matter of emancipation. If the initial impetus to enlist or become involved in the many support organizations devoted to the Union cause—the Sanitary Commission or the Christian Commission, for example—came from local loyalties and community pressures, that localism also prevented any overt or obvious association between the individuals concerned and the cause of abolition, a cause that had gained momentum but was still hardly universally accepted even after 1863. In effect, the Union cause generated a new American nationalism at the point when slavery was acknowledged to be a national crime rather than a sectional sin. When the Union population's attention turned to the assumption of a guilt that had, increasingly in the antebellum era, been assigned to the South alone, the grounds on which the nation, and the Union war effort in defense of that nation, rested began to shift.

At the national level, the representation of the war as the punishment for the national sin of slavery was most famously presented by Lincoln in his Second Inaugural, an address that has been described as the president's "election jeremiad." In it Lincoln summed up his position on "slavery and race, the meaning of nationhood, the purpose of government, [and] the role of God in the universe." It read, as Mark Neely has pointed out, "more like a sermon than a secular political appeal," but that is precisely the point. Although Neely argues that part of the power of the Second Inaugural lay in Lincoln's willingness to "tell people what they did not want to hear," in the broader spiritual climate, one overcast by the sacrifices of the war and infused with suffering, northern audiences were more open, by 1865, to Lincoln's interpretation of the nation's crime and punishment than they might have been in 1861. Writing to Thurlow Weed, Lincoln himself certainly expressed the view that the Second Inaugural might not be "immediately popular." "Men," he noted, "are not flattered by being shown that there has been a difference of purpose between the Almighty and them. To deny it, however, in this case, is to deny that there is a God governing the world. It is a truth which I thought needed to be told."[23]

By 1865, and for some time before, however, Lincoln was not the only one telling this particular truth. By the final stage of the conflict, northern preachers had already established the terms through which Union sacrifice would be contextualized, stressing the "new birth of freedom" that Abraham Lincoln had invoked at Gettysburg, a freedom for both the individual slave and the nation of which she was a part. In this context, Congregationalist theologian Horace Bushnell, in his 1865 oration to the alumni of Yale who had served in the war, chose to stress the Union's obligations to the dead, who were, he declared, "the purchase money of our redemption." It "is the ammunition spent that gains the battle," he advised his audience, and it was that ammunition, that terminal "shedding of blood," that had "cemented and sanctified" the unity of the nation. The establishment of the nation was Bushnell's main point in this funeral oration, in which the Civil War was presented as the culmination of what the Revolution had begun: "The sacrifices in the fields of the Revolution united us but imperfectly. We had not bled enough to merge our colonial distinctions . . . and make us a proper nation. And so, what argument could not accomplish, sacrifice has achieved," Bushnell declaimed, and "now a new and stupendous chapter of national history" awaited the American people.[24]

Northern preachers as well as politicians and pamphleteers turned to scripture both for solace and for confirmation that the struggle to hold the nation together in the face of the Confederate challenge and the sacrifices that entailed was worth the cost. Their ability to affirm a national faith during such a crisis derived in large part from the fact that, as Moorhead describes it, "Gabriel's trumpet resonated with national values in such a way that millennial symbols could shift, almost effortlessly, from a religious to a political context as the needs of the moment dictated." The "most dramatic example of such flexibility," he notes, "occurred in 1861 when Northern Protestants, who for several generations had seen the glory of the coming of the Lord in revivals and missionary societies, read the portents of his advent in the Army of the Potomac." Increasingly, as the war progressed, this "apocalyptic model" applied more broadly. And as this apocalyptic vision was taken up at the national level, it permitted individual suffering to find a place in a national redemption narrative that held out the promise of a new kind of law and order, a spiritual version of what had been, in 1861, only a secular faith. In part, of course, this interpretation of the war represented a polemic device, a means of selling the idea of emancipation to a broadly skeptical, possibly disinterested, and sometimes overtly racist northern public, who increasingly looked for evidence, and required reassurance, that the sacrifice, the suffering, and the loss of life were both necessary and divinely ordained, that the war was a test of American faith, a path to American nationality.[25]

The threads of what would by 1865 become a fully fledged reconstruction of American nationalism were, however, already present in the earliest discussions of the constitutional invalidity of secession. The first and most obvious of these, which Lowell's "E Pluribus Unum" is an example of, anticipated a reinvigoration of national sentiment emerging from the crisis and represented war as a nationalizing force and conflict as shared experience welding together hitherto disparate elements within the Union; as another writer put it, the "man who ever doubted that the first gun fired by the insurgents would instantly unite the nation against them knew as little of the American people as if he were editor of the London *Times*. There is no chemical solvent like gunpowder." Julian Sturtevant of Jacksonville, Illinois, also interpreted the war as a unifying force. As Lincoln would later do, he emphasized the experimental nature of America's democratic republic, but he also stressed that that did not exempt America "from a law of national progress to which all the past has been subjected," a progress achieved only through warfare. The "idea of a national government of limited powers has no firm hold on any portion of the national mind," he argued, because "it has not yet been subjected to the ordeal of the sword; it has not yet been written in blood. And the bloody handwriting of the sword is to nations the only intelligible writing."[26]

Yet what would become the strongest of these threads was the idea that the crisis offered a moral opportunity, and this thread came in time to be intertwined with the religious defense of the war and with the arguments in support of emancipation. Whereas Lowell, in 1861, saw the conflict as being less about slavery and more about "the re-establishment of order, the reaffirmation of national unity," Sturtevant, while grounding his argument in the unconstitutionality of secession, emphasized the morality of slavery. He believed that Americans had lived "too long and too much in the cool shade of prosperity" and required "the hot sunshine of national adversity" to develop as a nation and to develop nationalism. Even Lowell, however, shifted his ground over the course of the war (although he denied it was a change of heart and instead maintained that all that had happened was that "the real causes of the war" had become apparent to the population): by 1864, he drew from the war "an instinctive feeling that the very germinating principle of our nationality was at stake, and that unity of territory was but another name for unity of idea."[27]

Lincoln had, of course, set out the case with the greatest clarity in his July 4, 1861, message to Congress, in which he asserted that secession was a question that involved "more than the fate of these United States. It presents to the whole family of man, the question whether a constitutional republic, or a democracy— a government of the people, by the same people—can, or cannot, maintain its territorial integrity, against its own domestic foes."[28] By the time of his Second Inaugural, Lincoln, too, had moved toward a broader interpretation of the war as part of the divine plan, as punishment for the national sin of slavery; this was not an interpretation that all concurred in, but in the context of so much suffering and death, it undoubtedly had resonance. It was, after all, both the price and the challenge of the new nationalism.

The conclusions of historians on the outcome of the Civil War with respect to American nationalism can strike a downbeat note. Robert Wiebe, for one, argues that the reconstruction of American nationalism "began with secession itself," and in the end, what "all the bloodshed had settled was the issue of secession: Southern nationalism was no longer an option." The point was reinforced, of course, in *Texas v. White* (1869), which asserted that the "Union of the States never was a purely artificial and arbitrary relation. It began among the Colonies, and grew out of common origin, mutual sympathies, kindred principles, similar interests, and geographical relations." Yet the Civil War had done more than deny secession; it had also settled the issue of slavery and abolished it as a labor system within the United States.[29]

More significantly, in the context of emancipation the war led to American citizenship being defined for the first time via the Fourteenth Amendment. This was a citizenship based on the nation, not on the state, as it refers to all "persons born or naturalized in the United States." As Parish has noted, from a modern perspective this seems a fairly obvious statement, yet only a decade earlier the Supreme Court had ruled, in *Dred Scott v. Sandford* (1857), that African Americans could not be citizens and that "they had no rights that the white was bound to respect." Nevertheless, the "amount of permanent consolidation produced by the war," it has been argued, was "neither small enough to be called unimportant nor large enough to be called revolutionary. The principal achievement for American nationalism under Lincoln's leadership was the negative one of arresting a drift toward decentralization that had become a plunge into disintegration."[30]

This latter view derives from hindsight. Certainly in the postwar period, as has been shown, the most prominent theorists on nationalism—men such as Francis Lieber—struggled to marry up their civic national ideals with the ethnic challenges presented by the new American polity, and undoubtedly the shortcomings of their thinking on nationalism all too quickly became evident.[31] Yet the imperatives of the new nationalism, themselves products of the challenge involved in persuading a free people to conduct a long war, once established, could never again be dismissed. If the ideal and the reality diverged, and if future presidents disguised an impulse toward ethnic nationalism under a civic cloak, still their debt to the Civil War generation, to those who had sustained Union motivation and morale, had to be acknowledged. At the dawn of a new century, the inheritance of the crusading rhetoric of the Civil War era found its echo when Theodore Roosevelt, no inclusive civic nationalist, thanked "God for the iron in the blood of our fathers, the men who upheld the wisdom of Lincoln, and bore sword or rifle in the armies of Grant! Let us, the children of the men who proved themselves equal to the mighty days, let us, the children of the men who carried the great Civil War to a triumphant conclusion, praise the God of our fathers that the ignoble counsels of peace were rejected . . . for in the end the slave was freed, the Union restored, and the mighty American republic placed once more as a helmeted queen among nations." Many scholars would critique—and with good reason, perhaps—Roosevelt's conception of the nation, but the fact remains that it was not only the Union's ability to sustain a long war through to its conclusion but the methods it employed to do so that became the model for many—not all—future American conflicts and established the framework within which they would be fought and their nationalist ambitions defined.[32]

Notes

1. Charles Janeway Stillé, *History of the United States Sanitary Commission: Being the General Report of Its Work during the War of the Rebellion* (Philadelphia: J. B. Lippincott, 1866); Frank Freidel, "The Loyal Publication Society: A Pro-Union Propaganda Agency,"

The Mississippi Valley Historical Review 26, no. 3 (1939): 368; George M. Fredrickson, *The Inner Civil War: Northern Intellectuals and the Crisis of the Union* (New York: Harper and Row, 1965), 141–43; Frank Freidel, introduction, "How a Free People Conduct a Long War," in Frank Freidel, ed., *Union Pamphlets of the Civil War, 1861–1865*, 2 vols. (Cambridge, Mass.: Harvard University Press, 1967) 1:381; Abraham Lincoln, "Message to Congress in Special Session," July 4, 1861, in *The Collected Works of Abraham Lincoln*, 11 vols., ed. Roy Basler (New Brunswick, N.J.: Rutgers University Press, 1953–55), 4:438.

2. On the perception of the South as separate, see Kees Gispen, ed., *What Made the South Different?* (Jackson: University Press of Mississippi, 1990); on the lack of attention accorded the Union's perspective on secession, see Peter J. Parish, "Conflict by Consent," in his *The North and the Nation in the Era of the Civil War* (New York: Fordham University Press, 2003), 149–70; Phillip S. Paludan, "The American Civil War as a Crisis in Law and Order," *The American Historical Review* 77, no. 4 (1972): 1013–34; and Richard Franklin Bensel, *Yankee Leviathan: The Origins of Central State Authority in America, 1859–1877* (New York: Cambridge University Press, 1990), 18. Earl J. Hess, *Liberty, Virtue, and Progress: Northerners and Their War for the Union* (New York: New York University Press, 1988), is one of the few attempts to "understand how a society emotionally conducts a long, costly war effort" (1).

3. Kenneth M. Stampp, "The Concept of a Perpetual Union," *Journal of American History* 65:1 (1978): 6.

4. Brooks D. Simpson, "Olive Branch and Sword: Union War-making in the American Civil War," in *Aspects of War in American History*, ed. David K. Adams and Cornelis A. Van Minnen (Keele, U.K.: Keele University Press, 1997), 63–79, 63–4; Richard E. Beringer, Herman Hattaway, Archer Jones, and William N. Still, *Why the South Lost the Civil War* (Athens: University of Georgia Press, 1986), esp. chaps. 14, 16, 17 (for a challenge to their thesis see Gary W. Gallagher, *The Confederate War* [Cambridge, Mass.: Harvard University Press, 1997]); Herman Hattaway and Archer Jones, *How the North Won: A Military History of the Civil War* (Urbana: University of Illinois Press, 1983).

5. Paludan, "Civil War as a Crisis in Law and Order," 1013; John S. Preston, quoted in Manisha Sinha, *The Counter-revolution of Slavery: Politics and Ideology in Antebellum South Carolina* (Chapel Hill: University of North Carolina Press, 2000), 220; "A Declaration of the Immediate Causes Which Induce and Justify the Secession of the State of Mississippi from the Federal Union," in *Journal of the State Convention* (Jackson, Miss.: E. Barksdale, 1861) 86–88.

6. *New York Times*, Dec. 13, 1860.

7. James Russell Lowell, "E Pluribus Unum," *Atlantic Monthly*, Feb. 1861, 235, 236, 238, 237.

8. Stampp, "The Concept of a Perpetual Union," 6; Abraham Lincoln, "First Inaugural Address," Mar. 4, 1861, in *Collected Works*, 4:265; Joel Parker, *The Right of Secession:*

A Review of the Message of Jefferson Davis to the Congress of the Confederate States, in Freidel, ed., *Union Pamphlets,* 1:84.

9. Paludan, "Civil War as a Crisis in Law and Order," 1016; Don H. Doyle, *The Social Order of a Frontier Community: Jacksonville, Illinois, 1825–70* (Urbana: University of Illinois Press, 1978), 227; A. L. Peabody, "Loyalty," *The North American Review,* Jan. 1862, 158.

10. Lincoln, "First Inaugural Address," 4:268; "Where Will the Rebellion Leave Us," *Atlantic Monthly,* Aug. 1861, 238–39.

11. John Lothrop Motley, *The Causes of the American Civil War: A Paper Contributed to the London Times,* in Freidel, ed., *Union Pamphlets,* 1:31, 32, 36. Motley's letter appeared in the *Times* on May 23, 24, 1861.

12. George M. Fredrickson, *The Inner Civil War: Northern Intellectuals and the Crisis of the Union* (New York: Harper and Row, 1965); Peter Dobkin Hall, *The Organization of American Culture, 1700–1900: Private Institutions, Elites, and the Origins of American Nationality* (New York: New York University Press, 1984), 221.

13. Brian Holden Reid, "Command and Leadership in the Civil War, 1861–5," in *The American Civil War: Explorations and Reconsiderations,* ed. Susan-Mary Grant and Brian Holden Reid (Harlow, U.K.: Longman, 2000), 143; John Shy, *A People Numerous and Armed: Reflections on the Military Struggle for Independence,* rev. ed. (Ann Arbor: University of Michigan Press, 1990), 260–62; Paludan, "Civil War as a Crisis in Law and Order"; Doyle, *Social Order of a Frontier Community,* 228 (and more generally 227–41); J. Matthew Gallman, *The North Fights the Civil War: The Home Front* (Chicago: Dee, 1994), 188; Reid Mitchell, "The Northern Soldier and His Community," in *Toward a Social History of the American Civil War: Exploratory Essays,* ed. Maris A. Vinovskis (Cambridge: Cambridge University Press, 1990), 92.

14. Strong, diary entries, Oct. 23, Nov. 4, 5, 1862, in *The Diary of George Templeton Strong,* 4 vols., ed. Allan Nevins and Milton Hasley Thomas (New York: Macmillan, 1952), 3:270–72.

15. Edward Ingersoll, "Personal Liberty and Martial Law: A Review of Some Pamphlets of the Day," in Frank Freidel, ed., *Union Pamphlets,* 1:256.

16. *Chicago Times,* Jan. 3, 1863.

17. James W. Geary, *We Need Men: The Union Draft in the Civil War* (DeKalb: Northern Illinois University Press, 1991). See also Geary, "Civil War Conscription in the North: A Historiographical Review," *Civil War History* 32, no. 3 (1986): 208–28; Michael H. Frisch, *Town into City: Springfield, Massachusetts and the Meaning of Community, 1840–1880* (Cambridge, Mass.: Harvard University Press, 1972), 65; Doyle, *Social Order of a Frontier Community,* 235. See also Emily J. Harris, "Sons and Soldiers: Deerfield, Massachusetts and the Civil War," *Civil War History* 30, no. 2 (1984): 166–68.

18. Daniel Webster, speech, House of Representatives, Jan. 14, 1814, in *The Debates*

and *Proceedings in the Congress of the United States*, 18 vols. (Washington, D.C.: Gales and Seaton, 1834–36), 945–46.

19. Peter J. Parish, "The War for the Union as a Just War," in *Aspects of War in American History*, 83.

20. Francis Lieber, *What Is Our Constitution—League, Pact, or Government? Two Lectures on the Constitution of the United States . . . To Which is Appended an Address on Secession* (New York: Columbia Law School, 1861), 41.

21. Francis Lieber, *What Is Our Constitution?* 33, 12, 47.

22. Parish, "War for Union as a Just War," 89–90; Simpson, quoted in Parish, "War for Union as a Just War," 84. On this aspect of the war, see James H. Moorhead, *American Apocalypse: Yankee Protestants and the Civil War, 1860–1869* (New Haven: Yale University Press, 1978), 42–81, and James H. Moorhead, "Between Progress and Apocalypse: A Reassessment of Millennialism in American Religious Thought, 1800–1880," *Journal of American History* 71, no. 3 (1984): 524.

23. James Tackach, *Lincoln's Moral Vision: The Second Inaugural Address* (Jackson: University Press of Mississippi, 2002), 129, xiv; Mark E. Neely Jr., *The Last Best Hope of Earth: Abraham Lincoln and the Promise of America* (Cambridge, Mass.: Harvard University Press, 1993), 156; Abraham Lincoln to Thurlow Weed, Mar. 15, 1865, in *Collected Works*, 8:356.

24. Horace Bushnell, "Our Obligations to the Dead," 1865, in Mary Bushnell Cheney, *Life and Letters of Horace Bushnell* (New York: Charles Scribner and Sons, 1905), 485–86.

25. Moorhead, "Millennialism in American Religious Thought," 533, 538.

26. James Russell Lowell, "The Ordeal by Battle," *Atlantic Monthly*, July 1861, 89; Julian Sturtevant, "The Lessons of Our National Conflict: Address to the Alumni of Yale College, July 24, 1861," *New Englander*, Oct. 1861, 905–6.

27. Sturtevant, "The Lessons of Our National Conflict," 908; James Russell Lowell, quoted in Parish, "War for Union as a Just War," 99.

28. Abraham Lincoln, "Message to Congress in Special Session," 4:426.

29. Robert H. Wiebe, *Who We Are: A History of Popular Nationalism* (Princeton: Princeton University Press, 2002), 78–79.

30. Parish, "The Importance of Federalism," 104; *Dred Scott v. Sandford* 60 U.S. 393 (1856); Don E. Fehrenbacher, "Lincoln and the Constitution," in *The Public and Private Lincoln: Contemporary Perspectives*, ed. Culom Davis et al. (Carbondale: Southern Illinois University Press, 1979), 127.

31. On this point, see Dorothy Ross, "'Are We A Nation?': The Conjuncture of Nationhood and Race in the United States, 1850–1876," *Modern Intellectual History* 2, no. 3 (2005): 327–60.

32. Theodore Roosevelt, "The Strenuous Life," Hamilton Club, Chicago, Apr. 10, 1899, http://bartleby.com/58/1.html, accessed Oct. 18, 2007.

PAUL QUIGLEY

Secessionists in an Age of Secession

The Slave South in Transatlantic Perspective

Ours is not the first attempt to consider "secession as an international phenomenon." Secessionists in the American South and elsewhere did so themselves, reflecting on the international contexts of their movements and seizing on those comparisons that appeared to offer support.[1] For mid-nineteenth-century white southerners looking across the Atlantic, these were few and far between— not least because so many Europeans had by then come to view slavery, the basis of southern secessionism, as a barbaric relic of the past. However, the independence movements that sought to liberate peoples such as the Poles, the Irish, and the Hungarians from external domination appeared to offer a possible way of validating the effort to liberate southerners from the oppression of the North. Secessionists recognized the utility of comparing themselves with European nationalist movements, and it is their comparisons that have inspired this chapter.

In a speech delivered in 1859, the South Carolina fire-eater Robert Barnwell Rhett, a planter and politician who had been committed to southern secession for decades, placed the cause of southern independence within a transatlantic context. Referring to Europe, he saw what he termed "a bloody contest for the independence of nationalities." Nations had a God-given right to independence, he believed, which ought not to be denied by any external occupier. Aligning his own nationalist cause with others, Rhett asserted that "the people of England and Ireland, Russia and Poland, Austria and Italy, are not more distinct and antagonistic in their characters, pursuits, and institutions, their sympathies and views, than the people of our Northern and Southern

States."[2] Independence was deserved by any distinctive people subjugated by a foreign power—and for Rhett that included the American South.

Rhett's comparison indicates that southern secessionists were very much aware of the wider world around them.[3] And it was evident to them that the nineteenth century constituted an age of nationalism, especially in its middle decades, and especially in Europe. William Woods Holden, a North Carolina newspaper editor and politician, thus proclaimed in 1856, "As the great idea of the eighteenth century was that of *union against tyrants*, so is that of the nineteenth century, *the independence of nationalities*."[4] This context shaped the way white southerners conceived of and implemented their own separatist plans. The historian Joseph Leerssen has observed that "one of the outstanding features of nationalism is that it is a supremely international affair, spilling from one country to another, spreading ideas, books, and symbols freely across the map, spawning copycat movements at great distance." Like their contemporaries, southern secessionists recognized the benefits of this transnational concept that could be transplanted from place to place. Setting themselves within the ascendant trend of nationalism might allow secessionists not only to bolster their movement for independence in general terms but also to counteract the stigma that the slaveholding American South was retrograde, out of step with the rest of the Western world.[5]

Although historians have taken note of secessionists' forays into comparative history, they have not analyzed them in much depth. To be sure, there have been some attempts to situate the Civil War–era United States in the context of Europe's "age of nationalism." But these have mostly highlighted parallels between the Union's victory and the moderately analogous creation of strong, centralized nation-states in Italy and Germany.[6] There is good reason for this focus on unification: the story of nineteenth-century European nationalism *was* to a considerable degree the story of integration into centralized nation-states. Even some antebellum southerners protested that to secede from the United States would be to swim against the tide of history. The South Carolinian William Grayson, for instance, opposed secession in 1850 partly on these grounds, asking why southerners would want to break up the same sort of noble, beneficial union for which Italians and Germans were then striving.[7]

Yet the separatist impulse—the attempt to break up larger groupings rather than to join smaller components together—was also robust in Europe during this period. Although labeling the mid-nineteenth century an "age of secession" might go a little too far, separatism was more significant than we often assume.

This is true even of the prime examples of unification nationalism—Germany and Italy—both of which were faced in part with the problem of liberating territories from their occupiers (especially the Habsburg empire).[8] But even more pertinent were the vibrant separatist nationalisms in places such as Hungary, Poland, Bohemia, Norway, Serbia, Ireland, and (until it achieved independence in 1829) Greece. Most of these movements did not bear fruit until the twentieth century, but they were in many cases strong in the nineteenth.[9] Clearly, nationalism could be centrifugal, not just centripetal. Recognizing this reveals the value of putting the nationalism of the losing South as well as the victorious North into a comparative framework.

Secessionists themselves needed no convincing in that regard. They believed that transatlantic comparisons could bolster the cause of southern independence. This does not, of course, necessarily mean that their parallels were accurate. They contained major inconsistencies, mostly stemming from the proslavery basis of secession. But even so, the powerful resonance of these parallels in the Civil War–era South suggests the benefits of paying closer attention to the way southern secessionists deployed the concept of nationalism and attempted to align themselves with their European counterparts.

At the core of the comparison secessionists made lay the claim that southerners shared with certain European peoples a right to sovereign independence that was currently being denied them by another group of people. Thus the South Carolina secessionist Lewis Ayer observed that "the rights of sovereignty not unfrequently exist where they are not recognized, or, at all events, properly appreciated." In making this statement he was thinking not only of himself and his fellow white southerners but also of Europeans in Hungary, Ireland, and Poland. God had divided the world into separate nations, he believed, and human attempts to disrupt those national divisions could only lead to trouble. To do so was to go against nature: "From the habits of the honey bee, men might learn the important lesson that two nations should not inhabit the same hive, or attempt to work together under one government."[10]

As this beehive analogy suggests, southern secessionists based their claims in part on the assumption that nations (by which they meant distinctive groups of people) should be aligned with units of political governance. This same distinction underpinned European thinking on nationalism as well; as Mazzini memorably put it, "Every nation a state, and only one state for the entire nation." Consequently, in promising to correct the incongruous situation of the political

structure of the United States containing more than one national group, secessionists fell in with a transatlantic trend.[11]

After secession, white southerners understood the importance of being accepted as a nation-state in a world of nation-states. Henry Timrod, the Confederacy's foremost poet, gave notice of this recognition in a poem known both as
"Ethnogenesis" and "Ode on the Meeting of the Southern Congress." "At last,"
he wrote, "we are/A nation among nations; and the world/Shall soon behold in
many a distant port/Another flag unfurled!" But would the world—the world
of nation-states—agree that the Confederacy was indeed a nation? In their efforts to ensure that it would, Confederate diplomats in Europe made the most of
the broad correspondence between their independence movement and those of
others, aiming to capitalize on the sympathy Europeans had for certain independence movements. Thus in their initial instructions from Secretary of State Robert Toombs, Confederate diplomats were told that recent British policy toward
"the recognition of the right of the Italian people to change their form of government and choose their own rulers encourages this Government to hope that they
will pursue a similar policy in regard to the Confederate States." They went on
to contend that Britain's prior recognition of the nationality of Texas, Belgium,
Greece, Italy, and numerous countries in Latin America ought to influence Britain's current policy toward the Confederate States. Although aligning the South
with other independence movements—especially the successful ones—promised significant rewards, that promise was never realized. For a variety of reasons,
including European distaste for slavery, Union military successes, and European politicians' pragmatic calculation that recognizing the Confederacy would
not serve their own international interests, Confederate diplomacy failed.[12]

In arguing first for secession and later for Confederate nationality, southerners often placed particular emphasis on the oppression that resulted from the
denial of sovereignty. Southern critics of the Union had long been making this
claim. In the 1830 Webster-Hayne debates occasioned by conflicts over the federal tariff Robert Hayne compared the South's mistreatment by the United
States to Ireland's at the hand of the United Kingdom: "The fruits of our labor
are drawn from us to enrich other and more favored sections of the Union. . . .
The rank grass grows in our streets; our very fields are scathed by the hand
of injustice and oppression."[13] Two decades later, in 1851, the editor of an Alabama newspaper likewise compared southerners to downtrodden European
nationalists. The urgent and inescapable issue for southerners was, as he put
it, "whether they are to be free or slaves—whether they are to be subjugated as

Ireland and Hungary—whether they are to be partitioned as Poland, or erect themselves into an independent State."[14]

After secession, after white southerners had thrown off the supposed shackles of northern oppression, many of them interpreted the event in the same nationalist framework. Thus a broadside poem entitled "Hail! To the South" celebrated southern independence as the achievement of sovereignty:

> Another star arisen, another flag unfurled,
> Another name inscribed among the nations of the world!
> Another mighty struggle 'gainst a tyrant's fell decree,
> And again a burthened people have uprisen and are free![15]

During the war, white southerners continued to think along similar lines. The transatlantic context became especially pertinent in 1863, when Polish national- ists attempted to overthrow Russian rule. The Richmond *Enquirer* interpreted this as the revolt of "an ancient and glorious nation, against that crushing, killing union with another nationality and form of society. . . . At bottom, the cause of Poland is the same cause for which the Confederates are now fighting." Confed- erate diplomats in countries such as France, where sympathy for the Poles was extensive, tried to attract sympathy for their own cause by likening the Confed- erates to the insurgent Poles and the Union to the repressive Russian Empire.[16] Along similar lines, when confronted during the war with the possibility of de- feat, some southerners warned that the demise of the Confederacy would bring with it the same kind of treatment suffered by the peoples of Europe. An official 1864 address of the Confederate Congress, intended to steel the morale of the people, warned that "the fate of Ireland at the period of its conquest, and of Po- land, distinctly foreshadows what would await us." Likewise the South Carolina minister James Henley Thornwell predicted that "our history will be worse than that of Poland and Hungary" if the North were to win the war.[17]

The experiences of embattled European nations clearly resonated, then, in the secessionist and Confederate South. These were not happy tales but stories of woe—litanies of victimhood, oppression, and historical wrongs. And that is precisely why they held so much appeal for Civil War–era southerners. For narratives of victimhood at the hands of an oppressive North lay at the core of secessionist ideology and later of Confederate nationalism. These narratives contained several principal complaints: that the North threatened the white South's interest in slavery and therefore the racial order it engendered; that the North exploited the slaveholding South with an inequitable economic system;

and that the North unjustly denied southerners' right of equal access to federal territory. The Unionist-turned-secessionist John Ashmore, the subject of Charles Dew's chapter in this volume, made just such complaints in his writings. And for large numbers of his fellow white southerners, these grievances amounted to a general system of unreasonable oppression—oppression of such magnitude that national independence was deserved. As one secessionist resolution put it: "That in view of the humiliating condition of the Slaveholding States in this Confederacy—their rights violated—their Institutions proscribed—their character vilified—their offers of compromise rejected—and in view of the still greater dangers which are impending over them, we believe the time has come when this Union should be dissolved, and a new Government organized on the basis of a Southern Confederacy."

Humiliation, violation, proscription, vilification, rejection—these were the experiences that fueled the secessionist cause. And they were also precisely the experiences that southern secessionists claimed to share with downtrodden European nationalists.[18]

In Europe, too, narratives of suffering proved to be crucial stimuli of separatist nationalisms. According to one Irish historian, "Nationalism in Ireland has been reared less on the rights of man than on historical wrongs." The nineteenth-century nationalist John Mitchel, who was energized by his resentment over Britain's treatment of Ireland, is a case in point. Reflecting on his nationalist activism in a letter to an associate during the 1850s, he confessed, "I have found that there was perhaps less of love in it than of hate—less of affection to my country than of scornful impatience [that my country] suffered itself to be oppressed and humiliated by another."[19] Some of his contemporaries in continental Europe were similarly motivated. Thus the nationalist Polish historian Joachim Lelewel, reflecting on the "purpose of the historian," thought it was to "study peoples, their sufferings and their wrongs." And so he did—providing Polish nationalism in the process with much of its emotional substance. The Czech historian František Palacký similarly stressed the wrongs inflicted on his people by the Germans and the Magyars. From the Magyar perspective, though, *they* were the real victims: the 1849 Hungarian declaration of independence, written mostly by Louis Kossuth, consisted of a long compilation of injustices that the Magyar people had suffered at the hands of outsiders.[20]

Later in the century, thinking of his own country's treatment at the hands of a newly powerful Germany, the French writer Ernest Renan observed: "Suffering in common unifies more than joy does. Where national memories are concerned, griefs are of more value than triumphs, for they impose duties, and require a common effort." The perception of shared suffering, in other words, can promote national unity. More recently, the psychologist Joshua Searle-White has argued that victimhood is often central to nationalism because it brings with it the moral high ground, sharpening the line between a good "us" and an evil "them." As Searle White puts it, "We want to promote our own victimization and deny that of our opponents because victimhood confers power." The power of victimhood is clearly evident in the history of nationalism throughout the modern world—including Europe and the American South in the mid-nineteenth century—and helps explain the potency of the secessionists' exercises in comparative history.[21]

Southern secessionists, then, emulated the style and the language of many of their European contemporaries. This emulation, particularly the element of victimhood, reveals much about the intellectual and emotional rationalization of the movement. But even so, it is clear that these parallels were substantively limited. As the historian Carl Degler has observed, southerners had joined the Union as equals, not as subordinates, and if they suffered any genuine oppression at the hands of the North (which is doubtful), it paled in comparison with what their European counterparts went through.[22] There is also the matter of slavery. In basing their secession movement on so illiberal an institution, southerners appear to have negated whatever claim to nationality they might have had, for this was an era when nationalism—perhaps especially nationalism of the separatist variety—seems to have been very liberal. And in basing their secession movement on slavery, southerners also appear to have negated their claim to resemble nationalisms that seem to have rested on genuinely distinctive ethnicities and cultures. Both of these assumptions seem to be fairly unobjectionable. But both warrant further exploration.

Most commentators would agree that for most of the nineteenth century, unlike the twentieth, European nationalism was emphatically liberal in spirit. According to the historian David Potter for instance, "In both Europe and America, the forces of tradition and privilege tended to be arrayed against nationalism, while the forces of liberalism and democracy tended to support it."[23] There is certainly much to recommend this interpretation. Consider the following excerpt from a document issued by Mazzini and his associates in 1850: "Inasmuch as we believe in Liberty, Equality, Fraternity, and Association, for the individu-

als composing the State, we believe also in Liberty, Equality, Fraternity, and Association of Nations. Peoples are the individuals of Humanity. Nationality is
the sign of their individuality and the guarantee of their liberty: it is sacred."[24]
Clearly there was a close affinity between liberalism and Mazzini-style nationalism. As Otto Pflanze has argued, this was in large part the case because the two
shared both a constituency—the middle classes—and an enemy—autocratic
oppression. The symbiosis between liberalism and nineteenth-century nationalism has understandably caused historians to be skeptical that the American
South (as the champion of slavery) has a place in this story and to emphasize
instead the North (as the champion of freedom).[25]

Antislavery northerners certainly perceived common ground with liberal
European nationalists. Garrisonian abolitionists were particularly drawn to the
Irish movement, especially as embodied in the figure of Daniel O'Connell—
"The Liberator"—who provided enthusiastic support to American abolitionists and even lent his moniker to William Lloyd Garrison's famous newspaper.
As W. Caleb McDaniel has demonstrated, Garrison and like-minded abolitionists tied their own advocacy of disunion in the 1840s to O'Connell's Irish repeal movement of the same decade. Garrison desired the "repeal of the union
between England and Ireland . . . on the same ground, and for the same reason" as he desired the "repeal of the union between the North and the South."
Members of the free-soil movement of the late 1840s were particularly sympathetic to the European revolutions of 1848, aligning their own advocacy of
abolitionism with the liberal democracy they saw being advanced across the
Atlantic.[26]

For their part, European liberal nationalists tended to support the North
rather than the South in the sectional conflict and the Civil War. After all, they
saw themselves as engaged in a conflict between freedom on the one side and
slavery on the other. Hence in 1843 Daniel O'Connell warned Irish Americans (many of whom were in fact hostile to abolitionism and disagreed with
Garrison's claim that the two unions were alike): "If you . . . dare countenance
the system of slavery . . . we will recognize you as Irishmen no longer." Hence
Mazzini pointed to commonalities not only between nationalists in Italy, Poland, and Hungary but with abolitionists in the United States as well. Hence the
case of Ludwik Zychlinski, the Polish patriot who fought not only for Polish independence and Italian unification but for the Union army in the Civil War as
well. And hence too it was the Union and not the Confederacy that approached
Garibaldi with an offer of a commission in the Civil War—only to be urged by

Garibaldi to align the Union cause more explicitly with abolition. Although Edmund Ruffin, the Virginia fire-eater, sensed a kindred spirit in the romantic revolutionary figure of Garibaldi, his support for the Italian's cause was deeply ambivalent, compromised by Garibaldi's liberalism and opposition to slavery.[27] For the same reasons, conservative southerners, perhaps even more so than conservative Americans in general, had reacted with ambivalence if not outright hostility to the revolutions of 1848—which in their estimation had simply gone too far.[28] All of this supports the idea of a logical affinity between European liberal nationalism and the American North, not the American South.

Southerners themselves sometimes admitted as much. In a wartime letter the South Carolina planter and diplomatic historian William Henry Trescot emphasized precisely these connections: "The Black Republican Party of the United States is the same as the Red Republican party of Europe. Butler [the Union general] combines the principles of Mazzini with the practices of Haynau.... And the Radical of England, the Republican of France, the Conspirator of Italy, have recognized the brotherhood." Trescot freely admitted the congruence between northern ideals and European liberalism—including liberal nationalism.

Even so, in the same letter Trescot gave notice that he did not thereby relinquish the South's claim to the principle of nationality. Setting southerners' bid for independence within the broad stream of world history, Trescot suggested that they were only the latest in a line of peoples seeking to align the nation with the government. In 1861, as had happened many times before, an incongruity between nation and government had been resolved by what he described as "the restraint or destruction of overgrown empires, and the creation or recognition of new governments or nationalities." So even if Trescot did not wish to associate the Confederacy with Mazzini's brand of nationalism, he very much wanted to associate it with the general principle of nationality.[29]

There were some respects, then, in which southern separatists clearly could not align themselves with European nationalism, but there were others in which they might be able to. If they could overlook what Trescot called the "brotherhood" of international liberals and instead emphasize the right of self-determination, then separatist nationalisms in Europe might provide strong support. Thus, a few months into the war, an editorial in a Richmond paper drew attention to the apparent hypocrisy of what it described as,

> a denial of the right of self-government by a people [i.e., northerners] who
> have always professed the greatest obedience to the popular will. They were

all agog at the notion of freedom for Ireland. They exulted at the movement for Hungarian liberty, and rushed forward to flatter and fawn upon Kossuth when he landed on our shores. They raised a shout of gratulation at the overthrow of Austrian rule in Italy. They hooted at the idea of union between Ireland and Great Britain or between Austria and her dependencies.—Yet they deny, in effect, the claim of thirteen sovereign States to be free.[30]

This editorial was little troubled by the liberal bent of European nationalism. Some outside observers agreed that the South was more closely aligned with transatlantic nationalism than the North. The London *Times*, for example, claimed to find it difficult to understand how "a people fighting . . . to force their fellow citizens to remain in a confederacy which they repudiated, can be called the champions of liberty and nationalism."[31]

Both North and South used transatlantic comparisons for their own ends in the sectional conflict; as the historian Timothy Roberts has argued, "Their sense of transatlantic community at mid-century was selective and complicated." In 1850, for example, two congressmen, one northern and one southern, proposed greatly differing comparisons between the recent European revolutions and the American political crisis. Mississippian Albert Gallatin Brown warned his northern counterparts to reflect on the lessons of "Hungary, resisting the powers of Austria and Russia; and if Hungary, which had never tasted liberty, could make such stout resistance, what may you not anticipate from eight millions of southrons made desperate by your aggression." New Yorker William Seward, on the other hand, saw a quite different comparison. The slave South, he argued, was on the same side as the reactionary forces of monarchy and conservatism, whereas "emancipation is a democratic revolution." Clearly both sides deployed European events according to their own political positions. The difference turned on whether it was the slaves or the slaveholders who were the real victims.[32]

Although Mazzini, Garibaldi, O'Connell, and many others would not have lent support to the slaveholding South, some of their peers, to one degree or another, did so. The two most striking examples of this are the Hungarian Louis Kossuth and, especially, the Irishman John Mitchel. When he visited the United States in 1851–52, Kossuth appealed for aid from the South as well as the North. Visiting Alabama in 1852 he received an enthusiastic reception from that state's fire-eaters—presumably because the fire-eaters recognized him as a fellow secessionist. And Mississippians, like their counterparts in several northern states, demonstrated their approval by naming a town after him. White southerners were certainly troubled by the more radical elements of Kossuth's reputation, but they found reasons to admire him as well.[33] For his part, because he was essentially on a fund-raising mission for the Hungarian independence movement and was prepared to solicit support wherever he went, Kossuth pitched his message differently in the North and the South. Thomas Bender has found that "in the North he emphasized the integrity or autonomy of the nation . . . , freedom, and progress; in the South he was more likely to accent the evils of centralization (Austrian), the right to determine one's own local institutions, and independence." He was criticized by northern abolitionists such as William Lloyd Garrison for refusing to denounce slavery and follow his apparently liberal principles to their logical conclusion. So for Louis Kossuth—at least for the fund-raising side of Louis Kossuth—being a European nationalist did not necessarily preclude friendship with the slaveholding South.[34]

This was even more true of John Mitchel, a leader of the Young Ireland movement who was deported by the British government in 1848. After escaping from his Tasmanian banishment and making his way to the United States, he first settled in New York but ended up living in the South, a staunch supporter of slavery, secession, and Confederate independence. Historians have been perplexed by the apparent contradiction between Mitchel's radical Irish nationalism and his support for the slaveholding South. But in fact the ethnic exclusiveness of Mitchel's Irish nationalism fit quite well with the defense of racial slavery. And furthermore, Mitchel saw both Ireland and the American South as rural, localized communities that were being oppressed by overly powerful, industrialized nations. Thus he wrote in 1863 that he failed to understand how any Irish nationalist could support the North's attempt to impose an unwanted union—even the terminology, "union," was the same—on an unwilling people. And thus he sent his sons to fight and die for the Confederacy. In so doing, he disturbed the assumption that European nationalism was entirely liberal and could only share anything with the northern side in the American Civil War.[35]

Back in Ireland, the American Civil War divided the nationalist community. On the one hand, the United States had been a good friend to Ireland, and there was good reason to want this veteran of successful secession from Great Britain to survive and prosper, if only as an example for Ireland to follow. On the other hand, Irish nationalists could not easily deny the right of a group of people to secede from a purportedly unjust union—precisely the right that they claimed for themselves. Adding to the confusion were the problems of race and slavery, about which they also had mixed feelings. However, though the response of

Irish nationalists was by no means uniform, Mitchel was not alone in supporting the Confederacy. William Smith O'Brien, for example, took issue with the pro-Union Irishman Thomas Francis Meagher on the grounds that national self-determination was just as important in North America as in Europe and asked how Meagher could claim "that Ireland enjoys such a right—that Poland enjoys such a right—that Canada enjoys such a right," but that the southern states did not.[36]

O'Brien and Mitchel did not speak for all Irish nationalists, nor did Kossuth speak for all Hungarians. The majority of European nationalists supported the North, not the South. But these counterexamples encourage a rethinking of the conventional narrative of liberal nationalism versus conservative antinational-ism. They indicate that nationalism in the nineteenth century was not entirely liberal or entirely conservative. By the end of the century, to be sure, a general trend from the former to the latter had become evident. But along the way there were countervailing currents, and liberal and conservative strands of national-ism coexisted. Recognizing this state of flux necessitates a rethinking of ideas about how the American North and South fit into the transatlantic context.[37]

A central aspect of this uneven, incomplete shift in European nationalism from a liberal to conservative slant was the growing importance of ethnicity, cul-ture, and romanticism. Mitchel and Kossuth exemplify the romantic tone that came to characterize nineteenth-century European nationalism. But the south-ern movement, based on the defense of slavery, appears to have little in com-mon with this trend. At a time when nationalists made so much of distinctive ethnicities and time-honored cultural exceptionalism, was there any place for the slaveholding American South?

Ethnicity and culture were especially prominent features of the separatist na-tionalisms that southern secessionists liked to compare themselves to. In places such as Ireland, Bohemia, Hungary, and Poland, nationalist movements, their ideals inspired in part by the writings of Johann Herder, rested squarely on the claim of a unique and deep-rooted cultural community—within which ethnic-ity, language, and history were typically central features. In response to efforts on the part of imperial powers to impose German or Russian as official lan-guages, Czechs, Hungarians, and Poles celebrated and attempted to boost the use of their own national tongues. There were cultural revivals in Bohemia and Hungary. Young Irelanders such as Thomas Davis promoted the language, his-tory, music, poetry, art, and folklore of historical Ireland, all of which were proof that the Irish constituted a unique people with a noble past.[38]

History was especially important. John Hutchinson has emphasized that in these separatist nationalisms, "memories of former statehood, crowns and feudal constitutions provided a sense of historic nationhood."[39] But it took historians, of course, to create these histories and to endow them with political meaning. This is exactly what was undertaken by scholars such as Joachim Lelewel in Poland and František Palacký in Bohemia. Palacký devoted his life to archiving the primary sources of Bohemian history and to using those sources to construct a magnum opus, *The History of the Czech Nation*. He was dubbed the "father of the nation" for his efforts. Likewise, Joachim Lelewel authored numerous works of Polish historiography and history, including children's textbooks. As one of his biographers has put it, Lelewel "consciously used history to plead the Polish cause, to awaken national consciousness among the Poles."[40]

Did the American South have its own Joachim Lelewel? Could southern secessionists legitimately employ the mode of romantic nationalism? Could they reasonably point to a distinctive ethnicity, language, culture, history? The short answer, of course, is no. But it is very revealing that southerners did sometimes try to cast their nationalism in this mold.

They claimed, for instance, that there was a distinctive southern ethnicity to bolster their cause. A Richmond newspaper stated in 1864 that, like the Greeks, the Hungarians, and the Poles, "we are fighting for the idea of race." Such assertions typically rested on the notion that southerners were of a different ethnic stock than northerners. This stemmed, according to most versions of the story, from the early migration pattern in the American colonies. Whereas the Cavaliers of the English Civil War had settled in the South, their Roundhead enemies had settled in the North. Over the years, these ethnic differences had survived, festered, and ultimately produced secession and Civil War—the inevitable result of a fundamental ethnic difference between northerners and southerners. Here was an attempt, at least, to fit the southern cause into the mold of European ethnic nationalism.[41]

Another ethnic-style basis for southern nationalism derived from the central foundation of the whole enterprise, racial slavery. As they sought to convince fellow southerners of the benefits of leaving the Union, secessionists sometimes cast North-South difference in racial terms. Accusing northerners, and especially the "Black Republican Party," of advocating racial equality, white southerners contrasted the North's supposed racial "amalgamation" with their own dedication to racial purity and the unalloyed supremacy of the white race. After secession, this line of thinking received its most well-known expression from Alexander Stephens, vice president of the Confederate States. In his famous "cornerstone" speech of March 1861, Stephens posited "African slavery" as the "immediate cause" of secession. Unlike the United States, which held a misguided belief in "the equality of the races," the Confederacy recognized the divine truth of racial *in*equality. Indeed, Stephens said, the Confederacy's "foundations were laid, its cornerstone rests, upon the great truth that the negro is not equal to the white man; that slavery, subordination to the superior race, is his natural and moral condition." Herein, for Stephens, lay the essence of the Confederacy's claim to a distinct national identity. "Our new Government," he explained, "is the first, in the history of the world, based upon this great physical, philosophical, and moral truth."[42]

But this argument did not mimic particularly well the spirit of European ethnic nationalism. For one thing, it claimed not so much that a shared ethnic identity made southerners unique but rather that the Confederacy was taking to its extreme a principle—white supremacy—that was then shared, to one degree or another, by most white Americans and Europeans. It gave Confederate nationalism a racial element but not the ethnic distinctiveness of the kind asserted by the Poles, say, or the Irish. And besides, Confederate leaders recognized that their defense of white supremacy was inextricably tied to their far less expedient defense of racial slavery. While racism was broadly popular in the nineteenth-century transatlantic world, slavery was not. Identifying the Confederacy too tightly with slavery ran the risk of losing the crucial support of Europeans abroad and nonslaveholding white southerners at home.[43]

If ethnic distinctiveness was a stretch, what about a unique southern culture? Recognizing the importance of literature and culture to nationalism, southern partisans attempted to demonstrate—or, more often, to wish for—southern cultural independence. The South Carolina writer William Gilmore Simms was at the forefront of this movement. In 1858 he ranked "the formation of our own opinion" as the foremost ingredient of genuine national independence. And with Simms this was not just talk; in the early 1850s, planning to publish a volume of poetry that offered little promise of pecuniary gain, he took solace in the fact that such efforts constituted "one of the phases by which we are to secure home independence." Likewise, the Alabamian Alexander B. Meek, fellow writer and southern partisan, wrote to Simms in appreciation of what was probably the same volume, which, thought Meek, "will form a fit *avant courier* for Southern Literature and Southern Publication." "I am convinced," he went on, "that we cannot have *Home* independence of any kind,—in Commerce, Manufactures, Politics, or what not, until we have a Home Independence of *Mind*."[44]

In the months following secession and the creation of the Confederacy, the idea that a unique literature substantiated nationhood achieved new salience in the South. In addition to an outpouring of popular poetry and songs designed to celebrate and give weight to the new nation, 1861 also produced renewed calls for the support of southern literature. One Texan wrote to *De Bow's Review* that "I have never before taken interest enough in our periodicals or papers, but it is now a patriotic duty, as I consider, to use our efforts in getting our people to read our Southern writers." Praising the May 1861 issue of another long-running southern periodical, the *Southern Literary Messenger*, the editors of the Charleston *Mercury* declared that literary independence was as important a goal as political independence: "Let our writers write, as our soldiers fight, and our people cheer both parties, whether wielding sword or pen."[45]

There were similar efforts to claim a unique history for the South. Again, Simms was at the forefront. Thus he rejoiced when fellow southerners appeared to be taking an interest in their own history—especially when they transcended state lines and tried to make sense of the whole region's shared past. Other southern historians with secessionist proclivities agreed. In a secessionist pamphlet of 1850, William Henry Trescot argued that "history, in the action of its providential instinct," had produced fundamentally different peoples in the northern and southern United States. After the two different groups settled Plymouth and Jamestown, "the growth of the two great sections, radiated from different centres, diverged in different directions, were developed from different principles, and perfected through dissimilar experiences." Frederick Adolphus Porcher, a professor at the College of Charleston, later elaborated on the same premise. The founding philosophies of Virginia and New England were fundamentally different, he asserted: New England developed a tight-knit community ethos whereas Jamestown quickly became a society of independent individuals. The nineteenth-century gulf between North and South was, according to Porcher, the direct result of the different historical experiences of the two sections.[46]

Yet even after the Confederacy was established, calls for a southern history or literature never really became anything more than unfulfilled prescriptions. Serious commentators did not argue that a magnificent southern literature already existed—only that it *should* do so. And for all his bluster, neither Simms nor anyone else before the Civil War wrote a pansouthern history or demonstrated that the southern states shared a historical experience that was significantly different from that of the North. As Carl Degler has rightly pointed out, the lack of a shared, distinctive national history fundamentally distinguished southern nationalists from their counterparts in places like Hungary and Po-land.[47] Although they tried to imitate the form of ethnic and cultural European nationalisms, white southerners fell far short.

Still, although most European nationalisms had a considerably stronger case than the South for ethnic and cultural distinctiveness, we should not conclude that the southern movement was the binary opposite of European nationalisms. As the theorist Etienne Balibar has contended, the ethnic basis of any nation is a "fictive ethnicity." "No nation," Balibar explains, "possesses an ethnic base naturally, but as social formations are nationalized," groups of people become "ethnicized—that is, represented in the past or in the future *as if* they formed a national community."[48] This was certainly true of European nations in the nine-teenth century, which were not naturally occurring but were shaped by political and intellectual as well as cultural processes. John Breuilly has argued that na-tionalist claims are always political to one degree or another; the success or failure of any given nationalist movement is not exclusively dependent on the strength of its ethnic or cultural legitimacy. In places like Italy and Germany, nationalism arose more as a consequence than a cause of unification. And even the separatist nationalisms that did have more of a cultural or ethnic basis typi-cally owed their prominence as much to particular political circumstances and pragmatic interests as to the sentiment of nationality alone.[49]

Hence those nationalists who based their claims on ethnicity and culture tended to ignore those features when they clashed with other priorities. This was true of the Czechs, the Poles, and the Hungarians. All three groups demanded borders for their proposed nation-states that were determined more by historic political formations and pragmatic considerations than by language or ethnic-ity. The figurehead of the Hungarian nationalist movement, Louis Kossuth, was notoriously intolerant of the needs of non-Magyar minorities within lands that he claimed for Hungary. Not only was he prepared to compromise the pre-dominantly liberal bent of European nationalism by pandering to southern slaveholders; he was also prepared to disregard the ethnic and cultural claims of others when they threatened to upset his own agenda. If the ostensibly all-important correspondence between the ethnocultural nation and the unit of governance was not faithfully observed in the secessionist South, neither was it absolute in Europe.[50]

Amid the turmoil of 1848, the Hungarian writer Baron József Eötvös worried about the chaos that would ensue if the "fashionable sense" of ethnonationalism were used to redraw the political and historic borders of central and eastern Europe. "The great word 'nationality' blares out at us from every direction," he wrote, "but everybody wants to understand it differently."[51] As Eötvös recognized, nationalism is never only one thing. If southerners did not possess a "pure" nationalism, no one else did either. Even as nationalism traversed the globe, even as nationalist leaders sought to bolster their positions by likening themselves to each other, the concept never meant quite the same thing to everyone.[52]

Of course, we should resist the temptation to throw our hands up in the air and conclude that because nationalism is an unstable category we should not study it at all. Nor do I mean to suggest that the volatility of European nationalisms render them precisely equivalent to southern nationalism. That is clearly not the case. But critically exploring the comparisons southern secessionists drew between themselves and their European counterparts can help us understand both sides a little better. These parallels illuminate the intellectual and emotional justifications with which secessionists made their case. It is revealing that they emphasized the South's shared victimhood and likened it to the experiences of downtrodden European nationalists; it is revealing that they deployed the concept of nationalism, including its ethnic and cultural strands, in the effort to preserve their system of slavery. All of this suggests the extent to which white southerners—even at their most parochial, when they attempted to establish their uniqueness—lived in a transatlantic intellectual world.

Recognizing as much encourages us to modify the way we compare the Civil War–era United States and Europe. Comparing these very different places helps sharpen our understanding of the variety of nationalism and secessionism in both Europe and the United States. There is not just one story to be told here. Attending to the defeated South instead of focusing exclusively on the victorious North exposes multiple strands of nationalism—diverse yet interrelated, powerful yet always incomplete—on both sides of the Atlantic.

Notes

For their comments and guidance the author wishes to thank Don Doyle, Susan-Mary Grant, and the other contributors to this volume, along with Frank Cogliano, Owen Dudley Edwards, Susan Manning, Mark Newman, Gordon Pentland, and Andrew Newby. Participants in the "Secession as an International Phenomenon" conference in December 2007 and in the "Scotland's Transatlantic Relations" (STAR) seminar at the University of Edinburgh in October 2008 also provided valuable suggestions and questions.

1. Eugene Genovese's "The South in the History of the Transatlantic World" begins with a similar point: that while comparative history is a fairly recent development among southern historians, our subjects have long placed themselves in international contexts (in *What Made the South Different*, ed. Kees Gispen [Jackson, Miss.: University Press of Mississippi, 1990], 3–18).

2. Robert Barnwell Rhett, *The Political Life and Services of the Hon. R. Barnwell Rhett, of South Carolina, by a Cotemporary (the Late Hon. Daniel Wallace)* (n.p.: n.p., n.d), 42.

3. Michael O'Brien, *Conjectures of Order: Intellectual Life and the American South, 1810–1860*, 2 vols. (Chapel Hill: University of North Carolina Press, 2004).

4. William W. Holden, *Oration: Delivered in the City of Raleigh, North Carolina, July 4th, 1856* (Raleigh, N.C.: Holden and Wilson, 1856), 7. See also, Eric Hobsbawm, *Nations and Nationalism since 1780: Programme, Myth, Reality*, 2nd ed. (Cambridge: Cambridge University Press, 1992), 14–45; Eric Hobsbawm, *The Age of Capital, 1848–75* (New York: Scribner, 1975), 82ff.; Susan-Mary Grant, *North over South: Northern Nationalism and American Identity in the Antebellum Era* (Lawrence: University Press of Kansas, 2000); Drew Gilpin Faust, *The Creation of Confederate Nationalism: Ideology and Identity in the Civil War South* (Baton Rouge: Louisiana State University Press, 1988); Anne Sarah Rubin, *A Shattered Nation: The Rise and Fall of the Confederacy, 1861–1868* (Chapel Hill: University of North Carolina Press, 2005); Robert Bonner, "Americans Apart: Nationality in the Slaveholding South" (PhD diss., Yale University, 1998); and Robert Bonner, *Colors and Blood: Flag Passions of the Confederate South* (Princeton: Princeton University Press, 2002).

5. Joseph Leerssen, *National Thought in Europe: A Cultural History* (Amsterdam: Amsterdam University Press, 2006), 169. See also Don H. Doyle, *Nations Divided: America, Italy, and the Southern Question* (Athens: University of Georgia Press, 2002), 22–23.

6. Thomas Bender, *A Nation among Nations: America's Place in World History* (New York: Hill and Wang, 2006), 116–81; C. E. Bayly, *The Birth of the Modern World, 1780–1914: Global Connections and Comparisons* (Malden, Mass.: Blackwell Publishing, 2004), 162–65; Carl N. Degler, "One among Many: The Civil War and National Unification," in *Major Problems in the Civil War and Reconstruction*, 2nd ed., ed. Michael Perman (Boston: Houghton Mifflin, 1998), 442–50; Hans Kohn, *American Nationalism: An Interpretative Essay* (New York: Macmillan, 1957), esp. 100. For insightful exceptions, see Doyle, *Nations Divided*; Nicholas Onuf and Peter Onuf, *Nations, Markets, and War: Modern History and the American Civil War* (Charlottesville: University of Virginia Press, 2006); and Mitchell Snay, *Fenians, Freedmen, and the Southern Whites: Race and Nationality in the Era of Reconstruction* (Baton Rouge: Louisiana State University Press, 2007). Rollin G. Osterweis's classic *Romanticism and Nationalism in the Old South* (New Haven: Yale University Press, 1949) also contains suggestive, though often overly speculative, arguments about the influence of European nationalisms on the American South.

7. William J. Grayson, *Letter to His Excellency Whitemarsh B. Seabrook, Governor of the State of South-Carolina, on the Dissolution of the Union* (Charleston, S.C.: A. E. Miller, 1850), 3.

8. As Anthony D. Smith has observed, "The secessionist aspect of nationalist movements in the nineteenth century went hand in hand with the unification drive of some movements" ("Nationalism, Ethnic Separatism and the Intelligentsia," in *National Separatism*, ed. Colin H. Williams [Cardiff: University of Wales Press, 1982], 18).

9. In fact, it seems very likely that part of the reason why unification has been historiographically more prominent is precisely because it was so much more successful in the short term than was separatism. Moreover, success or failure often determines whether we label a given movement "separatist" or "nationalist." See also the essays in this volume by David Armitage and Peter Radan; Doyle, *Nations Divided*, 86; and David M. Potter, "The Historian's Use of Nationalism and Vice Versa," *American Historical Review* 67, no. 4 (1962): 924–50.

10. Lewis M. Ayer, *Patriotism and State Sovereignty: An Oration, Delivered before the Two Societies of the South-Carolina College, on the Fourth of December, 1858* (Charleston, S.C.: A. J. Burke, 1859), 9, 16.

11. Giuseppe Mazzini, quoted in Hobsbawm, *Nations and Nationalism*, 101. More recently, Michael Hechter has pointed out that there is a "broad consensus" that nationalism can be defined as the effort to equate a nation with a "governance unit" (*Containing Nationalism* [New York: Oxford University Press, 2000], 4–6.) Of course, much more dubious was the assumption that southerners *did* constitute a separate nation or "people."

12. Henry Timrod, "Ethnogenesis," in *The Poems of Henry Timrod*, ed. Paul H. Hayne (New York: E. J. Hale and Son, 1872), 100; Robert E. May, introduction, *The Union, the Confederacy, and the Atlantic Rim* (West Lafayette: Purdue University Press, 1995), 16; Robert Toombs to William L. Yancey et al., Mar. 16, 1861, in James D. Richardson, ed., *A Compilation of the Messages and Papers of the Confederacy*, 2 vols. (Nashville: United States Publishing Company, 1906), 2:5; Eric H. Walther, *William Lowndes Yancey and the Coming of the Civil War* (Chapel Hill: University of North Carolina Press, 2006), 317. See also William L. Yancey et al. to Earl Russell, Aug. 14, 1861, Records of the Confederate States of America, Library of Congress, Washington, D.C., and R. M. T. Hunter to James M. Mason et al., Sept. 23 1861, James M. Mason Papers, Library of Congress, Washington, D.C. The standard work on Confederate diplomacy remains Frank L. Owsley, *King Cotton Diplomacy*. More recent studies, which emphasize obstacles in the way of Confederate diplomats' success, are Charles M. Hubbard, *The Burden of Confederate Diplomacy* (Knoxville: University of Tennessee Press, 1998), and Gregory Mattson, "Pariah Diplomacy: The Slavery Issue in Confederate Foreign Relations" (PhD diss., University of Southern Mississippi, 1999).

13. Herman Belz, ed., *The Webster-Hayne Debate on the Nature of the Union: Selected Documents* (Indianapolis, Ind.: Liberty Fund, 2000), 8, 46.

14. J. Mills Thornton, *Politics and Power in a Slave Society: Alabama, 1800–1860* (Baton Rouge: Louisiana State University Press, 1978), 214. The article also included American revolutionaries in the comparison—another group of secessionists with whom southerners frequently identified.

15. *Hail! To the South*, n.d., Confederate Broadside Collection, Wake Forest University, Winston-Salem, N.C.

16. *Enquirer*, Mar. 16 1863, quoted in Faust, *The Creation of Confederate Nationalism*, 13; May, introduction 16–17. On the diplomatic consequences for the American Civil War, see John Kutolowski, "The Effect of the Polish Insurrection of 1863 on American Civil War Diplomacy," *Historian* 27, no. 3 (1965): 560–77.

17. Confederate States of America, *Address of Congress to the People of the Confederate States* (Richmond: n.p., 1864); James Henley Thornwell, *Our Danger and Our Duty* (Columbia, S.C: Southern Guardian, 1862), 4. As Snay has shown, after the Civil War, Fenians and white southerners compared themselves to each other using similar terms (*Fenians, Freedmen, and Southern Whites*, 12–13).

18. *Co-operation Meeting, Held in Charleston, S.C., July 29th, 1851* (n.p.: n.p., n.d.), 14. See also Onuf and Onuf, *Nations, Markets, and War*, 309, 314, 317.

19. K. H. Connell, quoted in D. George Boyce, *Nationalism in Ireland* (London: Routledge, 1991), 20; John Mitchel, *The Last Conquest of Ireland (Perhaps)*, ed. Patrick Maume (Dublin: University College Dublin Press, 2005), xviii.

20. Joan S. Skurnowicz, *Romantic Nationalism and Liberalism: Joachim Lelewel and the Polish National Idea* (Boulder, Colo.: East European Monographs, 1981), 133; István Deák, *Lawful Revolution: Louis Kossuth and the Hungarians, 1848–1849* (London: Phoenix, 2001), 261–64. For Palacký, see John Breuilly, *Nationalism and the State* (Manchester, U.K.: Manchester University Press, 1982), 59; Joseph Frederick Zacek, *Palacký: The Historian as Scholar and Nationalist* (The Hague: Mouton, 1970), 84; and David Armitage, *The Declaration of Independence: A Global History* (Cambridge, Mass.: Harvard University Press, 2007), 124.

21. Ernest Renan, "What is a Nation?" 1882, in *Nation and Narration*, ed. Homi K. Bhabha (London: Routledge, 1990), 19; Joshua Searle-White, *The Psychology of Nationalism* (New York: Palgrave, 2001), 91–94.

22. Degler, "One among Many."

23. David M. Potter, "The Literature on the Background of the Civil War," in his *The South and the Sectional Conflict* (Baton Rouge: Louisiana State University Press, 1968), 139; Bender, *A Nation among Nations*; Bayly, *Birth of the Modern World*, 163–64; Hobsbawm, *The Age of Capital*, 70, 97; Michael Rapport, *Nineteenth-Century Europe* (Basingstoke, U.K.: Palgrave, 2005), 65, 144; Emory M. Thomas, *The Confederate Nation, 1861–1865* (New York: Harper and Row, 1979), 167.

24. Giuseppe Mazzini, "A Basis of Central European Organization," in *Selected Writings*, ed. Nagendranath Gangulee (London: Lindsay Drummond, 2006), 149.

25. Otto Pflanze, "Nationalism in Europe, 1848–1871," *Review of Politics* 28, no. 2 (1966): 142. Although there were many exceptions, Europeans during the Civil War were more likely to have supported the Union if they were on the left and to oppose it if they were on the right. See James McPherson, "'The Whole Family of Man': Lincoln and the Last Best Hope Abroad," in his *Drawn with the Sword: Reflections on the American Civil War* (New York: Oxford University Press, 1996), 208–27.

26. W. Caleb McDaniel, "Repealing Unions: American Abolitionists, Irish Repeal, and the Origins of Garrisonian Disunionism," *Journal of the Early Republic* 28, no. 2 (2008): 244; Daniel W. Howe and Timothy M. Roberts, "The United States and the Revolutions of 1848," in *The Revolutions in Europe, 1848–1849: From Reform to Reaction*, ed. R. J. W. Evans (Oxford University Press, 2000), 168.

27. Edmund Ruffin, diary entries dated June 22, 1859, and May 23, 1860, in *The Diary of Edmund Ruffin*, 3 vols., ed. William Kauffman Scarborough (Baton Rouge: Louisiana State University Press,, 1972–89), 310–11, 422. For O'Connell, see Kevin Kenny, *The American Irish: A History* (Harlow, U.K.: Longman, 2000), 86; for Mazzini see Doyle, *Nations Divided*, 22–23; for Zychlinski see Norman Davies, *Heart of Europe: A Short History of Poland* (Oxford: Oxford University Press, 1986), 184–85.

28. See Frank Towers's essay in this volume; Timothy M. Roberts, "'Revolutions Have Become the Bloody Toy of the Multitude': European Revolutions, the South, and the Crisis of 1850," *Journal of the Early Republic* 25, no. 2 (2005): 259–83; and Elizabeth Fox-Genovese and Eugene D. Genovese, *The Mind of the Master Class: History and Faith in the Southern Slaveholders' Worldview* (Cambridge: Cambridge University Press, 2005), 45–55.

29. Public letter from William Henry Trescot to J. R. Ingersoll, printed in *The Record*, Aug. 27, 1863, 104, 99, copy in the William Henry Trescot Papers, University of South Carolina, Columbia. See also the *Richmond (Va.) Enquirer*, June 4, 1861.

30. *Richmond (Va.) Examiner*, Oct. 3, 1861.

31. Quoted in Norman Graebner, "Northern Diplomacy and European Neutrality," in *Why the North Won the Civil War*, ed. David Donald (Baton Rouge: Louisiana State University Press, 1960), 76.

32. Roberts, "'Revolutions Have Become the Bloody Toy of the Multitude,'" 276.

33. Thornton, *Politics and Power in a Slave Society*, 215; Roberts, "'Revolutions Have Become the Bloody Toy of the Multitude,'" 270. Elizabeth Fox-Genovese and Eugene D. Genovese emphasize white southerners' distaste for Kossuth's radicalism in their *The Mind of the Master Class*, 57–62.

34. Bender, *A Nation among Nations*, 129; Michael A. Morrison, "American Reac-

tion to European Revolutions, 1848–1852: Sectionalism, Memory, and the Revolutionary Heritage," *Civil War History* 49, no. 2 (2003): 111–32; Donald S. Spence, *Louis Kossuth
and Young America: A Study of Sectionalism and Foreign Policy, 1848–1852* (Columbia:
University of Missouri Press, 1977).

35. Bryan P. McGovern, "John Mitchel: Irish Nationalist and Southern Secessionist
in Mid-nineteenth Century America" (PhD diss., University of Missouri, 2003).

36. Joseph M. Hernon, *Celts, Catholics, and Copperheads: Ireland Views the American
Civil War* (Columbus: Ohio State University Press, 1968), 89–95.

37. Leerssen, *National Thought in Europe.*

38. Cf. István Deák (*The Lawful Revolution*, 44): "Modern nationalism in Hungary
began, as everywhere else in Central and Eastern Europe, in the form of a cultural and
linguistic revival, soon to be turned into a political and social reform movement." On the
general importance of language, literature, and history to nineteenth-century European
nationalism, see Lloyd Kramer, *Nationalism* (New York: Twayne, 1998), 42–61.

39. John Hutchinson, *The Dynamics of Cultural Nationalism: The Gaelic Revival and
the Creation of the Irish Nation State* (London: Allen and Unwin, 1987), 22.

40. Zacek, *Palacký*; Skurnowicz, *Romantic Nationalism and Liberalism*, 120. On the
importance of history and historians to nationalism in Western Europe, see *Writing National Histories: Western Europe since 1800* (London: Routledge, 1999).

41. *Richmond (Va.) Enquirer*, Nov. 2, 1864, quoted in James McPherson, *Is Blood
Thicker Than Water? Crises of Nationalism in the Modern World* (New York: Vintage,
1998), 61; Robert Bonner, "Roundheaded Cavaliers? The Context and Limits of a Confederate Racial Project," *Civil War History* 48, no. 1 (2002): 34–59. Some historians have
seen southern nationalism as an example of "ethnic" nationalism rather than as a "civic"
American nationalism. This schema overlooks the fact that both nationalisms contained
elements of each. See Osterweis, *Romanticism and Nationalism in the Old South*, and
McPherson, *Is Blood Thicker Than Water?*

42. Alexander H. Stephens, speech, Mar. 21, 1861, in Henry Steele Commager, ed.,
The Civil War Archive: The History of the Civil War in Documents (1950; rpt., New York:
Black Dog and Leventhal, 2000), 566–67. Thanks to Don Doyle for suggesting this
theme.

43. On the differing implications of racism and slaveholding for Confederate diplomacy, see Robert E. Bonner, "Slavery, Confederate Diplomacy, and the Racialist Mission
of Henry Hotze," *Civil War History* 51, no. 3 (2005): 288–316.

44. William Gilmore Simms to James Chesnut Jr., Feb. 5, 1852, and Simms to James
Henry Hammond, Mar. 27, 1858, in *The Letters of William Gilmore Simms*, 6 vols., ed.
Mary C. Simms Oliphant, Alfred Taylor Odell, and T. C. Duncan Eaves (Columbia: University of South Carolina Press, 1952–82), 3:158, 4:45; Meek quoted in O'Brien, *Conjectures
of Order*, 701. On the role of literature in southern nationalism, see John Budd, "Henry

Timrod: Poetic Voice of Southern Nationalism," *Southern Studies* 20, no. 4 (1981): 437–46; Eugene Current-Garcia, "Southern Literary Criticism and the Sectional Dilemma," *Journal of Southern History* 15, no. 3 (1949): 325–41; and John McCardell, *Idea of a Southern Nation: Southern Nationalists and Southern Nationalism, 1830–1860* (New York: Norton, 1979), 141–76.

45. "Editorial Miscellany," *De Bow's Review,* Mar. 1861, 384; *Charleston (S.C.) Mercury*, May 16, 1861.

46. William H. Trescot, *The Position and Course of the South* (Charleston, S.C.: Walker and James, 1850), 19; [Frederick Adolphus Porcher], "Southern and Northern Civilization Contrasted," *Russell's Magazine*, May 1857, 98–100; William G. Simms, "Pickett's History of Alabama," *Southern Quarterly Review* 5, no. 9 (1852): 182–209; [William G. Simms], "Ramsay's Annals of Tennessee," *Southern Quarterly Review* 8, no. 16 (1853): 337–68; Paul Quigley, "'That History is Truly the Life of Nations': History and Southern Nationalism in Antebellum South Carolina," *South Carolina Historical Magazine* 106:1 (2005): 7–33; Jon L. Wakelyn, *The Politics of a Literary Man: William Gilmore Simms* (Westport, Conn.: Greenwood Press, 1973), 115–36; Osterweis, *Romanticism and Nationalism in the Old South*, 137–38.

47. Degler, "One among Many," 444.

48. Etienne Balibar and Immanuel Maurice Wallerstein, *Race, Nation, Class: Ambiguous Identities* (London: Verso, 1991), 96.

49. Breuilly, *Nationalism and the State*, chaps. 4–5. See also Elie Kedourie, *Nationalism*, 4th ed. (Oxford, UK: Blackwell, 1993), 94.

50. In addition to Breuilly, see Pflanze, "Nationalism in Europe, 1848–1871," 136–37; Michael Hechter, *Containing Nationalism* (Oxford: Oxford University Press, 2000); Timothy Baycroft and Mark Hewitson, introduction, *What Is a Nation? Europe, 1789–1914*, ed. Timothy Baycroft and Mark Hewitson (Oxford: Oxford University Press, 2006), 11; Baycroft and Hewitson, conclusion, *What Is a Nation?* 331–32; and Mark Cornwall, "The Habsburg Monarchy," in *What Is a Nation?* 171–91. As Margaret Moore's essay in this volume shows, the same problem—how to reconcile political and historic borders with the boundaries between self-defined ethnic and national communities—persists.

51. József Eötvös, quoted in Cornwall, "The Habsburg Monarchy," 172.

52. A useful argument about "multiple nationalism" and the need for historians to approach nationalism not as a fixed category but as a malleable concept that different historical subjects have used in different ways can be found in Alexander Maxwell, "Multiple Nationalism: National Concepts in Nineteenth-Century Hungary and Benedict Anderson's 'Imagined Communities,'" *Nationalism and Ethnic Politics* 11, no. 3 (2005): 385–414.

FRANK TOWERS

The Origins of the Antimodern South

Romantic Nationalism and the Secession Movement in the American South

In 1861, New York City writer and architect Frederick Law Olmsted tacked a plea to suppress southern secession onto a reissued account of his travels in the slave states. To make that case, Olmsted argued that slavery had retarded the American South's economic and social progress. In the South, Olmsted wrote, "most of the people lived very poorly; that the proportion of men improving their condition was much less than in any Northern community; and that the natural resources of the land were strangely unused, or were used with poor economy."[1] In making this charge Olmsted joined other supporters of President Abraham Lincoln and the Republican Party who argued that slavery and its southern supporters lagged behind the pace of modernizing change set by the free North.

Southern secessionists agreed. In 1854, Benjamin Stringfellow, a Virginia planter's son who made a career in law and politics in western Missouri, penned a defense of slavery that accepted Olmsted's premise of an underdeveloped South but treated that condition as a point of pride rather than shame. "While in New England, we admit there are more overgrown fortunes, more towns, more seeming wealth and prosperity, in that distributed wealth, which marks real prosperity, in exemption from poverty with its ills, we assert that the slaveholding States are far in advance." As the head of Platte County, Missouri, Self-Defense Association ("border ruffians" to their free-soil enemies), Stringfellow wrote for a mostly nonslaveholding audience that because of its southern roots and ties to Missouri slaveholders were nonetheless open to his message. To reach them Stringfellow connected the struggle over slavery in neighboring Kansas to broader patterns of social and economic change that were transforming societies on both sides of the Atlantic. "Of necessity," he reasoned, "a slaveholding people must mainly be an agricultural people. Among such, whatever wealth there be, must be better distributed than among the inhabitants of the cities: there must be fewer paupers."[2]

Stringfellow and his friends in Platte County were among the many defenders of slavery and secession who promoted an image of the South as a communal, agrarian society critical of an urban, industrial, and individualist North. Promulgators of the idea that the South not only lagged behind the North but also benefited from its backwardness employed this narrative of sectional conflict in two important ways. They used it to provide a rationale for secession that went beyond the material interests of slaveholders, and they invoked it to justify building a modern state, complete with a powerful government and an industrial economy.

What at first looks paradoxical—politicians praising the South for avoiding cities, manufacturing, and a centralized state and then promising to give it these attributes—appears more intellectually consistent when considered as an expression of nineteenth-century nationalism. In justifying state building as a means of defending tradition, southern secessionists did something commonplace in the transatlantic world; they used the political implications of Romanticism to present their cause as a remedy for problems that transcended the here and now of local politics.

Coming to prominence in Europe after 1750, Romanticism complemented Enlightenment rationalism's interest in efficiency, methodical progress, and uniformity with a preference for impassioned heroics, anachronism, and organic community. In an effort to criticize the social changes engulfing England and its neighbors, Romantic writers often idealized homogenous agricultural society and contrasted its virtues to the vices of urban industrial capitalism. Regarding national affiliation, one scholar asserts that "Romanticism rejected the idea of a rational social contract between autonomous subjects as the basis for society emphasizing instead the primacy of community."[3] As Anthony Smith argues, Romanticism is operative in all nationalisms, "in that they all seek to measure the present by reference to a heroic past for moral purposes," but not all nationalisms resemble the archetypical Romantic ethnic nationalism fostered by German thinkers at the turn of the nineteenth century. Romanticism can serve the cause of a tightly defined ethnic nation, or, as in the case of the slave South, it can bolster a rights-and-interest-based argument for independent nationhood.[4]

Treating southern secession's stated aims as a mixture of civic, ethnic, and Romantic nationalism contributes to the debate over why the South left the Union. The preponderance of scholarship agrees with Don Doyle that "Confederate leaders made their strongest case for separation to the world and to their own people not on ethnic or cultural differences but on principles, interests, and rights."[5] Dissenters from this perspective argue that southern statements of white "America's common racial origins . . . virtually ceased after 1850" and that "by 1860" the Anglo-Norman myth that southern whites descended from English Cavaliers "had become diffused into the discourse of southern nationalism."[6] Critics of southern ethnonationalism argue that the rights-and-interest case for secession had a more established history and was used more often in critical moments of public persuasion.[7] Although southern secessionists talked about "ethnogenesis," Henry Timrod's title for his epic poem celebrating the Confederacy's founding, they spent more time discussing slavery, tariffs, and federal-state relations.

While each side of this debate has a case to make, trying to determine which brand of nationalism predominated—one based in civic principles or one grounded in ethnic identity—often obscures more than it clarifies given the confusing muddle of claims that nationalists often make. As one scholar states, "More interesting . . . are the ways ethnic and civic elements interact with one another in shaping political debates and agendas."[8] Accordingly, this chapter explores how the Romantic antimodern component of southern secessionism fit together with rights-and-interest arguments about the preservation of slavery and what that relationship says about the ways that localized separatist conflicts get attached to transnational debates over broader processes of social change.

As other contributions to this volume attest, historians have turned to transnational dimensions of southern secession as a means for unraveling some anomalies in prior scholarly accounts of the coming of the Civil War. Perhaps the most influential case for Romantic nationalism that was made in earlier works of scholarship on southern nationalism was Roland Osterweis's 1949 investigation of the "cult of chivalry" in the Old South. "Southern nationalism," he wrote, "stressed peculiarities of its particular institutions," which included a "chivalric ideal" that clashed with northern "respectability." Osterweis explained southern fascination with Sir Walter Scott and medieval jousts as a reflection of southerners' social order. "Behind the Southern social structure of the period lay a complex of traditions which, viewed as a whole, gave that structure a feudal character. Such structure offered an inevitable receptivity for chivalric notions."[9] Osterweis's argument that secessionists' criticism of modernity expressed their lived experience in a premodern slave society has had many adherents.[10] The turn back to transnational influences on the Old South, a strand of Osterweis's argument picked up here and elsewhere in this volume, responds to recent historical writing that disputes older claims for premodern southern society.

Scholars have had difficulty defining the place of the American South in nineteenth-century world history because in comparison to other parts of the globe, including much of Europe, the South was more advanced in its social modernization (shorthand for mass production, cities, rapid communication and transport, and middle-class culture), but its record was mixed when compared to the U.S. North. The North had more cities, industry, and schools, whereas the South had more wealth per free capita and, on balance, wielded more power in national politics. Slavery, of course, made the difference, and assessing the place of slavery in modern social development is central to evaluating the claim that the South was antimodern.

As a "property rights regime" slavery created unique incentives for southern whites. Command of labor enabled planters to settle new areas without having to create the infrastructure of roads, towns, and schools that northern real estate speculators built to attract free labor. Slaves were an incredible source of wealth in their own right, one that in 1860 surpassed the combined value of railroads, banks, and factories. Slaveholders viewed the market in slaves in the same ways that consumers and speculators viewed the market for other commodities. Slaves worked in leading industrial fields—they mined, they built railroads, they worked in factories, and they implemented mechanized agriculture. Slavery made the South a different kind of advanced society from the North rather than a less modern one. According to Gavin Wright, "the dominant figures in southern society, the slaveholders, could justifiably view themselves as winners of the [sectional] cold war in economic terms, using a scoreboard appropriate to their economy with their peculiar form of wealth." Newer research recognizes that slavery differentiated the sections, but it rejects the claim that slavery kept the South from modernizing.[11]

Secessionists' antimodern image of their society merits reevaluation in light of its disconnect from contemporary conditions. Although Osterweis ascribed

Romanticism's popularity to local conditions, he foreshadowed current scholarship in examining how southerners discovered Romanticism through transatlantic intellectual exchange.[12] New studies, including contributions to this volume, show that southerners learned about more than chivalric traditions from
the wider world. Paul Quigley's investigation of secessionist rhetoric's invocation of European nationalist movements suggests that the fire-eaters hoped to
"counteract the stigma that the slaveholding American South was retrograde."
Robert Bonner demonstrates how proslavery separatists considered to what extent "secession would rearrange that mixture of geopolitical threats and opportunities they had experienced within the Union" in their calculations about the
viability of a proslavery empire. In a separate study Nicholas and Peter Onuf
argue that secessionists changed their attitudes about nations, replacing a free-
trade vision of states as complementary partners in the global marketplace with
a protectionist stance that saw nations as self-reliant combatants in a war-prone
world. By 1860, southern disunionists had come to believe that "independence
could only be secured by recreating the powerful and protective nation state
that free traders had once sought to abolish." Looking beyond the South's internal social dynamics, Quigley, Bonner, and the Onufs consider southern secessionists as participants in a transatlantic dialogue about slavery, nationalism,
and modernity.[13]

The essay agrees that southern secessionists embraced elements of modern
nationalism, including the ambition to make a strong state and industrial economy. However, it disagrees with the implication that Old South disunionists were
always looking forward and endorsed all aspects of modernity, or "progress," as
contemporaries called the process. Embedded in the long-running discourse of
southern secession was the claim that the South represented a remnant of a
bygone age and that only independence from the Union could protect its antimodern social order from the ravages of nineteenth-century social change.

The pamphlets, speeches, and occasional book-length treatises that contained
this message had a wide circulation. Politicians printed thousands of copies of
their speeches and partisans republished them in newspapers across the South.
Pamphlet dissemination got a boost after Abraham Lincoln's election when the
1860 Association of Charleston, South Carolina, distributed more than two hundred thousand pamphlets throughout the slave states in two months.[14] Reader
reception of these documents needs further study, but given the money and effort secession's leaders spent on their production, we can assume that at least
they thought these tracts conveyed the ideas best suited to win mass support.

Unpacking these ideas is a tricky business given the authors' eclectic approach to their topic. Some secessionist tracts were composed after having been delivered repeatedly as speeches and showed careful editing and attention to argument. Others, particularly those churned out in the rush to shape public opinion in 1860–61, were, in one historian's judgment, "hurriedly delivered, hastily written, and clumsily edited." As a result those pamphlets "mainly lack clarity of expression, clear organization and consistent thoughts." In these documents, scholars can find secessionists invoking God, political economy, the family, history, and even the animal kingdom in an everything-but-the-kitchen-sink approach to reaching persuadable readers. Scattershot argumentation nonetheless served a purpose. In crafting far-flung analogies for their cause, fire eaters attached proslavery to broader principles and social visions that not only spoke to whites outside the planter class but also provided a vision of the new nation for everyone.

The antimodern image of the South presented in secessionist texts took the defense of slavery into the territory of metahistorical narrative. Should the Confederacy succeed, secessionists argued, southerners would travel a road into the future that bypassed the perceived ills of modern social change while reaping all of its rewards, including material riches and technological progress. Better yet, because of slavery, white southerners would commune as equal members of a like-minded nation that retained the best of traditional rural society. Although not the centerpiece, the Romantic narrative of an antimodern South was a necessary part of the case for secession.

Before the 1820s few southerners thought of their region as standing in opposition to modernity. First mentioned in scattered European travel writings before 1776, the idea of the South as locked in the past gained adherents after the Revolution among northerners trying to understand their own region, which diverged from the South by gradually abolishing slavery.[15] Accounts of southern backwardness appeared in the post–War of 1812 travel accounts written by northerners who journeyed to the slave states. Prior to the 1830s, these writings mixed praise and criticism and generally avoided lumping southerners together by way of a common stereotype. Indicative of how northerners could find virtue in southern social decline was James K. Paulding's *Letters from the South* published in 1817. Paulding was a New York City Jeffersonian Republican who believed that "we have too many people living in cities, in proportion to our farmers, who, after all, are the backbone of every country." Paulding worried that commercial speculation had eroded republican virtue. In a moral lesson for his fellow urban cosmopolitans, he portrayed rural Virginians as untouched by modernity and implied that this made them better mannered than their city-dwelling counterparts. "This liberal hospitality," which Paulding praised, "is more general in this part of the world, than where we have been educated, and is owing to the people being 'a century behind-hand with us.'" Paulding burnished the trope of southerners as tradition-bound agrarians to critique urban industrialism in his home state.[16]

These ideas took time to seep into sectional politics. A recent study finds that early nineteenth-century northerners acted on "the perception that slaveholders were encroaching on their own freedom" rather than on economic and cultural differences between the sections. Early 1800s abolitionists focused on the morality of slavery and largely ignored Adam Smith's charge that "the work done by slaves . . . is, in the end, the dearest of any" and that "slaves also perjorate the families that use them; the white Children become proud, disgusted with Labour, and . . . unfit to get a Living by Industry," a claim that defied the received wisdom that slave plantations were an advanced mode of production. Meanwhile, few southern whites thought their economy was backward.[17]

Fiction writers seized on southern antimodernism before economists did. The 1820s diffusion of Romanticism led to increased printed discussion of the "century behind-hand" southern plantation. As had Paulding, James Fenimore Cooper and Sarah Hale used the plantation to criticize Yankee materialism. Soon after, southern authors John Pendleton Kennedy, Beverly Tucker, and William Gilmore Simms furthered the plantation myth in novels that alternately praised and satirized southern manners. Southern writers absorbed many of their ideas from travel and study in Europe where they not only learned about the Romantic nationalism of Johann Gottfried von Herder but also found a prototype of American sectionalism in the ways that "the English and the Germans . . . had invented the counterpoint between North and South from their Italian experiences."[18]

In the 1830s abolitionists invoked the antimodern South to expand on Smith's case regarding the inefficiency of slave labor. In 1832, William Lloyd Garrison's *Liberator* characterized Virginia as a wasteland. "Slavery is ruinous to the whites—retards improvement—roots out industrious population. . . . [T]owns are stationary, . . . villages almost everywhere declining—and the general aspect of the country marks the curse of a wasteful, idle, reckless population." Later that decade Wendell Phillips said that "the South is in the thirteenth and fourteenth centuries." By the 1850s northern readers were ready to receive as common sense the popular critiques of southern social decay penned by Olmsted, Harriet Beecher Stowe, and Hinton Rowan Helper.[19]

Like their abolitionist foes, proslavery southerners came to the antimodern image through sectional political struggle and embellished this narrative as tensions mounted. Although they had railed against centralization since the founding, southern politicians launched their first sustained critique of what they perceived to be a northern-dominated federal government during the 1819–21 crisis over the extension of slavery to Missouri. Referring to political rather than economic power, southern editorialists claimed that banning slavery from Missouri "would lead directly to dissolution of the Union, by giving an unjust influence in the National Councils, by which the Southern people would become the 'hewers of wood and drawers of water' for those of the North." Accompanying the strong showing by antislavery forces in the Missouri crisis was the 1820 census's revelation that the North had twice the number of whites as the South and would gain the upper hand in the population-apportioned federal House of Representatives. During the administration of John Quincy Adams, only the second northerner to occupy the White House, slaveholders complained about federal policy with respect to Indian land, slavery on the high seas, and free-black colonization. The South generally got its way on these issues, suggesting that its charge of northern domination was both overblown and politically effective.[20]

In the Missouri crisis and lesser battles with the Adams administration southern sectionalists emphasized the danger of central power, not social underdevelopment. However, charges of political inequality resonated with ideas about regional decline that had already been aired in print. The two arguments fused during the nullification crisis of 1828–32 when South Carolina threatened secession should its stand against protective import duties not be respected. The need to make the abstract issue of customs rates relevant to ordinary southern whites pushed free-trade activists to connect complaints about federal domination to the compelling story of colonial underdevelopment at the hands of a self-aggrandizing metropole. In this construction of the sectional conflict, agriculture had made the South the wealthier section, but it had been robbed of its capital by industrialists and their corrupt politics. In his 1827 pronouncement that protective tariffs had forced the South "to calculate the value of the Union," Thomas Cooper, president of South Carolina College, said that federal trade policy constituted "a system by which the earnings of the South are to be transferred to the North . . . by which inequality of rights, inequality of burthens, inequality of protection, unequal laws, and unequal taxes are to be enacted and rendered permanent—that the planter and the farmer under this system are to be considered as inferior beings to the spinner, the bleacher, and the dyer."[21]

Robert J. Turnbull, another widely read antitariff writer, shared Cooper's belief that protectionism had impoverished the South. "Our trade is diminished; real property is depreciated; our mechanics are without employment—many of them emigrate to the North," he lamented. "Confidence is lost, and despondency and gloom universally prevail." Robert Bonner's essay in this volume shows that Turnbull considered the idea of making an independent South a satellite of a European empire, yet Turnbull also claimed that colonial vassalage was the South's problem. "With resources that few countries can boast of," Turnbull continued, "we are, nevertheless, becoming to the North as Ireland is to England."[22] Like Cooper, Turnbull tried to add immediacy to his constitutional arguments by claiming that current policy had stalled southern progress.

When South Carolina political leaders Robert Y. Hayne and John C. Calhoun took up the antitariff fight they adopted Cooper and Turnbull's argument that protectionist politicians had turned the South into an underdeveloped colony of the North. In his famed 1831 Senate debate with Daniel Webster, Hayne said that the South stood "towards the United States in the relation of Ireland to England. The fruits of our labor are drawn from us to enrich other and more favored sections of the Union. . . . The rank grass grows in our streets; our very fields are scathed by the hand of injustice and oppression."[23] The same dependency metaphor ran through *The Exposition*, a pamphlet authored by Calhoun in 1828 for mass distribution. "We are the serfs of the system," Calhoun wrote, "out of whose labor is raised, not only the money paid into the Treasury, but the funds out of which are drawn the rich rewards of the manufacturer and his associates in interest. Their encouragement is our discouragement."[24]

Calhoun continued to support economic modernization, a cause he championed as secretary of war under James Monroe, but in his newfound opposition to tariffs he adopted a critique of factory work that made an industrial economy seem like a nightmare. According to Calhoun, manufacturing economies "make the poor poorer, and the rich richer" and generate class war. "Heretofore, in our country, this tendency has displayed itself . . . as regards the different sections—but the time will come when it will produce the same results between the several classes in the manufacturing States. After we are exhausted, the contest will be between the capitalists and operatives. . . . The issue of the struggle here must be the same as it has been in Europe."[25] In turning against

Henry Clay's American System of federally supported internal improvement, Calhoun adopted arguments from more radical proslavery thinkers who regarded the North as a parasite on southern development.

The nullifiers' critique of northern industrial expropriation found an audience among pro-Union southern modernizers, which shows just how malleable the idea was. The commercial convention movement, which began in the 1830s, tried to rally southern businessmen behind the project of developing a home market. "Under the pretext of encouraging 'domestic industry,'" resolved an 1838 gathering in Savannah, Georgia, "duties on foreign goods were imposed to an amount *greatly exceeding the wants of the government.* . . . Hundreds of millions of dollars were thus DRAWN FROM THE SOUTH and expended North of the Potomac." As a response, conventioneers declared their support for lower tariffs and the "great principle of FREE TRADE AND UNRESTRICTED INDUSTRY," yet they simultaneously appealed to "Planters, Capitalists, and others" to deposit their money in southern banks, buy from southern merchants, and invest in southern industry. According to the logic of this critique of northern exploitation, the only way for southerners to defeat their rivals was to develop the same economic weaponry.[26]

My fellow contributor Paul Quigley looks at the nullification debate and finds in Hayne's comparison of the South to Ireland an effort to identify with European ethnic groups who would be nations but for the domination of a metropolitan imperial core. Quigley shows that while slaveholders did not fully identify with the liberal creed of the revolutions of 1848 they perceived a "shared victimhood" with Europe's suppressed nationalists. What southern secessionists said in distancing themselves from these revolutions suggests why they were attracted to the antimodern narrative. While in France, South Carolina planter Charles Manigault feared that "if the Insurgents had succeeded . . . [injury] would . . . have been inflicted upon all the residents of Paris whose means or apparent wealth held out any inducements to the bloodthirsty designs of these 50,000 horrible assassins." Comparing nationalist revolutions in Europe to American sectional conflict, proslavery clergymen James Henry Thornwell wrote that each case pitted "atheists, socialists, communists, red republicans, jacobins, on the one side, and the friends of order and regulated freedom on the other." None of this undermined the sincerity of secessionists' claims that they shared the same dream of national liberation espoused by Poles, Hungarians, and the Irish, yet it pointed out the boundaries of southern nationalism. The need to explain how to change governments drew the South's fire-eaters to Europe's nationalist revolutions at the same time that their fear of unleashing an internal class rebellion made conservative defenses of tradition attractive to them.[27]

Secessionists employed the antimodern narrative of the South to mobilize nonslaveholders while avoiding the nationalist class rebellions in Europe that they criticized. Competing with disunionists' need to rally mass support was their fear that democracy tended to mob rule and that poor southern whites might decide that planters were an oppressive aristocracy. Doubts about non-slaveholders were strongest in South Carolina, the engine of secession and the state with the most restrictions on mass democracy. In 1860, Daniel H. Hamilton, a Charleston public official and future Confederate officer, warned a friend that "when the battle comes in earnest . . . you will find an element of great weakness are our non-slave holding population. . . . We must travel through blood and carnage to some better and stronger form of Government than that which can be controlled by a popular majority." Trapped in a democratic republic, secessionists had to construct arguments that dissolved the differences among white voters without undermining the power of slaveholders.[28]

Typical of these formulations was *The Union: Its Past, Present, and Future*, a pamphlet written by Muscoe R. H. Garnett that went into multiple printings and periodical syndication. Along with defending property rights in slaves, Garnett, a delegate to Virginia's constitutional convention of 1850–51 and the nephew of states' rights leader Robert M. T. Hunter, presented southern traditionalism as a virtue threatened by the modernizing North. "The free states are filled more and more with a manufacturing and town population," Garnett asserted, but "the slave states preserve the old country character. The people of the former are losing their Revolutionary associations which were one of the bonds of our union." To buttress his case for the South as virtue's fortress, Garnett identified the patriarchal family, which encompassed the master-slave relationship, as an attribute of traditionalism. In the South the "relations of parent and child, of husband and wife, of master and slave, and the right of property . . . all go to make up the great cornerstone of the social edifice[.] . . . [G]overnment rests its authority not upon force but upon universal consent; there is no despotic public opinion to stifle freedom of thought; no King Numbers to flatter; no rapacious majority can use the forms of law to gratify its ravenings for plunder."[29] Writing in the aftermath of Europe's failed revolutions, Garnett told white southerners that their agrarian slave society saved their democracy from the class-war politics endemic to urban, industrial society.

Secessionist politicians repeated these ideas during the tumultuous sectional battles of the 1850s. Speaking before the House of Representatives in 1857, South Carolinian Lawrence Keitt, who later published his remarks, explicitly linked class conflict to humanitarian reform.

> Need I ask to what extent modern philanthropy and modern progress have burst the bands of the slaves? Need I ask how the doctrine of "universal equality" has been inaugurated? In Paris it has been baptized behind barricades, and torrents of blood. In London it has been pressed back into the gutter by disciplined steel. All over Europe it has risen in insurrection, and been crushed beneath the tread of armies. . . . Does not yonder city [New York] pay $1,000,000 to save her quiet from brawl and fray, and her people from theft and murder and arson?

Echoing the well-known writings of Richmond editor and sociologist George Fitzhugh, Keitt portrayed free labor as an unstable basis for social order. "The legal bands of slavery may be dissolved," Keitt wrote, "but necessity imposes a still sterner one. . . . Capital and muscle are facing each other, and the antagonism between them in a free society seems to be beyond the reach of legislative lead-line."[30]

This antimodern argument informed the so-called mudsill appeal to non-slaveholders. In 1858, South Carolina senator James Henry Hammond asserted that "in all social systems there must be a class to do the menial duties, to perform the drudgery of life." By confining manual labor to blacks, slavery elevated whites. Hammond's appeal rested on drawing a contrast between the situation of poor southern whites and what he asserted was the condition of urban white workers in the North, who, Hammond said, "are hired by the day, not cared for, and scantily compensated, which may be proved in the most painful manner in any of your large towns."[31]

Two months before Lincoln's election, Charleston's 1860 Association persuaded New Orleans publicist James D. B. De Bow to write a pamphlet aimed at nonslaveholders. Reprinted in the New Orleans and Charleston press and among the most widely circulated of the association's tracts, De Bow's *Non-Slaveholders of the South* reinforced Hammond's message that slavery protected poor whites from the ravages of urban industrialism. "The non-slaveholders, as a class, are not reduced by the necessity of our condition," De Bow wrote, "as is the case in the free States, to find employment in crowded cities, and come into competition in close and sickly workshops and factories, with remorseless and untiring machinery. They have but to compare their condition . . . with the mining and manufacturing operatives of the North and Europe, to be thankful that God has reserved them for a better fate." De Bow then told nonslaveholders that slavery protected their moral character from the snares of modern ideology. "Adhering to the simple truths of the Gospel, and the faith of their fathers, [southern nonslaveholders] have not run hither and thither in search of all the absurd and degrading isms which have sprung up in the rank soil of infidelity. . . . They . . . prefer law, order, and existing institutions, to the chaos which radicalism involves."[32] By 1860, secessionists had tightly fastened the defense of traditional society to their larger case for disunion. Ironically, the logic of national independence mandated that the Confederacy develop the material attributes of modernism—that is, manufacturing, cities, and a strong central government.

This contradiction appeared in an 1860 speech made by John Coles Rutherfoord to the Virginia legislature. He cited urban industrialism as a problem that could be avoided by quitting the Union. "Let us leave to Old England and New England their hives of suffering humanity, their Manchesters and Lowells, their Chartist mobs and 'labor strikes,' their social evils, in the present, and their alarming social problems, in the future." A future southern nation, Rutherfoord pledged, would "pass laws . . . to whiten the sea with our sails; but not to fill our atmosphere with the smoke of factories." Shortly thereafter, he outlined the next steps toward nationhood. "Let all the Southern States 'adopt a regular plan of opposition in which they can combine all the resources of the community;' let them, in pursuance of this plan, organize and arm the military forces of the South, and go to work building forts, armories and powder mills."[33] Rutherfoord thus wanted to maintain what he saw as the agrarian South's exemption from urban industrialism while simultaneously building up a military complete with an industrial supply network.

For Rutherfoord as for other secessionists, the home that the Confederacy would guard was rooted in an antimodern agrarian culture. In his inaugural address, Confederate president Jefferson Davis devoted most of his time to a rights-based justification of secession. He nevertheless proclaimed that the Confederates were "an agricultural people, whose chief interest is the export of a commodity required in every manufacturing country." Here Davis evoked the familiar free-trade vision of the slave states. But he quickly went on to recommend that the Confederacy build a navy and an army, which would strengthen the central state and home industries. Davis's plans followed through on De Bow's promise to nonslaveholders "to build up our towns and cities, to extend our railroads, and increase our shipping."[34] Seceding to fend off progress implicitly required the South to develop a modern nation-state.

By embracing the Romantic distortion of the South as a place resistant to the tide of nineteenth-century change, secessionists gave potential followers another rationale for supporting their cause. In addition to secession providing a way of defending southern whites' material interests in slaves and slaveholders' rights, it also offered a means of defending something called home, a geographically and culturally specific setting to which they belonged by dint of their upbringing. That home had the added advantage of being antimodern; that is, of being a fortification against the trends of industry, urbanization, and bourgeois individualism that observers on both sides of the Atlantic feared would erode the foundations of human community. Southern whites' embrace of an antimodern self-image did not signify their opposition to change but rather originated in their very attempt to make a modern nation.

Notes

1. Frederick Law Olmsted, *The Cotton Kingdom: A Traveller's Observations on Cotton and Slavery in the American Slave States*, vol. 1 (New York: Mason Brothers, 1861), 8.

2. Benjamin F. Stringfellow, *Negro Slavery No Evil* (St. Louis: M. Niedner, 1854), 22; Nicole Etcheson, *Bleeding Kansas: Contested Liberty in the Civil War Era* (Lawrence: University Press of Kansas, 2004), 30–33.

3. Michael O'Brien, *Conjectures of Order: Intellectual Life in the American South, 1810–1860*, 2 vols. (Chapel Hill: University of North Carolina Press, 2004), 1:21; Michael Lowy and Robert Sayre, *Romanticism Against the Tide of Modernity* (Durham: Duke University Press, 2001), 16–19; Thomas Rohkrämer, *A Single Communal Faith? The German Right from Conservatism to National Socialism* (New York: Bergham Books, 2008), 60.

4. Anthony D. Smith, *Nationalism and Modernity* (New York: Routledge, 1998), 53; Josep Llobera, *The God of Modernity: The Development of Nationalism in Western Europe* (Oxford, U.K.: Berg, 1994), 171–74.

5. Don H. Doyle, *Nations Divided: America, Italy, and the Southern Question* (Athens: University of Georgia Press, 2002), 80; Peter Kolchin, *A Sphinx on the Land: The Nineteenth-Century South in Comparative Perspective* (Baton Rouge: Louisiana State University Press, 2003), 89–90; William W. Freehling, *The Road to Disunion*, 2 vols. (New York: Oxford University Press, 1990–2007), 2:529; Charles Dew, *Apostles of Disunion: Southern Secession Commissioners and the Causes of the Civil War* (Charlottesville: University Press of Virginia, 2001).

6. Ritchie Devon Watson Jr., *Normans and Saxons: Southern Race Mythology and the*

Intellectual History of the American Civil War (Baton Rouge: Louisiana State University Press, 2008), 26; James M. McPherson, *Is Blood Thicker Than Water? Crises of Nationalism in the Modern World* (New York: Vintage, 1999), 45; Wolfgang Schivelbusch, *The Culture of Defeat: On National Trauma, Mourning, and Recovery* (New York: Metropolitan Books, 2003), 48.

7. Robert E. Bonner, "Roundheaded Cavaliers? The Context and Limits of a Confederate Racial Project," *Civil War History* 48, no. 1 (2002) 34–59.

8. Aviel Roshwald, *The Endurance of Nationalism* (New York: Cambridge University Press, 2006), 258.

9. Rollin G. Osterweis, *Romanticism and Nationalism in the Old South* (1949; rpt., Gloucester, Mass.: Peter Smith, 1964), 16, 56, 137–38.

10. Influential variations on this theme include Frederick Jackson Turner, "The South, 1820–1830," *American Historical Review* 11:3 (1906), 559–573, 560–61; Charles A. Beard and Mary R. Beard, *The Rise of American Civilization*, rev. ed. (New York: Macmillan, 1927); Ulrich B. Phillips, *The Course of the South to Secession*, ed. E. Merton Coulter (1939; rpt., New York: Hill and Wang, 1964), 90, 101, 125, 145; Eugene D. Genovese, *The Political Economy of Slavery: Studies in the Economy and Society of the Slave South* (1965; rpt., New York: Vintage, 1967), 23, 30, 33–36; John Ashworth, *Slavery, Capitalism, and Politics in the Antebellum Republic*, vol. 2, *The Coming of the Civil War, 1850–1861* (Cambridge: Cambridge University Press, 2007), 294, 616; and Bertram Wyatt-Brown, *The Shaping of Southern Culture: Honor, Grace, and War, 1760s–1880s* (Chapel Hill: University of North Carolina Press, 2001), 88.

11. Robert W. Fogel, *Without Consent or Contract: The Rise and Fall of American Slavery* (New York: Norton, 1989), 81–92; Steven Deyle, *Carry Me Back: The Domestic Slave Trade in American Life* (New York: Oxford University Press, 2005); Walter Johnson, *Soul by Soul: Life inside the Antebellum Slave Market* (Cambridge, Mass.: Harvard University Press, 1999); Mark M. Smith, *Mastered by the Clock: Time, Slavery, and Freedom in the American South* (Chapel Hill: University of North Carolina Press, 1997); James L. Huston, *Calculating the Value of the Union: Slavery, Property Rights, and the Economic Origins of the Civil War* (Chapel Hill: University of North Carolina Press, 2003), 27–30; Kenneth W. Noe, *Southwest Virginia's Railroad: Modernization and the Sectional Crisis* (Urbana: University of Illinois Press, 1994), 69, 82; Richard Follett, *The Sugar Masters: Planters and Slaves in Louisiana's Cane World, 1820–1860* (Baton Rouge: Louisiana State University Press, 2005), 31–39; Gavin Wright, *Slavery and American Economic Development* (Baton Rouge: Louisiana State University Press, 2006), 55–70, 82.

12. Osterweis, *Romanticism and Nationalism in the Old South*, 24–40.

13. Nicholas and Peter Onuf, *Nations, Markets, and War: Modern History and the American Civil War* (Charlottesville: University of Virginia Press, 2006), 325. Also see O'Brien, *Conjectures of Order*, and Edward B. Rugemer, *The Problem of Emancipation:*

The Caribbean Roots of the American Civil War (Baton Rouge: Louisiana State University Press, 2008).

14. William W. Freehling, *The Road to Disunion*, 2:390–91; Jon C. Wakelyn, *Southern Pamphlets on Secession*, Nov. 1860–Apr. 1861 (Chapel Hill: University of North Carolina Press, 1996), xiv–xix, xxi.

15. Jack P. Greene, "The Constitution of 1787 and the Question of Southern Distinctiveness," in *The South's Role in the Creation of the Bill of Rights*, ed. Robert J. Haws (Jackson: University Press of Mississippi, 1991), 11.

16. James K. Paulding, *Letters from the South*, 2 vols. (New York: James Eastburn, 1817), 2:100–101, 126–27; Eric William Plaag, "Strangers in a Strange Land: Northern Travelers and the Coming of the American Civil War," (PhD diss., University of South Carolina, 2006), 11, 39.

17. Matthew Mason, *Slavery and Politics in the Early American Republic* (Chapel Hill: University of North Carolina Press, 2006), 46, 130; Adam Smith, quoted in Seymour Drescher, *The Mighty Experiment: Free Labor versus Slavery in British Emancipation* (New York: Oxford University Press, 2002), 20–21; Joyce Chaplin, *An Anxious Pursuit: Agricultural Innovation and Modernity in the Lower South, 1730–1815* (Chapel Hill: University of North Carolina Press, 1996), 357.

18. Susan-Mary Grant, *North over South: Northern Nationalism and Sectional Identity in Antebellum America* (Lawrence: University of Kansas Press, 2000), 42; William R. Taylor, *Cavalier and Yankee: The Old South and American National Character* (New York: George Braziller, 1961), 115, 133, 149; O'Brien, *Conjectures of Order*, 1:127, 147–48, 2:598.

19. "Effects of Slavery Upon the White Population," *Liberator*, July 14, 1832; Wendell Phillips, quoted in Richard N. Current, *Northernizing the South* (Athens: University of Georgia Press, 1983), 33; Patrick Gerster and Nicholas Chords, "The Northern Origins of Southern Mythology," *Journal of Southern History* 43:4 (1977), 567–82, 569.

20. Don E. Fehrenbacher, *The Slaveholding Republic: An Account of the United States Government's Relationship to Slavery* (New York: Oxford University Press, 2001), 265; Mason, *Slavery and Politics in the Early Republic*, 199; Donald J. Ratcliffe, "The Nullification Crisis, Southern Discontents, and American Political Process," *American Nineteenth-Century History* 1:2 (2000), 4–8.

21. Thomas Cooper, quoted in John A. Logan, *The Great Conspiracy: Its Origin and Its History* (New York: A. R. Hart, 1886), 22.

22. [Robert J. Turnbull], *The Crisis; or, Essays on the Usurpations of the Federal Government* (Charleston, S.C.: A. E. Miller, 1827), 21.

23. Herman Belz, ed., *The Webster-Hayne Debate on the Nature of the Union: Selected Documents* (Indianapolis, Ind.: Liberty Fund, 2000), 8, 46.

24. John C. Calhoun, "Exposition," in *Reports and Public Letters of John C. Calhoun*, vol. 6, ed. Richard Cralle (New York: D. Appleton, 1855), 18.

25. Calhoun, "Exposition," 10, 26.

26. Convention of Merchants, *Minutes of the Proceedings of the Second Convention of Merchants and Others, Held in Augusta, Georgia, April 2d, 1838* (Augusta, Ga.: Benjamin Brantley, 1838), 15, 16, 21; Frank J. Byrne, *Becoming Bourgeois: Merchant Culture in the South, 1820–1865* (Lexington: University Press of Kentucky, 2006), 52.

27. Charles Manigault to Mr. Jackson, July 21, 1848, Manigault Family Papers, South Carolina Historical Society, Charleston; J. H. Thornwell, *The Rights and Duties of Masters: A Sermon Preached at the Dedication of a Church, Erected in Charleston, S.C., for the Benefit and Instruction of the Coloured Population* (Charleston, S.C.: Walker and James, 1850), 14, 12; Timothy M. Roberts, "'Revolutions Have Become the Toy of the Multitude': European Revolutions, the South, and the Crisis of 1850," *Journal of the Early Republic* 25, no. 2 (2005), 259–83.

28. Daniel Hayward Hamilton to William P. Miles, June 23, 1860, William Porcher Miles Papers, Southern Historical Collection, Wilson Library, University of North Carolina, Chapel Hill.

29. [Muscoe R. H. Garnett], *The Union, Past and Future; How It Works and How to Save It* (Washington, D.C.: J. T. Towers, 1850), 16, 26–27; Henry T. Shanks, *The Secession Movement in Virginia, 1847–1861* (1934; rpt., New York: AMS Press, 1971), 67.

30. Lawrence Keitt, *Slavery and the Resources of the South* (Washington, D.C.: Congressional Globe, 1857), 10.

31. James Henry Hammond, "Speech on the Admission of Kansas . . . in the Senate of the United States," Mar. 4, 1858, in *Selections from the Letters and Speeches of James Henry Hammond, of South Carolina* (1866; rpt., Spartanburg, S.C.: Reprint Co., 1978), 319.

32. James D. B. De Bow, "The Non-slaveholders of the South: Their Interest in the Present Sectional Controversy Identical with That of the Slaveholders," *De Bow's Review*, Jan. 1861, 67–77, 72–73; Eric H. Walther, *The Fire-Eaters* (Baton Rouge: Louisiana State University Press, 1992), 220.

33. John Coles Rutherfoord, *Speech of John C. Rutherford, of Goochland, in the House of Delegates of Virginia, 21 February, 1860, in Favor of the Proposed Conference of Southern States* (Richmond, Va.: William H. Clemmitt, 1860), 18, 20.

34. Jefferson Davis, "Speech at Montgomery, Alabama (Inaugural Address as Provisional President)", Feb. 18, 1861, in *Jefferson Davis: The Essential Writings*, ed. William J. Cooper (New York: Random House, 2003), 200–201; De Bow, "The Non-slaveholders of the South," 77.

PART 3

Turbulence in the Gulf of Mexico

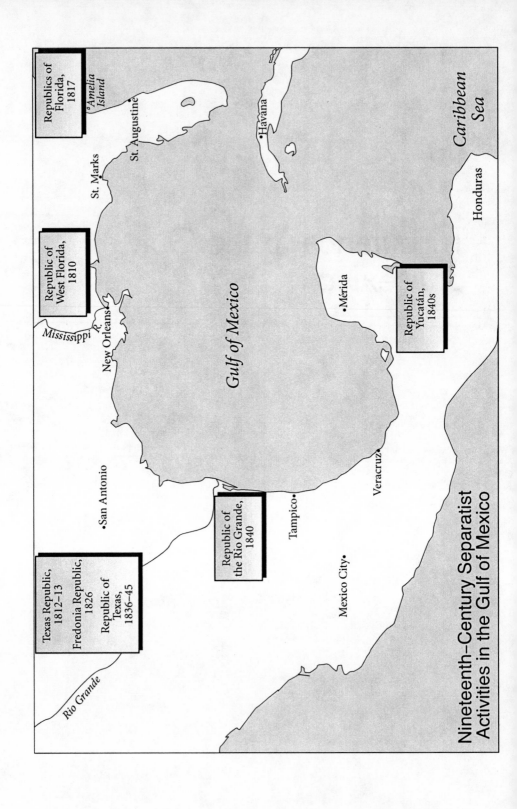

Republics of Florida, 1817
°Amelia Island
St. Augustine
St. Marks

Republic of West Florida, 1810

Mississippi R.
New Orleans

Gulf of Mexico

Havana

Caribbean Sea

Honduras

Mérida

Republic of Yucatán, 1840s

Veracruz•

Tampico•

Republic of the Rio Grande, 1840

Mexico City•

•San Antonio

Texas Republic, 1812–13
Fredonia Republic, 1826
Republic of Texas, 1836–45

Rio Grande

Nineteenth-Century Separatist Activities in the Gulf of Mexico

ANDRÉS RESÉNDEZ

Texas and the Spread of That Troublesome Secessionist Spirit through the Gulf of Mexico Basin

The Texas Republic is one of the most celebrated cases of secessionism in the Americas. Texas remained viable and independent for nine full years, between 1836 and 1845, fending off repeated attempts by Mexico to reconquer it. During its existence Texas had all the attributes of a proper state: a functioning government, a constitution, effective control over its territory, and a very active international diplomacy. Even today Texans take pride in being heirs to a real nation (not a mere state) and are still moved by a national saga that starts with the settlement of American families in Mexican Texas and ends with the dramatic events of the Alamo and San Jacinto.

Yet this retelling of the Lone Star story that emphasizes its peculiar pantheon glosses over the fact that by the time of the Texas Revolution, secessionism was already a well-established type of political movement in the Gulf of Mexico basin. Ever since the 1780s and 1790s groups of Tennesseans and Kentuckians had been conspiring to wrest Louisiana away from Spain. During the tumultuous 1810s East and West Florida seceded—a recent book refers to West Florida after its 1810 secession as "the original Lone Star Republic." As early as 1824, Yucatán was vowing to break away from Mexico to protect its commerce with Cuba.[1] Texas itself weathered secessionist plots for thirty years before breaking off completely: in 1805–6 the province became a principal target of the Aaron Burr conspiracy; in 1812–13 a combined army of Mexican patriots and American filibusters declared Texas free of Spanish domination and separate from the rest of New Spain; the 1819 filibustering expedition of James Long in 1819 declared the independence of Texas yet again; and in 1826 a coalition of American colonists and Cherokee Indians established the so-called Fredonia Republic, which spanned much of the territory of Texas.[2]

These various secessionist schemes may have been short lived, self-interested, and destined to failure, but nonetheless they naturalized the idea of a breakaway republic and gave rise to an international cast of adventurers and politicians willing to undertake secessionist projects long before the Texas Republic came into being. In turn, the unprecedented success of the Texas Republic gave added impetus to various movements throughout the region at a time when European empires in the Americas were being replaced by independent republics.

This chapter is a very preliminary sketch of the secessionist impulse that washed over the Gulf of Mexico seascape from the 1780s to the 1840s. Few historians conceive of the Gulf of Mexico as a unit of analysis, because it contains discrete portions of the United States, Mexico, and the Spanish Empire. Yet in the nineteenth century this smallish sea and its coastal lands and cities were intimately connected by sailing ships, trade ties, and a human geography that favored the dissemination of political ideologies, harebrained ideas, arms, and alternative national and imperial visions. Owing to the large scope and interpretive nature of my argument, I don't address specific cases as much as I attend to the mechanisms and human connections that facilitated secessionism. This machinery of secession, so to speak, included an international cadre of leaders with firsthand experience in launching such movements, the emergence of New Orleans as a preeminent recruitment and outfitting center, and a language and method of secession.

EARLY SEPARATIST ATTEMPTS: CRASS EXPANSIONISM OR LEGITIMATE ANTICOLONIAL MOVEMENTS?

The Gulf of Mexico basin was originally an "interior sea" completely under Spanish control. It became a site of imperial rivalry as early as the seventeenth century when the "French thorn," as Robert S. Weddle styles it, first became lodged in the northern gulf coast. But the first recognizably secessionist movements—as opposed to imperial colonization and countercolonization schemes—were organized in the period from the 1780s through the 1810s.[3]

These early separatist movements, all clustered on the northern rim of the Gulf of Mexico coast, conformed to a particular pattern. The impetus invariably originated farther north, among residents of the landlocked western states of the Union who promoted the independence of the Spanish possessions along the northern rim of the gulf coast—Louisiana and the Floridas—in order to secure an outlet into the Gulf of Mexico. Time and again residents of Kentucky, Tennessee, and other areas along the Ohio and Mississippi rivers attempted to throw open the doors to the Gulf of Mexico by exporting their successful anticolonial struggle to Louisiana and the Floridas. And thus, from inception, secessionism in the Gulf of Mexico seascape combined America's yearning for expansion with anticolonial rhetoric.

The catalyst for these separatist attempts was Spain's decision to close the lower Mississippi to all but Spanish shipping in 1784. The reaction was swift. One Frenchman who traveled through the western states in 1788 captured the mood well: "Men who have shook off the yoke of Great Britain, and who are masters of the Ohio and the Mississippi, cannot conceive that the insolence of a handful of Spaniards can think of shutting rivers and seas against a hundred thousand free Americans. The slightest quarrel will be sufficient to throw them into a flame; and if ever the Americans shall march toward New Orleans, it will infallibly fall into their hands."[4]

The earliest American attempts to pry open the Gulf of Mexico combined crude expansionism with appeals to "throw off the Spanish yoke" and follow the example of the British colonists in North America. Perhaps the earliest such scheme dates back to an early spring day in 1793, when Edmund Charles Genet, France's plenipotentiary minister in the United States, arrived in Charleston, South Carolina, from Paris to revolutionize the New World. One of his most immediate objectives was to rally support in the western states to launch an attack at the mouth of the Mississippi and to sweep along the Gulf of Mexico so as to aid the United States in its efforts to incorporate the Floridas. Genet's goal was to satisfy both America's territorial yearnings and France's universal revolutionary aspirations.[5] The mission was aborted in the end, however, in part owing to the fall of the Girondins in France and the recall of Genet. But other westerners felt free to pursue the idea without France. In 1796 William Blount, a senator from Tennessee, came up with a scheme to raise a buckskin army in his home state, float down the Mississippi River, and wrest New Orleans and the Floridas away from the Spanish Empire. Blount's plan was discovered prematurely and discussed on the floor of the Senate, which resulted in his expulsion from the august chamber amid shouts of "treason."[6] But even after the failure of

Blount's scheme, Louisiana remained the main target of America's expansionist drive until the 1803 purchase at last provided a vital outlet to the western states by means of diplomacy rather than internal upheaval and secession.

The Floridas, however, were a different matter. East and West Florida were ripe for secession because they were largely settled by Anglo-Americans, even though they were Spanish possessions. In effect, a handful of Spanish officials and soldiers, clustering in dilapidated presidios, attempted to rule over vast areas inhabited only by Indians and Anglo-Americans whose loyalties to Spain were questionable at best. The 1810 rebellion in West Florida, which produced the Lone Star Republic, constituted the first successful, full-fledged separatist movement and provided a model for future republics. Taking advantage of their numerical superiority, a group of Anglo-Americans from the Bayou Sara marched on Baton Rouge on the night of September 23, 1810, overwhelming the Spanish garrison. The rebels raised a blue flag with a white star in the middle (not the last time the lone star would be flown to signal secession). Three days later a convention of hastily assembled representatives declared West Florida to be "a free and independent state" possessing a right to institute "such form of government [as] conducive to their safety and happiness" and the ability to "form treaties," "establish commerce," "provide for their common defense," and "do all acts which may, of right, be done by a sovereign and independent nation."[7] For seventy-two days West Florida existed as the Lone Star Republic. This national experiment would only end when President Madison claimed West Florida for the United States as part of the Louisiana Purchase.[8]

One cannot help but ask whether the launching of the West Florida republic constituted a travesty—America's peculiar form of national aggrandizement—whether it was just a link in a chain of machinations of territorial expansion. The answer is far from simple. There were certainly some who conceived the independence of West Florida as a necessary step toward incorporation into the United States. Indeed, the West Florida declaration of independence was accompanied by a formal address to the American government urging Congress to admit West Florida into the American union immediately.[9] But there were others within the movement who conceived a compact with Great Britain or even France. As one witness observed, "Succors are now offered by the French equal to our present wants. And many true Americans who are well acquainted with the Cautious Policy of the United States have no confidence in their interference and are willing to accept."[10] The promoters of the 1810 rebellion in West Florida ultimately opted for independence, a risky course that made them vulnerable to reprisals from Spain, indifference from the United States, and even possible attacks from Great Britain and France. In the last analysis, it is impossible to disentangle American expansionism, a host of self-interested parties, and a raging anticolonial struggle that was engulfing all of Spain's colonies in the New World.

Before considering other secessionist movements, I wish to emphasize two interrelated factors that may explain how separatism became possible elsewhere in the Gulf of Mexico basin. First, the cases of Louisiana and the Floridas show that secessionist schemes did not succeed on the first try. Instead, they had to be attempted time and again, and sometimes they spanned decades. Conspirators spent years trying to seize Louisiana and the Floridas from Spain. These early schemes may have been wide eyed, but they generated a momentum of their own; new leaders launched subsequent separatist ventures, imitating the most successful aspects of prior attempts and at the same time learning from past mistakes. For instance, the 1810 march from Bayou Sara to Baton Rouge that culminated in the seizure of the Spanish garrison and the proclamation of the West Florida republic had already been rehearsed, point by point, by the Kemper brothers in 1804, who were arrested only because the Spanish commander of the garrison received early intelligence of the insurrection. The undaunted Reuben Kemper made another attempt in 1805. Toward the end of 1806 there were persistent rumors that Aaron Burr's agents would attempt yet again a similar maneuver against Baton Rouge and that the liberation of West Florida featured in this new conspiracy.[11] By 1810 the march on Baton Rouge had been long in the making. And West Florida was not the only territory repeatedly visited by secessionist ambition. Texas, as noted, likewise experienced half a dozen secessionist attempts from the 1800s through the 1830s; Tamaulipas toyed with separatism in 1839–40 and again in 1846 at the outbreak of the Mexican-American War; Yucatán threatened to break with the rest of Mexico in 1824 and in the 1840s; and so on. Practically every secessionist movement in the Gulf of Mexico seascape had multiple iterations.

Second, such repeated secessionist attempts facilitated the emergence of a cadre of statesmen, commanders, and adventurers with experience in such ventures. The aforementioned Reuben Kemper not only made repeated attempts to establish West Florida as an independent nation but also later took part in the 1812–13 expedition that declared the separation of Texas from the Spanish Empire. Perhaps the most obvious example of the seasoned secessionist is James Wilkinson, an American frontier commander and intermediary with the

Spanish authorities. Wilkinson would be a protagonist of practically every intrigue that unfolded in Louisiana, the Floridas, and Texas for thirty years. In the
winter of 1796–97 Wilkinson (along with Thomas Jefferson, another conspirator extraordinaire) was present at a dinner given by Senator William Blount in
which the latter revealed his plans to "win the Southwest from Spain by means
of the British aid and the active support from the Indian tribes."[12] Wilkinson was
also Aaron Burr's main partner during the alleged conspiracy of 1805–6. Over
the following few years Wilkinson played an instrumental role in the secession
and ultimate incorporation of the Floridas into the United States, advising the
Spanish authorities on how to hold on to its possession (and getting paid for
his services) while at the same time advancing the interests of the United States
in the region.[13] In later years Wilkinson became keenly interested in the affairs
of Texas and supported the 1819 filibustering expedition of Dr. James Long, a
Natchez resident who was married to Wilkinson's niece.[14]

Wilkinson's life points to a broader network of human connections worth
sketching out if only in the broadest outlines. Easily the most important meeting ground of filibusters, financiers, and politicians of all ethnicities and the
key vehicle for the dissemination of political ideas was Freemasonry. Indeed,
Freemasons played leading roles in every secessionist movement around the
Gulf of Mexico (and elsewhere) from the Florida rebellion of 1810 and the Republic of Texas of 1836 to the Cuban separatist attempts of the late 1840s and
early 1850s. As Antonio Rafael de la Cova has shown, the fraternity's own ideology impelled its members to join such movements; it was their "sworn obligation," as he notes. For instance, Scottish Rite Masons attaining the ninth and
tenth degrees vowed to assist "those who struggle against oppression" and in
the thirty-second degree swore to become "soldiers of freedom" and wage war
against tyranny and despotism.[15]

There was also an institutional dimension to the filibustering and separatist ventures of the Freemasons. Masonic lodges became privileged sites where
members could meet one another regularly, exchange information, and organize
rebellions and movements without fear of reprisal. Masons could provide in-
troductions to other Masons occupying important posts, and they were always
able to recognize each other through secret signs and rely on one another, as
they swore on the Bible to "'always aid and assist all poor, distressed, worthy
Master Masons' and to 'fly to his relief' upon seeing the Grand Hailing Sign of
Distress."[16] In the absence of political parties within the Spanish Empire in the
1800s and 1810s (and even after parties were established in Mexico in the 1820s),

it was only natural that the more established lodges and grand lodges in Louisiana and elsewhere in the South would sponsor new lodges all around the Gulf of Mexico basin. Grand lodges of Louisiana and South Carolina chartered some of the earliest lodges in Cuba, and prominent Louisiana Masons—beginning with Stephen F. Austin of the Louisiana no. 109 Lodge—became influential colonists and politicians in Coahuila and Texas.[17] Even the symbols employed in these insurrections and breakaway republics were of Masonic inspiration. The ubiquitous lone star—the five-pointed star that was in the symbol of the West Florida Republic, the Texas Republic, and the proposed project to liberate Cuba in 1848–49—represented the Masonic five points of fellowship. While Freemasons represented small minorities in each of the gulf provinces and colonies, they predominated in all filibustering/separatist movements during the first half of the nineteenth century.[18]

THE CAPITAL OF SECESSION

Prior to the Louisiana Purchase of 1803, the main aim of agents like Genet and Blount had been to secure for the United States free passage through the length of the Mississippi River. Once Louisiana became a part of the Union, New Orleans became the jumping-off point of further filibustering adventures and political movements launched against various parts of the Gulf of Mexico controlled by Spain and Mexico.

New Orleans was the tip of a continent-wide funnel—a vast region of North America locked in by the Appalachian Mountains but linked together by a network of waterways around the Ohio, Missouri, and Mississippi rivers. By 1830 it was the second largest port on the Gulf of Mexico, boasting some seventy thousand inhabitants, rivaling Havana (which may have had as many as one hundred thousand) and dwarfing all other ports in the region including Veracruz, Mexico's gateway to the world. New Orleans's diverse population was constantly replenished by men, women, and children who drifted down the Mississippi River and by scores of transients coming from the Gulf of Mexico basin and the wider Atlantic world.

New Orleans's vigorous demography was especially felt in neighboring Texas. Prior to around 1800 there were virtually no Anglo-American residents in Spanish Texas. Americans were so rare and conspicuous that Spanish authorities were able to keep track of them (many were involved in the smuggling of horses, such as the legendary Philip Nolan, whose party was captured in 1803). By the 1810s Anglo-American settlers began to make Texas their home, but it was only in the following decade that Mexican officials formally opened the door to American colonists. The results were immediate and dramatic. From 1823 to 1830 Anglo-Americans entered Texas at a rate of nearly one thousand persons per year, increasing to nearly three thousand annually during the early 1830s. On the eve of the Texas Revolution in 1835, the Anglo-Texan and slave population outnumbered Mexican Texans by a ratio of ten to one, totaling nearly twenty-five thousand.[19]

It is remarkable that this wave of settlers was able to take possession of much of the coast of Texas and the border area with Louisiana so quickly, virtually overnight in historical time. But what is even more impressive is that all who made up this relentless human torrent from the United States completed virtually the same migratory pathway. The majority of these settlers originated in the landlocked American states—Kentucky, Missouri, Tennessee, and so forth—floated down the Mississippi, made a stopover in New Orleans, and finally completed the journey with a leisurely three-day sailing trip to one of the new Anglo-American colonies that mushroomed up and down the Texas coast in the 1820s and 1830s.

Stephen F. Austin, the man most directly responsible for the tidal wave of Anglo-American colonists that washed over Spanish and Mexican Texas, pioneered this very route. He grew up in Virginia and Missouri and as a young man moved to Arkansas hoping to claim a tract close to the Red River. In the fall of 1820 he made his way to New Orleans seeking a fresh start. "I came here with the hope of finding employ," Austin would later admit. "I offered to hire myself out as clerk, as an overseer, or anything else."[20] And from New Orleans he began to hear about the opportunities in Spanish Texas. The preeminent *empresario* of Texas had found his calling in New Orleans, and thousands would follow in his tracks.

And demography went hand in hand with economy. New Orleans possessed the best port facilities in the Gulf of Mexico and the largest fleet. Lorenzo de Zavala, a Mexican politician who would go on to become vice president of the breakaway Republic of Texas, passed through New Orleans in 1830 and described it in this way: "The general appearance of the city is not pleasing to the traveler, there are no domes or towers or columns, nor any handsome buildings of exquisite architecture . . . [but] at the approach of the levee rises a jungle of masts. . . . At my arrival, there must have been more than a thousand ships, small and large, and at least five thousand seamen."[21] New Orleans also had the banks with the deepest pockets in the Gulf of Mexico and the most important merchants and suppliers of the region. Residents of places like Havana, Mérida, Campeche, or Veracruz regularly procured goods that had been imported or smuggled from New Orleans.

The economic impact of Louisiana on Texas was enormous. In 1823 Mexican officials, desirous to promote the development of Texas, decided to waive import duties within the province for a period of seven years.[22] This tax exemption created an immediate trading rush and resulted in the colonies along the coast of Texas becoming totally dependent on Louisiana markets. They imported everything from the Big Easy from house frames, china, and silverware to shovels and cotton mills. Conversely, they sent back to Louisiana all the products obtained through their toils, primarily bales of cotton. Even the Mexican towns in Texas like San Antonio and Goliad fell under the orbit of New Orleans's economy. And thus the rhythms of town life in Texas were set by the arrival and departure of schooners and steam packets shuttling back and forth between Louisiana and Texas.

Unquestionably, New Orleans was the preeminent port on the Gulf of Mexico. But its pivotal political role throughout the basin was defined as much by its demographic and economic might as by its intrepid and visionary leaders. A small cadre of individuals charted the future of New Orleans with unmatched optimism. These leaders formed organizations that were partly social venues and partly business and political forums, often the natural outgrowth of pre-existing organizations such as Masonic lodges or business associations. The best-known example was the Mexican Association, also known as the Association of Three Hundred and later as the New Orleans Association, which consisted of three hundred American and Creole businessmen and politicians whose main goal was to bring about the emancipation of Mexico from the Spanish Empire as well as to encourage the promotion of American ideals and the selling of goods in Spanish America. The Mexican Association was possibly a party to the Burr conspiracy of 1805–6 but came into its own in the 1810s when it began financing arms and ammunition for Mexican patriots fighting against the Spanish Crown and promoting filibustering expeditions against Texas. The business of outfitting rebel armies in New Orleans grew to such an extent that the Louisiana legislature and the U.S. Congress both passed laws to curb it.[23]

But in spite of an outright ban, the outfitting business and the activities of such bodies as the Mexican Association continued to flourish. The Committee on Texas Affairs is a better-documented example of how influential residents from Louisiana injected themselves in the affairs of Texas, promoting secession while at the same time speculating with tracts of land in east Texas. The Committee on Texas Affairs came into being in October 1835, just as Mexican Texas was plunging into turmoil due to an all-out partisan conflict that had been simmering since the 1820s. Mexican "centralists," an amorphous political coalition particularly strong in the area around Mexico City, insisted on restricting state rights and limiting popular participation. They were opposed by an even more amorphous "federalist" camp, particularly well represented in fringe areas like Coahuila and Texas, which strove to uphold the autonomy of the states.[24] As President Antonio López de Santa Anna spearheaded a crackdown of recalcitrant, federalist-dominated states, Texas braced for an outright military conflict with Mexico City. In these trying circumstances, a group of powerful financiers and merchants gathered at the Banks Arcade in New Orleans to discuss how to respond to the impending crisis in Texas. The Committee on Texas Affairs would go on to raise the extraordinary sum of $250,000 on behalf of Texas. More significantly, the committee was able to recruit and organize two companies of soldiers—the New Orleans Greys—that saw action in Texas campaigns leading toward secession from Mexico, including the crucial battles of Goliad and the Alamo.[25]

In short, by the 1830s New Orleans had become a locus of insurrectionist intrigue in the Gulf of Mexico basin. Its large population and vibrant economy made it the ideal ground for any recruiter in search of funds and volunteers willing to embark on even the most outlandish expeditions of conquest, rebellion, and secession. Its large fleet facilitated the chartering and purchasing of vessels and provisions. Its competitive print culture—New Orleans possessed no less than thirteen newspapers by the early 1840s—provided the means to advertise and promote every conceivable venture. It is no wonder that the Crescent City had lured men of action with bold schemes like Wilkinson and Burr and would again become attractive to the captains of the various expeditions launched against Texas in the 1810s, including Bernardo Gutiérrez de Lara and Francisco Javier Mina. When Mexican centralists gained the upper hand in the mid 1830s, New Orleans emerged once again as a haven of deposed Mexican federalists. The list of Mexicans residing in New Orleans at that time reads like a *Who's Who* of the Mexican federalist movement—former vice president Valentín Gómez Farías, former secretary of the treasury (and soon-to-be vice president of the Texas Republic) Lorenzo de Zavala, federalist governor of Coahuila and Texas Agustín Viesca, Brigadier General José Antonio Mexía (who led a disastrous expedition into Tampico in 1835), and Colonel Martín Peraza (who would play a prominent role in Yucatán's secessionist movement in the 1840s) all lived in the city. Over the following two decades New Orleans served as a principal staging ground for a series of filibustering/separatist movements in the Gulf of Mexico basin.[26]

ONE, TWO, MANY TEXAS: THE MACHINERY AT WORK

After the northern rim of the Gulf of Mexico became formally incorporated into the United States, settlers, adventurers, and secessionists turned their sights on Texas. Texas constitutes an obvious link between the early secessionist movements in Louisiana and the Floridas and later movements farther south. Texas also exposes the workings of the machinery of secession that had emerged in the area since the times of Genet and Blount. The Texas Revolution was neither a case of simple ethnic antagonism—American colonists against Mexican authorities—nor an instance of naked expansion on the part of the United States. Ethnic tensions were undeniable, as were the machinations of American officials in their efforts to acquire this Mexican province. But the Texas Revolution was all along a complex, multiethnic movement—scores of Mexican Texans and high-ranking Mexican federalists took part as well—effectively sustained by money, men, and arms that came from many parts of the United States and were channeled through Louisiana. The Texas Revolution thus illustrates some of the aforementioned themes: it was a movement that had been in the making since the 1800s; it combined America's expansionist aspirations with a liberationist rhetoric that made it attractive to Mexican federalists in their bitter struggle against centralists; and it was an insurrection sustained by resources from Louisiana and beyond and raised by such groups as the Committee of Texas Affairs. Texas, however, is only the best-known example of a series of insurrections that had secessionist potential. Unfortunately for Mexico, the internecine struggle between centralists and federalists (later known as the conservatives and the liberals) remained unabated in the 1830s and 1840s, and therefore the machinery of secession continued to operate all along Mexico's gulf coast.

The insurgency that rocked Tamaulipas in the late 1830s and that culminated in the creation of an "independent government" in 1840 shows just how close other Mexican provinces came to becoming other "lone star republics." The Tamaulipas movement was centered in the northern villages and consisted of scores of rancheros described as "badly-armed citizens of the six towns of the frontier of the North from Matamoros to the town of Laredo."[27] Since 1838 these independent Mexican towns along the border with Texas had raised a federalist army of some eight hundred men capable of defying the centralist national government and of exercising political control throughout northern Tamaulipas.

As was the case in other secessionist movements, the Tamaulipas rebels were motivated by concrete economic goals—in this instance they wanted to preserve free trade with the Texas Republic. Since the days of the Texas Revolution, frontier Mexicans had carried out a lucrative trade with the Texas rebels. Local federalist leaders along the border encouraged this economic activity by licensing Mexican merchants and issuing passports permitting them to cross into Texas. But centralists strenuously opposed the Tamaulipas-Texas trade, claiming—quite rightly—that liberal commercial and colonization policies had resulted in the loss of Texas and could have similar consequences in Tamaulipas.[28]

Aside from trade, the federalist insurrection of the northern villages pursued far more ambitious political objectives. According to Lieutenant Anson G. Neal, a Texas auxiliary fighting with the Tamaulipas federalists, the objective of the federalist rebels of Tamaulipas was nothing less than to accomplish "the union of the Northern States of Mexico to Texas as one large Independent Govt."[29] The New Orleans and Texas press repeatedly asserted that the ultimate goal of the rebels was to separate off Tamaulipas, Coahuila, Nuevo León, and other northern Mexican states and territories from Mexico and to form an independent republic called the North Mexican Republic or the Republic of the Rio Grande (a common variation was that these states would enter into some sort of confederation with the Texas Republic).[30] In September 1839 the *Telegraph and Texas Register* reported on the activities of General Juan Pablo Anaya, a high-ranking federalist leader who was in Texas at the time seeking aid for the movement. The *Register* reported that General Anaya "represents it as within the power of the Federal party to establish a good and stable government over six or seven of the Northern Mexican States—pay off their proportion of the National Debt and assume a respectable standing among the nations of the earth," a claim that General Anaya vigorously disputed a few days later.[31]

After months of speculation, the directors of the federalist movement in northern Tamaulipas convened a general meeting on January 18, 1840. The convention took the momentous decision to establish an "independent government" and proceeded to appoint a *president* and a *council*.[32] On January 29 the newly elected administration was inaugurated. According to one witness, "A Federal

Flag was planted in the center of the square; the soldiers all marched under it, kissing it as they passed; which was considered as an oath of allegiance to the new Govt—A great Ball was given at the House of [Antonio] Zapata, and all were welcomed who chose to attend; many, however, were unable to go for the want of suitable clothes; they were literally naked.—After the party each soldier recd. $2.00 in part pyt for past services."[33] Basilio Benavides, the alcalde of Laredo, recounted that after the government was elected, civilian leaders and the entire army went to Laredo, which was established as the seat of government. There an Anglo-Texan guard of sixty men protected the newly elected president.[34]

The newborn republic was shrouded in ambiguity from the start. While some contemporary participants refer to it as the Republic of the Rio Grande or the North Mexican Republic other sources do not go that far.[35] Nonetheless there is clear evidence that the conventionist government of 1840 remained deliberately silent about the true nature of the "independent government" in an effort to keep together a heterogeneous coalition that included Mexican patriots who wished solely to restore a federalist regime in Mexico as well as Anglo-American auxiliaries who pushed for total separation from Mexico. Centralists typically branded the federalist movement along the border as treasonous: "There are among us, I am forced to say, men so vile, so destitute of modesty, lastly, so traitorous, that they have no hesitancy in making common cause with the enemies of [our] territorial integrity and . . . independence."[36] The conventionist government could not afford to confirm these charges by breaking away completely from Mexico. But at the same time, the ambiguity surrounding the movement discouraged the Anglo-American auxiliaries, some of whom became quite disillusioned and went back to Texas or Louisiana. An open letter published in a Texas newspaper in May 1840 urged the federalist leadership to dispel the mystery: "Nothing short of an absolute independence of the states of Río Grande and Chihuahua will ensure the happiness of your people. . . . Declare yourselves at once absolutely independent from Mexico and then you shall not be in want of [Anglo-American] auxiliaries to sustain you."[37] Historian Josefina Vázquez makes the interesting point that during the period of the so-called Republic of the Rio Grande, secessionist rhetoric invariably came from printmen and filibusters in New Orleans and Texas, while Mexican participants preferred to speak of a "provisional" government that had withdrawn its allegiance to the centralist regime "temporarily" but would rejoin the nation once the federalist constitution was reestablished. This observation underscores how the machinery of secession had acquired a life of its own and was able to disregard the compromised course charted by the federalists from Tamaulipas.

In the end the "independent government" of northern Tamaulipas was unable to please God and the devil at the same time. The movement became fragmented and was irresistibly pulled in different directions. By November 1840 the remaining federalist forces had surrendered to the national government. But the specter of secessionism remained alive in the decades that followed, as the Texas-Tamaulipas border turned into a collection of fiefdoms that threatened to break free from the nation during the Mexican War—when rumors surfaced of a so-called Republic of the Sierra Madre—and again in the 1850s during the Merchant Wars.

Along with Texas and Tamaulipas, Yucatán is another example of the secessionist impulse washing over the Gulf of Mexico basin. As Terry Rugeley's essay in this volume makes clear, in May 1841 the Yucatán rebels went through many of the same motions as their counterparts in Texas and Tamaulipas by setting up a provisional government, promulgating a constitution, and raising a flag. At that point the Yucatán insurgents did not opt for complete separation like Texas, nor did they adopt an ambiguous stance like the rebels of the northern villages. Instead the insurgent Yucatecans clarified the meaning and scope of their "provisional government" by including a provision stating that Yucatán would rejoin the Mexican federation once the centralist regime was defeated and a federalist system reestablished. In other words, the Yucatecans were claiming that Yucatán's movement was to unfold within Mexico's national framework, at least in theory. In practice, however, the movement veered between defiant federalism and outright separation.

For an account of the internal dynamics of the secessionist project in Yucatán I refer readers to Rugeley's illuminating essay. But I do want to point to Yucatán's bold decision to establish a defensive alliance with the Texas Republic, a move that underscores how the forces of secession emanating from New Orleans and Texas became inevitably intertwined with the fierce political infighting on the peninsula and that indeed epitomizes the workings of the gulf's machinery of secession. The origins of the alliance hark back to a letter exchange between Mirabeau Buonaparte Lamar, president of Texas, and Miguel Barbachano, governor of Yucatán, in the summer of 1841. Governor Barbachano unambiguously declared that Yucatán desired "to draw closer its relations with the people of Texas, and unite with them to sustain the cause of liberty which has been proclaimed against the oppressive Government of Mexico."[38] But the effusive governor was interested in more than words and immediately sent Colonel Martín F. Peraza, one of the highest-ranking Yucatecan conspirators who had resided in New Orleans during the Texas Revolution, as a special commissioner to Texas to negotiate "on such points as may be of common interest; not only as regards the policy, but also for the aggrandizement and good of both countries."[39] Clearly Yucatán was acting as a sovereign nation in spite of protestations to the contrary. "The republics of Yucatan and Texas, though separated by the Gulf of Mexico, are the persecuted and exiled daughters of an unnatural mother [Mexico]," one eloquent but partisan contemporary explained. "They now meet like sisters to mourn over the woes of a heartless exile, and to look forward to brighter days in prospect."[40]

Colonel Peraza's mission led to a defensive agreement under which Texas pledged to use its newly created navy to uphold Yucatán's independent status by keeping Mexico's few ships at bay. The geometry of the arrangement could not be more enlightening: a Texas navy outfitted in New Orleans and deployed on the coast of Tabasco, Campeche, and Yucatán. In essence Texas was to send three or more ships to Yucatán to attack Mexico's centralist ships and coastal cities. The two countries would share "such sums as may be received from captures by sea, or from the custom houses or other public offices, or property belonging to the Central Government, of such towns and cities as may be occupied by said forces during the period our vessels may co-operate with those of Yucatan"—an article that was tantamount to piracy.[41] In return for these services, Yucatán agreed to pay $8,000 per month to help defray the cost of maintaining the Lone Star's Navy.[42]

In December 1841 the Texas Navy under Commodore Edwin Moore began arriving in Sisal, Mérida's closest port. By then, however, the situation had changed completely in Yucatán. A more moderate faction was in control and had begun negotiations with Andrés Quintana Roo, a representative from Mexico's central government, over the terms of Yucatán's reentry into the Mexican fold. One of the preconditions of Yucatán's readmission was that it had to cease all diplomatic relations with Texas immediately. As Quintana Roo himself put it, "The solemn alliance celebrated between the governments of Texas and Yucatán, as spelled out in the papers in my possession, was nothing less than a scandal and had to stop as soon as possible. . . . I demanded as a precondition the end of all relations with Texas and with the Navy which was to arrive shortly, as indeed it was seen shortly thereafter in the waters of Sisal."[43] Commodore Moore made his way from Sisal to Mérida and attempted to compel Yucatán's government to live up to its agreements. He went so far as to issue an ultimatum: should Yucatán reenter Mexico it would be immediately considered an enemy of Texas and therefore her ships and harbors would be open to capture by Moore's navy. In an attempt to placate both Texas and Mexico, Yucatán agreed to continue paying the $8,000 subsidy and at the same time carried on its negotiations with the central government.[44] Yucatán's secessionist drive receded for the moment, but, as in the case of Tamaulipas, it resurfaced from time to time over the following few years.

In 2003 a group of scholars gathered to discuss and historicize such categories as "seascapes" and "littoral societies." The idea was to identify coastal societies that, at least potentially, had more in common with one another than with their inland neighbors.[45] The Gulf of Mexico basin during the first half of the nineteenth century is a case worthy of analysis in light of such categories. By dint of a peculiar geography that facilitated coastal travel, the spread of political ideologies, and close economic ties, the Gulf of Mexico basin possessed its own inertia. At the same time, however, it is also important to recognize that these regional networks were invariably opposed to or at least in competition with national projects unfolding in the region—the divvying up of the Gulf of Mexico basin among the United States, Mexico, and the Spanish Empire.

The spread of secessionism around the gulf coast admirably demonstrates the extent to which tensions obtained between regional ties and national imperatives. In this chapter I have tried to highlight the regional linkages that formed around the gulf coast: the emergence of New Orleans as a privileged outfitting station for filibustering/separatist ventures; Masonic lodges as crucial sites, where leaders from different nationalities could come together; the common political lexicon and symbols, such as the five-pointed star employed by different secessionist movements; the cadre of American, Spanish, and Mexican leaders who were able to move from one area of the gulf to another and who took part not only in one but in several such movements (Wilkinson, Carvajal, Peraza, etc.). This regional network was real. But it was in constant tension with the national and imperial forces in the region. And it was precisely the articulation of this machinery of secessionism with larger national projects that determined the ultimate outcome. Thus the virulent rhetoric of emancipation and support for states' rights served America well in its efforts to consolidate its hold on the region, as the cases of Louisiana, the Floridas, and Texas attest. Conversely, Mexico's federalists and liberals were torn between supporting their political ideals and maintaining the integrity of their nation along the Gulf of Mexico shores.

Notes

1. General Antonio López de Santa Anna was dispatched to Yucatán to quell that separatist attempt in 1824. His instructions included the following: "The state of Yucatán remains in a state of total separation from the rest of the republic since the latter adopted a federalist regime. . . . It is said that the government of Mérida remains dependent on Spain and persists in paying inordinate attention to commerce with Havana, subordinating the entire cause of Anahuac to its mercantile advantages" (Instrucciones al Sr. General de Brigada don Antonio López de Santa Anna, Mexico City, Apr. 21, 1824, expediente de Antonio López de Santa Anna, tomo II, foja 437, Archivo Histórico de la Defensa Nacional, Mexico City).

2. The literature on the Burr conspiracy is vast. The actual aims and scope of the conspiracy will remain forever nebulous, but tellingly a very detailed map of Texas was found among Burr's possessions when he was apprehended. For the events of 1812–13, see Harry McCorry Henderson, "The Magee-Gutiérrez Expedition," *Southwestern Historical Quarterly* 55, no. 1 (1951): 43–61, and Henry P. Walker, ed., "William McLane's Narrative of the Magee-Gutiérrez Expedition, 1812–1813," *Southwestern Historical Quarterly* 66, no. 4 (1963): 569–88. For Long's expedition see John Henry Brown, *Long's Expedition* (Houston, Tex.: Union National Bank, 1930), and Harris Gaylord Warren, *The Sword Was Their Passport: A History of American Filibustering in the Mexican Revolution* (Baton Rouge: Louisiana State University Press, 1943). For a panoramic and more recent view in neighboring Louisiana, see Peter J. Kastor, "'Motives of Peculiar Urgency': Local Diplomacy in Louisiana, 1803–1821," *William and Mary Quarterly* 58:4 (2001): 819–48. For a brief treatment of the Fredonia Republic, see my own *Changing National Identities at the Frontier: Texas and New Mexico, 1800–1850* (New York: Cambridge University Press, 2005).

3. Any discussion of the history of the Gulf of Mexico basin has to start with Weddle's three-volume opus. He charts the early colonial history of the region in *The Gulf of Mexico in North American Discovery, 1500–1685* (College Station: Texas A&M University, 1985). That volume was followed by *The French Thorn: Rival Explorers in the Spanish Sea, 1682–1762* (College Station: Texas A&M University, 1991) and finally by *Changing Tides: Twilight and Dawn in the Spanish Sea, 1763–1803* (College Station: Texas A&M University, 1995).

4. Brissot de Warville, *Nouveau Voyage dans les États-Unis* (Paris: Buisson, 1791), quoted in Frederick Jackson Turner, "The Origin of Genet's Projected Attack on Louisiana and the Floridas," *The American Historical Review* 3, no. 4 (1898): 654.

5. The Genet affair is well explained in Turner's "The Origins of Genet's Projected Attack on Louisiana and the Floridas," 650–71.

6. See William H. Masterson, *William Blount* (Baton Rouge: Louisiana State University Press, 1954), passim, and Buckner F. Melton Jr., *The First Impeachment: The Constitution's Framers and the Case of Senator William Blount* (Macon: Mercer University Press, 1998), esp. 78–88.

7. West Florida declaration of independence, quoted in David A. Bice, *The Original Lone Star Republic: Scoundrels, Statesmen, and Schemers of the 1810 West Florida Rebellion* (Clanton, Ala.: Heritage Publishing Consultants, 2004), 199.

8. For a study of these events from the Spanish perspective, see Elena Sánchez-Fabrés Mirat, *Situación histórica de las Floridas en la segunda mitad del siglo XVIII (1783–1819)* (Madrid: Gráficas Cóndor, 1977). For the English-language classic, see Isaac J. Cox, *The West Florida Controversy, 1798–1813* (Baltimore: Johns Hopkins Press, 1912), passim. For a more recent rendition, see Bice, *The Original Lone Star Republic*, passim.

9. Cox, *The West Florida Controversy*, 415.

10. John Ballinger to Harry Toulmin, n.p., Nov. 10, 1810, quoted in Cox, *The West Florida Controversy*, 419.

11. Sánchez-Fabrés Mirat, *Situación histórica de las Floridas en la segunda mitad del siglo XVIII*, 257–61; Cox, *The West Florida Controversy*, chap. 6.

12. James Ripley Jacobs, *Tarnished Warrior: Major-General James Wilkinson* (New York: Macmillan, 1938), 173.

13. Jacobs, *Tarnished Warrior*, 206, 243, 280–81

14. Jacobs, *Tarnished Warrior*, 184.

15. Antonio Rafael de la Cova, "Filibusters and Freemasons: The Sworn Obligation," *Journal of the Early Republic* 17:1 (1997): 100.

16. Quoted in de la Cova, "Filibusters and Freemasons," 99.

17. For a more detailed analysis of the role of Freemasonry in Texas see James David Carter, *Masonry in Texas: Background, History, and Influence to 1846* (Waco, Tex.: Committee on Masonic Education and Service for the Grand Lodge of Texas, 1955).

18. The Cuban revolutionaries adopted the five-point star only after having considered and rejected even more explicit Masonic emblems like the equilateral triangle and the Masonic All-Seeing Eye in the center of the triangle (De la Cova, "Filibusters and Freemasons," 106).

19. See Juan Nepomuceno Almonte, *Informe secreto sobre la presente situación de Texas*, 1834, ed. Celia Gutiérrez Ibarra (Mexico City: INAH, 1987), 20, 26, 31, and David

Weber, *The Mexican Frontier, 1821–1846: The American Southwest under Mexico* (Albuquerque: University of New Mexico Press, 1982), 159–62, 166–67.

20. Quoted in Greg Cantrell, *Stephen F. Austin: Empresario of Texas* (New Haven: Yale University Press, 1999), 78.

21. Lorenzo de Zavala, "Viaje a los Estados Unidos del Norte de América," in *Obras*, 2 vols., ed. Manual González-Ramírez (Mexico City: Porrúa, 1966–), 2:14.

22. "Instrucciones para el diputado Refugio de la Garza. . . ," San Antonio, Jan. 30, 1822, Nacogdoches Archives, box 2q297, no. 190, 8–17, Barker History Center, University of Texas at Austin. See also Refugio de la Garza to San Antonio *ayuntamiento*, Mexico City, Apr. 30, 1822, Béxar Archives, microfilm roll 70, 494–96, and Aug. 8, 1822, microfilm roll 72, 455–57, Barker Center, University of Texas at Austin, and "Decree of Freedom of Commerce," in José Antonio Saucedo to Juan Martín de Veramendi, San Antonio, Apr. 13, 1825, Béxar Archives, microfilm roll 80, 548–49, Barker Center, University of Texas at Austin.

23. See Jacobs, *Tarnished Warrior*, 221, 326.

24. For a more detailed discussion of how the centralist-federalist cleavage unfolded in Coahuila and Texas, see my *Changing National Identities at the Frontier*, passim.

25. On the activities of the Committee of Texas Affairs, see Edward L. Miller, *New Orleans and the Texas Revolution* (College Station: Texas A&M University Press, 2004), passim.

26. See especially Alan C. Hutchinson, "Mexican Federalists in New Orleans and the Texas Revolution" *Louisiana Historical Quarterly* 39, no. 1 (1956): 26–35, and "Valentín Gómez Farías and the 'Secret Pact of New Orleans,'" *The Hispanic American Historical Review* 36:4 (1956): 471–89.

27. Anonymous account (my translation), [Laredo?], May 30, 1847, in *The Papers of Mirabeau Buonaparte Lamar*, 6 vols., ed. Charles Adam Gulick Jr. et al. (Austin: Pemberton Press, 1968), entry 2333 (hereafter *Lamar Papers*).

28. On federalist leaders issuing passports to Mexican merchants and on other matters relating to trade, see Antonio Canales to Mirabeau Buonaparte Lamar, Reynosa, Dec. 17, 1838, in *Lamar Papers*, entry 934.

29. Anson G. Neal, Laredo, May 30, 1847, in *Lamar Papers*, entry 2333.

30. *Houston (Tex.) Telegraph and Texas Register*, Apr. 10, 1839. New Orleans resident Orazio de Attellis Santangelo, a Neapolitan officer, naturalized Mexican, and ardent federalist banished twice from Mexico, was an early proponent of this daring scheme. As evidence of the secessionist sentiment prevalent in the north of Mexico, Santangelo copied a letter signed by a "federalist Zacatecan." For discussions of the relevance and impact of these letters, see Joseph Milton Nance, *After San Jacinto: The Texas-Mexican Frontier, 1836–1841* (Austin: University of Texas Press, 1963), 173–79, and Josefina Vázquez, "La

Supuesta República del Río Grande," *Historia Mexicana* 36, no. 3 (1986): 58–60. For Sant-angelo's story as told by himself, see Orazio de Attellis Santangelo, *Statement of Facts Relating to the Claim of Orazio de Attellis Santangelo, a Citizen of the United States, on the Government of the Republic of Mexico* (Washington, D.C.: Peter Force, 1841).

31. *Houston (Tex.) Telegraph and Texas Register*, Sept. 18, 1839 (see also Sept. 11, 1839); Vázquez, "La Supuesta República," 60.

32. The most valuable source on the results of the convention is a letter by George Fisher to the editor of the *Morning Star* dated February 29, 1840 (*Houston (Tex.) Morning Star*, Mar. 3, 1840). The five-member council consisted of Jesús Cárdenas (who was also president), Francisco Vidaurri y Villaseñor (who was also vice president), Juan Nepomuceno Molano (representative of Tamaulipas), Manuel María del Llano (representative of Nuevo León), and Francisco Vidaurri y Villaseñor (representative of Coahuila). The supplementary members were Antonio Canales, José María de Jesús Carvajal, and Pablo Anaya. See Nance, *After San Jacinto*, 252–53.

33. Anton G. Neal, Laredo, May 30, 1847, in *Lamar Papers*, entry 2333.

34. Basilio Benavides (my translation), [Laredo?], May 30, 1847, in *Lamar Papers*, entry 2333. Constant harassment from the centralist troops forced the conventionist government to move from Guerrero to Laredo and finally to Casa Blanca on the Nueces River.

35. In an address to the troops under his command, Canales referred to the "Provisional Government of these States" and likened it to "the Swiss cantons [that] did not owe their liberty to the potentates, [but] nevertheless until today exists the government, which some few shepherds set up" (Antonio Canales, to troops, Guerrero, Feb. 8, 1840, in *Lamar Papers*, entry 1709a). But in a letter to President Lamar he went a step beyond, representing that "very soon, when the ties that now unite us to proud Mexico shall have been torn asunder, we shall have [oc]casion to prove to your Excellency and to all [the in]habitants of this Republic, that those of that of [the] Rio Bravo know how to appreciate and comply [with] the duties imposed by gratitude" (Antonio Canales to Mirabeau Buonaparte Lamar, Austin, Apr. 29, 1840, in *Lamar Papers*, entry 1794). See also discussion in Vázquez, "La Supuesta República," 63–64, 78–79.

36. *Diario del Gobierno* (Mexico City), Dec. 1839, quoted in Nance, *After San Jacinto*, 220.

37. George Fisher to Jesús Cárdenas, Houston, Apr. 25, 1840, *Houston (Tex.) Morning Star*, May 23, 1840.

38. Miguel Barbachano to Mirabeau Buonaparte Lamar, Mérida, Aug. 24, 1841, in *Correspondence of the Secretary of State of the Texas Republic* (Austin, 1842), 4.

39. Martín Peraza to Samuel A. Roberts, Austin, Sept. 11, 1841, in *Correspondence of the Secretary of State of the Texas Republic*, 18.

40. Quoted in George Folsom, *Mexico in 1842: A Description of the Country, Its Natural and Political Features* . . . (New York: Wiley and Putnam, 1842), 252.

41. The articles of the agreement can be found in Samuel A. Roberts to Martín F. Peraza, Austin, Sept. 27, 1841, in *Correspondence of the Secretary of State of the Texas Republic*, 9.

42. See Jonathan W. Jordan, *Lone Star Navy: Texas, the Fight for the Gulf of Mexico, and the Shaping of the American West* (Washington, D.C.: Potomac Books, 2007), and Tom Henderson Wells, *Commodore Moore and the Texas Navy* (Austin: University of Texas Press, 1982).

43. *Manifiesto del gobierno provisional a la nación, acerca de los negocios de Yucatán* (Mexico City: Imprenta de Lara, 1843), 16.

44. Wells, *Commodore Moore and the Texas Navy*, 68.

45. The conference was entitled "Seascapes, Littoral Cultures, and Trans-Oceanic Exchanges" and was held February 13–15, 2003, at the Library of Congress.

TERRY RUGELEY

The Brief, Glorious History of the Yucatecan Republic

Secession and Violence in Southeast Mexico, 1836–1848

Political secession is the scourge of postcolonial states, and although in this hemisphere it is most often associated with the ill-fated Confederate States of America, secession was endemic to nineteenth-century Latin America as well. Indeed, had nations adhered to the layout of late Bourbon and early national redistricting, continental Latin America might have coalesced into only six political entities: Chile, Peru, Brazil (with Uruguay), Mexico (including the five Central American states), New Granada (encompassing Venezuela, Colombia, and Ecuador), and Río de la Plata (with Argentina, Paraguay, and Bolivia). Instead, by 1840 the original groupings had splintered into sixteen, after which there were numerous attempts at secession that ultimately ended in failure and reunification.

This chapter explores one of the most important cases—the rise of the Yucatecan Republic and its descent into ethnic revolt and civil war—in an effort to shed light on the dynamics that tore apart so much of the Americas. In 1836, Yucatecans, infuriated by Mexican attempts to curtail regional autonomy and impose greater metropolitan rule, launched a four-year revolt that led to the formation of a new political entity. Yucatecans initially won the battle and maintained an intermittent independence until 1848. But the price was high. Their separation led not to prosperity and national health but rather to decades of entrenched violence. How did this dream go awry, and why did a people seemingly intent on creating their own nation succumb to civil wars, ethnic and otherwise? This chapter proposes there are links between the separatist movement in Yucatán and the later peasant uprisings and military revolts there and concludes by exploring how Mexican secession differed from its counterpart in the nineteenth-century United States.

YUCATECAN SECESSION AND THE FAILED RECONQUEST

The Yucatán Peninsula is an enormous limestone shelf jutting out from Mexico's extreme southeast into the Caribbean. Prior to 1858 it constituted one of the Mexican republic's largest provinces (this term being preferred over "state"), second only to the thinly populated Chihuahua in sheer geographical expanse. Given that Yucatán boasted five hundred thousand inhabitants in a nation of some nine million, it might have formed a significant political force, but the vast majority of its inhabitants were Maya-speaking peasants with no access to power and with little reason to rejoice in the glories of the Mexican nation. Most Mayas still lived by independent subsistence farming in the 1840s, but an increasing number were becoming permanent servants on Hispanic-owned commercial properties known as haciendas.

Several features separated Mexico from its southeastern province. For one, the province was geographically isolated; until the 1970s both Yucatán and Tabasco remained accessible only by boat. Even marine access was poor, for the shallow coasts forced vessels to weigh anchor farther out; smaller vessels of limited draft had to be used to transport both goods and people to the shore. Differing patterns of conquest and colonization also distinguished Mexico from the Yucatán. The decentralized, almost anarchic, conditions of late fifteenth-century Maya society retarded Spanish conquest until 1546, by which time central New Spain had already assumed a certain coherence and had established stable Hispanic institutions. The peninsula's overall poverty retarded commercial development and confined Spaniards to a handful of European-style cities until the early 1700s. Maya, not Spanish or Nahuatl, reigned as the language of the countryside. Yucatán lacked many of the accouterments of Mexico City, and as sugar and cattle production grew in commercial importance, Yucatecan entrepreneurs began to resent metropolitan attempts to restrict their trade options. These matters came to a head after Mexico won its independence in 1821.[1] The new Mexican statesmen tried to eradicate former dependency on Spain, and in so doing restricted trade with Spain's Cuban colony, thereby severing Yucatecans from their principal market.

Yucatecan Hispanics lived in a cultural atmosphere that antebellum southern planters would in some ways have found made to order. Elites prized gentility, knowledge of classical literature, and honorific militia commands for prominent landowners. In their youth, Hispanic women lived "the most hothouse existence that Europeans could imagine," but they married young, bore many children, managed enormous households of extended family and servants, and found refuge from the patriarchal order in the rival patriarchy of the Catholic church, with its slate of activities, festivals, and lay organizations.[2] But much of Hispanic gentility went no deeper than the frock coat. Outside of Mérida, almost all rural people spoke some Maya, particularly on the haciendas, and by 1821 a certain medium of folk culture prevailed throughout. People shared a belief in folk healings, apparitions, and the saints' daily intervention in human affairs. Popular folk dances known as *jaranas* attracted both Mayas and Hispanics.

Despite the southeast's almost entirely peaceful role in the independence struggle, it was ultimately driven from Mexico's political system. Conflict began in the years 1834–36, when proponents of centralism revoked the federalist constitution of 1823 and dispatched collaborators throughout the provinces. Acting under the guidance of conservative counselors such as Lucas Alamán, Antonio López de Santa Anna imposed a system known as the Siete Leyes, under which most decision making was made by the chief executive, who was supported in turn by clerics, military officers, and men of property. Governorships became appointed offices. These changes infuriated the provinces, and the most prosperous, not surprisingly, proved the most reluctant to part with their newfound authority. By mid-decade a good half of all Mexican provinces were either up in arms or nearly so.[3]

Integrally linked to these internal political developments was the Texas problem. When Anglo settlers in Texas rebelled in early 1836, Mexico conscripted peasants from the four corners of the republic in an effort to reclaim its defiant province. To do so it tapped into local militias known as the active battalions. Despite their dynamic name, the active battalions had before independence typically consisted of a landowner-officer and his peons and clients; local units had functioned less as bulwarks of military readiness and more as a part of a neocolonial system for controlling men and labor. But all this began to change as centralist officials—both civilian and military—came to oversee a huge levy of rural manpower in the national army. Attempts to convert the active battalions into real fighting units failed to reclaim Texas, but they did bite deeply into the Yucatecan workforce.[4]

In the summer of 1836 news of Santa Anna's loss and capture in Texas inspired Yucatán's first serious revolt under the leadership of an irascible merchant and property owner named Santiago Imán y Villafaña. The uprising initially faltered but got its second wind in 1838 as attempts to reconquer Texas once more caused a massive dragooning of provincials. This time Imán took steps to develop a popular base by promising to liberate Maya peasants from the hated church taxes known as obventions. This platform proved the magic formula that had previously eluded him, and within a year Imán and his followers managed to expel the Mexican army from the peninsula.[5]

At first all was joy. Imán himself said nothing about independence—his idea of liberation was simply to run out centralist *políticos* and military officers and stop the draft—but Mérida's opportunistic political class stepped in. The urban gentry that supported federalism had been too weak and disconnected from the peasantry to take the measures Imán had, but Imán's victory emboldened them, and in order to make the Yucatecan secession stick they set about harassing their centralist opponents out of office and out of the peninsula. Quickly setting up a provisional government, they proclaimed independence on the morning of May 16, 1841, a proclamation accompanied by a constitution, a flag, anthems, and other requisite trappings of nationalism.[6]

But Yucatán's euphoria over its independence concealed intractable problems. The new republic worked from a limited resource base, while manufacturing remained almost entirely artisanal (a famous cotton mill being the exception that proved the rule).[7] As B. A. Norman, a New Orleans book dealer who visited the peninsula in 1842, remarked, Yucatán possessed no mineral wealth, little variety in agriculture, no rivers, and few adequate roads.[8] Literacy remained confined to a handful of elites; indeed, only a small percentage of the population spoke Spanish, and most Maya peasants harbored an instinctive distrust of Hispanics and urbanites. Norman's remarks on the perils of secession proved prescient, even if his home state of Louisiana repeated the same mistake nineteen years later, in 1861. More prophetic still was Norman's warning that the upheavals of secession could spark an uprising among the Maya underclasses. Indeed, although not evident during the euphoria of national birth, the dynamics of secession led the peninsula directly into a violence that took Yucatecans forty years to suppress. Leaders fell victim to that paranoia common to victorious separatists and revolutionaries. They immediately launched a campaign to root out enemies in the peninsula and intimidated, imprisoned, or expelled anyone who expressed public opposition to the break from Mexico.[9] Not surprisingly, many of these opponents were clergy, and the 1841 Constitution imposed restrictions on church power far exceeding anything found in the mother republic. Church taxes were abolished, along with the *fueros*, or special court privileges, that priests had enjoyed in Spain since medieval times. The separatists' belief that there was a fifth column had some foundation, but their harsh display of political intolerance, which helped set the tone for civil war, was also payback for the centralists' ostracizing of the peninsula in 1835. Fearful Yucatecans also launched an armaments campaign that brought in rifles, munitions, and thousands of cannon balls from such places as Spain, France, and the United States.[10] Campeche's arms and cannon foundry, closed since late colonial times, now reopened for business.[11] Those living in the southeast strengthened their ties with contraband arms smugglers in British Honduras. Finally, Yucatán did away with the hated active battalions but replaced them with defense militias under the command of local planters. All these tendencies fed political intolerance, military mobilization, and subregional power struggles.

Mexico and Yucatán soon came to blows over secession, but unlike the United States in its civil war, Mexico failed miserably in its plan of reconquest. Mexico shared many of the same structural weaknesses of its renegade province, only on a grander scale. The brief economic buoyancy of the years 1841–44 misled Santa Anna into imagining he was in a stronger position than he really was. Beneath the surface lay numerous problems: unstable currency, inadequate financial institutions, ethnic division, a weak manufacturing sector, and poor educational and transportation infrastructures. Though Mexico enjoyed a far greater tax base and pool of draftable men than Yucatán, its advantages over the separatists were more apparent than real.

The Mexican army arrived at the island of Carmen, off the Yucatecan Republic's west tip, in September 1842 in numbers that would reach six thousand, but a typhus epidemic seriously weakened their force. Many had died in route and were buried at sea. Survivors remained prostrate in makeshift hospital wards on the island. Mexico's limited naval capacity made it impossible to blockade the Yucatecan coast (in fact, during the 1842 invasion Mexicans had to contract British merchant vessels to transport their troops). More dangerous than typhus were the misconceptions that Mexicans brought with them. Misled by the reports of conservative observers (particularly Mexico's consul in Cuba, who witnessed the early euphoria of independence), the invaders expected a large and enthusiastic fifth column to welcome their overthrow of the essentially liberal separatists.[12] Mexican generals also bought into the stereotype of Yucatecan debt slavery and imagined that the Maya peasants would receive them as liberators. Neither expectation proved correct. Instead of inspiring a popular reunification, Mexican officers found themselves leading sick and dispirited troops through a harsh terrain devoid of resources and support.[13]

Mexican operations on the Campeche coast quickly bogged down. The determined Yucatecans proved more resourceful than the Mexicans had anticipated in mobilizing both men and resources. Peasants not only failed to support the invasion but, in fact, encouraged by their gains under Santiago Imán, formed militias in hopes of making still greater advances once the war had ended. The state had scant liquidity but offered to reward soldiers, officers, and financial backers with grants of public land. And while both sides suffered frightful desertion rates, it was easier for Yucatecans to dragoon new conscripts from among its own people. Stymied, the Mexicans gambled on a stratagem. They left one group near Campeche and sent a second force to sail northeastward around the Yucatecan coast, the idea being that the second force would make a drive toward Mérida from the north of the peninsula. But the plan soon went awry. Yucatecans conducted a scorched-earth campaign that denied the invaders resources. They poisoned wells and emptied the villages of all but old men. As the ill-fed units marched toward Mérida they found themselves harassed by small bands of partisans, many recruited from the eastern part of the peninsula. Two months of this was all Matías de la Peña, the general leading the forces, could stand, and in May he found himself forced to negotiate extremely humiliating terms of withdrawal. The Yucatecans had seceded, and unlike separatists in other Mexican provinces, they alone had made it stick.

Smarting from military defeat, the central republic reopened diplomatic channels and showed itself to be far more flexible. Yucatecan statesmen, conversely, drove a flinty bargain. They insisted on the legitimacy of the 1840 separation and their subsequent military actions and argued that the lack of internal uprisings during the 1843 defense offered proof of Yucatecan unanimity (a statement that within four years would prove to be utterly falsified). From a southeastern point of view, the basic problem was that Mexico's governing document, the highly conservative Bases Orgánicas, set the property-requirement bar too high to allow for regional elites' participation. Few had the amount of *capitalinos* needed, and provincial leaders were thus forced downward into the same uncomfortable cellar as the Mexico City poor.[14] Moreover, the problem of military conscription continued to fester. Not only did Yucatecans and other provincials resent being drafted for service in the Texas wars; they also hated being impressed into the Mexican Navy, notorious for its low pay, awful food, and institutionalized brutality. If there were to be Yucatecan soldiers, the idea ran, then better to let them guard the peninsula itself. Yucatecan secession was also a project of Yucatán's liberal vanguard, many of whom had come to resent the priesthood for its economic privileges. Mindful of their own need for peasant labor, the new statesmen feared that Mexico's overtly proclerical tendencies would mean a peasant diaspora into the forests and remote hinterlands.[15] Finally, Yucatecans insisted that in the proposed reunification Yucatán would be an ally of Mexico, not a *departamento* or state, and as such, the Yucatecans would have no obligation to cover either military expenses or the cost of maintaining the national senate.[16] In sum, Yucatán was proposing little more than a trade arrangement between essentially sovereign powers, a framework for near-total autonomy. Mexico capitulated on all these terms; with political conflict simmering in some dozen other provinces, there was little choice.[17]

THE DESCENT INTO VIOLENCE

The República de Yucatán's downward spiral into civil war followed directly from the 1843 victory. Warfare is expensive, and in those days Yucatán suffered from dire poverty. Far from rivaling King Cotton, the peninsula's assortment of cattle, sugar, and henequen fiber exports did not even rank as minor nobility. The empty treasury meant that the state had to pay would-be defenders with promises of public land. This problem, coupled with disputes over who would represent local leadership in the new order, generated considerable internal conflict. Under such conditions, the claims of Yucatecan unity proved a tissue of lies. Indeed, even before Mexican sails ever appeared over the horizon, a series of subregional revolts had racked the peninsula. For example, an 1841 revolt centered in the southern town of Tekax appears to have been a gamble for greater local control of land and tax revenues.[18] The most important revolt took the form of an attempt to protect corrupt eastern officials from being prosecuted for embezzling money during the Mexican invasion. The revolt failed but rehearsed almost point for point the coming Caste War, in which prominent Hispanic conspirators would mobilize Maya clients in the area from Valladolid to Tihosuco.[19] Thus beneath claims of sovereignty lay deep subregional and ethnic conflicts that the recent secession wars had stoked and encouraged.

In 1846 Zachary Taylor brought U.S. troops to Mexican soil, and in so doing reawakened the demons of federalism. Fearful of the deepening U.S. naval blockade of Mexican ports and resentful of Mérida control, leaders in Campeche launched their own rebellion in December 1846. This time the proseparatist conflict meshed with deeply rooted caudillo politics, and each side had its own strongman, regional base, and economic agenda. Campeche-based Santiago Méndez represented Campeche interests and was more stridently separatist owing to Campeche's vulnerable position as a port. Miguel Barbachano, Méndez's rival, spoke for the Mérida crowd, northwestern exporters to the Cuban market, and the expanding southern sugar economy. Yucatecan elites squared off through rival armed bands, but far more importantly, for the first time violence fell on Maya caciques, posing a serious threat to a colonial order that for three centuries had kept the peace, or at least something resembling it.[20] Campechanos won the contest by February, but Yucatán never recovered from this fratricidal episode, which exceeded all others for bloodletting.

Yucatecans managed to escape a U.S. invasion but ended up with something far worse: a race war that in turn spawned social and economic chaos and fomented a raft of rebellions and civil war. The Caste War emerged out of a series of cabals that cannot be precisely reconstructed. Essentially, it grew from an eastern revolt of a line of communities that enjoyed a separate economic and social network and that were deeply engaged in a smuggling trade with British Honduras. The 1840s had been a time of great promise for prominent Mayas. They had shared in the prosperity of the sugar and smuggling economy. But the violence of the same period, together with the difficulty of dealing with the unstable tax base and the shrinking reserve of public land, led a certain number of Maya headmen to dissociate themselves from their Hispanic partners and to contemplate an ethnic uprising. The aims of the original Caste War fighters remain uncertain, and doubtless the participants weren't sure either. The original motivation was probably the leaders' desire to redress recent abuses of political violence and aggressive Hispanic usurpation of local politics and economy, but these leaders' appeals to the peasant masses also awoke ancient racial hatreds. Hispanics' attempts to suppress the early uprising in turn fanned what began as limited conflict into a full-scale ethnic uprising.

Historians both popular and academic have exaggerated the Maya rebels' success. Legends notwithstanding, they came nowhere close to expelling Hispanics from the peninsula, and within six months the movement had already overextended itself. Only the chaos and incompetence of the Yucatecan state, together with sheer racial panic, concealed rebel weaknesses and inflated rebel gains. The state ultimately beat back disintegrating Maya forces, but they managed to survive in the south and southeast, where they drew strength from the poorly watered and deeply wooded terrain, the availability of British arms, and the encouragement of an ad hoc oracle, the famous Speaking Cross that preached inevitable victory and a war to their enemy's death.[21] At the same time, campaigns to suppress the rebels produced a group of military officers that existed as a virtual caste and that garnered both wealth and social prestige through leadership in the various campaigns. Between 1853 and 1876 the military caste launched at least a dozen revolts and small-scale civil wars.

Violence infiltrated virtually every aspect of life during these hard years. The first casualty was state solvency, because the Caste War seriously disrupted agriculture, commerce, and the raising of revenues. The war also caused a rapid military expansion that drained the few resources then available. To make ends meet the still-sovereign Yucatecan Republic resorted to a variety of desperate stratagems, allowing military officers to claim pacified territory and granting them power to control the labor of dislocated noncombatants. Funds for soldiers' pay quickly ran dry, and the state compensated by allowing enlisted men to claim abandoned goods like tools and furniture. This too proved insufficient in a world beset by material scarcity, and during the entirety of the Caste War, loan sharks known as *agiotistas* accompanied the troops. These unscrupulous individuals gleaned large profits from the war, as did quartermasters and finance ministers who learned to skim funds from the payrolls. Insolvency perpetuated violence by giving ambitious officers reason to revolt. It also created unhappy troops, who remained susceptible to promises by those same officers, and it depleted army ranks through chronic desertion, thus preventing the formation of a military force strong enough to quash the ethnic rebellions and civil wars.

The mayhem of the Yucatecan Republic also generated a population diaspora. A handful of planters and *políticos* relocated to places like New Orleans and Havana, but a far greater number of people remained internal refugees. Many eastern Hispanic families fled to Mérida or to west coast communities such as Campeche, Calkiní, and Champotón.[22] Some relocated to islands like Holbox, Cozumel, and Isla Mujeres, creating island communities where none had existed before.[23] Another group crossed the southern border. The first of these, a group composed primarily of southeastern Hispanic elites but that also included a good number of Maya milpa farmers, settled in northern British Honduras, around Corozal, Orange Walk, and Punta Consejos. Here they attempted to re-create their old lives, complete with sugar cane farming, Catholicism, and bullfights, but found that British Honduras's social structure and poorly developed system of internal controls limited their ability to install peonage. The

British Honduran refugee communities also carried on a love-hate relationship with Maya rebels to the north, trading with warlords in good times but finding themselves vulnerable to retribution when those same warlords thought themselves cheated or victims of conspiracy.[24] Further to the west, a large group of Maya refugees settled in the Petén district of Guatemala, a land where peasant farmers could live untroubled by the demands of either church or state.[25]

Still another type of violence was the harm done to human knowledge. The war destroyed most paperwork in the south and east, the only exceptions being documents that had already been sent to Mérida. Church records, censuses, town council reports, notarized papers, all of which might have shed more light on the origins of Yucatán's secessionist movement and its subsequent descent into chaos, not to mention, on a more personal level, such quotidian landmarks as birth and marriage records—all were lost. For an entire generation it became virtually impossible to prove who was married to whom, how old anyone was, or who owed debts to whom. The price of secession ultimately was a Yucatán that for the next half century abounded in imposters of various stripes, including ersatz priests, bogus diplomats, wandering con men, and forgers of money, debt vouchers, and land titles.

Secession came to its anticlimactic conclusion with reunification in 1848. There was no bargaining now, no dissenting opinions, or profound philosophical differences, as there was in 1843. Yucatán had grown so desperate for aid that it was willing to return to Mexico under almost any terms. Fortunately for the wayward peninsulars, Mexico itself was in no condition to punish. The Treaty of Guadalupe-Hidalgo stripped it of 40 percent of national territory and threw central politics into a profound crisis. But, by the same token, Mexico could not provide much help, either. The larger republic was virtually prostrate, while its military resources remained dedicated to suffocating rebellions and uprisings that had exploded in the wake of the U.S. occupation. The best that Mexico had to offer was a series of generals who dedicated as much time to dabbling in local politics as to fighting rebellious Mayas. For all these reasons, the three decades following reunification were every bit as troubled as the period during which the Yucatecan Republic existed.

Reunification witnessed the peninsula's dismemberment. Mexico supported Campeche's 1857 separation from Yucatán, in no small part as a way of keeping former secessionists divided. Even the destruction in 1867 of the tragicomic French Empire, whose representatives had reached Yucatán by late 1863, did not bring peace. The empire had foundered on its pledge to win the Caste War once and for all, and even the postimperial years remained a time of banditry, military revolt, and comeback attempts by unrepentant supporters of Maximilian, Mexico's French-imposed "emperor."[26] During the last three decades of the nineteenth century, Yucatán went from being the nation's poorest state to being its richest, the result of an international boom in henequen fiber, which was used to service the mechanized wheat industry of the North American Great Plains.[27] Fearing the return of a too powerful sister republic, the dictator Porfirio Díaz assigned the reconquest of the eastern territories (1898–1901) to federal troops and saw to it that the new province of Quintana Roo, together with its wealth of chicle and lumber, remained in metropolitan (and foreign) hands.[28] Although the peninsula as a whole demonstrates profound similarities of culture, language, and family networks to this day, the once-sizeable Yucatecan Republic was never to return.

YUCATÁN AND THE ANTEBELLUM SOUTH: A COMPARATIVE PERSPECTIVE

The Yucatecan Republic constitutes the longest-lived (one hesitates to use the word "successful") secessionist movement in the history of Mexico. Following the centralist coup of the mid-1830s, a series of ephemeral republics emerged characterized as much by inadequate resources as by poor planning and execution. Most of the supposed separations were more bargaining positions than real efforts at state-building. In this group we can place the comically short-lived Republic of Durango, which played out its national existence in less than a week in October 1841.[29] Zacatecas presented a more serious challenge, owing to its prosperity from silver mining. The list might also include the Texas movement, even though to some degree it was a land grab by an alien people, not a political schism originating among people of a shared culture. Given its size and centrality in Mexican history, then, it is safe to assume that the history of the Yucatecan Republic has something to say about secession in general. One way of answering the question of what that is is to compare the Yucatecan secession with its counterpart, the ill-fated Confederate States of America.

Both the early republics of Mexico and the United States embraced political ideals that they were not prepared to carry out in practice. Most obviously, the early United States suffered from the problem of slavery: how was it that slaves, who were all too evidently human, came to be excluded from ideals of life, liberty, and the pursuit of happiness? Mexicans too had their unresolved contradictions. True, they abolished slavery in 1829, by which time it was largely a dead institution. But peonage and state-sanctioned drafts of Indian labor were far cheaper, and though it would be intellectually indiscriminate to categorize peonage as slavery, the two did share some family resemblances. Both systems generated a culture strongly disdainful of labor. Moreover, both the U.S. and Mexican social orders acquired strong moral economies that outlived the legal trappings of the institution. And although Mexican political documents spoke of citizenship and equality, in people's hearts a caste system and colonial hierarchy persisted. Early Latin America's constitutions and legal frameworks functioned more as a way of perpetuating oligarchic privilege than abolishing it.

Both Yucatán and the antebellum South were lesser developed, largely agricultural regions; and, as events were to show, they lacked the wherewithal to maintain their independence. Although in 1821 it was the largest state in Mexico, Yucatán had neither the population density, urban concentration, market abundance, or print culture of the center. Manufacturing and even artisan production paled in comparison to that of other regions. Yucatecan and southern politics alike operated within a democratic framework, but each made participating in that democracy subject to certain preconditions strongly linked to issues of land and labor control often characteristic of lesser developed regions. Planters exercised greater control in Yucatán than in the antebellum South, and while both Hispanic and Maya adult males voted, balloting was indirect (male voters elected electors, who tended to be clients of powerful individuals). Moreover, economic factors bound lower-class electoral decisions to the interests of their land-owning and money-lending patrons. Participation was somewhat broader in the South, owing to the presence of small freeholders and the absence of the profound linguistic and cultural barriers endemic to postcolonial Mexico. Still, a shared vision of racial superiority connected southern oligarchs and poor whites and helped the landowning class guide their at times antidemocratic agenda through a system of limited democratic participation.[30]

Both underwent independence processes that led them to conceive of an expanded federalism as the logical consequence of independence. Mexican federalist politics traced preexisting forms of organization; holdovers from the colonial period included tax districts, militia service, and political representation in the form of provincial elites. Greater provincial decision making also represented a more explicit reversal of policy under Spanish imperialism—what was the point of breaking with Spain, only to re-create the same relationship with Mexico City?[31] Not surprisingly, then, both Yucatán and the antebellum South felt slighted by rule from without. Governance had always been concentrated in Mexico City, even in pre-Columbian times. Yucatecans persistently saw themselves as victims of trade restriction and of import tariffs for Yucatecan sugar. On almost any issue, the presecessionists found themselves politically outflanked and outnumbered.

Hemispheric geographical realignments also affected the secession processes in Mexico and the United States, although in somewhat different ways. Earlier Mexican secessionism was triggered by the related and twin crises of centralist takeover and the loss of Texas, together with subsequent attempts to regain that lost territory. The 1846 U. S. naval blockade precipitated the last pre–Caste War rebellion, which proved to be the most powerful catalyst to a rural violence— and for the first time explicitly interethnic violence—that the Caste War merely amplified. Similarly, the national challenges that prompted Confederate seces- sion spun out of the 1848 acquisition of two-fifths of Mexican territory, for that acquisition reawakened the issue of slavery vs. free soil. The Compromise of 1850 postponed the crisis, but it also enabled ten years of northern industrial- ization and growth. At the same time, the deal's endorsement of popular sov- ereignty (soon to be violently enacted in the Kansas territories) and its fugitive slave law fostered future controversy.

Yucatecans and Confederates suffered reunifications that were in some ways disappointing or punitive and designed to weaken regional power as a hedge against future secessions. The American South became an investment target for wealthy northern interests (much like Mexico itself in the nineteenth century's final quarter). In southeast Mexico, however, the losses were more self-inflicted. Here secession had a domino effect (a recurring fear of the Confederacy itself). During the ensuing Caste War, Yucatán lost Campeche, as well as the territory that later became the state of Quintana Roo. Lesser known, however, is that at various points in the 1840s the southern part of Yucatán, clustered around the city of Tekax, sought to break away as well.

But if there were underlying similarities between early national Mexico and the antebellum South, there were also defining differences. To begin with, the secession crisis happened sooner in Mexico. This was a direct function of the greater poverty of the former Spanish colony but was also related to its relatively static population. Rather than migrate in search of better opportunities, Mexico's people tended to remain glued to their place of birth. Northern Mexico was more arid than the western territories of the early American republic, and following the wars of 1836 and 1846–48, there was a lot less of it. Ancient practices of commu- nal land rights, together with a more feudalistic ethos overall and a strong ethnic "rootedness" to place of birth, discouraged geographical mobility. In contrast, western expansion provided a critical option for the early United States, up to a point, at least, allowing Union control over the fundamental resource of land.

This precocity of rebellion seems odd when one considers that there was greater homogeneity between Mexico's center and its southeastern periphery than between the U.S. North and South. The North was dominated by religiously motivated communities of individual farms and trading concerns; the South, by contrast, was more akin to Latin America, where colonial settlements were economic projects, runoff systems for social undesirables, and as time went by, became agroexport economies based on coerced labor. In Mexico, the center and the southeast shared similar origins: they were both Hispanic-dominated tributary societies molded by conquest. Debt peonage was standard practice in both regions. What separated Mexico and Yucatán was that they had different indigenous cultures (Nahua vs. Maya) and that Yucatán was geographically isolated compared to Mexico and was much poorer than Mexico. Regarding Yucatán's poverty, it was the absence of mining and agricultural wealth that perpetuated tributary relationships far longer there than in central Mexico. Beyond these shades of difference, no fundamental cause existed to unify southeastern elites by pitting them against national counterparts.

This absence of underlying ideological divide related directly to another point: the striking silence of Yucatecan ideologues and the nonexistence of incendiary writings. Here there were no fire-eaters, no *De Bow's Review*, no corps of propagandists and pamphleteers who inflamed public opinion.[32] Santiago Imán himself penned no manifestos and seems to have been more interested in practicing his brand of cowboy revolt than in promulgating any sort of political theory. In no small part, this was a product of the lower literacy of Mexican society. No more than 5 percent of the southeast could read at the time of secession, and printing presses had only been introduced twenty-four years earlier. But the rhetorical muteness also points to fundamental continuities of thought and social practice throughout early national Mexico. Even those literary journals that did exist in the 1840s, such as the *Registro yucateco* or the *Mosaico*, concerned themselves mostly with explorations of regional history and culture, not independence.

Internal fragmentation tore more deeply at the Yucatecan project. The antebellum South never suffered significant divisions of class, regionalism, personal ambition, and ideological hue, no doubt owing to the fact that secession there remained more or less confined to its original project, again owing in large part to the binding ideology of slavery.[33] In Mexico, secession went beyond its original intention and degenerated into ethnic violence and separatism. Prior to the spring of 1848, Yucatán demonstrated less unity than the more geographically and politically diverse Confederacy. As is well known, early Mexico suffered from significant transportation problems. Rivers were few, and most pre-Hispanic settlements were settled according to access to rain-fed lands or natural wells; pre-Hispanic cities later became Hispanic ones. No rivers (or subsequent canals) connected provinces, and there were no railroads to speak of until the 1880s. The dynamic of secession in Mexico thus had a more decentralized and fragmenting cast than it did in the American South. Even adjoining provinces like Yucatán and Tabasco failed to create a unified front against Mexico, one of the reasons for the failure of their secessionist projects. Antebellum southerners did a somewhat better job of holding their society intact, but they too faced a certain amount of dissension: the border slave states of Maryland, Missouri, and Kentucky remained with the Union, while slave resistance and political discontent on the part of poor whites posed significant problems to the Confederate cause throughout the Civil War.[34]

Many differences between the U.S. South and Yucatán traced back to the matter of ethnic composition and mobilization. Spanish colonialism almost invariably Catholicized and incorporated native peoples of its far-flung empire, establishing with them a relationship that was oddly protective and exploitative at the same time. This resulted in a complex and highly unequal caste system in which each ethnic group had its own rights and responsibilities. Mexico entered its national period with the caste system's colonial safeguards and corporate identities relatively intact. Maya peasants constituted the vast majority. Even cities had a significant Maya underclass. And from the late 1600s onward, Maya populations had begun to grow, straining thereby old colonial systems of governance and land usage.

Given the paucity of Hispanic political elites and the abundance of disfranchised Maya farmers, the Yucatecan Republic found itself forced to depend on ethnic militias. No matter how statesmen wrote the rules, prohibitions on Indian service consistently fell by the wayside, even in the days of the Spanish. Southern secessionists, on the other hand, generally opposed the idea of slaves with weapons, and for the obvious reasons. The South *overall* had a slave minority, with majorities only in Mississippi and South Carolina. Rendered into commodities that serviced the expanding capitalist agricultural empire of cotton, sugar, and tobacco, slaves had far more reason to turn on their masters than did the still largely free peasants of southeast Mexico. For this reason, nearly half of the South's male population remained excluded from military service, and even in the last, desperate days of the Confederacy, the many ill-conceived plans to admit black soldiers to the ranks never got off the drawing board.[35]

The Confederacy's own brief history ended with military defeat and a humiliating surrender, followed by a conflictive period of occupation. In large part, this owed to the presence of the Union army, for although the southern planter class managed to reclaim much of its social ascendency over freedmen and a discontented lower class, the presence of occupational soldiers still generated resentment.[36] The victorious Union had far greater power to impose its political vision than did central Mexico, which was itself mired in chaos and lacked a communications and transportation infrastructure and where the civilian political structure exercised only nominal control over an ambitious military. Mexico's prolonged (1854–76) fall into civil wars and foreign occupation meant that for Yucatán the reunification process, while hardly eliminating internal conflict, was relatively uncontroversial. Yucatecan elites were discount versions of their central Mexican counterparts, but the reestablishment of law and order took place under Yucatecan supervision, not that of an occupying army. Nothing resembling Reconstruction took place until 1915, when the revolutionary army of General Salvador Alvarado entered the peninsula. Alvarado abolished debt peonage, attacked the power of the Catholic Church, took control of the henequen purchasing houses, channeled funds to socially constructive measures such as schools and hospitals, and encouraged the formation of popular political organizations. His efforts resulted in the same mixed legacy as southern Reconstruction and inspired the same sort of (distorted) black legend that redeemer historians pinned to the period of Union occupation.[37]

If the brief, glorious history of the Yucatecan Republic teaches anything, it is the fragility of early national Latin America's first nation-states. Poor transportation over an often forbidding topography separated province from province; the colonial caste system made it difficult to enact uniform laws; a decade of independence wars wreaked havoc on economies; and lack of experience in self-government translated into political institutions that often collapsed under pressure. But the southeastern story also points to another lesson: the fragility of the secessions movements themselves. Indeed, despite Yucatán, Texas, and a dozen other lesser cases, the bulk of Mexico managed to cohere. The limited potency of separatism in what is generally recognized as a society of weak states seems odd, but at least three considerations help clarify the picture. First, if states were weak, provinces like Yucatán were weak in corresponding measure. Second, the two and a half centuries of Aztec hegemony, followed by three more centuries of Spanish colonialism, had introduced a certain commonality of thought and practice among the people of Mesoamerica. A third, and perhaps more important, check on secession, derived from the often ethnically based class divisions of the society. Though abolished on paper, the Latin American caste system still reigned in most people's hearts, and widespread acceptance of the idea of different races with correspondingly different rights and privileges hamstrung attempts to develop nation-states. Hispanic elites who propounded secession found themselves in the bind of Latin America's early independence leaders: how was it possible for a tiny class of elites to raise the huge ethnic underclass without themselves falling victim to popular rage, like the French planter of the Americas' *other* eighteenth-century secessionist movement, the Haitian revolution?[38] It was no accident, then, that early national Mexico's largest Indian uprising scotched its most developed separatist movement.

The relationship between the provinces and the center after the turmoil of the first half of the nineteenth century was not necessarily hostile or unhappy. Mexico's hand over late nineteenth- and early twentieth-century peninsular affairs remained light. Privileged Yucatecans resented the imposition of revolutionary programs, but many other southeasterners thrilled to the idea of destroying the colonial fetters of the hacienda and the de facto mechanisms that kept Maya-speaking peoples away from power. And while hardly a racial paragon, modern-day Yucatán, like the contemporary United States, proves the degree to which determined federal policy, applied with consistency across successive administrations, can help reduce racial hatreds and inequalities. Perhaps the greatest proof of union's advantages came in the 1970s and 1980s. When another nearby country with a Maya peasant majority—Guatemala—fell victim to levels of violence and genocide unimaginable to the nineteenth-century caste warriors, Yucatán remained peaceful and in fact experienced considerable social advances in virtually all areas.

What ghostly remains of the Yucatecan Republic still flicker in the present day? Talk of secession enjoyed a brief if ersatz renaissance in the early twentieth century, when a momentary boom in henequen fiber catapulted Yucatán to riches. This rhetoric's real intent was to stave off revolutionary land redistributions and modification of the debt peonage system that assured a cheap and pliant workforce. But the collapse of global henequen markets from the 1920s onward led to profound economic stagnation that persists to this day, the extent of which is made all the more apparent when juxtaposed against industrial surges in central and northern Mexico. In this sense, secession seems even less viable now than when B. A. Norman wrote his pessimistic prognosis 150 years ago. The development of transportation and communication infrastructures may not have stripped Yucatecans of their unique identity, but they have helped dissipate dreams of going it alone. The republic did leave at least one legacy, however, and that was a profound sense of difference on the part of Yucatecans themselves. Even today, the term *hermana república* ("sister republic") occasionally crops up, warming the hearts of southeasterners and stirring consternation among Mexico City statesmen. But until the day that southeasterners discover some new source of wealth, reject the unifying force of national media, and find a compelling reason to sunder old political bonds, the República de Yucatán seems destined to exist only as a bumper sticker on the automobiles of Mérida's upper-middle-class suburbs.

Notes

I would like to thank Don Doyle for his generous invitation to participate in the secession symposium in Charleston, South Carolina, in December 2007. This chapter greatly benefited from comments and suggestions that I received in a subsequent workshop held in Athens, Georgia, in June 2008.

1. Regarding the Yucatecan role in Mexican independence, see Justo Sierra O'Reilly, *Los indios de Yucatán: Consideraciones históricas sobre la influencia del elemento indígena en la organización social del país*, 2 vols. (Mérida: Compañía Tipográfica Yucateca, 1954); Terry Rugeley, *Yucatán's Maya Peasantry and the Origins of the Caste War, 1800–1847* (Austin: University of Texas Press, 1996), chap. 2; and Melchor Campos García, *Que los yucatecos todos proclamen su independencia* (Mérida: Universidad Autónoma de Yucatán, 2002).

2. See Terry Rugeley, *Of Wonders and Wise Men: Religion and Popular Cultures in Southeast Mexico, 1800–1876* (Austin: University of Texas Press, 2001), chap. 3. The remark about hothouse lifestyles comes from Methodist missionary Alfredo Giolma. See Wesleyan Methodist Missionary Society Archives, Oct. 29, 1868, Corozal (a portion of this letter is reproduced in Terry Rugeley, *Maya Wars: Ethnographic Accounts of Nineteenth-Century Yucatán* [Norman: University of Oklahoma Press, 2001], 115–16).

3. On the centralist takeover, see Michael P. Costeloe, *The Central Republic in Mexico, 1835–1846: Hombres de Bien in the Age of Santa Anna* (Cambridge: Cambridge University Press, 1993), chaps. 2 and 3, and Timothy E. Anna, *Forging Mexico, 1821–1835* (Lincoln: University of Nebraska Press, 1998), 246–68.

4. On the Texas secession movement, see Andrés Reséndez, *Changing National Identities at the Frontier: Texas and New Mexico, 1800–1850* (Cambridge: Cambridge University Press, 2003); see also Reséndez's chapter in this volume.

5. On Imán's life, see also Rugeley, *Yucatán's Maya Peasantry and the Origins of the Caste War*, 116–45, and "Imán, Santiago," xi/iii/2–378, 1838–1839, ff. 32–38, and June 10, 1850, ff. 26–27, Archivo Histórico de la Defensa Nacional, Mexico City (hereafter AHDN). Other important material on the revolt is found in xi/481.3/1493 and xi/481.3/1546, 1838–40, AHDN.

6. This description of Yucatán's independence ceremonies comes from a letter by Mexico's consul in Cuba, xi/481.3/1690, July 26, 1841, ff. 628–38, AHDN.

7. Howard F. Cline, "The 'Aurora Yucateca' and the Spirit of Enterprise in Yucatan, 1821–1847," *Hispanic American Historical Review* 47, no. 1 (1947): 30–60.

8. B. A. Norman, *Rambles in Yucatan; or, Notes of Travel through the Peninsula, Including a Visit to the Remarkable Ruins of Chi-Chen Itaza, Kabah, Zayi, and Uxmal* (New York: J. and H. G. Langley, 1843), 233–34.

9. See Rugeley, *Yucatán's Maya Peasantry and the Origins of the Caste War*, chap. 5.

10. Poder ejecutivo 46, milicia, VI, 133, Mar. 24, 1841, Archivo General del Estado de Yucatán, Mérida (hereafter AGEY); poder ejecutivo 46, milicia, VI, 122, Nov. 30, 1841, AGEY; poder ejecutivo 46, milicia, V, 107, June 25, 1841, AGEY.

11. Poder ejecutivo 46, milicia, III, 55, Aug. 28, 1841, AGEY.

12. On the persecutions of reunionists, see the lengthy account by Mexico's consul in Cuba in xi/481.3/1690, July 1841, ff. 628–638, AHDN, and libro copiador del poder ejecutivo, correspondencia del gobernador, bk. 12, Mar. 15, 1842, 26, AGEY.

13. On the failed Mexican invasion, see Serapio Baqueiro, *Ensayo histórico sobre las revoluciones de Yucatán desde el año 1840 hasta 1864*, vol. 1 (Mérida: Manuel Heredia Argüelles, 1878), 79–120. To this we can add three lesser-known sources. The first is the report of Antonio López de Santa Anna to the Ministro de Guerra y Marina, xi/481.3/1992, May 30, 1853, AHDN, originally published in the *Diario del gobierno de la república mexicana*. The second is the report of General Matías de la Peña y Barragán, xi/481.3/1992, May 30, 1853, AHDN (also originally published in the *Diario*). The third and most complete is by General Manuel María Sandoval, xi/481.3/1986, Dec. 11, 1843, AHDN.

14. Much of our understanding of the Yucatecan-Mexican problem comes from "Carta del Gobernador de Yucatán Santiago Méndez al General Antonio López de Santa Anna, relativo a la incorporación de Yucatán a la nación mexicana," manuscripts, XXXVII, 002, Aug. 29, 1843, Centro de Apoyo a la Investigación Histórica de Yucatán, Mérida (hereafter CAIHY).

15. Again, see "Carta de Gobernador," manuscripts, XXXVII, 002, Aug. 29, 1843, CAIHY.

16. For the Yucatecan analysis of the situation, see Pantaleón Barrera, Isidro Rejón,

Joaquín Ruiz de León, and Crescencio Boves, "Observaciones sobre la actual situación política del Departamento de Yucatán," manuscripts, IV, 14, Nov. 26, 1845, CAIHY.

17. Costeloe, *The Central Republic in Mexico, 1835–1846*, 230.

18. Retrospective reports on the event can be found in poder ejectuivo 47, milicia, I, 37, Dec. 18, 1842, AGEY.

19. Hemeroteca Pino Suárez, *Siglo XIX*, Sept. 9, 1843, 4; Sept. 16, 1843, 4; and Dec. 9, 1843, 4.

20. Rugeley, *Yucatán's Maya Peasantry and the Origins of the Caste War*, 169–170.

21. Nelson Reed, *The Caste War of Yucatan* (Stanford: Stanford University Press, 1968); Ramón Berzunza Pinto, *Guerra social en Yucatán* (México: Costa-Amic, 1965); Don E. Dumond, *The Machete and the Cross: Campesino Rebellion in Yucatán* (Lincoln: University of Nebraska Press, 1997).

22. Poder ejecutivo 67, gobernación, jefetura política of Campeche, Apr. 30, 1848, AGEY; decretos y oficios, Sabancuy, Apr. 2, 1848, Archivo Histórico del Arzobispado de Yucatán (hereafter AHAY); poder ejecutivo 67, gobernación, jefetura política of Campeche, Apr. 18, 1848, AGEY; AGEY, poder ejecutivo 67, gobernación, correspondencia, Apr. 18, 1848, AGEY.

23. Poder ejecutivo 78, población, "Padrón que comprende todos los hombres que forman el pueblo de San Miguel en la isla de Cozumel," AGEY; poder ejecutivo 99, justicia, Juzgado de Mérida, Nov. 18, 1853, AGEY; poder ejecutivo 86, justicia, Juez de Paz de Dolores, Feb. 12, 1851, AGEY; poder ejecutivo 283, milicia, Sept. 15, 1893, Holbox, AGEY; Mar. 19, 1862, 73–75, Archivo Notarial del Estado de Yucatán, Mérida; poder ejecutivo 99, hacienda, "Explotación de guano," Sisal, misc. dates, 1854, AGEY.

24. Record 36, Dec. 30, 1850, 123–32, Belize Archives and Records Service, Belmopan; poder ejecutivo 101, gobernación, prefectura, Feb. 23, 1855, AGEY; British Foreign Office Records 39–5, Mar. 13, 1858, Bancroft Library, University of California, Berkeley.

25. Section B, legajo 28624, expediente 270, Dec. 5, 1870, and legajo 28594, expediente 1, Aug. 2, 1859, Archivo General de Centroamérica, Guatemala City.

26. For a detailed examination of national traumas that played out in the southeast, see Terry Rugeley, *Rebellion Now and Forever: Mayas, Hispanics, and Caste War Violence in Yucatán, 1800–1880* (Stanford: Stanford University Press, 2009).

27. Moisés González Navarro, *Raza y tierra: La guerra de castas y el henequén* (Mexico City: El Colegio de México, 1970); Allen Wells, *Yucatán's Gilded Age: Haciendas, Henequen, and International Harvester, 1860–1915* (Albuquerque: University of New Mexico Press, 1985); Allen Wells and Gilbert M. Joseph, *Summer of Discontent, Seasons of Upheaval: Elite Politics and Rural Insurgency in Yucatán, 1876–1915* (Stanford: Stanford University Press, 1996); Sterling Evans, *Bound in Twine: The History and Ecology of the Henequen-Wheat Complex for Mexico and the American and Canadian Plains, 1800–1950* (College Station: Texas A&M University Press, 2007).

28. Carlos Macías Richard, *Nueva frontera mexicana: Milicia, burocracia y ocupación territorial en Quintana Roo* (México: Universidad de Quintana Roo, 1997).

29. José de la Cruz Pacheco Rojas, *Breve historia de Durango* (México: Colegio de México, 2001), 149–50.

30. On southern oscillation between elitism and egalitarianism, see William W. Freehling, *The Road to Disunion*, 2 vols. (New York: Oxford University Press, 1990–2007), 1:39–58.

31. Anna's *Forging Mexico*, 34–70, explores many of the dynamics behind the federalist movement.

32. On the centrality of slavery to the ideological formation of southern politics, see William A. Link, *Roots of Secession: Slavery and Politics in Antebellum Virginia* (Chapel Hill: University of North Carolina Press, 2004).

33. Freehling, *The Road to Disunion*, vol. 1.

34. On the matter of slave and lower-class white resistance to the Confederacy, see Armstead L. Robinson, *Bitter Fruits of Bondage: The Demise of Slavery and the Collapse of the Confederacy, 1861–1865* (Charlottesville: University of Virginia Press, 2005), particularly chaps. 7–9.

35. On the many plans for black Confederate units, see Bruce Levine, *Confederate Emancipation: Southern Plans to Free and Arm Slaves during the Civil War* (New York: Oxford University Press, 2006).

36. Take, for example, the case of Louisiana, in Rebecca J. Scott, *Degrees of Freedom: Louisiana and Cuba after Slavery* (Cambridge, Mass.: Harvard University Press, 2005), chaps. 2 and 3; on freedmen struggles to maintain and advance the gains of liberation, see Stephen Hahn, *A Nation under Our Feet: Black Political Struggles in the Rural South from Slavery to the Great Migration* (Cambridge, Mass.: Harvard University Press, 2003).

37. On the Alvarado period in Yucatán, see Gilbert M. Joseph, *Revolution from Without: Yucatán, Mexico and the United States, 1880–1924* (Cambridge: Cambridge University Press, 1982). For a treatment considerably more hostile to Alvarado, see Franco Savarino Roggero, *Pueblos y nacionalismo, del régimen oligárquico a la sociedad de masas en Yucatán, 1894–1925* (México: Instituto Nacional de Estudios Históricos de la Revolución Mexicana, 1997). On the matter of "redeemer" histories of southern Reconstruction, see Kenneth M. Stampp, "The Tragic Legend of Reconstruction," in *Reconstruction: An Anthology of Revisionist Writing*, ed. Kenneth M. Stampp and Leon F. Litwick (Baton Rouge: Louisiana State University Press, 1965), 3–21.

38. C. L. R. James, *The Black Jacobins: Toussaint L'Ouverture and the San Domingo Rebellion* (1938; rpt., New York: Vintage Books, 1989); Carolyn E. Fick, *The Making of Haiti: The Saint Domingue Revolution from Below* (Knoxville: University of Tennessee Press, 1990).

PART 4

European Separatism

Separatist Activities in Contemporary Europe

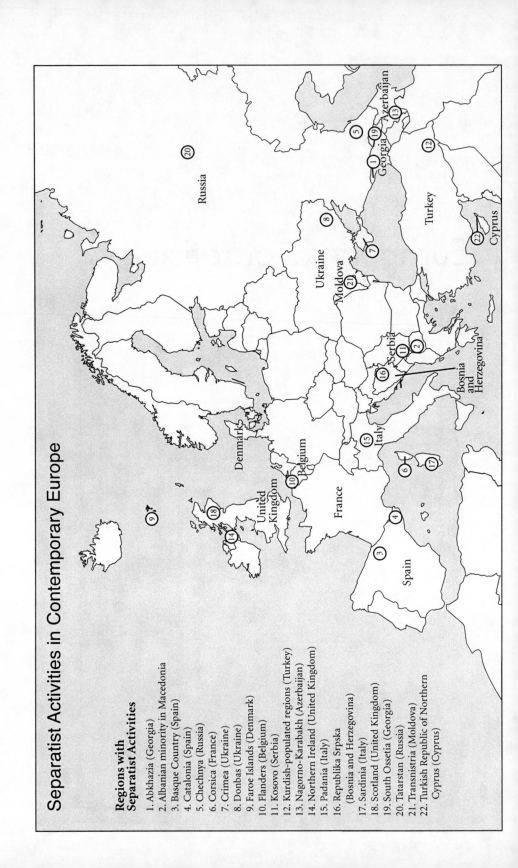

**Regions with
Separatist Activities**

1. Abkhazia (Georgia)
2. Albanian minority in Macedonia
3. Basque Country (Spain)
4. Catalonia (Spain)
5. Chechnya (Russia)
6. Corsica (France)
7. Crimea (Ukraine)
8. Donbas (Ukraine)
9. Faroe Islands (Denmark)
10. Flanders (Belgium)
11. Kosovo (Serbia)
12. Kurdish-populated regions (Turkey)
13. Nagorno-Karabakh (Azerbaijan)
14. Northern Ireland (United Kingdom)
15. Padania (Italy)
16. Republika Srpska
    (Bosnia and Herzegovina)
17. Sardinia (Italy)
18. Scotland (United Kingdom)
19. South Ossetia (Georgia)
20. Tatarstan (Russia)
21. Transnistria (Moldova)
22. Turkish Republic of Northern
    Cyprus (Cyprus)

BRUNO COPPIETERS

Secessionist Conflicts in Europe

Since the beginning of the twentieth century, all European states have in one way or another been confronted with secession. But the ways in which they have experienced secession are extremely varied. In the case of the European Union (EU), a number of its members (France, Britain, Italy, Spain, the Netherlands, Portugal, Belgium, and Germany) are former imperial powers, and the process of decolonizing their empires was often a violent one. Three European states (Ireland, Cyprus, and Malta) are former British colonies. Six of the ten states that joined the EU in 2004 are products of the dissolution of federal socialist states: the Czech and Slovak republics resulted from the dissolution of Czechoslovakia; the Baltic republics seceded from the Soviet Union; and Slovenia broke away from Yugoslavia. Some EU member states, such as Spain, Belgium, and the United Kingdom, are confronted with secessionist threats on their own territory. Since the fall of the Berlin Wall, meanwhile, the Federal Republic of Germany has gone through a process of state reunification.

This chapter analyzes the various secessionist conflicts in Europe and the various European responses to these conflicts. The chapter introduces the concept of a strategic culture relating to secession in order to provide a better understanding of the divergences between the EU's member states in their responses to the conflicts, either within their own territory or in other European states. Has, the chapter asks, a strategic EU culture relating to secession emerged, or is one emerging, that could support a common EU response to the division of nations and states?

An overview of secessionist conflicts in Europe must of necessity refer to U.S. policies on divided states and nations, which are important for two reasons. There is, first of all, the profound impact of the American Revolution and the U.S. Civil War on European discussions about the right to secession. The American disputes over federalism during the debate on the ratification of the U.S. Constitution in the 1780s also influenced debates in Europe. The vitriolic criticism of confederations to be found in *The Federalist Papers*, the replacement of the Articles of Confederation by the 1787 Constitution, and the outcome of the Civil War were among the ideological and historical factors that weakened the ideological appeal of decentralized confederations in Europe.[1]

The second way in which the United States influences European separatist conflicts has to do with its powerful role in post–World War II world affairs. The involvement of the United States in all security issues on the continent of Europe necessitates a clear U.S. position on all issues having to do with intrastate wars and the delimitation of international borders. The way the two security organizations—North Atlantic Treaty Organization (NATO) and Organization for Security and Cooperation in Europe (OSCE)—frame the question of European security illustrates the deep involvement of the United States. For example, the United States has led NATO in the Balkans, as its heading up of NATO's military interventions in Bosnia (1995) and Kosovo (1999) demonstrates. The American government gave effective support to Croatia in the military buildup that enabled it to destroy the breakaway Serb state of Krajina (1995). The United States has also participated in UN and OSCE mediation efforts in Nagorno-Karabakh, Abkhazia, South Ossetia, and Transnistria. The United States was, in addition, centrally involved in the facilitation of the Good Friday Agreement on Northern Ireland (1998) and it took a leading role in the diplomatic recognition of Kosovo's independence (2008).

There is a certain division of labor between the United States and the European Union with respect to secessionist conflicts. Some of these are addressed primarily, or even exclusively, by European diplomacy, but with American backing. The EU received full American support, for instance, in its policies of conflict prevention in Macedonia (which was confronted with the threat of secession by its Albanian minority). And it was clear to U.S. policy makers that a resolution of the Cyprus conflict would require the full integration of the island into the EU.

Individual states' views about the nation are determined by their diverse experiences. These experiences have shaped their positions on national identity and on the right of other nations to exist as sovereign states and are, furthermore, influential when it comes to the political recognition of new states. In 1991 and 1992, for instance, within the European Community Germany was a driving force in the process leading to the recognition of Slovenia, Croatia, and Bosnia. The right to national self-determination was central to all domestic dis-

courses on German unity, and this affected their Balkan policies, which significantly differed from those of some other EU members.[2]

Differences among member states came into the open in 2008 during discussions on Kosovo's unilateral declaration of independence (UDI). Spain,
Greece, Romania, Slovakia, and Cyprus were opposed to the establishment of
diplomatic relations with Pristina, but a large majority of EU member states—
a majority that totaled twenty-two in October 2009—were for it.[3] These five
countries are fearful that the recognition of Kosovo's UDI might strengthen separatist forces on their own territory or on the territory of a close ally—Greece
in the case of Cyprus, for example.

STRATEGIC CULTURES FRAMING POLICIES ON SECESSION

Nations thus have very diverse strategic cultures when it comes to secession.
The concept of "strategic culture" refers in this context to the ways nations perceive particular threats to the principle of territorial integrity or how they view
the right of a nation to constitute an independent state.[4] Each strategic culture
offers a particular interpretation of the principle of national self-determination.
Choices in policies on secession are made not on the basis of formalized doctrines but with the help of individual historical experiences. Institutional memories of past secessionist conflicts and their outcomes will guide a nation's selection of policy options from among various alternatives, and this selection
will be made in line with perceived state interests and national values. Political
leaders will reason by historical analogy to exclude particular strategies that
conflict with what they regard as state interests or national values or that are
associated with past failures. Such analogies with events from their national
past may also strengthen particular preferences, when these are in line with the
country's interests and accepted values. The strategic cultures framing European policies on secession are of necessity diverse, reflecting the great variety of
experiences in nation building and nation splitting.

Some states have a twofold historical experience with separatism. On the
one hand they achieved independence through popular mobilization against a
regime they considered oppressive, but on the other they have had to contend
with secessionist movements within their own territory. In many of these cases,
these secessionists accuse them of being oppressive as well. Belgium and Cyprus have had such a dual historical experience, as has the United States, whose

revolution was followed by a civil war. But the two European countries face threats of secession in the present, whereas the American Civil War has now become a distant historical memory.

In defining their policies on secessionist conflicts elsewhere, countries with a dual experience of secession may support secession in other countries by referring to the first type of experience, or they may condemn such attempts by reference to the second. Which of the two options they choose depends on a number of factors, such as the type of justification they used to advocate their own independence or have invoked to condemn secessionist attempts within their own territory, the strategic interests they have in a particular secessionist conflict, the ties they have with the parties in the conflict, and the consequences of such a conflict for their own domestic policies.

The references that the United States has had occasion to make to the protection of territorial integrity against separatism go back to the American Civil War. This is the historical analogy that sprang to mind for Bill Clinton at the Moscow summit of April 1996, when he had to comment on how Russia was dealing with separatism in Chechnya. The American President took the position that the conflict should be regarded as an "internal" Russian matter and that the military operation should be carried out as quickly as possible. President Clinton suggested a parallel between Boris Yeltsin's war against Chechnya and Abraham Lincoln's readiness to defend the territorial integrity of his country: "I would remind you that we once had a civil war in our country . . . over the proposition that Abraham Lincoln gave his life for—that no state had a right to withdrawal from our Union."[5]

In the case of Kosovo, the United State likewise drew lessons from its national past. In 2003, in a 4th of July speech, Reno L. Harnish, the American chief of mission in Pristina, drew a series of parallels between the difficulties faced by the Pristina political elites in forming a coherent leadership and the problems faced by the leaders of the American independence movement in establishing a united front on account of their differing political views. He argued that the Kosovar political elite should follow the example of the American founding fathers by attempting to compromise on difficult issues, such as building the national economy. Harnish made no direct reference to the right to secession—the speech was given in 2003, and it would be five more years before the United States officially recognized Kosovo's independence—but the historical link between the two independence movements was already clear to U.S. policy makers.[6]

Belgium and Cyprus likewise seceded themselves only to have separatist movements subsequently spring up within their territories. Unlike the United States, however, they have so far failed to resolve their domestic conflict over sovereignty. They thus have to take into account the potential consequences recognizing breakaway states might have for their own domestic conflicts. But this does not mean that both countries adopt the same policy on the recognition of new states. The case of Kosovo is illustrative in this respect. In February 2008, when the Belgian government had decided to recognize Kosovo's independence, Karel De Gucht, the minister for foreign affairs, drew a parallel with the secession of Belgium from the Netherlands in 1830. In this case too, independence was conceivable only as a unilateral move. He denied that the recognition of Kosovo may have negative repercussions with respect to Belgium's own internal conflicts over sovereignty.[7] The Belgian government assumed that it was far more important to secure stability in the Balkans by acting in accordance with the Kosovo policies adopted by its main Western allies.

A contrary position was then taken by Cyprus. This country has a firm anticolonial heritage borne of its struggle against the British. In the case of Kosovo, however, it remained adamantly opposed to recognition. From the Greek Cypriot perspective, the fear of creating a legal and political precedent prevailed over all else.

The manner in which the American, Belgian, and Greek Cypriot governments framed their positions on Chechnya and Kosovo demonstrates the way a dual experience of secession—both as political emancipation from foreign rule and as a threat to national unity—can be selectively mobilized depending on the particular interests and values the government is eager to defend.

THE VARIETY OF SECESSIONIST CONFLICTS AND POLICIES ON SECESSION

There are currently some twenty to twenty-five significant separatist movements in Europe seeking to break their territory away from the control of a central government. They are significant in the sense that central governments have to take them into account. Their importance can be measured by the number of votes they receive in elections, the potential they have to influence governmental policies, and their ability to use force or even to control their territory through the creation of a de facto state. This does not mean that such secessionist movements receive majority support from the population of their territory or that it is even conceivable that they could ever achieve independent statehood in the future.

Corsica is a good example of a territory where there is a secessionist movement that receives only marginal popular support. It is inconceivable that it should ever obtain a political majority on the island. Nevertheless, the French government had to take demands for decentralization and autonomy seriously, partly owing to pressure from the secessionist movement itself.[8] Scotland provides another interesting case: according to opinion polls conducted in 2008, Scottish nationalists would be unable to count on more than 19 percent of the population voting in favor of full independence from the United Kingdom, but majority support for that option is not considered inconceivable in the long term.[9]

There are significant political movements striving to withdraw from the control of the central government in the following territories or countries: Abkhazia (Georgia), South Ossetia (Georgia), Corsica (France), Transnistria (Moldova), the Basque Country (Spain), Flanders (Belgium), Kosovo (Serbia), the Turkish Republic of Northern Cyprus (Cyprus), Republika Srpska (Bosnia and Herzegovina), the area occupied by the Albanian minority in Macedonia, Catalonia (Spain), Padania (Italy), Sardinia (Italy), the Kurdish-populated regions of Turkey, Nagorno-Karabakh (Azerbaijan), Chechnya (Russia), Tatarstan (Russia), Faroe Islands (Denmark), Northern Ireland (United Kingdom), Scotland (United Kingdom), and Crimea (Ukraine).[10] Some of the secessionist movements in these territories or countries oppose both the central and the regional governments, but others either constitute or are part of the regional government or—in the case of de facto states—are in control of a population and a territory.

The unresolved secessionist conflicts in Europe are extremely diverse. At first sight there does not seem to be much in common between Nagorno-Karabakh and Flanders, between Transnistria and Scotland, or between the Republika Srpska and the Basque Country—to mention only a few of the constituent states, autonomous regions, and de facto independent entities that may become recognized independent states in our lifetime. We turn next to take a closer look at these movements and the attributes that, despite their many differences, they share.

Because these conflicts are taking place in Europe, these secessionist movements have in common at the very least the fact that they have to strive for international recognition within a European framework. The process of European integration does not necessarily oppose attempts to build sovereign statehood. Secessionist movements and entities generally regard the process of European integration as favorable to their cause. This is reflected in their state-building programs, which mostly favor inclusion in a broader, supranational framework. In their view, the inclusion of their state and nation within the EU would support their statehood and facilitate their integration into a globalized economy.

The eagerness of secessionist movements to obtain international recognition gives European states and organizations a certain amount of leverage. When addressing secessionist crises, European organizations such as the EU and the Council of Europe make serious attempts to negotiate the differences in the ways that national cultures strategically manage secession. European integration, therefore, has far-reaching implications for all secessionist conflicts. It will not necessarily resolve them, but it will affect how the parties to a conflict perceive their own interests and identities. That influence may be positive (it could narrow the gap between the secessionist movement and the central government) or negative (it could create even more divergence and make conflict resolution thus more difficult).

When addressing secessionist conflicts, European institutions such as the EU, the OSCE, and the Council of Europe explore a great variety of options, ranging from strengthening minority rights to proposing shared sovereignty and federal solutions. Among the federal options, their preference has traditionally been for establishing a federation in cases where the secession yields a single sovereign state. But where a federation has seemed out of reach, they have also endorsed the alternative option of a confederation—that is, a union of sovereign states—as a second choice. As a final option, they have accepted and even been supportive of mutually agreed on processes of dissolution, preferably according to clearly defined constitutional rules. In these cases, the EU and its member states have then recognized the legitimacy of this dissolution process and established diplomatic relations with the new state or states.

In the case of the crisis of the Soviet federation, the Western European countries—and the United States—initially gave their full support to Gorbachev's reform plans. Confronted, however, with the failure of the attempt to rebuild the Soviet federation in accordance with democratic norms, and worried about the potential security implications of disorderly fragmentation, Western Europeans and the United States spoke out in favor of a confederation and, as a last resort, supported the peaceful dissolution of the Soviet Union. A similar three-step approach to the question of secession was evident in the case of the dissolution of Yugoslavia.

Where owing to the resistance of the central government there is no mutual agreement on such a dissolution process, a separatist group may take unilateral steps to achieve independence. This is far more problematic than mutually agreed on forms of dissolution and secession. Recent European experience confirms if the separatist group and the central government do not accept a common constitutional framework and then the separatist group takes unilateral steps, the central government is likely to resort to the use of force. In most cases in the recent past in which the secessionist group and the central government were unable to agree on common decision-making procedures, their conflict led to a full-fledged armed conflict.

Unilateral steps may include secessions from secessions—a kind of partition that is not enshrined in any constitutional right to secede. Georgia's independence happened before any agreement was worked out between the various members of the Soviet Union as to how dissolution should proceed. The Georgian push for independence paralleled attempts at secession from Georgia by South Ossetia and Abkhazia. The Croatian and Bosnian attempts to secede from Yugoslavia triggered further fragmentation within their own territories. These recursive secessions represent the most violent episodes of the Soviet and Yugoslav disintegration.

In some of the violent cases of unilateral secession, such as the secession of the Baltic states from the Soviet Union or of Slovenia from Yugoslavia, the use of force was limited. Most violent were those secessions that led to the creation of de facto states or de facto independent entities that fell short of statehood.[11] Eight such states or entities emerged in Europe in the last twenty years of the twentieth century: the Turkish Republic of Northern Cyprus, Chechnya, Republika Srpska, Krajina, Transnistria, Abkhazia, South Ossetia, and Nagorno-Karabakh. Two of them—Chechnya and Krajina—have been destroyed by the central government by military means and one—the Republika Srpska—has been forcibly reintegrated into the state of Bosnia as a constituent state. So out of the eight cases where force led to the creation of de facto independent states or entities, three have seen their de facto independence canceled, while the five others remain, legally speaking, in limbo.

It is with respect to the question of unilateral secession and the use of force that the American approach differs most from the European one. Concerning the secessionist conflicts taking place in the Balkans, the United States has been far more decisive in urging forceful steps such as the use of military force to end conflict than the vast majority of European governments. This was particularly clear during the Bosnian civil war and in the debate over whether to intervene in the humanitarian crisis in Kosovo in 1999—without the authorization of the UN Security Council. The United States also took the lead in recognizing Kosovo's independence.

By contrast, European governments were often divided on the issue of the recognition of new states. They were also more attentive to prudential considerations—in line with their lack of military strength—and more ambivalent concerning the idea of comparative justice, that is, that one side must be more in the right than the other.[12] They often stressed that in none of these conflicts could just cause be found exclusively on one side, and this ambiguity underlay their lack of resolve.

A systematic description of the diversity of secessionist movements and policies on secession in Europe requires answering the following questions:

1. What is the model of governance in the disputed territories? Is there a centralized administration operating from the capital or have de facto independent states been established?

2. What kinds of strategies have been adopted by the secessionists? Reformist parties but also terrorist organizations may be in favor of independence.

3. How have the central governments responded? Responses range from power sharing to the use of military force.

4. What kind of nationhood and citizenship do the secessionists envision? An inclusive or exclusive type?

5. What justification has been offered for seceding? Are the secessionists making a just cause or a free choice type of argument in claiming they have the right to secede?

6. What degree of external backing exists for the secessionist party or secessionist state entity? Is the party or entity isolated or is it dependent on a foreign power or powers?

7. To what degree are the parties involved in a secessionist dispute linked to European structures?

Other potential issues are not taken into account here. Religious differences, for example, may be crucial in building identity, but they seem far less important in determining external support and do not appear to play a critical role in the recognition process. The Chechen de facto state, largely dominated by fundamentalist Islamic forces when the second war started in 1999, was recognized by the Taliban-led Afghan government in 2000. This recognition owed in significant part to the fact of their shared fundamentalist Islamic policies. In other cases—Kosovo, for instance—external support was not based on religious affinity. By January 2009, a surprisingly small number of countries with a Muslim-majority population and only one Arab country had recognized Kosovo's independence.[13]

MODELS OF GOVERNANCE

The extent to which a territory and its population have broken away from the authority of the central government as well as the population's degree of self-governance vary. In some cases the central government retains strong control over the disputed territory—as, for instance, Turkey does over the Kurdish-populated regions. France has given Corsica autonomous powers as part of wider decentralization reforms. Flanders and Wallonia are constituent states with exclusive competences in the Belgian federation, including treaty-making power in foreign relations.

Some secessionist movements have completely broken away from the authority of the central government, creating de facto independent entities. There are at present five such entities in Europe: the Turkish Republic of Northern Cyprus, Transnistria, Abkhazia, South Ossetia, and Nagorno-Karabakh. These entities have the objective features of a state to a certain degree, but none of them are recognized as such by the international community. But the international community cannot ignore these entities either, as the leaderships of them exercise effective control over a territory and population. This has far-reaching implications for international security and trade.

STRATEGIES AND GOVERNMENT RESPONSES

The strategies of secessionist movements differ widely. In the Basque Country, for instance, Eusko Alderdi Jeltzalea/Partido Nacionalista Vasco (EAJ/PNV), the party that constituted the Basque government up until the local parliamentary elections of March 1, 2009, supports the idea of a free association between the Basque Country and Spain, a long-term objective that would be achieved gradually, by democratic means, such as a referendum. Free association implies sovereignty for the Basque Country, which is strongly opposed by the main Spanish government parties. The EAJ/PNV is fiercely opposed to the terrorist activities of the organization Euskadi Ta Askatasuna (ETA), which strives for an independent Basque state.

There is a wide variety of possible responses to secessionist demands. There is also a broad-ranging discussion on the appropriate responses to such demands, and here, choice of words is considered crucial. The central authorities may regard federalism, and even federalist constitutional terminology, as too radical an option, on the grounds that such a response to secessionist threats might strengthen existing ethnic identities, increase institutional divisions, and lead to the division of the country. Belgium has chosen federalism, which has been enshrined in its constitution, but Spain and the United Kingdom have made less radical choices. Madrid opposed federal terminology—considered to be too divisive—and has created "autonomous communities." The United Kingdom has employed the term "devolution" to describe a similar process of granting autonomy to particular territories, such as Scotland and Wales.

There is also a wide variety of responses to the problem of the reunification of states. The governments of Georgia and Moldova diverge in their views on the potential role of federalism in restoring the territorial integrity of their countries. A process of federalization was envisaged by the Georgian constitution of 1995 as a means of achieving reunification with the breakaway entities of Abkhazia and South Ossetia. Such a process has been rejected, however, by the Moldovan Parliament, with respect to Transnistria. Instead, it favors a unitary state in which Transnistria would be made an autonomous region.

The two Cypriot communities are divided on the question of which type of federalism would be most appropriate for reunifying the island. The Greek Cypriots have traditionally favored a type of federation in which the federal institutions would retain strong powers. The Turkish Cypriots would prefer, on the contrary, to give maximum powers to the two constituent communities—a position the Greek Cypriot leaders call "confederalism."

EXCLUSIVE AND INCLUSIVE SECESSIONIST MOVEMENTS

Secessionist movements have to determine the extent their conception of nationhood is exclusive or inclusive. The EU condemns exclusive types of nationalism as morally retrograde and conducive to conflict. This position is fully in line with that of the United States. That a movement be inclusive and, in particular, that it fully respect the rights of ethnic minorities are the main political conditions for international recognition by Western countries.

This issue of exclusiveness vs. inclusiveness is raised by de facto states whose creation went hand in hand with the ethnic cleansing of one community by the other. In de facto states where the ethnic community that supports independent statehood is in a minority position, the minority community may feel threatened by having to acknowledge the right of members of the majority population to return. Peace proposals then have to design a way to turn an exclusive conception of citizenship into an inclusive one—into a conception where all communities are integrated within a shared view of state sovereignty.

The island of Cyprus has been divided along ethnic lines as a result of violence and war. The 2004 UN plan for the reunification of Cyprus—the so-called Annan plan—entailed turning the de facto state of Northern Cyprus into a constituent state within a reunited Cyprus that would then join the EU.[14] The Annan plan accepted territoriality as one of the basic principles of the Cypriot federation but provided for territorial readjustments between the Greek and Turkish Cypriot communities and for the right of members of each group who had been expelled from their homes either to reclaim their property or to receive compensation. According to this plan, the right to return, which would allow for ethnically mixed communities, would be implemented gradually and would not jeopardize the political hegemony of the Turkish community over the northern territory.

The Turkish Cypriot community was deeply divided as to whether or not this plan threatened its survival. A large majority eventually voted in favor of it, in an April 2004 referendum, accepting it as the main condition for joining the European Union. But the restrictions on the right to return that were built into the plan constituted one of the primary reasons why it was rejected by the Greek Cypriot community in a separate referendum. A month after that, a divided Cyprus, represented by a Greek Cypriot government, joined the European Union.

For Kosovo, a territory under UN administration since 1999 and partially under EU supervision since 2008, the integration of minorities and the protection of their rights are critical to ensuring the multiethnicity and representativeness of the state institutions. The principle of "standards before status" adopted by the UN in 2002, the proposals for supervised independence, which were discussed—but not accepted—by the UN Security Council in 2007, and the 2008 draft Constitution were all directed toward the creation of a multiethnic society. Albanian and Serbian are both recognized as official languages. Decentralization aims at increasing Serb minority participation. The present Kosovar Constitution is based on respect for the highest level of internationally recognized human rights and fundamental freedoms.

JUST CAUSE OR CHOICE

There are two main types of justification for increasing the self-governance of a secessionist entity up to the point where it achieves full independence from the central government. One series of arguments in favor of independence advances a case based on just cause. Such arguments refer to historical experiences of injustice at the hands of the central government, flagrant injustices that are to be corrected or prevented through some form of local autonomy or, as a last resort, via outright independence.

Other arguments for independence are grounded in the idea that secession is justified if it constitutes a sovereign choice made by the majority of a population. The choice approach in the ethics of secession maintains that any group aspiring to national self-determination has the right to claim a separate political identity and to make demands up to and including independence, provided certain conditions are satisfied, such as that the group intends to support democratic rights and respect minorities. The right to national self-determination may thus override the principle of territorial integrity.

Both types of argument intermingle in most discourses on secession, but it is still possible to make a distinction between secessionist movements based on the use they make of these two types of normative argument. The cases for the recognition of Kosovo, Chechnya, Abkhazia, and South Ossetia as independent states are founded on the argument that this is the only way to redress past injustices or prevent their repetition. Transnistrian nationalists, on the other hand, argue that their independence is justified by the fact that their population has freely chosen it. Scottish nationalists state that a referendum would enable their nation to make a free choice as to its future. The discourses of some secessionist movements—such as the Flemish nationalist movement—reflect a shift from a type of justification based on just cause to a choice type.

The distinction between the two types of justification helps us better understand European strategic culture regarding secession and European motives for supporting, or opposing, UDIS. Massive human rights violations (like those committed by Serbia in Kosovo) may increase the legitimacy of the claim to independence as a last resort. The just cause argument carries particular weight in situations in which highly repressive measures are adopted by the central government, as when the Serbs forcibly expelled some seven hundred thousand Kosovars from their homes in 1998–99.

European governments will, however, resolutely oppose unilateral moves toward independence if they are based mainly on a choice type of justification, as in the case of Republika Srpska and Transnistria. In these two cases the EU argued that no massive human rights violations had been committed against the populations of these territories that could justify abolishing the authority of the central government or overriding the principle of territorial integrity.[15]

The choice argument may be powerful only in cases where secession can be peacefully negotiated and where a referendum can take place in accordance with constitutional law, as happened with the State Union of Serbia and Montenegro in 2006. In the latter half of the 1990s, the EU and its member states opposed Serbia's domestic and foreign policies and accused Belgrade of committing human rights violations in Kosovo.[16] In their view, the policies of Serb leader Slobodan Milosevic severely destabilized the Balkans. At the time, after the secession of Slovenia, Croatia, Macedonia, and Bosnia, Serbia together with Montenegro constituted a rump federation: the Federal Republic of Yugoslavia. But tension was mounting between the leaderships of the two constituent states, and it gained momentum in 1999, when Montenegro made the Deutschmark its official currency.[17] Montenegrin criticism of Serb policies in Kosovo and its generally pro-Western line spoke in favor of EU support. The Montenegrin government's declarations that the democratization of Serbia was the *conditio sine qua non* for the survival of the Yugoslav federation received open support in European capitals. But the risk of an armed confrontation with Serbia, a civil war within Montenegro between the supporters and opponents of independence, and the risk that Montenegro would turn into a failed state spoke also for cautiousness.[18] Brussels backed certain steps toward a separation from Belgrade, without, however, overtly acknowledging Montenegro's right to strive for unilateral independence. This implicitly meant that Milosevic's authoritarian rule gave Montenegro just cause to take gradual steps toward separation but not to seek full independence.

This just cause for gradual separation disappeared with Milosevic's fall from power in October 2000. Serbia organized democratic elections, and Montenegrin demands for independence from the Yugoslav federation then had to rely mainly on choice arguments. But Brussels now had other interests to defend in the region. It wanted to strengthen the democratization of all the Balkan states through their progressive integration into the EU. Brussels therefore preferred a renewal of the federal arrangement between Serbia and Montenegro to dissolution. Integration into and future membership in the EU were even made contingent on the ability of Serbia and Montenegro to integrate as a single state.

In 2002 an agreement was reached between Belgrade and Podgorica, under strong pressure from the EU, to create the State Union of Serbia and Montenegro. As a concession to the Montenegrin desire for independence, it was then agreed that a referendum on it could take place no sooner than three years after the creation of the state union. This referendum was held in Montenegro in 2006, and a clear majority came out in favor of independence. The EU then had to recognize Montenegro as an independent state. The case of Montenegro shows that choice arguments still carry a certain democratic weight with the EU but that they are considered acceptable only within the framework of a mutually agreed-on process of separation.

Just cause is a necessary, but not necessarily sufficient, condition for receiving EU support for a UDI. In the case of the two Chechen wars of 1994–96 and 1999–, the EU made a series of appeals to the Russian government to uphold human rights and international humanitarian law and to enter into political negotiations with the separatists, but it did not question the right of the central government to enforce its authority on the region by force. None of the EU's member states thought the EU should support independent statehood for Chechnya, in contrast to the position they took with respect to Kosovo in 2008. Doubt that the secessionist forces would implement democratic norms, the rule of law, or international humanitarian law was one important reason for their unwillingness—several European governments regarded the Chechen leaders as terrorists. The high degree of interdependence between the EU and the Russian Federation was another reason (whereas Serbia is dependent on the EU, facilitating the EU's imposition of policies it deems appropriate).[19]

INTERNATIONALIZATION

Demands for sovereignty and independence have their roots in the domestic political sphere, but their achievement requires international recognition. This goal may be achieved progressively. Fear of such an outcome explains why several central governments have avoided any form of Europeanization or internationalization of the secessionist conflicts they are confronted with. This is the case, for instance, in Spain, where the government has addressed the Basque conflict at the European level only under the auspices of antiterrorist cooperation.

France has traditionally been wary of moves toward autonomy and federalization in other countries, conscious of the fact that such moves could negatively affect its own interests. For example, the French have regarded with suspicion the treaty-making power of constituent entities in Belgium, even though this right was formally enshrined in the Belgian constitution of 1993. Paris feared that its recognition of such a constitutional right—which is exceptional even for federations—might be perceived as a form of support for potentially divisive institutions and might create a dangerous precedent in other cases where the unity of the state was at stake. Belgium's federal government had to speak on behalf of its regions and communities in order to make such treaties with France possible.[20]

Cyprus, Georgia, and Moldova are all three confronted with breakaway territories and consider that it is in their interest to receive external support for their cause. As Cyprus became a member of the EU in 2004, the Greek Cypriots may count on support from Brussels, while the Turkish Cypriots may rely on Ankara.

The recognition of Kosovo by Western governments had a major impact on all secessionist conflicts in which external actors have a strong presence.[21] The possibility that external powers may recognize a secessionist entity without the consent of the central government was raised in the context of Russia's policy toward secessionist conflicts in Georgia. At first, Russia did not seem to have any great interest in adopting the kind of policies toward South Ossetia and Abkhazia that Western Europe and the United States had adopted with respect to Kosovo, for a number of reasons. First, since few other countries would follow suit, it would simply demonstrate Russia's international isolation. Second, even if Moscow does not fear secession in Chechnya or Tatarstan in the short term, it has no interest in encouraging domestic debates on a unilateral right to independence. Moscow could, moreover, deepen its relations with the breakaway territories in Georgia without recognizing them as independent states. It could thus preserve "strategic ambiguity" as regards recognition, whereby it reserves the right to recognize secessionist entities without necessarily choosing to do so. By defending the principle of territorial integrity, Moscow retained the moral and legal high ground in its position on secessionist conflicts. This proved helpful in legitimizing its role as a peacekeeper in Georgia's internal conflicts. Furthermore, Russia kept alive the possibility that it might play an active role in the reunification of Georgia in a later stage. But the war in August 2008 changed the Russian proportionality calculation in favor of recognizing South Ossetia and Abkhazia, which was perceived as the best means, in the long term, of preserving the Russian military presence there, as it would then be made dependent on the exclusive decision of the authorities of these entities.

Georgia has actively striven to draw the West more deeply into the negotiations with Abkhazia and South Ossetia, while they, for their part, lean on Moscow and its peacekeeping forces. Up until the war of August 2008, Tbilisi had hoped that an internationalization of the peacekeeping forces in the two entities would weaken Russia's stronghold on the negotiation process, but after its military defeat by Russia in August 2008 Georgia had to relinquish these hopes. According to the Kremlin, its recognition of South Ossetia and Abkhazia rendered null and void all Georgian declarations that Russian troops had to leave its territory. Moscow stated that the two territories were no longer part of Georgia and that all questions relating to the presence of foreign troops or monitors there had to be negotiated directly with their governments. But Tbilisi did not give up all hope of internationalizing its conflict with Russia, Abkhazia, and South Ossetia. The Abkhaz and South Ossetian authorities have refused to allow EU monitors on their territories, but the deployment of these monitors along the disputed borders of the two entities, on the territory controlled by the Georgian government, is a sign of the further involvement of Brussels.[22]

CORE AND PERIPHERY

The outcome—but not necessarily the origin—of secessionist conflicts is strongly affected by the degree to which the territories involved are integrated into the EU and other European structures. A distinction needs to be made here between secessionist conflicts taking place at the core of the European integration process and those at the margins, and as the EU must be regarded as the main European institution, the distinction has to be framed in terms of secession processes taking place within and outside the EU enlargement process, or, to be more concrete, between divided states that either are or have a reasonable prospect of becoming EU member states and those that are not EU members and do not have a reasonable prospect of joining the EU.

EU integration provides arguments for and against secession, as illustrated by the debate preceding Kosovo's UDI.[23] The argument against secession was that EU integration would strengthen the legal and political guarantees of Kosovo's autonomy within Serbia and that the exercise of considerable competences by Brussels would decrease the points of friction between Serbs and Albanians and the significance of international boundaries. Why, some asked, should Kosovo strive for full sovereignty if it would then share sovereignty with Serbia within a common EU framework?

There were also strong arguments in favor of secession in the face of Kosovo's and Serbia's EU integration. A federal relationship between Serbia and Kosovo would necessarily lead to conflict. This would make their common integration within the EU more cumbersome. And why strive for shared sovereignty between Serbia and Kosovo and oppose independence for Kosovo if both would ultimately be reunited within the EU? The potentially negative consequences of secession could thus be addressed through integration within broader European structures.

In the case of Kosovo and Serbia, the EU member states that had recognized Kosovo based their conflict resolution policies on the possibility that EU membership would function as a common framework for these two sovereign states, facilitating the process of reconciliation within a multilateral framework. Serbia's refusal to accept equal status with its former province, however, and the refusal of some EU member states to recognize Kosovo, challenged these conflict resolution policies.

In the case of Georgia, Abkhazia, and South Ossetia, there is no realistic possibility of EU membership in the foreseeable future. Unlike with Kosovo and Serbia, and all the other cases in which full EU integration through membership is a realistic goal, a peaceful outcome to the conflict is thus not perceived as being institutionally linked to EU structures. As a consequence, there is significantly less EU involvement in the conflict resolution process. The potential role of the EU at the European periphery is restricted to that of an actor who mainly initiates or supports mediation processes, facilitates conflict transformation, and gives security guarantees to the parties.

A STRATEGIC EUROPEAN CULTURE WITH RESPECT TO SECESSION

Each European state has its own history of secession, and many are confronting secessionist threats today. States decide individually on the political criteria they wish to apply in recognizing other states. Their criteria are generally based on interests and values that form part of a broader strategic culture that informs how they approach secession, and they legitimize their choices on the basis of analogies with their own historical experiences—either of their own emancipation from foreign rule or of dealing with threats to their own national unity.

The EU is severely weakened in its foreign and security policies by divergent positions on secession and state recognition. These differences in opinion were already problematic back in the 1990s when its member states were confronted with the question of whether or when to recognize the new states that emerged from the dissolution of Yugoslavia. The question of Kosovo's UDI then created even deeper divisions within the EU.

A strategic EU culture that shapes European countries' response to secession is emerging, however, based on the following common preferences. First, there is a clear support within the EU for models of regional self-governance that respect the principle of territorial integrity. Second, the EU regards reformist strategies working toward higher levels of self-governance and even toward independence as legitimate, and in line with a democratic system, and rejects terrorist strategies. Third, the use of force is considered legitimate only if used against terrorist groups or in other exceptional circumstances. All three preferences are based on the fear that policies and strategies that encourage unilateral steps may lead to conflict escalation.

If member states of the EU take unilateral steps in a secessionist conflict or support those taken by one side (as they did when Kosovo issued its UDI in 2008), they will simply deny that such a move should be regarded as unilateral, owing to the strong support it has received from Western countries. The diplomats of the countries that recognized Kosovo, for instance, described its declaration of independence as a "coordinated declaration of independence" rather than as a UDI. Other rhetorical strategies used to deny a contradiction with their standard policies on secession include its justification as "unique" and therefore as not having any legal consequences or value as a precedent for any other secessionist conflict. They will thus not explicitly admit that such a policy should be considered a legitimate exception. And indeed, the justification of exceptions would require a number of formalized rules or possibly even a doctrine on policies on secession, which the EU is unwilling to draw up.

The EU and its member states will generally prefer inclusive concepts of the nation and citizenship to exclusive ones. Just cause and choice arguments for secession do not have the same value. If the EU or its member states were to support a UDI, as they did with Kosovo, they would attempt to legitimate that support by way of reference to just cause arguments. A secessionist discourse based mainly on choice arguments would only be accepted in the event of mutually agreed-on forms of state division.

Central governments may regard the internationalization of attempts to resolve secessionist conflicts as being either supportive of or detrimental to their cause, which will then determine the degree of involvement of the EU. Conflicts in which the EU was strongly involved include those in Moldova, Georgia, and Cyprus; they also had a large presence in the disputes between Serbia and Montenegro and between Serbia and Kosovo. Secessionist conflicts may take place either within the EU or at its periphery, and this too will have an impact on the form its involvement takes.

In the case of EU member states or prospective member states, the EU will be perceived as a potential institutional framework within which conflict transformation and resolution may take place. This, for instance, was how those Greek and Turkish Cypriots who were in favor of the Annan plan in 2004 saw the EU. The State Union of Serbia and Montenegro in 2002 was likewise built on the prospect of common integration of both constituent states within the EU. The EU member states in favor of Kosovo's independence expected that membership prospects for Kosovo and Serbia would promote conflict transformation and resolution within EU structures. In countries that do not have any prospect of membership in the foreseeable future, the EU is, instead, perceived as an actor. This has been the case, for instance, with Moldova and Georgia.

This means that there is a great variety of secessionist conflicts the EU has to cope with. A strategic European culture related to secession would no doubt help the EU to forge common policies in all these cases.

Notes

I am grateful to Aleksandar Pavković and Peter Radan for their comments on this paper and to Don H. Doyle and Veronica Kelly for their language corrections.

1. See Frederick K. Lister, *The European Union, the United Nations, and the Revival of Confederal Governance* (Westport, Conn.: Greenwood Press, 1996), 26–32; Xiaokun Song, "Confederalism: A Review of Recent Literature," in *Federal Practice: Exploring Alternatives for Georgia and Abkhazia*, ed. Bruno Coppieters, David Darchiashvili, and Natella Akaba (Brussels: VUB University Press, 2000), 181–82.

2. On European recognition policies in Yugoslavia, see Richard Caplan, *Europe and the Recognition of New States in Yugoslavia* (Cambridge: Cambridge University Press, 2005).

3. An overview of the process of recognizing Kosovo can be found in "Who Recognized Kosova as an Independent State?" http://www.kosovothanksyou.com, accessed Oct. 16, 2009.

4. On the concept of strategic culture, see, among others, Wyn Rees and Richard J. Aldrich, "Contending Cultures of Counterterrorism: Transatlantic Divergence or Convergence?" *International Affairs* 81, no. 5 (2005): 905–23. The concept of a strategic culture is traditionally used in security studies but not in relation to secession.

5. "America's New Hard Line on Chechnya," *BBC News Hotline*, Nov. 3, 1999, http://news.bbc.co.uk/1/hi/world/europe/503804.stm, accessed Jan. 11, 2009. Such analogies were already being made at the start of the first Chechen war (1994–96). In stating that the United States would likewise prevent secession by force, a spokesman for the U.S. State Department compared the attack on Chechnya with the American Civil War. See John J. Maresca, "Where is the Moral Leader of the West?" *International Herald Tribune* (Paris), Jan. 6, 1995, http://www.iht.com/articles/1995/01/06/edjohn.php, accessed Jan. 11, 2009.

6. Reno L. Harnish, "America's Founding Fathers Speak to Kosovo," July 4, 2003, http://pristina.usembassy.gov/press20030704.html, accessed Jan. 12, 2009.

7. These statements were made on the television program *Terzake*, Vlaamse Radio en Televisieomroep, Feb. 18, 2008.

8. See Gunter Lauwers, "Discussing Autonomy and Independence for Corsica," in *Contextualizing Secession: Normative Studies in Comparative Perspective*, ed. Bruno Coppieters and Richard Sakwa (Oxford: Oxford University Press, 2003), 49–70.

9. "Où l'on reparle de l'indépendance de l'Écosse," *Courrier International* (Paris), May 15–21, 2008, 18.

10. The broad definition of secession used in this chapter includes irredentist and anticolonial movements.

11. A distinction has to be drawn between de facto states and entities that fall short of statehood. This chapter does not examine the extent to which the de facto independent entities that exist in Europe have acquired the fundamental characteristics of statehood such that they could be considered de facto states.

12. On the notion of comparative justice, see Bruno Coppieters, Carl Ceulemans, and Anthony Hartle, "Just Cause," in *Moral Constraints on War: Principles and Cases*, ed. Bruno Coppieters and Nick Fotion (Lanham, Md.: Lexington Books, 2008), 48–49.

13. Countries with a Muslim majority were relatively slow to recognize Kosovo. Albania, Senegal, Turkey, and Afghanistan recognized Kosovo in February 2008. Sierra Leone followed in June and the United Arab Emirates and Malaysia in October 2008. By January 2009, no other Muslim country—of the fifty or so with a Muslim majority— had established diplomatic relations with Pristina.

14. See Nathalie Tocci and Tamara Kovziridze, "Cyprus," in *Europeanization and*

Conflict Resolution: Case Studies from the European Periphery, ed. Bruno Coppieters et al. (Ghent: Academia Press, 2004), 63–106.

15. Nationalists in the Transnistrian referendum of September 17, 2006, justified secession mainly by reference to choice arguments based on the principle of national self-determination and—in opposition to Kosovar nationalists—only marginally by reference to previous injustices. Arguments in favor of Transnistrian independence are to be found in S. I. Beril, I. N. Galinsky and I. M. Blagodatskikh, eds., *The Pridnestrovian Moldavian Republic as a Full-Fledged State* (Tiraspol: CSPR Perspektive, 2006).

16. On the EU's Montenegro policies, see Raymond Detrez, "The Right to Self-Determination and Secession in Yugoslavia: A Hornets' Nest of Inconsistencies," *Contextualizing Secession*, 126–129.

17. *Financial Times* (London), Nov. 3, 1999.

18. *The Economist*, Jan. 29, 2000.

19. On European policies in relation to the Second Chechnya War, see Céline Francis, "'Selective affinities': The Reactions of the Council of Europe and the European Union to the Second Armed Conflict in Chechnya (1999–2006)," *Europe-Asia Studies* 60, no. 2 (2008): 317–38.

20. On foreign policy making in Belgium, see Maarten Theo Jans and Patrick Stouthuysen, "Federal Regions and External Relations: The Belgian Case," *International Spectator* 42, no. 2 (2007): 209–20.

21. On the following, see my "Kosovo Hampers Conflict Negotiators," *Oxford Analytica*, Mar. 7, 2008.

22. On the 2008 August war, see Roy Allison, "Russia Resurgent? Moscow's Campaign to 'Coerce Georgia to Peace,'" *International Affairs* 84, no. 6 (2008): 1145–71.

23. On the consequences of European integration for secessionist conflicts at the European periphery, see *Europeanization and Conflict Resolution*.

ALEKSANDAR PAVKOVIĆ

By the Force of Arms
Violence and Morality in Secessionist Conflict

The basis of statehood, and of unity, can only be general acceptance by the participants. You cannot kill thousands of people, and keep on killing more, in the name of unity. There is no unity between the dead and those who killed them.

Julius K. Nyerere, "Why We Recognized Biafra"

How does a group acquire the right to secede from an existing state? This is the central question that contemporary normative theorists of secession—including Christopher Wellman in this volume—address. The question I address in this chapter is quite different: *can the use of military force in order to achieve or to prevent a secession be justified on moral grounds?* Even if a group does have a right to secede, this does not necessarily imply that it is morally justified to use military force and to kill people in an attempt to secure secession or independence. Whether or not there are rights to independent statehood, one can still ask, *is independent statehood worth the sacrifice of human life and the misery that attends any military conflict?*

The word "independence" has, partly as a consequence of decolonization, gained honorific connotations that may incline us to answer this question unhesitatingly in the affirmative. This chapter attempts to offer some reasons to resist this inclination.

Nyerere's eloquent plea against the use of force to secure the unity of a state raises a parallel question: *is maintaining the unity of a state—its territorial integrity—worth the sacrifice of human life and misery that attends any military conflict?*

In economic parlance, do the benefits of having a unified state outweigh the costs in human life and other social costs that using military force to maintain its unity exacts? The two questions suggest that the two relevant aspects of statehood—its territorial integrity and its independence from other states—are goods whose maintenance or possession could be *assessed* in terms of the loss of human life; in consequence, the two—independent statehood and human lives—are *morally commensurate* goods. This chapter presents a few reasons to question this assumption.

Moral considerations are here regarded as distinct from political ones; the latter but not the former concern the exercise of power over people and territories. Hence the issues of political power (control) and who exercises it are, by themselves, not moral issues. The *ways* in which one attempts to gain or maintain political control over people and territory are, however, open to moral assessment. Accordingly, if we say that an action is morally justified or permissible, we are assuming that it *can* be ranked on a scale of other morally comparable or commensurate actions or goods. The value of maintaining control over territory, I argue, is not a value that can be placed on a scale of moral values on which human life is placed.

As many chapters in this volume suggest, in the initial stages of violent secessionist conflicts the question of their human costs is rarely raised, at least not before human costs become too large to be ignored. Yet the question of whether the pursuit of a secessionist or antisecessionist cause is justifiable in terms of its human cost is, I believe, central to any *moral* assessment of secession attempts that involve the use of lethal force. Here I attempt to assess normatively the use of violence in secessionist conflict, and thus my perspective is restricted to universal humanism. In its application, my normative assessment is limited to four secessionist conflicts—in Slovenia (1991), Kosovo (1998–99), Chechnya (1994, 1999), and Biafra (1967–70). Universal humanism, according to which human life is the highest moral value and every human life is of equal value, is a moral worldview present in a variety of religious and secular doctrines (for example, Christianity, Buddhism, Kantianism). Universal humanism allows the use of lethal force in self-defense and in the defense of the defenseless; in this, it is distinct from pacifism, which rejects any use of lethal force.

A normative moral assessment of violence in attempts at secession also presupposes an account of the conflict that highlights those aspects of the use of violence that are relevant for such an assessment. I offer such an account of the secessionist conflicts in Slovenia, Kosovo, Chechnya, and Biafra. Most violent secessionist conflicts, I think, resemble one (or more) of these four conflicts, both in the ways in which lethal force is used and in the objectives for which it is used.

VIOLENT ATTEMPTS AT SECESSION: SLOVENIA, KOSOVO, CHECHNYA, BIAFRA

In each of the four cases (1) the secessionist movement had an almost complete and effective *political control* over its target population or national group (the majority group in the territory); (2) the secessionist military forces presented a serious challenge to the host state's *military control* over the territory; and (3) the secessionist movement demanded *independent statehood* (external self-determination) since its leaders had, for a variety of reasons, rejected any form of self-government short of that. In each case, *prior* to the outbreak of violence, the secessionist population had some form of representation in the central government and a degree of self-government in its territory; the host state, in each case, had not denied the latter *internal* self-determination. The host state was using military force against the secessionist forces primarily in order to prevent the realization of their demand for *independent statehood*. How that was done will be briefly outlined below.

Slovenia

Slovenia was one of six federal units (republics) in the Yugoslav federation, which the Communist Party of Yugoslavia created in 1946 on the model of the USSR. A day before its declaration of independence, (June 24, 1991), the Slovenian defense force (a territorial militia created under the Yugoslav Communist government to resist foreign invasion) took over Slovenia's international border crossing from the Yugoslav federal authorities, created new border crossings with Croatia (a neighboring federal unit that declared independence at the same time), and blockaded all Yugoslav federal army garrisons in Slovenia. This was a part of a media campaign to present Slovenia as a democracy under brutal Communist attack, and it was accompanied by Slovenia's urgent request that the Organization for Security and Cooperation in Europe (OSCE) and the European Community (EC) intervene in the conflict; the EC and OSCE quickly complied with this request. Only after Yugoslav federal armored units retook the international border crossings from Slovenia's defense forces did the EC broker an agreement. Under the terms of the agreement, Slovenia lifted its blockade of Yugoslav garrisons and consented to a three-month moratorium on its independence. During this time most Yugoslav army units left Slovenia.

The primary aim of the Yugoslav federal army operation was to wrest away control over its international border crossings from Slovenia. No attempt was made to take control of the territory or population. The Slovene secessionist forces knew of the limited aims of the militarily superior Yugoslav army and avoided full-scale engagement with it. Because the military operation was restricted in its scope and the secessionist response was restrained, the estimated death toll was forty-five Yugoslav army conscripts and officers, twelve Slovenian conscripts, and several civilians caught in cross fire.[1]

Kosovo

The current secessionist conflict started with large-scale violent demonstrations by Kosovo Albanians in 1981 demanding the secession of Kosovo, a subfederal province, from Serbia, a federal unit of the Yugoslav federation. In 1990, responding to Serbian government legislation that severely restricted the legislative autonomy that Kosovo had enjoyed in the Communist-ruled Yugoslav federation since 1974, the majority Kosovo Albanian deputies in the provincial assembly (elected under the one-party Communist system) voted to secede unilaterally from Serbia. Following the reiterated declarations of independence of Slovenia and Croatia, in October 1991 the same deputies declared independence from the Yugoslav federation. From 1991 until 1999 the new majority Kosovo Albanian party, the Democratic League of Kosovo, ran a parallel state that provided education, health, taxation, and rudimentary judiciary services for Kosovo Albanians, separate from the Serbian state. The Serbian government tolerated this state while suppressing by force any secessionist public manifestation by Kosovo Albanians. In 1996 the Kosovo Liberation Army (KLA), a secessionist organization that had formed outside the peaceful mainstream movement, started to target Serbian officials and (alleged) Kosovo Albanian collaborators for assassination and government targets for bombing; in 1998 it raised a mass armed rebellion that received widespread support from the Albanian population. By June 1998 a large Yugoslav/Serbian military campaign using armor, heavy artillery, and air support had forced the KLA units to fragment and to withdraw to mountain areas. Following the refusal of the Serbian leaders to sign an agreement with the Kosovo Albanian secessionist leadership brokered by the United

States in March 1999 NATO began an air bombing campaign against Serbia. Soon after, around seven hundred thousand Kosovo Albanians were forced to leave Kosovo for neighboring countries. Serbia's military forces were able to contain the KLA, denying them access to most of the territory of Kosovo, despite the significant military aid that NATO provided to the KLA. Under a May 1999 cease-fire agreement with NATO, Yugoslav/Serb forces were ejected from Kosovo and a UN administration was installed supported by a NATO-led military force. The Kosovo Albanian refugees then returned, the KLA assumed political power, and most of the non-Albanian population of Kosovo fled to Serbia.

The primary aim of the Yugoslav military operation was to destroy the KLA as an effective fighting force and to neutralize it by severing its contact with its supporting Kosovo Albanian population. No attempt was made to establish political control over the population by, for example, installing collaborationist political authorities. During the military campaign against the KLA, Kosovo Albanians were evicted from the area in which military operations were being carried out. However, after the NATO bombing campaign began, the Albanian population was also forced out of areas of Kosovo that had not previously been affected by military operations.[2]

Chechnya

On November 1, 1991, Jokhar Dudaev, the newly elected president of Chechnya-Ingushetia, an autonomous republic within the Russian federation (which was at the time a union republic of the USSR), proclaimed its independence. The Russian government regarded both his election and the declaration illegal and, while negotiating with the Chechen officials, supported attempts of Chechen opposition groups to remove him from power by force. In December 1994 a combined force of Russian army and Chechen opposition forces invaded Chechnya. Facing determined resistance, the Russian forces used massive aerial and artillery bombardment, destroying the civilian infrastructure of the capital and causing tens of thousands of civilian casualties. In August 1995, they installed a collaborationist Chechen government in Grozny, the capital, but in 1996 the Chechen secessionist forces encircled the Russian forces there. Following this defeat, in August 1996 a cease-fire and in 1997 a peace treaty were signed that left the secessionist authorities in control of Chechnya.

Following the 1999 invasion of Dagestan (a neighboring federal unit in Russia) by the private army of a leading Chechen military commander and a series of bombings of civilian targets elsewhere in Russia (attributed to the Chechen secessionists), Russian forces invaded Chechnya again. Using large-scale bombardment and armor, the Russian army forced the Chechen secessionists into the sparsely inhabited mountains and installed a collaborationist native government that, at the time of writing, together with the Russian forces, controls the country.

The primary objectives of both the 1994 and 1999 Russian military campaigns were to destroy the military forces of the secessionist authorities and to remove the secessionist authorities from power and replace them with a collaborationist government. When the first proved to be impossible to achieve, the Russian government settled in 1996 for a de facto recognition of secession. In their second military campaign in 1999, the Russian forces achieved all three objectives.[3]

Biafra

Biafra's (Eastern Region) secession from Nigeria in 1967 was preceded, in 1966, by a series of military coups in Nigeria that were followed by pogroms and massacres of Igbo people who were settlers in the Northern Region of Nigeria. Around a million Igbo settlers subsequently fled to their homeland in the Eastern Region and hundreds of thousands of non-Easterners were in turn expelled from that region. In April 1967 the military government of Nigeria imposed martial law on the whole of Nigeria and divided the country into twelve new states or federal units; the Eastern Region was to be divided into three states, and the Igbo would be allowed a majority in only one of these. In response, the Igbo military governor Chukwuemeka Odumegwu Ojukwu declared the whole Eastern Region to be the independent Republic of Biafra. In September 1967 the federal forces, with the military aid and diplomatic support of Nigeria's former colonial power, the UK, invaded Biafra. Owing to the well-organized defense of the Igbo homeland, it took two and a half years for the federal army to force the surrender of the much smaller and lightly armed Biafran army. An estimated one million people died during and immediately after the end of the war, mostly as a result of famine and disease.

The aim of the Nigerian government was the unconditional surrender of the secessionist forces, the reimposition of its authority on the territory, and the administrative restructuring of the territory into three federal units. After the surrender, the host government reintegrated the remnants of the civil and military corps of Biafra into this federal structure and attempted reconciliation under the slogan "One Nigeria."[4]

A Variety of Military Objectives

In all four cases, the host state used its military forces primarily in order to deny the secessionist movement military and political control over the territory required for their achievement of independence. Yet in each case, the specific objectives of the military operations differed considerably. In Slovenia, the host state aimed only to remove the secessionist forces from international border crossings—that is, from the symbolic space of a fully independent state. In Kosovo, the host state's forces fought to deny the secessionists military but not political control over territory and its population. In Chechnya, the host state wanted to remove the secessionist leaders from power (and to kill them) and to replace them with native but nonsecessionist leaders. In Biafra, the host state removed, by force, the secessionist leaders from power (but did not attempt to kill them) and reintegrated the territory and remaining state officials into the new host state structure. Only in the case of Nigeria did the host state demand that the leaders of the secessionist forces accept defeat and transfer their allegiance to it.

Why Use Indiscriminate Violence against Civilians?

In Slovenia, civilians were not a target of the military operations because the military conflict was restricted to the control of symbolic spaces that were not populated. In the other three conflicts, civilians were targets of indiscriminate violence, which appeared to have had the following three objectives:

1. To reduce the capacity of secessionist military forces to resist the host state, for example, launching heavy bombardment of their suspected positions, including civilian-inhabited buildings and areas, to accomplish their aim. This tactic of indiscriminate bombardment (characteristic of much of modern warfare) was used the most in Chechnya, causing the majority of civilian casualties there, but it was also extensively used in Kosovo and in Biafra.

2. To intimidate, "paralyze," and punish the secessionist population suspected of assisting the secessionist forces. In all three conflicts, the host state forces indiscriminately fired on civilian habitations, refugee columns, refugee camps, and nonthreatening civilians.[5]

3. To remove the opposing population from the targeted territory ("ethnic cleansing") by deploying random violence against individuals and groups.

Removal of "disloyal" or hostile national groups that provide support and refuge to the enemy forces may appear to be the most effective and least costly way of securing and maintaining political and military control over the contested *territory* as opposed to its inhabitants. Consequently, in periods when secessionists in these conflicts exercised military superiority over the host state, they expelled or condoned the expulsion of members of populations hostile to the secessionist project.[6] Unlike the host states of Kosovo and Chechnya, the Nigerian government appears not to have engaged in systematic expulsion of the Igbo (the "disloyal" population) from their homeland, Biafra. Prior to its invasion of Biafra, it also issued a general code of conduct to every member of its military forces prohibiting violence against civilians and allowed the UN-organized international military observer team to monitor (in a restricted way) its forces' conduct toward civilians. However, its effective blockade of the secessionist territory greatly contributed to the large number of Biafran deaths from starvation and disease. Moreover, *before* the start of the war, Easterners were forced (under the threat of massacre) to leave many parts of Nigeria and return to their homeland and non-Easterners were forced to leave the Eastern Region (Biafra).

THE MORALITY OF THE USE OF LETHAL FORCE IN SECESSIONIST CONFLICT

As Bruno Coppieters suggests in his chapter, a host state's use of indiscriminate violence against civilians on a part of its territory may be used to justify the denial of its sovereignty over that territory and to legitimate the consequent resistance to and military attack on the host state. One can argue, for example, that the host state military operations in Kosovo, Chechnya, and Biafra (but not in Slovenia) were *morally* impermissible because they involved indiscriminate use of violence against civilians. If so, the secessionist authorities were morally justified in using force against the host state as a means of preventing it from carrying out morally impermissible actions.

However, in these three cases the secessionist forces also used various forms of violence against potentially hostile civilians often belonging to the national groups supporting the host state. The secessionists' violence against civilians was more restricted, discriminate, and targeted than that of the host state. The secessionist forces, which operated in a potentially friendly environment and had no heavy weaponry, normally did not fire on civilian targets and when they did, they targeted primarily (but not exclusively) those civilians whom they believed to be supporters of the host state. As noted above, in Kosovo, Chechnya, and Biafra secessionists used or condoned indiscriminate violence to evict potentially hostile populations from the contested territory.

If one still wants to argue that the secessionist resistance to the host states' military was *morally* justified because the host states used violence against civilians indiscriminately, then one has either to claim that

1. secessionist killing of civilians was *morally* different from the killing carried out by the host state; or
2. the secessionist political cause—the liberation from foreign rule or the achievement of independent statehood—*morally* justifies or excuses their killing of civilians.

The first line of argument is difficult to sustain because the secessionist forces targeted civilians for the same reason the host state did—namely, because they were perceived as being hostile to the chosen political cause, in this case, secession. In this respect, their killing of civilians did not seem to be morally different from the host state's killing, and if that is so, then only their political cause could provide the required justification or excuse for the killing of civilians.

Eradicating Oppressive Foreign Rule: How Many Human Lives Is It Worth?

As Coppieters indicates, EU member states justify their recognition of Kosovo's secession by referring to acts of indiscriminate violence on the part of the host state—Serbia—against its own *minority* population—Kosovo Albanians. In the view of the member states, this gave Kosovo Albanians a just cause for their secession. But in their view, the secessionists' acts of violence against the supporters of the host state—mostly Serbs, but also Kosovo Albanians—did *not* give those Serbs and Kosovo Albanian supporters a just cause to secede from Kosovo. This seems to imply that the secessionist violence against the supporters of an unjust or oppressive host state is in some sense permissible, while the host state's is not. But why is that so?

In his *Wretched of the Earth* (1961), Frantz Fanon argued that any form of colonial rule—the rule of foreigners backed by the use of force—is a form of moral degradation and subjugation. The oppressors keep their rule over colonial subjects with the help of superior military technology and organization and use random violence against civilians in order to terrorize them into submission. In opposing this kind of oppression, the use of indiscriminate violence against civilians *who belong to the oppressor group* is, Fanon believed, morally justified. The civilians of the oppressor group are part of the system of oppression and are, even if not intentionally, helping maintain its injustice. Moreover, indiscriminate killing of civilians by the liberation forces may prove to be an effective instrument for the liberation from oppression because the oppressor state might end its oppression if the cost in civilian lives is too high. In short, Fanon's argument is that in the cases of oppressive foreign rule, the end justifies the means: because foreign rule is an injustice of such a scale, its removal justifies the use of instruments that perhaps in other contexts could not be legitimately used.[7]

But was foreign rule in our four cases morally degrading or morally unjust? Colonial rule did degrade its subjects in many ways, often by denying them the political and civil rights that their (usually white) rulers enjoyed. But in our cases, prior to the outbreak of the violence the members of the secessionist population enjoyed, as citizens, political and legal equality in the host state, and the secessionist group enjoyed a form of internal self-determination (that is, self-government). Moreover, prior to the outbreak of the secessionist conflict, the secessionist population was not exposed to the kind of state-sponsored random violence that, according to Fanon, characterizes oppressive colonial rule. The violence to which Igbo settlers in the Northern Region of Nigeria were exposed in 1966–67 was not state organized. While many Igbo at the time rejected the rule of the host state and regarded it as oppressive, its rule was not comparable to that of a colonial power as Fanon describes it. Another question is whether the value of the host state's removal belongs to the same scale of values as human life. This question is addressed in the sections that follow.

Secession: Rectifying a Moral Injustice by Lethal Force?

In our four cases, *prior* to the outbreak of violence, the host state neither systematically denied equal political and civil rights to the members of the secessionist population nor organized or sponsored random violence that led to its (alleged) moral degradation. What else could have led to moral degradation or moral injustice for the minority group? Perhaps we should approach this question by asking first what the host state in each of our four cases denied to the members of the minority national group the secessionist movements sought to liberate.

In each case, the host state denied external—but not internal—self-determination to the national groups that were a minority in the state but the majority population in the (secessionist) territory; that is, they denied these groups independent statehood. At the time of writing, Serbia, Russia, and Nigeria refuse to recognize the independent statehood declared by secessionists in Kosovo, Chechnya, and Biafra, but they nevertheless offer a high degree of legislative and political autonomy to these groups. Liberal democratic political systems have not (as yet) consolidated in Nigeria and Serbia, and Russia, in spite of its liberal democratic institutions, has an authoritarian regime. But the establishment of a liberal democracy was not the primary aim of the secessionist authorities in Biafra, Kosovo, and Chechnya; the issue of liberal democracy or the lack of it was not central to any of these secessionist conflicts. For the sake of the present discussion, then, we can ignore the issue of liberal democracy and focus on the effects that the denial of independent statehood has on the secessionist population.

Does the absence of external (but not internal) self-determination affect the moral integrity of members of the national groups that lack external self-determination? In their federal or administrative unit, members of the minority have the right to use their language, celebrate their cultures and their religious and other holidays, and display their national symbols. In their unit, their language and culture are not only equal to the majority language and culture of the host state but dominate over all other cultures and languages. Yet even in a consolidated liberal democratic host state it is highly unlikely (but not impossible) that members of national minorities would come to wield sovereign powers by holding the highest offices in the host state. Further, certain decisions regarding, for instance, the economy, security, and military and foreign affairs are, even in a liberal democratic host state, made jointly with members of other national groups, including the majority national group. This makes it impossible for representatives of a national minority to have a *veto* power with respect to such decisions. In this sense, a minority group, as a group, has less political power than the majority group. However, the lack of power, as a group, to veto these decisions and to elect officials wielding sovereign powers does not imply that members of these groups are not *morally* equal to the members of the majority group. In short, the denial of specific political powers to minority *groups* does not entail the denial of the equal moral status of their *members*.

Does the lack of these political powers *necessarily* negatively affect the well-being of the group? In our four cases, the lack of these political powers did not, prior to the outbreak of violence, thwart the flourishing of these minority national groups in the host state. On the contrary, in cultural as well as in economic and political matters the target groups had flourished either in their territorial units or in the host state at large. Moreover, within the federal political system of the host members, members of the four national groups—Slovenes, Kosovo Albanians, Chechens, and Igbo—held the highest state offices in their respective host states. However, initially many Kosovo Albanians (in 1912) and Chechens (from 1830 to 1859) opposed, by the force of arms, the incorporation of their homelands into these host states, and in 1918 many Slovenes would have probably chosen another host state or independence, had they at the time been offered any such choice. Because their opposition originated in the rejection of a foreign state and alien political domination and not in any obstacles to the well-being of their national group, it was possible to keep alive the idea of independent statehood of these groups as long as they were inhabiting a foreign host state even when their well-being was not under threat. In the case of Biafra, the demands for independent statehood were made in response to the indiscriminate violence to which the settlers from that territory were exposed in the Northern Region of Nigeria; this had certainly endangered the well-being of the Igbo people in Nigeria at the time. Yet several years after the defeat of Biafra, partly as a result of the host state's attempts at reconciliation, the Igbo citizens no longer faced discrimination or obstacles to their well-being in Nigeria and in the successor-federal units of Biafra. Ojukwu, their erstwhile secessionist leader, returned to Nigeria in 1982 and ran as candidate for the presidency of Nigeria in 2007.

National minorities having to inhabit a foreign state—a state in which the majority of the population is foreign—is sometimes represented as an injustice they have to bear; it is an injustice because they lack the institutions that would allow them to give expression to their identity on par with the majority.[8] But if being a national minority leads only to a denial of certain *political* powers, this is no good reason to regard it as *moral* injustice or degradation. Further, even if one were to concede that the denial of these or any other political powers is morally unjust, the fact of such injustice would not by itself entail that rectification by any means, including lethal force, is morally justified or permissible. Killing for the sake of rectification of that particular (allegedly) moral injustice—killing for the sake of achieving independent statehood—may still be morally impermissible.

How might one go about proving otherwise? The first step in such an argument would be to show that independent statehood—as the only way to rectify the moral injustice of being a minority in a foreign state—is a value on par with human life; that is, that the two values are morally commensurate. In the writings of academic advocates of the right to unilateral secession (including the work of Yael Tamir), I can find no argument that the value of independent statehood, for those who are denied having an independent state, can be compared to the value of human life.[9] This does not prove, of course, that the two values are not comparable; it only suggests a lack of reasoned argument for their moral comparison.

Secession as a Self-Defense of Last Resort: Does It Justify Killing?

Yet many theorists of secession believe that unilateral secession, that is, independent statehood, is an instrument of last resort in self-defense.[10] Individuals are morally permitted or justified to kill the people who endanger their lives; killing in self-defense is justifiable or permissible. If independent statehood is only an instrument of self-defense, then it is morally permissible or justified to kill people who violently oppose this use of independent statehood. If so, one can argue by analogy that killing people in *secessionist* self-defense is justified or permissible.

There are two questions that arise here. What is the "self" that is being defended in secessionist conflict generally and, in particular, in our four cases? And does the defense of this particular self justify or allow killing people who are, allegedly, attacking that self? In reply to the first question, one should note that both sides in a secessionist conflict allege to be defending the same self: the population and the territory settled by the target secessionist group. The host states claim they are defending the population and territory from the secessionist organizations and leaders. These organizations discriminate against, expel, or attack their opponents (who usually belong to the majority national groups in the host states) and are illegally using armed force against the lawful authorities. The secessionist authorities, on the other hand, claim they are defending the population and territory from the host state, which they consider illegitimate, discriminatory, and oppressive and which they assert uses armed force against the members of their national group. Each side is thus arguing that its use of force is justified self-defense against an armed aggression by the other side.

In many violent secessions, as in our four cases, it is sometimes difficult to establish who is the defender and who the aggressor. The deck is stacked against the host state because, as a state, it claims monopoly over the use of force on the territory and claims the right to exercise its monopoly against any political movement that threatens it. Moreover, an armed secessionist movement is usually significantly inferior in terms of its military force and, therefore, the host state, armed to the teeth, is pitted against a mostly unarmed and seemingly defenseless population that rejects its legitimacy. For these reasons, then, host states often appear as aggressors. Even though it was the secessionist armed forces—on the admission of their own leaders after the event—that pulled the trigger first in Slovenia and Kosovo, that mattered little, if at all, because a host state in such secessionist conflicts is regularly regarded as the aggressor for the simple reason that it is using armed force against its own (allegedly) unarmed citizens. But the secessionist forces also used or threatened to use lethal force against both the host state agents who were not attacking (or preparing to attack) them and/or "disloyal" civilians. In other words, the secessionist forces used or threatened to use lethal force in cases that were not, strictly speaking, those of self-defense or the defense of the defenseless. In short, if the secessionist use of lethal force is not confined to self-defense—the "self" here being understood as constituted by the members of the secessionist population—then the host state is not the only aggressor in the conflict.

The objectives of the secessionist organizations in our four conflicts appear to confirm this conclusion; they gained political control over their target populations or national groups in the secessionist territory prior to the outbreak of warfare. One of their objectives was to deny the host state military control over the territory and to expel their military forces from it. As Terry Rugeley, Peter Sluggett, and Raphael Chijioke Njoku point out in their chapters, in other attempts at secession one can discern a similar overall objective of securing military control over the secessionist territory. For any authority that claims to exercise sovereign powers, securing military control over a territory is necessary to securing its independence from other states. The monopoly over the use of force is still the distinguishing mark of independent statehood—and, in consequence, any secessionist authority attempting to establish its claim to independent statehood would need to secure military control over the territory it claims. Moreover, in our four cases the secessionist authorities had some reason to believe that unless they expelled the host state's military forces, the host state would always be in a position to deny them political control over their target populations.

But do attempts to deny the host state's military control over its territory count as self-defense? David Rodin argues in *Wars and Self-Defence* (2003) that defending a territory by lethal force from the armed forces of another state is not necessarily analogous to the paradigmatic cases of individual self-defense. In many cases of national territorial defense, he points out, there is no immediate or immanent threat to the lives of the soldiers or the civilian population of an invaded state. The aim of the invading state in such cases is to gain control over the territory (with or without its population), if possible without killing anyone; the invading state threatens to kill anyone who resists its invasion, but not anyone who is found on or living on the territory.

Rodin argues that a state's legitimate claim to control over territory cannot, in *every case* of military invasion of such a state, *morally* justify or excuse killing the invading soldiers. This conclusion, Rodin notes, contradicts the doctrines of just war theories that regard as morally justified the killing of the invading soldiers (of a foreign state) by the state that is being invaded. The same argument, I think, can be applied to the use of armed force *both* by the host state *and* its secessionist adversaries: killing armed soldiers whose objective is to gain or maintain military control over territory *cannot* be *morally* justified, no matter who the killer is—a secessionist or a soldier of the host state. In my opinion, killing people is not an action that can be ranked on the same scale of moral values as military or political control over territory. I am thus claiming that to rank the value of military or political control over territory higher than the lives of many armed combatants of both sides is wrong because then we are putting human lives on a scale that cannot or does not measure the value of lives. In other words, military control over a territory is not morally commensurate with human life, at least within a universal humanist framework. Since the value of every human life is within such a framework equal, the value of an individual life is commensurate only with the value of another life. For this reason, I am morally justified in taking someone's life only if that person threatens, immediately or immanently, the life of another person or, as in the case of mercy killing, when the life of that person is not worth living (for the kind of ending of life (by killing) that we call mercy killing can be ranked on the same scale of moral values as that of life lived in unremitting pain without any hope of recovery and on that moral scale, it can be argued that the ending of such life ranks higher than the life lived in unremitting pain).[11] I am not justified in killing that person if that person is engaged in a military operation that I *only think or fear* will result in the killing of unarmed and unresisting civilians. In Biafra (and perhaps in Chechnya) many secessionist fighters probably feared that the host state's military occupation of the territory in which their unarmed co-nationals lived would result in their killing. In Biafra they feared this because their co-nationals had indeed been killed in pogroms in the very same host state only a short time earlier. Their fear may indeed *excuse* their killing of the host-state soldiers invading their homeland. Fearing for one's safety or the safety of other defenseless people often excuses the killing of those who are the source of the fear, but these fears do not make that killing a case of justified self-defense. In the humanist view, too, the fear for one's safety and for the safety of others, however justified the fear is, does not, by itself, *morally justify* the killing of the host state's agents or soldiers—let alone the unarmed supporters of the host state.

In violent conflicts or war, the prescriptions of universal humanism are usually breached for two different reasons: on one hand, people who fear their adversaries' violence often engage in preemptive violence even when not under attack and, on the other, political leaders and their followers often measure the value of human life in ways that override such prescriptions. Nationalist ideologies in particular suggest a valuation of human life according to which the life of any member of the enemy nation—for instance, the Serbs for Kosovo Albanians or Kosovo Albanians for the Serbs—is regarded as being of lower value and therefore, at least in warfare, as expendable. According to such ideologies, killing members of the enemy nations in warfare is not only justified but also commendable. Contrary to those who regard nationalism as an ethical doctrine, I do not think that nationalist ideologies provide good reasons to regard the actions to which such ideologies exhort their followers as morally justified. I do not think that nationalist ideologies are or contain moral doctrines for the simple reason that they privilege, on no justifiable grounds, one group against all other groups and individuals.

This chapter is not a plea for excuses (to refer to the title of J. L. Austin's essay on moral questions); it is not intended to defend the actions of host states, not least host states' use of armed force against secessionists. In all four cases, the host state flouted universal humanism as much if not more than the secessionists; this is not surprising, given that both sides were (and still are) motivated by nationalist ideologies. The aim of this chapter had been to encourage us to examine critically the uses of lethal force by both sides of secessionist conflict and to challenge a few popular justifications of the secessionist use of lethal force. My tentative conclusion, that there is no moral justification, within the framework of universal humanism, for the use of lethal force by either side in certain kinds of secessionist conflicts, is not surprising. Nor do I expect this conclusion to prevent or stop such use of lethal force. Political leaders in secessionist and other conflicts will continue to claim that they have morality on their side when they advocate, for purely political reasons, the use of lethal force. From this, many—including the politicians themselves—infer that their justifications for using lethal force are of a moral nature too. I hope that I have offered some reasons to question rhetoric of this kind.

Notes

1. Susan L. Woodward *Balkan Tragedy: Chaos and Dissolution after the Cold War,* (Washington, D.C.: Brookings Institution Press, 1995), 165–67; Aleksandar Pavković, *The Fragmentation of Yugoslavia: Nationalism and War in the Balkans* (Basingstoke, U.K.: Palgrave, 2000), 135–41.

2. Pavković, *The Fragmentation of Yugoslavia,* 184–200.

3. Matthew Evangelista, *The Chechen Wars: Will Russia Go the Way of the Soviet Union?* (Washington, D.C.: Brookings Institution Press, 2002).

4. John de St. Jorre, *The Nigerian Civil War* (London: Hodder and Stoughton, 1972).

5. As Stathis N. Kalyvas notes, indiscriminate violence against civilians can result in civilians cutting off support (both in supplies and in recruits) to the insurgents; the violence thus appears to "paralyze" the civilians (*The Logic of Violence in Civil War* [Cambridge: Cambridge University Press, 2003], 167).

6. For the expulsions in Chechnya prior to the outbreak of the first war, see Anatoly V. Isaenko and Peter W. Petschauer, "A Failure That Transformed Russia: The 1991–94 Democratic State-Building Experiment in Chechnya," *International Social Science Review* 75, nos. 1/2 (2000): 3–13.

7. For a further discussion, see Aleksandar Pavković "Terrorism as an Instrument of Liberation: A Liberation Ideology Perspective," in *Ethics of Terrorism and Counterterrorism,* ed. George Meggle (Frankfurt: Ontos, 2005), 245–61.

8. Yael Tamir, *Liberal Nationalim* (Princeton: Princeton University Press, 1993).

9. For a discussion of this issue, see Aleksandar Pavković, "Liberalism, Secession and Violence," in *Sovereignty and Diversity,* ed. Miograd Jovanovic and Kirstin Henrard (Amsterdam: Eleven International Publishing, 2008), 15–31.

10. For example, Alan Buchanan, "Theories of Secession," *Philosophy and Public Af-*

fairs 26, no. 1 (1997): 31–61; Paul Gilbert, *New Terror, New Wars*, (Washington, D.C.: Georgetown University Press, 2003); and Aris Gounaris, "Self-Determination and Secession: A Moral Theory Perspective," in *On the Way to Statehood*, ed. Aleksandar Pavković and Peter Radan (Burlington, Vt.: Ashgate, 2008), 117–32.

11. For a further elaboration of this argument, see Aleksandar Pavković, "Killing for One's Country," in *Patriotism: Philosophical and Political Perspectives*, ed. Igor Primoratz and Aleksandar Pavković (Burlington, Vt.: Ashgate, 2008), 219–34.

PAUL KUBICEK

Structure, Agency, and Secessionism in the Soviet Union and Post-Soviet States

Any comparative consideration of secessionist movements should take into account the Soviet and post-Soviet experience. Although ethnopolitical mobilization did not occur in all Soviet republics or regions, the implosion of the Soviet empire produced the most successful wave of secessionism in modern times. Fifteen independent countries now exist in the post-Soviet space. The end of the Soviet Union, meanwhile, has not seen the end of separatist movements in post-Soviet states, as demonstrated by ongoing conflicts in Chechnya, Abkhazia, Transnistria, and Nagorno-Karabakh. The Soviet and post-Soviet experience therefore represents a wonderful opportunity for those interested in secessionist movements, offering as it does numerous cases to study and compare.

Although many strong secessionist movements have materialized in the former Soviet Union, there are also many dogs that did not bark: ethnic groups or regions that one thought might witness secessionist mobilization but did not. In addition, there have been several cases in which groups mobilized but in which the crisis was defused peacefully. While it is perfectly natural to want to examine the often dramatic cases of Soviet and post-Soviet secessionist movements, one should not forget the more quiescent peoples and regions when trying to explain why secessionist movements occur and how they fare. In social science parlance, one should not select cases on the dependent variable.

This chapter first reviews the literature associated with the development of secessionist movements in the Soviet Union and puts forward several hypotheses about secessionism that one can apply to the Soviet context and, hopefully, to other contexts as well. Second, it examines in more detail the cases of Moldova and Ukraine, focusing in particular on their experiences in the post-Soviet environment. Located on the western edge of the post-Soviet space, parts of both Ukraine and Moldova were, for long periods of time, ruled by states other than Russia. Both have significant minorities that could make separatist claims. Of the two, Moldova has faced the greater threat from its Transnistria region, but it has managed to defuse ethnic Gagauz separatism. Meanwhile, despite marked regional fissures in Ukraine, its main separatist crisis, in Crimea, was resolved and a secessionist movement it was threatened with in the eastern region of Donbas did not occur. This chapter argues that although there are structural factors that facilitate secessionism, human agency—more specifically, the agency of political elites—matters greatly. Where it is possible for elites to achieve "voice" within a state, secessionism is less likely or can be defused. If there is little prospect for gaining "voice" within the state, "exit," or separatism, becomes far more likely.[1]

EXPLAINING SECESSIONISM IN THE SOVIET UNION

The collapse of the Soviet Union was brought about by two failures: that of Communist ideology to deliver on its promises and that of the Soviet government to maintain control over its disparate peoples and regions. What led to these failures is hotly debated, but this lies beyond the scope of this chapter. Instead, my focus is on the collapse of the Soviet state in the face of ethnoseparatist mobilization. This is not to say that there was nothing unique about the Soviet experience but rather that we should not treat the Soviet experience as sui genesis because of its ideology.

One should note at the outset that secessionism in the Soviet Union came as a surprise to many observers. Various groups held grievances against Russian/Soviet rule for decades, but it wasn't until Gorbachev's reforms in the 1980s that political mobilization around nationalist-secessionist causes became possible. The net result, as Mark Beissinger notes, was that the "seemingly impossible" became "seemingly inevitable."[2] Nonetheless, not all ethnic minorities mobilized in the waning days of the Soviet Union. Some ethnic groups developed sizeable separatist movements. Others did not. The factors that account for the appearance of ethnoseparatist movements in the Soviet case fall into four categories: institutional, cultural/historical, economic, and agental.

Institutional Factors

The Soviet Union was a federal state. For much of its history, this had little practical relevance, but it did mean that the various regions of the USSR had both geographic boundaries and their own political and economic administrations, even though these administrations were largely under the control of Moscow. This division, which had the effect of creating republic-level institutions, was important for a variety of reasons. First, the republics were not merely geographic entities or administrative divisions; they were designed to be ethnopolitical units. For example, Ukraine and Moldova were, in theory at least, "homelands" of ethnic Ukrainians and Moldovans. In this respect, Soviet republics were qualitatively different from, let's say, South Carolina or Michigan. Some observers argue that the very carving out of geographic boundaries for various republics, particularly those in Central Asia but also arguably in Moldova, contributed to the formation of a "Kazakh," "Kyrgyz," and "Moldovan" nation or consciousness where there had been none before.[3] Soviet institutions, in other words, helped create ethnonational identities that, eventually, were activated and that then rebelled against central authority.

Cultural/Historical Factors

While an institutional or structural account is part of the explanation, it leaves many cold. Why, one might ask, would peoples and elites seek secession—typically a radical solution—instead of simply more decentralization and local governance? What, in other words, was the *motive* behind separatism?

For some, the fact that the secessionist movements in the Soviet Union had an ethnocultural component is central to the story. Nationalist and secessionist arguments were not, publicly at least, primarily about explicit material interests. Masses mobilized because they wanted to assert their distinctive cultural rights and preserve their identities against what they saw as a cultural threat from Soviet rule, which many equated with Russification. They wanted to be Estonian or Latvian, not Russian or Soviet. Moreover, because republican-level institutions already were in place, the cultural/nationalist card was the easiest one to play against the central authorities. Political action thus came to crystallize around ethnic identification.

In addition, one could argue that it is not culture per se but the historical experience of different ethnocultural groups that is most critical. Years of repression, so this argument goes, account for why different ethnic groups want to separate. Thus, for example, memories of Soviet brutality during World War II and in its immediate aftermath are invoked to explain Baltic, Crimean Tatar, and Chechen resistance to Soviet authority. The Balts, Moldova, and Western Ukraine, which were not ruled by Moscow until the 1940s, also had a different historical experience that made them less amenable to the idea of remaining in the Soviet Union.

Economic Factors

Economic considerations may make some regions more prone to separatism than others. The desire to control natural resources (as in the case of Biafra) or to preserve certain economic policies or structures (as in the case of the Confederate States of America) can provide an additional, "rational" explanation for secessionism. Indeed, economic arguments did emerge during ethnonationalist mobilization against Soviet rule. What was striking, however, was that it was the relatively richer republics—those who relied less on subsidies from Moscow and who thought they would have far better economic prospects as independent states—that were the leaders in the drive to escape Soviet rule. Thus, one sees the richer Baltic republics spearheading secessionism, while populations and elites in the poorer Central Asian states remained conspicuously unmobilized. Moreover, one could argue that a higher standard of living provides a strong material or social capital basis for mass secessionist movements.

Agental Factors

Various structural or historical factors may make one region more prone to separatism than another. However, secessionism is also a choice—a program adopted by political actors. In the Soviet case, one saw both a mass secessionist movement in several republics and, at a certain point, the adoption of the secessionist agenda by political elites, who until then had been loyal Communist Party stalwarts.

How does agency fit into the Soviet cases? Beissinger, in an effort to resolve the structure-agency debate, emphasizes the dynamic or "tidal" factor in late Soviet-period separatist movements.[4] The catalyst was Gorbachev's reforms, which created new incentives and possibilities for separatism at the mass and elite level. The Baltic states, which possessed a "latent nationalist frame" and a "high degree of pre-existing facilitating structure," were best poised to take advantage of Gorbachev's opening.[5] Their example provided inspiration and emboldened would-be separatists elsewhere. As events unfolded, initial demands for cultural autonomy, language rights, and environmental protection gave way to more radical demands for independent statehood.[6]

What about the political elites? One could start with an institutional perspective that argues that a decentralized political structure, however pro forma, creates psychological and material instrumentalist incentives for elites to begin to think about defending *their* own turf, procuring *their* resources, or expanding their rights and powers; the emergence of such strategic thinking can be seen as analogous to the development of "states' rights" rhetoric prior to the U.S. Civil War. Republic-level elites, particularly those who realized that their careers would not carry them to Moscow, became bosses of their own little fiefdoms. In the 1970s and early 1980s, this arrangement facilitated graft and corruption. In the latter half of the 1980s, when Gorbachev's reforms opened up possibilities for economic decentralization and popular input into policy, republican elites became "national Communists"; they became interested in securing more rights for the republic vis-à-vis the center. Later, realizing that communist authority was doomed and that nationalism would win them popular support, many of them shed communism completely, becoming "fathers" of their new country.[7]

The core notion here is that institutions make agency possible. Republic-level elites had much greater opportunity for "voice" and power in a separate country than in the Soviet Union. For most of the Soviet period, of course, "exit" was not an option. By the late 1980s, however, it was, and many elites eventually made the decisive choice to embrace the separatist impulse. Although less parsimonious than an explanation that focuses on just one or two factors, this narrative—which can also acknowledge the role played by factors such as size of ethnic group (bigger is better), linguistic assimilation (the less assimilated to Russian, the better), and urbanization (a facilitating variable)—does a nice job of accounting for the dynamic wave of separatism in the Soviet Union.

POST-SOVIET SEPARATISM

The breakup of the Soviet state did not spell the end of separatism among post-Soviet peoples. However, whereas one might say that a separatist wave washed over much of the Soviet Union during the period from 1988 to 1991, in the post-

Soviet context separatist movements have been the exception, not the rule. For example, out of the twenty-one ethnically defined republics within the Russian Federation, only Chechnya has seen a sustained, violent separatist movement. Elsewhere, despite fears, especially among ethnic Russians and other minority groups, that "nationalizing states" would be established and alienate minorities, there has been just one case (an unsuccessful one at that—Crimea) in which an area with an ethnic Russian majority has spearheaded secessionism.[8] With the exception of Chechnya, the most dramatic cases of separatism have unfolded beyond Russia's borders. The common pattern among separatist regions such as Abkhazia, South Ossetia, Transnistria, and Crimea has been for local populations to claim ethnic or historical distinctiveness and to turn to Moscow for political, economic, and/or military support. Yet not all regions or ethnic minorities have rallied for secession, and some have been willing to settle for new political arrangements short of independence.

How can one account for differences across cases, taking into account both active secessionist movements and the "dogs that don't bark"? By looking at differing outcomes in Ukraine and Moldova, one can put forward hypotheses that explain secessionism in the post-Soviet context.

SEPARATISM IN POST-SOVIET UKRAINE AND MOLDOVA

As new countries that lacked prior experience of statehood and that were inhabited by ethnic minorities who exhibited ambivalence and/or hostility to their very formation, Ukraine and Moldova faced significant challenges. Both states also had acute economic difficulties and problems in making the transition to a more democratic political system. Historical/cultural factors as well as economic and political weakness created a ripe environment for separatism.

Outcomes between the two states have differed markedly. Ukraine, despite the persistence of marked regional divisions, has maintained its territorial integrity. Its most significant separatist crisis—Crimea—never became violent and was peacefully resolved. There were other separatist movements percolating, but in the end no others emerged. In contrast, Moldova has been unable to establish control over the breakaway Transdniestr region. The Gagauz separatist crisis, like that in Crimea, however, was resolved through political negotiations. What accounts for the differences in these cases? What broader lessons can be learned from a comparison of them? It is to these questions that we now turn.

UKRAINE: SEPARATISM AVERTED

By many conventional measures, Ukraine seemed ripe for separatism. It had no experience of statehood, a relatively weak sense of national identity, historically based regional divisions, ethnic minorities, and, especially in the early 1990s, economic hardship.

Ukraine, however, survived. Regionalism has been persistent, but it has not given way to a successful separatist movement. One writer in the late 1990s even described separatism as a "myth."[9] Why has this been the case, particularly when other post-Soviet states have seen sustained and violent separatist movements? Let us examine the two major regions of Ukraine that had the greatest potential for separatism.

Crimea

For numerous reasons, Crimea has been the site of the most concerted separatist movement in Ukraine. Crimea is the only region in Ukraine with a majority (67 percent in 1989) of ethnic Russians. Most were born in Russia, suggesting they would have strong ties to Russia as their "homeland." Crimea has a long association with the Russian Empire, and it is well enshrined as "Russian" land thanks to its conquest by Catherine the Great at the end of the eighteenth century. It was transferred to Ukraine only in 1954, a symbolic gesture to commemorate three hundred years of unity between Russia and Ukraine. Finally, the Soviet Black Sea Fleet was headquartered there, and a large percentage of the population was active-duty or retired Soviet military.

Separatist mobilization began in 1989, a direct result of Ukrainian national mobilization. Crimean elites lobbied for restoration of the region's autonomous status (revoked in 1946) and worked to prevent the return of the exiled Crimean Tatars, the people native to the region. By 1990, with the prospect of an independent Ukraine becoming more likely, many in Crimea began to call for the region to be returned to Russia. In January 1991, in defiance of Kyiv, Crimean authorities held a referendum in which 93 percent of voters declared their desire to see Crimea awarded autonomous status in the federal structure of the Soviet Union. Ukrainian authorities granted the region an autonomous status within the borders of Ukraine in February 1991, giving Crimea its own parliament and control over local social and cultural matters. This strengthened the hand of Crimea's political elites and gave them resources and means to pursue their own independent agenda. As Taras Kuzio and David Mayer put it, Crimea "possessed institutions that the Russian local majority could use in the process of ethno-political mobilization" to "marshal[] resources and channel[] ethnic grievances into formal interest articulation and policy formation."[10]

A bare majority of Crimean residents—54 percent—voted in favor of Ukrainian independence in December 1991, and, as Paul Pirie has noted, this slim majority vote reflected an "ambivalent" political consciousness in the region.[11] Indeed, very quickly many in Crimea embraced the idea of Crimean independence or unification with Russia. In May 1992, the Crimean Parliament declared the region independent and proposed a referendum on the matter, but the Ukrainian government declared such actions illegal. It ordered the Crimean authorities to desist their movement toward separatism but kept the door to dialogue open. In June 1992 the Ukrainian Parliament passed a law delineating powers between the national government and Kyiv that gave Crimea a large measure of autonomy. Kyiv also pledged economic assistance to Crimea. These proved to be temporary solutions, however, as in 1994 a separatist candidate, Yuri Meshkov, was elected to the new post of president of Crimea. Meanwhile, public opinion surveys in 1995 showed that only 6 percent of Crimeans would vote for Ukrainian independence from the Soviet Union.[12]

Crimean separatists received political support from Russia. Various Russian politicians claimed Crimea as Russian territory. In May 1992, the Russian Parliament declared the transfer of Crimea to Ukraine an illegal act. Alexander Rutskoi, the Russian vice president, argued that actions taken by Khrushchev in 1954 "under the influence of a hangover or sunstroke" did not "cancel out the history of Crimea."[13] Negotiations over the status of the Black Sea Fleet complicated matters as well, and in July 1993 the Russian Parliament adopted a resolution declaring Sevastopol, the Crimean city that headquartered the fleet, Russian territory. Given the line Russia had adopted and the strong separatist sentiment within Crimea, there were real fears of military conflict.

This did not occur. By 1996 Crimea's status as an autonomous region within Ukraine had been agreed on by the relevant parties.

Several factors help explain why Crimean separatism did not succeed. The first is that outside support, although vocal, was not that significant. Russians were not funneling arms to Crimean separatists. The Black Sea Fleet did not, unlike the Russian Fourteenth Army in Moldova, ally with separatists and confront Ukrainian forces. Why not? Part of the answer is that Boris Yeltsin did not want to risk hostilities with Kyiv. On many occasions he distanced himself from actions taken by the more nationalist-oriented Russian Parliament. Secondly, by early 1995, Russia was bogged down in Chechnya and was not in a strong position to lend a hand to separatists in Crimea. Third, unlike in Transnistria, where separatist forces had declared their independence prior to the collapse of the Soviet Union, Crimea was part of Ukraine when it became independent. Battling Ukraine over Crimea therefore would be an open violation of Yeltsin's commitment to respecting the republican borders of the Soviet Union.

In addition, political forces within Crimea were divided. Although Meshkov was elected with solid support in 1994, he alienated the Crimean Parliament by asserting strong presidential powers. This caused political divisions within Crimea and prevented Crimeans from presenting a united front. When Kyiv acted in March 1995 to strip Meshkov of his post and pursue criminal prosecution against him, many in Crimea welcomed the move, as they thought Meshkov had overstepped his authority. Noting the failure of the population to rally to Meshkov's defense, Pirie again highlights the ambivalent or vacillating political culture in the region. Most Crimeans had contradictory attitudes; they desired that Crimea become part of Russia at the same time that they wished not to secede from Ukraine.[14]

Finally, one should emphasize that the Ukrainian government issued, both in 1992 and in 1995, a strong response to Crimean separatism. Both of Ukraine's presidents in the 1990s refused to discuss border changes or federalism. Declarations of independence by Crimean authorities were swiftly condemned. In March 1995, the Ukrainian Parliament voted to suspend Crimea's constitution, abolish the post of the Crimean president, and place the Crimean government under the control of the national government. This narrowed the range of institutions available for ethnopolitical mobilization. These measures undertaken to maintain Ukraine's borders enjoyed broad public support throughout Ukraine—even among the country's ethnic Russians.[15]

This is not to suggest that Kyiv simply strong-armed Crimea. The Ukrainian government adopted a relatively liberal policy toward ethnic minorities, making it clear that there would be no rapid or forced "Ukrainianization." Crimean autonomy within Ukraine was also never taken off the table, making it possible for the parties to negotiate a compromise that recognized Crimea's special status. Put differently, the possibility that Crimea might gain voice dampened its desire for exit.

Since 1995, the authorities in Crimea have been dominated by Tatar, centrist, and left-wing parties opposed to separatism. The majority of the pro-Russian forces have "forgotten about their slogans calling for the annexation of Crimea to Russia" and have focused instead on issues such as protection of the Russian language and the formation of closer ties between Ukraine and Russia.[16] In 1997, Moscow and Kyiv finally concluded agreements on the status of the Black Sea Fleet and signed a treaty that definitively recognized Ukrainian sovereignty over Crimea.

Donbas

One might have thought that Donbas in southeastern Ukraine would present at least as much of a separatist challenge as Crimea. The majority (66 percent) of its population, like Crimea's, claim Russian as its native language, although, unlike Crimea, ethnic Russians do not constitute a majority of the population.[17] It was incorporated into the Russian Empire in the 1600s; its links with Russia are thus even more long-standing than Crimea's. It is heavily industrialized, and its industries (coal mining; steel, chemical, and armaments production) were heavily integrated into the Soviet economy. It also borders Russia, making it more likely that it might consider leaving Ukraine for Russia than it would if it didn't border Russia. However, although leaders and publics in Donbas have pushed for economic autonomy and rights for the Russian language, there has been, with a brief exception during the 2004 Orange Revolution, little discussion of Donbas separatism.

Why not? One could advance several explanations. On cultural grounds, while it is true that large numbers of the region's inhabitants are ethnically Russian, most were born in Ukraine. There is some nostalgia for the Soviet Union among Donbas residents, but regardless of their ethnicity, few see Russia as their motherland, and there is a long tradition in the region of intermarriage and intermixing of languages and cultures of the two countries.[18] In 1991, 89 percent of Russians in Donbas agreed that "I do not feel myself to be a stranger in this Republic."[19] Moreover, it is worth mentioning again that the central government in Kyiv did not pursue immediate Ukrainianization. While Ukrainian was introduced in the schools, Russian was not pushed out, and in 1994 the government even adopted a program to protect both the Russian language and Russian culture. Interestingly, the Ukrainian census in 2001 revealed that the percentage of people in Donbas claiming to be ethnically Russian declined to 39 percent from 45 percent in 1989.[20] This is not primarily due to out-migration; rather, it indicates that more individuals now view themselves as Ukrainian.

Perhaps, however, regionalism rather than ethnicity per se may be the spur for separatist movements. Multivariate analysis of public opinion data shows that ethnicity, occupation, and income are less reliable predictors of political attitudes than region.[21] Surveys in the 1990s revealed that residents of Donbas were much more likely to favor closer ties with Russia and were more skeptical about the benefits of market reform. Indeed, it was the dire economic situation in the Ukrainian rustbelt that produced the largest mass action in Donbas: strikes by miners and other industrial workers in the summer of 1993 that called for early elections, federalism, and economic autonomy for the region. Donbas voters indicated in a regional referendum in 1994 that they supported a federal Ukraine and more rights for the Russian language, but Ukrainian remained the sole state language, federalism was not adopted, and Donbas acquired no special regional privileges.

Donbas does not, unlike Crimea, have political institutions to facilitate secessionism. Its elites, however, also have less incentive to pursue separatism. Local elites in Donbas have secured immense wealth thanks to the region's resources as well as to their serving in important national-level political positions. In the aftermath of the 1993 miners' strike, for example, a Donbas mine director was made acting prime minister. Other leaders from Donbas have risen to political prominence, including Viktor Yanukovych, who served as prime minister (2002–4, 2006–7). In other words, working within the system, many Donbas elites have found voice. Over time, they have become loyal to the state. They are not interested in exit. Kuzio notes that the "Donbas elites understand that they have better opportunities within Ukraine than within a Russia which does not require another decaying industrial region with more troublesome coal miners. . . . Asked whether the Donbas would be better in Russia the Chairman of Donets'k oblast council, Vladimir Shcherban, replied: 'There are no "what ifs" in history. We have what we have. And we have to work from this reality instead of engaging in guesses. Donbas is an inalienable part of Ukraine.'"[22]

The time the idea of Donbas separatism was floated proves the point about the importance of having a political voice. Throughout the 1990s, the more populous regions of eastern Ukraine had the votes and insider connections to control national politics. During the 2004 Orange Revolution, however, Viktor Yushchenko, whose strongest base of support was in western Ukraine, prevailed over Donbas's Yanukovych. By this point, Yanukovych's own shenanigans and ties to the widely discredited president of Ukraine, Leonid Kuchma, meant that much of central and even east-central Ukraine was willing to vote for the allegedly archnationalist Yushchenko. Faced with the prospect of Yanukovych's defeat, some in Donbas suggested that they have a referendum on separatism. This was widely denounced throughout Ukraine, and it was never held. In 2006 Yanukovych's Party of Regions won the largest number of votes in parliamentary elections, and he became prime minister again. The Ukrainian economy at that time was performing relatively well, thanks in part to rising prices for steel manufactured in eastern Ukrainian regions such as Donbas. Donbas is one of the richest regions in Ukraine. There is little talk of Donbas separatism today.

Lastly, one should note that unlike Crimea, Donbas would not be able to rely on any external support for separatism. In simple terms, Donbas, full of slag heaps and smokestacks, lacks the charms of Crimea. In asserting the Russianness of Crimea, one Russian acknowledged that Donbas is "another question."[23]

MOLDOVA: DIVERGENT SEPARATIST OUTCOMES

Independent Moldova has wrestled with two major separatist crises in Transnistria and Gagauzia. The first erupted into violence and is one of the most intractable post-Soviet secessionist movements. The second, which appeared to be quite serious when Moldova became independent, was resolved peacefully in the mid-1990s.

Transnistrian Secessionism

Transnistrian separatism, which calls for independence for a narrow strip of territory east of the Dniestr River that borders Ukraine, posed a major challenge to the nascent Moldovan state.[24] Two weeks after Moldova declared itself independent in August 1991, the Transnistrian government—which had already proclaimed itself a separate republic in 1990 and was openly pro-Soviet and pro-Communist—announced its intention to remain with the Soviet Union. In December 1991 elections, 95 percent of the region's electorate supported the creation of the Transnistrian Moldavian Republic (TMR), and Igor Smirnov, who had been arrested in August of that year for supporting the Communist coup in Moscow, was elected president. The TMR organized its own defense forces and, crucially, received political and material support from volunteer Cossacks from Russia and the Soviet (later Russian) 14th Army, which was stationed on its territory. Fighting erupted along the Moldovan-TMR border, and in June 1992 the Russian Army intervened on the side of the TMR forces. A thousand people died in the conflict. A cease-fire, concluded between Russia and Moldova in July 1992, marked the end of major hostilities, and under its terms, peacekeepers were sent in. Questions of the TMR's final status, as well as that of the Russian Army, were deferred pending further negotiations.

The conflict has been essentially frozen since that date.[25] Smirnov remains president of the TMR. Despite pledges by the Russians to withdraw their forces from the TMR, in 2007 Russian personnel as well as twenty-thousand tons of munitions remained. On the Moldovan side, defeat in the 1992 war was politically disastrous for those who wanted Moldova to unify with Romania (Moldovans and Romanians essentially share a common language), and subsequent Moldovan governments showed a willingness to negotiate a settlement.[26] For example, the 1994 Moldovan Constitution assured the Transnistrian region would have a "special status." Nonetheless, negotiations over the fate of the TMR, in which representatives from Moldova, the TMR, Russia, and Ukraine are participating, have made little progress. In 2002 and 2003, the Moldovan government proposed creating a federal state, and the Russian-backed Kozak Plan of 2003 proposed establishing a single Moldovan state and allowing Russian troops to remain in the TMR. At the last minute, allegedly because of pressure from the EU, the Moldovan government refused to sign on. Meanwhile, the TMR has built its own quasi-state structure—it has its own military, currency, and citizenship—and has became a transit point for smugglers. Many observers accuse the TMR government of being nondemocratic and of committing human rights violations.[27] In 2004 new tensions developed when TMR authorities shut down Moldovan language schools that were using the Latin ("Romanian") alphabet, as opposed to the Cyrillic-based version of Moldovan authorized by the TMR. In September 2006, TMR voters overwhelmingly (97 percent) backed a referendum supporting TMR independence and union with Russia. It is hard to envision how, especially with such a result (though one should note that no internationally recognized third-party observers were present), the two sides can forge a common state.

What accounts for TMR separatism? Its rise coincided with that of forces in Moldova that pushed for Moldova to unify with Romania. Although the 1989 census revealed that a plurality (40 percent) of the population of Transnistria was ethnically Moldovan, many are Russified. In any event, they are outnumbered by Russians and Ukrainians, who comprise the majority in the TMR. Russian is the TMR's de facto language. Transnistria, unlike the rest of Moldova,

also has ties to Russia dating to the late 1700s. The TMR's leaders could therefore make a plausible historical-cultural argument supporting separatism, particularly given the possibility that Moldova would join with Romania. However,
ideological factors were also important. Transnistrian separatists have a nostalgia for the Soviet Union; indeed, one goal was to create "an island of Soviet
power."[28] Living in Moldova would make it impossible to realize these ambitions; thus voice within Moldova was not an attractive option. In addition, the
TMR's industries were tightly integrated into the Soviet economy. By remaining part of the Soviet Union, the TMR could more easily preserve economic ties
with Moscow and factory directors in the region could be assured of retaining
their positions and ties to patrons in Moscow.[29] Economic resources—coupled
with confidence that the Soviet army would back their separatist claims—made
up for the fact that Transnistria had no recognized separate political status that
would enable it to build an institutional structure.

The more interesting question, perhaps, is why this conflict is so intractable.
After all, one of the original causes of the conflict—the prospect of Moldova
unifying with Romania—is no longer an issue. It seems that no one has sufficient incentive to resolve the conflict.[30] Elites within the Moldovan government,
although they reject the TMR's secessionist claims and have put forward some
proposals to resolve the conflict, recognize the potential problems of reintegrat-
ing this region with the rest of Moldova, especially given the current hard-line,
pro-Russian orientation of the TMR's leadership. More seriously, the TMR leadership sees little reason to negotiate. The two main political parties in the TMR
oppose reintegration, and it is safe to say that TMR elites are faring well with an
economy that, in addition to having significant industrial assets, relies heavily
upon smuggling of contraband. Their relatively well-stocked army and Russian
support ensures that they cannot be ousted from their position. The crisis resolution formula adopted in the early 1990s requires that the TMR leadership be
a party to any talks. The elites' subsequent hard-line position makes the conflict *seem* intractable.[31] The fact that civil society—both in Moldova and in the
TMR—is unable or unwilling to put pressure on the elites to end the conflict is
also a key consideration, as well as the fact that the weak Moldovan economy
does not offer a strong material incentive to Transnistrians for reintegration.[32]
Perhaps the relative lack of democracy in the TMR is a factor, as settlement plans
suggested by Ukraine and European actors call for democratization of the TMR.
One could even argue that the fighting in 1992 has strengthened a "Transnistrian identity."[33] Lastly, one cannot forget the Russian presence. Russian sup-

port for the TMR and various economic sanctions it has placed on Moldova make it clear that Russia is not a neutral bystander. By providing key props to the TMR regime, it creates few incentives for TMR leaders to reach a settlement with Chisinau.

Gagauzia: Thwarted Separatism

The Gagauz, ethnically Turkish Christians residing in Moldova, mobilized for their rights in the waning days of the Soviet Union. Like the ethnic Slavs, the Gagauz did not want Moldova to unify with Romania and they wanted to ensure protection for their language and culture. Five days after Moldova declared its independence, in September 1991, delegates to a Gagauz congress in Comrat (the largest city in Gagauzia) issued a declaration of independence, which proposed a confederation among Moldova, Transnistria, and a Gagauz republic. In December 1991, voters in the self-declared independent Gagauzia supported the region's independence and elected Stepan Topal, who like Igor Smirnov had been arrested for his support of the communist coup, as president.

It looked like Gagauzia might turn out the same as Transnistria. However, Gagauz leaders did not embark on a military campaign for independence. Instead, they attempted to negotiate with the central government. Arguably, they made a virtue out of necessity.[34] The Gagauz did not have military materiel or a Soviet army on their territory. Gagauzia was the poorest region in the poorest country in Europe. The Gagauz relied on subsidies from the central budget for provision of basic services. Its protogovernment lacked the means to exercise control over the five districts under its purported administration. In short, Gagauzia, which also had ill-defined borders and a relatively small population, lacked the wherewithal to be a viable independent state. Moreover, the Gagauz, unlike the Transnistrians, also had a more moderate faction that was willing to accept Moldovan sovereignty if they were granted a degree of political autonomy.[35]

The Moldovans were willing to cut a deal. The hard-liners in Chisniau had been discredited by the failure to militarily subdue the Transnistrians. By 1993, pan-Romanian figures had been pushed out of the leadership. Moldovan leaders also hoped that settlement of the Gagauz question would help resolve the crisis in Transnistria in their favor.[36] The Turkish government and the Council of Europe supported an autonomy plan, and the Turkish government also helped convince the Gagauz that their rights would be respected within Moldova. Various gestures—development of a Latin alphabet for Gagauz by the Moldovan Academy of Sciences and measures to allow teaching in Gagauz— also ameliorated Gagauz concerns.

In 1994 the status of Gagauzia was finally resolved. First, the Moldovan Constitution provided for autonomy for both Transnistria and Gagauzia and gave parents the right to choose the language of their children's schooling. In December 1994, the Moldovan Parliament passed a law on the special legal status of Gagauzia, which, inter alia, affirmed the region's status as an autonomous territorial unit, gave it three official languages, created a parliament for it, defined its borders, and transferred powers to it enabling it to oversee education, culture, local economic development, and policing. Gagauzia also has the right to secede should the status of Moldova change (e.g., if it unifies with Romania). The Gagauz thus gained a strong voice—particularly as far as running their own affairs is concerned. Exit, on the other hand, did not look to be a very viable alternative. Although some still complain about excessive interference by Chisinau in the affairs of Gagauzia and inadequate resources devoted to supporting the Gagauz language, the Moldovans and Gagauz have managed to resolve their differences peacefully.

Does the resolution of the Gagauz case provide a model for others to follow? Certainly the Moldovan government hoped so, but to date there is still no final settlement with Transnistria. In addition to observing that the agreement between Chisinau and Comrat was facilitated by the limited prospects for a fully independent Gagauzia, there are other points worth noting. First, there was little prior history of conflict between Moldovans and Gagauz. Secondly, moderate political forces were strong enough in both cases to put down demands by radical hard-liners. Third, the central government, given the larger problem of Transnistria, had strong incentives to resolve this conflict. Finally, the international environment favored a settlement, as would-be separatists could not rely on outside support. In sum, these may constitute an "uncommon conjuncture of favorable circumstances," making its exportability limited.[37]

What can one glean from the examination of both the collapse of the Soviet Union and secessionism in post-Soviet Ukraine and Moldova? First, consideration of the Soviet case leads one to believe that institutions, in the form of ethnically and territorially defined republics, were of paramount importance in encouraging secession. Separate political institutions also, arguably, facilitated

Crimean separatism and their absence worked against secessionism in Donbas. On this front, Moldova is more interesting: neither the TMR nor Gagauzia had their own political institutions, yet separatism materialized in both regions. In the former case one can point to a distinct history as well as a clear geographic conception defined by the Dniestr River that facilitated at least the emergence of a Transnistrian identity. Gagauz separatism was weaker than that in the TMR in part because the boundaries of Gagauzia were ill defined.

Secondly, foreign support matters. This is clearest in the case of the TMR, which relies heavily on Russian military support. As the cases of South Ossetia, Abkhazia, Nagorno-Karabakh suggest, outside assistance can be crucial. The Gagauz and Donbas residents could not count on it, and Russia was unable or unwilling to clash with Ukraine over Crimea. Russian intransigence during efforts to settle the Transnistrian conflict has also bolstered TMR separatists.

What of economic considerations? These do not appear to be decisive. On the one hand, Transnistria does have sizeable economic resources, making its bid for independence, compared to Gagauzia at least, more viable. In the Ukrainian case, however, Donbas possesses more wealth than Crimea and was no less integrated with the Soviet/Russian economy. It, however, did not try to secede.

These factors can all be critical in helping would-be separatist elites exercise their own agency. When would-be states have institutional and economic resources and they either have outside support or will face limited resistance from the central government, "exit" becomes a more viable option. This was the case in the waning days of the USSR, when a variety of factors fed separatist movements, thereby generating popular support for secessionism. In the context of a democratizing state, republic-level elites also ultimately made the choice to embrace secessionism. In the TMR, Russian support, economic resources, and the fact that it possessed clear geographic boundaries made up for the lack of formal political institutions. Moldova's push for independence between 1989 and 1991 created opportunities for political elites in the TMR to pursue their own exit option. Unlike pro-Russian or Communist parties in Crimea—who could make common cause with parties in eastern Ukraine—the leaders of the TMR would be isolated in a Moldova committed to either joining with Romania (now a moot issue) or seeking EU membership (definitely on the agenda). Their open sympathies for the Soviet Union and disdain for anything Moldovan would rankle even their erstwhile comrades in the significantly reformed Moldovan Communist Party. If elites do not believe they can at least potentially win in a given political environment, they are unlikely to play the game. In short, from the perspective of the leaders of the TMR, so long as exit is still a viable option, there is little incentive to seek voice within Moldova.

The other cases play out differently. Gagauzia could not survive on its own. When offered voice by the Moldovan government, the Gagauz leadership signed on. In Ukraine, "exit" was far more feasible for Crimea than Donbas, but the Crimeans lacked outside support and were internally divided as well. The offer of "voice" within Ukraine helped quell Crimean separatism and arguably prevented the emergence of Donbas separatism. The notion that elite choice between "exit" and "voice," driven by available resources and identifiable political and economic motives, gives one purchase on understanding the various outcomes of the cases examined in this chapter, and examination of this interplay between structure and agency could be made in other post-Soviet states as well.

Notes

1. These terms and the model of behavior come from Albert Hirschman, *Exit, Loyalty, and Voice* (Cambridge, Mass.: Harvard University Press, 1970).

2. Mark Beissinger, *Nationalist Mobilization and the Collapse of the Soviet State* (Cambridge: Cambridge University Press, 2002), 3.

3. Valerie Bunce, *Subversive Institutions: The Design and the Destruction of Socialism and the State* (Cambridge: Cambridge University Press, 1999).

4. Beissinger, *Nationalist Mobilization*.

5. Beissinger, *Nationalist Mobilization*, 166.

6. Beissinger, *Nationalist Mobilization*, 399.

7. Alexander Motyl, *Sovietology, Rationality, Nationality* (New York: Columbia University Press, 1990).

8. Rogers Brubaker, "National Minorities, Nationalizing States, and External National Homelands in the New Europe," *Daedalus* 124, no. 2 (1995): 107–32.

9. Taras Kuzio, *Ukraine: State and Nation Building* (London: Routledge, 1998), 69.

10. Taras Kuzio and David Mayer, "The Donbas and Crimea: An Institutional and Demographic Approach to Ethnic Mobilization in Two Ukrainian Regions," in *State and Institution Building in Ukraine*, ed. Taras Kuzio, Robert S. Kravchuk, and Paul D'Anieri (New York: St. Martin's, 2001), 310.

11. Paul Pirie, "National Identity and Politics in Southern and Eastern Ukraine," *Europe-Asia Studies* 48, no. 7 (1996): 1094.

12. Pirie, "National Identity and Politics in Southern and Eastern Ukraine," 1099.

13. Quoted in Roman Solchanyk, "The Politics of State Building: Centre-Periphery Relations in Post-Soviet Ukraine," *Europe-Asia Studies* 46, no. 1 (1994): 54.

14. Pirie, "National Identity and Politics in Southern and Eastern Ukraine," 1097.

15. Kuzio, *Ukraine*, 80.

16. Kuzio and Mayer, "The Donbas and Crimea," 313.

17. From the 1989 Soviet census, www.ukrcensus.gov.ua/eng, accessed Dec. 23, 2009.

18. Surveys in 1995 found that a narrow plurality (32.8 percent) of respondents considered the USSR their homeland; 29.6 percent said Ukraine, 20.4 percent said their region, and only 2 percent said Russia (reported in *Politychnyi Portret Ukrainy* 13 [1995]).

19. Kuzio and Mayer, "The Donbas and Crimea," 304.

20. 2001 Ukrainian Census, www.ukrcensus.gov.ua/eng, accessed Dec. 23, 2009.

21. Paul Kubicek, "Regional Polarization in Ukraine: Public Opinion, Voting, and Legislative Behavior Over Time," *Europe-Asia Studies* 52, no. 2, (2000): 273–94.

22. Kuzio, *Ukraine*, 83.

23. Anna Reid, *Borderland: A Journey through the History of Ukraine* (Boulder, Colo.: Westview Press, 1997), 174.

24. Stuart Kaufman, "Spiraling to Ethnic War: Elites, Masses, and Moscow in Moldova's Civil War," *International Security* 21, no. 1 (1996): 108–38.

25. Christopher Borgen, "Thawing a Frozen Conflict: Legal Aspects of the Separatist Crisis in Moldova," St. John's University School of Law, paper 06-0045, July 2006.

26. Shale Horowitz, *From Ethnic Conflict to Stillborn Reform: The Former Soviet Union and Yugoslavia* (College Station: Texas A&M University Press, 2005).

27. Borgen, "Thawing a Frozen Conflict."

28. Horowitz, *From Ethnic Conflict to Stillborn Reform*, 108.

29. Pal Kolsto, *Political Construction Sites: Nation-Building in Russia and the Post-Soviet States* (Boulder, Colo.: Westview Press, 2000), 139.

30. Stuart Hensel, "Moldova Strategic Conflict Assessment," paper, UK Global Conflict Prevention Pool, Nov. 2006.

31. Borgen, "Thawing a Frozen Conflict," 8.

32. Hensel, "Moldova Strategic Conflict Assessment."

33. Kolsto, *Political Construction Sites*, 148.

34. Charles King, "Moldovan Identity and the Politics of Pan-Romanianism," *Slavic Review* 53, no. 2 (1994): 362.

35. Horowitz, *From Ethnic Conflict to Stillborn Reform*, 118.

36. Kolsto, *Political Construction Sites*, 239.

37. Ted Robert Gurr and Michael Haxton, "The Gagauz of Moldova: Settling an Ethnonational Rebellion," in Ted Robert Gurr, *Peoples Versus States: Minorities at Risk in the New Century* (Washington, D.C.: U.S. Institute of Peace Press, 2000), 222.

STEFAN ZAHLMANN

"Our Cause Was Foredoomed to Failure"

Secession in Germany and the

United States

THE FAILURE OF THE CONFEDERATE STATES OF AMERICA (CSA) AND THE GERMAN DEMOCRATIC REPUBLIC (GDR) IN AUTOBIOGRAPHICAL REMEMBRANCE CULTURES

Both the American Civil War and the Cold War were followed by a grimly waged "war of recollections." The failures of 1865 and 1989 and the subsequent process of political unification mark the beginning of debates about the respective countries' former double statehood and the citizens' living conditions in the newly reunited societies, which have lasted to the present day. In both critical discussions about such patterns and in efforts to find alternative ways of perceiving past and present, the debates show a persistence of thinking within patterns of former enmity. One might expect ongoing disputes to mildly influence any "war of recollections" between former adversaries. But in the case of East German and the American South, the authors who engage in this war express extreme views and an outsized hostility.

What follows is a comparison of two cultures of remembrance that emerged following reunification. They took place more than 140 years apart in very different situations, and yet we see almost identical ways of handling national schism and the failure of the "weaker" society.[1]

A comparison of America's remembrance culture after 1865 and Germany's after 1989, however, is not rooted in the similarity of Confederate and East German societies. That said, comparing some of their social structures, the attempts of the ruling elites of each to legitimize their states as superior societies, and the autobiographical reconstruction of the societies' rise and fall is reasonable in this context. As such, the term "secession" becomes central. The term was explicitly invoked by the CSA and implicitly appealed to by the GDR. Secession coined the self-image of political players, as well as the perception and the memories of a failed society throughout all social strata.

For the southern states, secession meant the disengagement of a region—one might even say a cultural space—from political and economic developments taking place in another part of the country. Furthermore, it meant the preservation of the Constitution, which favored the interests of slaveholding southerners, at least insofar as those who seceded interpreted it. The foundation of the GDR in 1949 and the successively increasing self-isolation of East German society until 1961 put an end to the romantic dream of unifying a Germany that had been divided after 1945. The interpretation of the GDR's role within German history as an independent and progressive new social order informs its characterization as a secessionist state. The GDR separated itself politically, culturally, and physically by an almost insurmountable border from an image of Germany as hopelessly capitalistic, fascist, and hawkish—and intrinsically tied to West Germany. Both the CSA and GDR's concepts of secession are thus connected to a temporal horizon. Yet, unlike the CSA, which linked its republican ideal to the foundation of the United States and fought for the continuance of the status quo, the GDR focused on the future. The social ideal of communism was to enlighten citizens' lives, and the dawning of a better age was already adumbrated by the pre-stage of socialism. For East German communists, the "real existence" of socialism would have meant the political and cultural perfection of the GDR's secession. Hence, both the CSA and GDR legitimize the particularities of their social orders by arguing that these social orders were a principally positive civilizing achievement.

In both nations, elites played a significant role in initiating the move toward secession, enforcing and defending the idea of the separate nation against their own fellow countrymen as well as against the "other" Americans or Germans in the North or West, respectively. The term "elite" is slippery; southern and East German elites have redefined the term as they have redefined themselves in their struggle to defend their memories. But still one can provide a basic outline of the elite class in the CSA and the GDR. There are three social groups within the category that one can identify. One are the "old elites," those decision makers who "significantly and continuously participate[d]" in the social realm, having a measurable impact on politics, the economy, religion, or the military.[2] Another group is the counterelites—that is, persons who, because of the power structures in the CSA and GDR, were denied or had limited *direct and independent* participation in relevant social decisions but nevertheless claimed to take part.[3] A third group consists of former CSA and GDR citizens who, in their reunited nations, remain influential in all areas of society, even beyond the boundaries of their former state. This group of new elites includes people who advanced after 1865 or 1989, as well as former members of the counterelites or old elites.

TYPE-A MEMORIES: "WE WERE RIGHT" VERSUS "THE EXTERNAL AND DOMESTIC ENEMY"

Texts advancing a "We were right" argument were written by members of the old elites in both the CSA and GDR. The lives of such elite authors, both male and female, was interpenetrated with the political existence of the CSA and GDR and their specific social order to such an extent that for a large portion of the population these authors became and remain symbols of a perished state. This is especially true in the case of leading politicians (Jefferson Davis, Walter Ulbricht, Erich Honecker) who are regarded as personifications of the state's strengths and weaknesses, even by other members of this elite group. Even though the individual biographies among the different groups of elites are different, perceptions of the old elite in the failed society are connected to perceptions of the counterelites and the new elites by the fact of their former elite position.

These authors' interpretations of the past are self-referential and concern their own group and the close circle of people around them. We can assume a wide circulation and acceptance of these texts, which include military accounts and political pamphlets, among southern readers, but they appear to have met with no response in the northern states. Meanwhile, the memoirs of the former members of the Politburo and the GDR legislature that appeared in the 1990s mainly address themselves to an East German audience, and most of the books were published by small houses located in the former East Germany.

In both cases, authors from the old elite attentively take note of other members of their group and refer to what they have read. There is an obvious tendency toward carrying out a kind of inner-circle discourse with former colleagues and friends in both remembrance cultures, which has the result that some works can only be understood by simultaneously reading the respective referential texts. The old-elite authors set out to create a collective identity for the societies they designed before 1865 or 1989. The texts of these writers, homogenous in content, revisit old patterns of representation and legitimization of the failed state in their demand for a new social order. This approach requires authors to maintain distance between themselves and their former opponents and does not look for similarities or present links within the unified nation.

In this group's remembrances, national identity is rooted not in the unity but in the division of the nation. For some, such as Jefferson Davis, this division was simply a matter of circumstance:

> It is well known that at the time of the adoption of the federal Constitution African servitude existed in all the states that were parties to that compact. . . . The slaves, however were very numerous in the Southern, and very few in the Northern, states. This diversity was occasioned by differences of climate, soil, and industrial interests—not in any degree by moral considerations, which at that period were not recognized as an element in the question. It was simply because negro labor was more profitable in the South than in the North that the importation of negroes had been, and continued to be, chiefly directed to the Southern ports.[4]

Though the division of the country was based on "circumstance," old elites still showed preference for living in the South. Former Confederates loved the South after 1865 as much as they did before 1861—the vanished past very often seemed to be even more attractive than the present South.

German party elites, too, recalled their lost state with emotion. Karl Eduard von Schnitzler remembered his decision to move to eastern Germany from western Germany as a journey back home:

> For almost 31 years I was searching for my fatherland. It could not have been the Kaiser's Empire. . . . It could not have been the Weimar Republic, because during her existence I pledged my allegiance to the working class, which had not found a fatherland yet. This class could not have a fatherland as long as it was deprived of political power. The working class made itself a fatherland, after it acquired political power and the ability to shape things to their liking [in the aftermath of World War II]. I know when exactly my search had ended: after I had fulfilled the order of the party to broadcast on Democratic Radio the election of the first president of the German Democratic Republic Wilhelm Pieck. That was when I had found my fatherland.[5]

Secession, in a larger sense seen as the struggle for national independence, its shaping, and its perpetuation, is by the old elites comprehended as the climax of their individual biography. Maintaining a different way of life than those in the North and West was for them an individual way to embrace a secession worth fighting for.

Both the American and German authors follow similar models in their memoirs. The formula typically begins with proof of origin and a description of individual experiences that link the authors' identities, family histories, and national histories together in a positive way. Southern memoirists often trace themselves back to patriotic ancestors. Secession thus is portrayed as an inherited form of patriotism reenacted by descendants to preserve a state of divine order that is "beautiful and just and benign."[6]

Such an Elysium was the state the Communists were fighting for too. The family legends of East Germany's old elites linked them one way or the other to almost all revolutionary movements since the first half of the nineteenth century. For example, Kurt Hager, the leading ideologist of the Sozialistische Einheitspartei Deutschlands, remembers proudly that his last name is "listed three times" in the 1836 records of the revolutionary national alliance Das junge Deutschland—but, he adds as a joke, it shows up only once in a bourgeois context, one predecessor having been an imperial snooper at the court of Vienna during the congress of 1814–15.[7]

Not only is family history intimately connected to the nation's most characteristic moments; both family history and national history also serve as an orientation for the author's own personal biography. By this biography the old-elite authors legitimize their own status within the failed society.

The authors thus underline the ongoing validity of the cause of secession after the failure of their respective states. Neither individual nor collective failure can be integrated into their lived concept of biography because the canon these biographies are based on illustrates the history of the cause's victory. According to them, the cause did not fail because it was per se immoral or wrong; rather, it failed because it "was failed." "Overwhelmed but not defeated" or "Socialism will prevail" sounds the angry creed of their memory. Old-elite authors demand solidarity among the population against the former enemy in the North and West, even after the failure of the state. They demand a defiant "We were right!"

They are humiliated by the way their own careers ended and the way they were treated after the fall of their state and see this denouement as a denial of their achievements to which their biographies attest. They are stubbornly convinced of the legitimacy of the way they lived their lives, so they vehemently defend the righteousness of their state. For them its end marks also the decline of the nation: "Ours is a decaying civilization."[8]

For the authors of this group, the principles that governed how southerners and East Germans lived with one another relied on a certain knowledge that, in their understanding, was supertemporal and not to be challenged. In their memory, the state they helped to build represented not only a better political system but also one that was inevitable, given the assumptions of Marxism-Leninism in the GDR and a certain interpretation of the Bible and the Constitution in the CSA. This knowledge has a global dimension, allowing the authors to legitimize the division of a nation and to regard the seceding part of the nation as superior to the flawed one from which it separated. In addition, they portray their society as an ideal international example and represent the victorious United States and Federal Republic of Germany (FRG) as a form of foreign rule that drives them to external or internal emigration.

The success of the authors' effort to vindicate their state in the face of its failure depends on their being able to depict the conditions of that failure as being beyond their personal control. They speak of the fact that the "cause" was not yet capable of being realized; disturbances caused by political opponents meant it could not be "perfected."[9] The old elites see the military superiority of the North and the economic power of the West as evidence of an unfair fight. The failure of their state for them means defeat of their "cause" at the hands of a stronger opponent, but not their moral victory. Thus the members of the old elite take no responsibility for the demise of their state.

For authors of this type, reconciliation with the victorious opponent presents a severe challenge. They often despise their former compatriots for the indifference, relief, or even joy with which they accepted their state's decline. Honecker even shouted after the East Germans who fled into the West in 1989 that "one should not shed a tear for them."[10] For them, any expression of doubt regarding the rightfulness of the cause and the necessity of the means adopted to further it and any sympathy with the politics of the opponent after the collapse is seen as an outrageous betrayal for those loyal leaders of the cause. They discredit them in their autobiographies by lodging false accusations against them and by blaming "renegades" such as General Longstreet, whose disastrous leadership cost the Confederates a victory at Gettysburg, or Günter Schabowski, whose press conference led to the surprising opening of the inner German border on November 9, 1989.[11]

These authors take consolation in the idea that their opponent only won a Pyrrhic victory and that they will be proven right in the eyes of posterity. For them the failure of their state is only temporary, a failure of just one manifestation of their "cause." The legal strengthening of the single state's independence and socialism's victory are still political long-term objectives advertised in their texts. The authors are victims, not failures. By keeping that in mind, they are able to persuade themselves that their creed, as well as the life they've lived in obeisance to it, is not in vain.

TYPE-B MEMORIES: "WE WERE BETTER" VERSUS "WE WERE RIGHT"

Many southerners had longed for the downfall of the Confederacy. Who were these persons and what were their motives? Miss Abby, a northerner by birth and citizen of Atlanta, wrote when the war came to an end that "There are three classes who are looking anxiously for the coming of the victors. Those who love their Country and their Government with true loyalty of Soul—the poor who are suffering for the commonest comforts of life, and this nation of negroes who have patiently waited through long years for their deliverance to come."[12]

Obviously these classifications are not necessarily exclusive. One group is defined by patriotism, one by income, and one by race; probably many critics of the Confederacy belonged to all of them. But most of the very small group of counterelites who published books after 1865 belonged to the first two groups. Miss Abby, though owning a few slaves, never accepted the separation of the South, and Daniel Ellis, from the Tennessee mountains, never gained an impressive fortune, in part because he used to give away his published memoirs. He never imagined that, more than a century later, his recollections might inspire a novel and movie called *Cold Mountain*.[13]

Certainly he and Miss Abby would have been proud that their secret longing for reunification had come to be appreciated and (in Ellis's case) honored by the affection of an audience of millions of people from all over the world. Both of them considered themselves to be true American patriots and, for this reason, felt that their stories deserved telling. Like memoirs of the first type, their recollections connect a "cause" with individual biographies. But unlike other memoirs, these authors see defeat as a kind of justice. Whether by critiquing the legal defense of secession, aligning themselves with the partisan fight against the old elites by rule of force, or meticulously pointing out daily injustice within the established secessionist state, the authors do not delegitimize the failed state on political but instead on moral grounds. Their arguments are most striking when they measure the seceded state against the core values the old elites claimed to be fighting for. Who, for example, in the GDR, would have expected that the presence of the most common among "the people" would be considered a sort of punishment?

> It was one of the peculiarities of our dear GDR, to order people to be in the presence of regular or working class people and for people to see this as a form of punishment, or even as a time for repentance and atonement. Certain behavior could lead to this, e.g., a tendency to think and speak independently, to contradict superiors or the official party line, to express a dislike for subordination under the collective, to be late, to have unshined shoes, to neglect assigned homework or earmarks in exercise books. . . . Until today I could not comprehend why the working class put up with this. Why was the "sphere of production," where the workers created the very modest wealth of the country, used as a boot camp for the young people who were imperfect but hungry for education? Did being a member of the working class (*Proletariat*) really mean nothing at all?[14]

Within the group of counterelites there were several representatives who publicly articulated their protest against the old elite's politics even before Appomattox or the fall of the Berlin Wall. They took courage from the same source as their political opponents, namely, their heritage. By giving proof in the form of a biography of having lived lives no less honorable than that of those devoted to the "cause," counterelites were able to claim the same authority and attention as the representatives of the old elites. A self-perceived "We were better" thus contrasted with the old elites' totalitarian "We were right" used to coerce solidarity.

East German texts of this type are more distinctive than their Confederate counterparts in that they remember a double failure: the failure of the GDR under Honecker and the failure of their own efforts to consolidate a socialist alternative. They regret that they were not able to impart their political convictions to a population that was not patient enough for another socialist experiment or had doubts about the continuation of a two-state system and already wanted reunification in the fall of 1989. Yet this group of authors from the southern states as well as from East Germany regard reunification as positive, even though they might be critical of the way it was carried out.

Most important, authors in this group seek to reexamine the myths that supported secession. These myths were built by the old elites in the process of seceding or in the years following secession, and after the failure of secession they were used to justify opposition to the reunited society. These myths provided the foundation for secession by establishing a permanent and steadfast solidarity between the people and the elites and by positing the fundamental superiority of the failed social orders compared to those of the opponent or the united society.

TYPE-C MEMORIES: "WE ARE THE PEOPLE"

The authors of this group belong mostly to the new elites of the American South or German East and they typically draw a positive image of the reunification era. Henry Watterson, for example, links his assessment of the new order to an aspect frequently discussed in memoirs from the Restoration South, slavery: "Under the old system we paid our debts and walloped our niggers. Under the new we have to pay our niggers and wallop our debts. We have no longer any slaves, but we have no longer any debts. . . . Bless the Lord! I'm gettin' fatter and fatter!"[15]

These authors separate the "cause" of the secession from the failure of the states that followed. Both factors are evaluated in a different way. Some discuss the political idea that stood behind the formation of the Confederation or the socialist society, while others concentrate on the nonpolitical aspects of everyday life in their former states. The analytical approach in both instances does not prevent the authors from reliving emotional experiences of their past: "My mind was inflamed with pure hate. There were things for which I could not forgive the GDR. The destruction of families was part of it. That was different from shortages of certain foods like fruit or parades before the party elite. This system brought parents to give up their children forever. Such wounds will never heal."[16]

This kind of memory illustrates that critics of the secession movements were not complaining about minor inconveniences in an otherwise good political system. Those authors who focus on their memories of everyday life rather than of the "cause" first of all recall the private ways of living in the lost state. Some confess to their readers that they were even convinced of the necessity of the Confederacy or of socialism and that they committed to it up to the collapse of the system. Most, however, remember that after being initially willing to commit themselves to the state and also the "cause" (or else just submitting to necessity), they later lost the motivation to stand up for the political goals of their new states. These authors illustrate how, owing to both domestic and external factors, the societies they inhabited came to be incapable of self-correction or even development. They make it quite clear to readers that the political pressure to avoid failure resulted in the seceded states eventually committing acts that in other societies would have been considered immoral or a violation of human rights. The GDR government, for example, imprisoned citizens who sometimes did nothing except express a desire to leave their country without having given them a proper trial—and subsequently offered these prisoners' freedom to West Germany in exchange for "valuta" (i.e., Western currency desperately needed by the weak socialist economy) or high-tech equipment. Consequently, the authors imagine their nation reunited and try to overcome whatever former historical differences led to separation. For this, they either choose irony (as Henry Watterson does, mimicking the slang of former plantation slaves) or adapt to the prejudices of their former "opponents," who in these texts never appear as adversaries but rather as partners. Thus Mary Pickett recalls at length a dialogue she had with Abraham Lincoln about the burning of Richmond, noting how the U.S. president kissed her baby boy while mentioning Jefferson Davis at the same time without any emotional weight, only as required by a chronicler's duties.[17]

Reconciliation for the southerner was the noble act of internal unification of the American nation and not the mere political reentry of the South into the Union. For East Germans in the fall of 1989 the equivalent was the motto "We are the people!" It was not the society that had failed in the memories of this group of new elites but the former rulers and their political vision. The authors criticize the old elites' attempts to preserve the rights of the single states or to realize socialism and are especially critical of the means certain members of the old elite adopted to carry out these endeavors. These endeavors were contrary to the original character of the goal and undertaken to the disadvantage of the people. Alexander Hamilton Stephens, former vice president of the Confederacy, admitted that the South had cause to defend itself militarily but no reason to keep southerners under arms all the time:

> The war was for principles and rights, and it was in defense of these, as well as of their property, that the people had taken up arms. They could always be relied on when a battle was imminent; but, when no fighting was to be done, they had best be at home attending their families and interests. As their intelligence was equal to their patriotism, they were as capable of judging of the necessity of their presence with the colors as the commanders of armies, who were but professional soldiers fighting for rank and pay, and most of them without property in the South.[18]

This quotation is found in the memoirs of Richard Taylor, a brother-in-law of Jefferson Davis and diehard secessionist, who used it against Stephens, whom he accused of being close to insanity. Stephens remembered that he always insisted on consistent enforcement of the secession's original purpose. The problems that led to the population's not fully accepting the new state could be blamed on its mistrust of the elites and on the elites' despotic pretense that their politics alone were an adequate instrument to achieve their goals. Their protective measures in favor of the "cause," which they justified by appealing to the living conditions in the South and GDR and by referring to the alleged attacks of the enemy, proved more detrimental to the cause than the actual work of the enemy himself. Authors like Stephens denounce the leaders, arguing that over the course of national development the struggle for survival of the CSA and the GDR had become a struggle for personal power among the old elites during the course of which they forgot the needs of the people. A political program less geared toward the old elites, their personal vanity, and their impertinent emotions might have saved the "cause" and the nation.

FAILURE AND CULTURAL COMMEMORATION

Linking personal memories of life with the failures of society at first might seem to contradict the character of the literary genre of autobiography because for at least the last two hundred years this genre has spoken the language of success. It has become a typical means of narrating a positive view of life.

Few of the CSA and GDR authors remember the failure of their state as a simple interruption in an otherwise "successful" personal life or as a "normal" historic event. For some, like Jefferson Davis or Erich Honecker, the failure verges on a personal catastrophe because it was a part of their personal vita. Others, like Miss Abby or Claudia Rusch, welcomed reunification as liberation. The means by which they express their memories in their autobiographies are as individual as the reasons for which they broach the subject of the changes in their lives after the end of their nation. However, we can clearly distinguish three types of autobiographical texts within both societies. The exploration of the failure of the state and the evaluation of the reunited society in these autobiographies reflects a process whereby the failure is "*biographized*," *objectified*, and finally *neutralized*.

The majority of the texts published immediately after the failure of secession were not typically titled "memoirs" or "autobiography," even though their form and content suggest that is what they are. Instead, old elite or counterelite authors try to "disremember" the significance of failure by focusing on a certain period of time during the downfall or by concentrating on aspects of their state they consider "approved" and positive. These texts are full of dramatic and abusive descriptions of alleged traitors from their own ranks and former opponents under the spell of the recent collapse of the social order. However, the authors often try to objectify the highly emotional content of their texts. Despite their autobiographical character they serve as a cross-examination in front of an audience, as a chronicle on a failed state, or in some cases even as a future-oriented political manifesto.[19] The final judgment on their own role in the old society is not yet determined. The value of the Confederate and East German secession is still negotiable and their careers have not yet ended. An unbroken sense of mission gives them a boost up against their critics and enemies one last time.

After this first phase in the development of the autobiographical remembrance culture, which lasted until 1867 in the southern states and until 1991 in Germany, authors of the old elites also began to biographize their state's failure. In these texts, the end of the CSA and the GDR is remembered as a significant but not main event in the elites' lives, whereas the secession or foundation of the failed state always remains central. The authors highlight their justification for secession and their criticism of the united society and tie these points to their own life histories. The extensively justified belief that that their states had been failed rather than that they had failed them serves as the background against which the elites wrote their autobiographies. Until the 1880s in the United States and through the 1990s in Germany the predominant formal feature of this autobiographical remembrance culture was the telling of "great history" rather than spontaneous autobiographical introspection. For a final time they review their attempt to realize an alternative society, a life in a different version of modernity, and their impeded life as individuals and the history of the failed state become one. Even in this double negation we can clearly see how their autobiographies are directed toward the reckoning of their success and failure.

In the final phase, autobiographies by members of the new elites are predominant, especially by women from the southern states and representatives of a younger generation of GDR citizens who emphasize the advantages of the overthrown two-state system more than their personal disadvantages after unification. Their accounts demonstrate that the failure of state is not a loss but a new biographical opportunity. That these authors use "classical" autobiographical tropes and that their texts can be read as stories of success might be attributable to the fact that they have found value in reunification.

AUTOBIOGRAPHY AND MODERNITY

The autobiographies of authors from the southern states occupy an important place in late nineteenth- and early twentieth-century American culture. The autobiography of Benjamin Franklin, which had been posthumously published in several editions by the middle of the nineteenth century, already refers to the young American nation's great demand for texts that would help its citizens identify with the state. Through the memories of southern authors the reading public was offered a retrospective of a common past through which it could acquire a national self-perception, complemented by many new immigrants from Europe.

For the American authors, the genre of autobiography was quite an obvious choice because it was a means of self-portrayal that was accessible and popular. In several cases, parts of the authors' memoirs were simultaneously published in the new mass medium of newspapers, thus demonstrating the genre's adaptability. GDR elites' decision to write autobiographies is, however, less explicable. Why did authors not use modern audiovisual media to portray their lives instead of falling back on a genre that clearly belongs to the nineteenth-century bourgeois tradition? The answer is probably because in the reunited nation such authors could not find an uncritical audiovisual public. A documentary, a talk show, or some other TV format would have exposed them to their critics' direct and clear interrogation. Only the controllable medium of print gave them the freedom to portray themselves as they liked.

Unlike the southern elites, however, the new German elites detached themselves and their narratives from other elite groups and underlined the democratic and present-oriented character of today's GDR autobiographies. They gained their elite status as intellectuals because they reminded the people not only of their past but also of the challenges they shared in present time. Their works took on the guise of popular literature rather than reportage; these texts adopted an audience-oriented style of writing that in actualizing forms of national commemoration *and* manifesting the character of the autobiographical genre mirrored the works of the new elites of the southern states. Writing was the means by which female authors of the former Confederacy in particular realized the democratic rights of equality. Autobiography allowed them to influence social and political debates that they were not able to partake in since they lacked the right to vote. By playing with the principles of autobiographies (i.e., by fictionalizing their memories) they add popular texts and new, attractive content to the U.S. national memory.

THE SECESSIONS OF THE CSA AND GDR AS SYMPTOMS OF IMPERFECT MODERNITY

The fate of the CSA and GDR will be captured only incompletely if they are understood only as sui generis events of national history. To make these two autobiographical remembrance cultures comprehensible, one has to see the structural parallels between them in an international context.

In both cases, the failure of state can be seen as a consequence of a "double revolution" that started in the middle of the eighteenth century, whereby economic modernization (industrialization processes in England beginning around 1760) combined with the triumphant principles of liberty and equality (which became a political factor after the American (1776) and French (1789) revolutions).[20] In the southern states of 1861, the old elites were faced with different social and economic developments from that of the northern states and with slavery's obvious contradiction of the principles of the Declaration of Independence. Secession was the only means of countering the no longer politically controllable processes of modernization in the northern states.[21] There might have been ways to cover the problems of southern modernity with a decorative varnish, but this could not mend the cracks between different social groups and races in the South.

The GDR was the political representative of an ideologically interpreted modernity based on a nineteenth-century theory. Marxism provided an explanation of the social problems unleashed by the industrialization of the nineteenth and early twentieth centuries. The economic boom in the Soviet Union in the 1930s and its victory in World War II made it possible to carry over this theory into the Soviet zone of occupation. In the 1960s, GDR elites embraced Marxist thinking, but their concept of socialism could not keep pace with the accelerating and further globalizing modernity of the twentieth century.

The "enemies" remembered by the GDR were the Germany of capitalism and the Germany of fascism in the first half of the twentieth century. The "fight" the GDR engaged in up until 1989 against these opponents consumed the economic energy that might have been invested in modernizing socialism and finding up-to-date answers to the social problems of East Germany. The struggle against pre-1945 opponents did not have to be justified or proven practicable and in fact served as the raison d'être of the GDR—that is, of the East German secession. Hence "the fight against the enemies" could be used as a knockdown argument against any aspiration to reform socialism.

The CSA and the GDR countered developments in the other part of their nations with a concept of modernization that, in their eyes, maintained a society more easily. It was based on only a few certainties: that slavery was God-given and that socialism did not exploit the people. Leaders in each society created the impression that they were in possession of a practicable principle based on scientific knowledge that promised a better way of organizing society than that of the opponent. In everyday life these principles only withstood challenge and won plausibility through external pressure or repressive measures, which indicates the extent to which the modernity of both CSA and GDR was deficient. In long passages, the old elites struggle to explain and legitimize their concept of modernity. Yet even these efforts cannot make readers forget that the enemy of the failed states was not the arsenals of the Union or NATO but their own inability to effectively modernize their societies. When the inevitable consequences of their deficient modernity became unbearable for the people of the CSA and GDR, they began to undermine the political project of their leaders.

MEMORIES OF THE ELITES AS NATIONAL MEMORIES?

"At least they should remain silent!"[22] This is what the writer Monika Maron disgustedly demanded in 1992, referring to the self-important rhetoric of former political rulers. Indeed the writings of elites attest less to a critical self-reflection than to a continuing claim to a monopoly on knowledge of the nation's past. They did not remain silent—not for long anyway. Nor did the Confederate leaders in America.

In the case of the southern states, the influence of the "memory work" of former rebels on U.S. national identity is so overwhelming that Wolfgang Schivelbusch is led to conclude that the reunited nation owes "her true destiny and perfection" to the grandeur of thought in the South.[23] The results of thorough research make it clear that both male and female authors of the South could only write themselves into the memory of the united society by throwing overboard certain southern idioms and formulating their memories in the language of the North and in terms of its achievements and its protagonists. In their memory, "southern" is only that which does not startle the readers in the North. But it is not only members of the new elite that manage to have an impact on American remembrance culture. Some representatives of the old elites also do so by assimilating themselves to the narratives of the new elites.

The Confederate secession and the Civil War are vital events in the national memory of the United States. Up to the present day, the thinking of southern authors can still be recognized in both what scholarship and the popular media selects to remember. This points to a problematic aspect of autobiographical remembrance culture, namely that for decades, only texts written by white authors found entry into social memory. Before the 1960s, the voices of other ethnic groups were shut out of the memory-making process.

Even though former East Germans are not done yet producing autobiographical forms of cultural commemoration of the GDR, it is possible to draw a preliminary conclusion about these texts. So far these autobiographies have failed to solve economic and social problems that emerged after 1989 or answer questions pertaining to the domestic unity of East and West. Rather, they strictly focus on their own group and the political beliefs from the first half of the twentieth century. Because the authors of these autobiographies were significantly responsible for the failure of the GDR, their memories can only be understood as voices from a past overcome. Against the background of the injustice that was done to East Germans in the name of socialism and antifascism, sentimental nostalgia for East Germany would only be possible if we assume a planned "oblivion" or rigorously defended "not wanting to know" in which the GDR is not remembered as part of real history but as a mythic utopia. These authors try harder than any other German elite group to construct a national memory that declares the former social order of their "New Germany" to be an example for the whole nation. Their memories of the GDR and the communist struggle neither productively process the failure of the state nor develop a means of allowing West Germans to identify with East Germans. Hence they do not help produce unity.

A reason the memoirs of the counterelites fail to connect to the present social debates is that they do not envision a consistent and practicable alternative. They themselves recognized the theatricality of their conception of socialism and understood that their "revolutionary play" had been closed by the people.[24] The fact that they were not, as former critics of the East German system, permanently given attention, gratitude, and respect by the united German society might also have sped up their retreat from public debates. Even though most of these authors do not take part in constructing the public opinion of the united Germany, they harbor a critical perspective that could be voiced at any time. In the face of growing trivialization of the crimes committed in the GDR by former perpetrators who now speak up—especially members of the Ministry of State Security—it is the counterelites who take a stand.[25] Hence autobiographies up to the present give insight into the still hard-fought battles to depict the weaknesses of the East German social order.

The texts that currently affect the debates on East German identity and the character of a united Germany the most were written by authors of the new elite. The backgrounds of the elite authors, just like those of American southern new elites, seem to be hazy. The East German authors remember their lives in the GDR as "unfinished" because they had not been able to achieve their career goals before the collapse of 1989, even though their plans had been well suited to the GDR. Younger representatives remember the failure of the GDR as a break in their lives that separates their youth in the GDR from their adult life in the FRG. The adolescence—or childishness—of the "Zonenchildren" is generalized as "we" and relieves them of any entanglement in aspects of GDR history that might be found problematic by West German readers.[26] And there is yet another tendency within autobiography by former East Germans. Representations of the GDR in a novel like *My First T-Shirt* connect seamlessly with memories of the early years of the united Germany. In his autobiography, Jakob Hein does not separate the failure of state from his life plans but rather focuses on his individual perspective. The success of many young writers underscores that a new type of popular author has emerged through their work on cultural forms of memory, a "commemoration elite" whose members can be accounted "intellectuals"—a social group that in German history traditionally patterns national self-perception.[27]

Within the new elites of East Germany we can observe a social shift that owes to the participation of very young authors; popular authors rather than members of clearly determinable groups (old elites and counterelites) now do the work of producing cultural memory. Such a shift had likewise occurred in the United States with the emergence of southern female autobiographical writers. The impact of the work of the new elites makes them "prominent," but their prominence is not a function either of their having been part of the elite in the GDR or of their being part of the new elite in a unified Germany; rather their prominence derives from their role in shaping the popular memory of the GDR. Between the texts of the old elites and the counterelites and those of the new elites, we can see a change from "cultural memory as *elite memory*" to "popular memories of the commemoration elites." Further, the texts of cultural memory are unmoored from the social origin of their authors.

The changes in the autobiographical remembrance cultures of the American South and East Germany can be attributed to two factors. The first is the displacement of authors from the old elite by those of new elite. The second, far more important element is the changing taste of the audience, which at first defended secession and later came to support a future of national unity. The analysis of secession in memoirs shows that the historic battles are fought again on literary fields, and their predictability comforts the critical reader. "The past does not repeat itself, but it rhymes," Mark Twain observed. Even with new protagonists and a new setting we can look forward to a "happy ending" in Germany.

Notes

1. Stefan Zahlmann, *Autobiographische Verarbeitungen gesellschaftlichen Scheiterns: Die Eliten der amerikanischen Südstaaten nach 1865 und der DDR nach 1989* (Cologne: Böhlau, 2009).

2. Wilhelm Bürklin, "Die Potsdamer Elitenstudie von 1995: Problemstellung und wissenschaftliches Programm," in *Eliten in Deutschland: Rekrutierung und Integration,* ed. Wilhelm Bürklin and Hilke Rebenstorf (Opladen: Leske und Budrich, 2007), 16.

3. Rainer Eckert, "Widerstand und Opposition: Umstrittene Begriffe der deutschen Diktaturgeschichte," in *Macht, Ohnmacht, Gegenmacht: Grundfragen zur politischen*

Gegnerschaft in der DDR, ed. Erhart Neubert and Bernd Eisenfeld (Bremen: Temmen, 2001), 32–33.

4. Jefferson Davis, *The Rise and Fall of the Confederate Government*, 2 vols. (New York: Appleton, 1881), 1:1.

5. Karl-Eduard von Schnitzler, *Meine Schlösser oder Wie ich mein Vaterland fand* (Hamburg: Nautilus, 1995), 212.

6. Josiah C. Nott, "Climates of the South in Their Relation to White Labor," *De Bow's Review*, Feb. 1866, 59.

7. Kurt Hager, *Erinnerungen* (Leipzig: Faber and Faber, 1996), 11.

8. Dosia Williams Moore, *War, Reconstruction, and Redemption on Red River: The Memoirs of Dosia Williams Moore*, ed. Carol Wells (Ruston: Dept. of History, Louisiana Tech University, 1990), 88.

9. *Der Sturz: Erich Honecker im Kreuzverhör*, ed. Reinhold Andert and Wolfganz Herzberg (Berlin: Aufbau, 1990), 291.

10. Erich Honecker's statement was broadcast nationwide on televison on October 1, 1989.

11. Günter Mittags, *Um jeden Preis: Im Spannungsfeld zweier Systeme* (Berlin: Aufbau, 1991), 26–27; Jubal A. Early, *Autobiographical Sketch and Narrative of the War between the States* (Philadelphia: Lippincott, 1912), 272–73.

12. Thomas G. Dyer, *Secret Yankees: The Union Circle in Confederate Atlanta* (Baltimore: Johns Hopkins University Press, 1999), 285–86.

13. *Cold Mountain* (2003) was based on Charles Frazier's *Cold Mountain* (Hampton Falls, N.H.: Beeler, 1997).

14. Reinhard Lakomy, *Es war doch nicht das letzte Mal: Erinnerungen* (Berlin: Das Neue Berlin, 2000), 63.

15. Henry Watterson, *The Compromises of Life* (New York: Fox, Duffield, 1903), 290.

16. Claudia Rusch, *Meine freie Deutsche Jugend* (Frankfurt am Main: Fischer, 2003), 134.

17. La Salle Pickett, *The Heart of a Soldier as Revealed in the Intimate Letters of General George E. Pickett* (New York: S. Moyle, 1913), 14ff.

18. Alexander H. Stephens, quoted in Richard Taylor, *Destruction and Reconstruction: Personal Experiences of the Late War* (Nashville, Tenn.: J. S. Sanders, 1879), 21–22.

19. For autobiography as cross-examination, see the answers of Erich and Margot Honecker in *Erich Honecker im Kreuzverhör*. For autobiography as a chronicle of a failed state, see Edward A. Pollard, *The Lost Cause: A New Southern History of the War of the Confederates* (New York: E. B. Treat, 1866). For autobiography as manifesto, see Edward A. Pollard, *The Lost Cause Regained* (New York: G. W. Carleton, 1868), and Margot Honecker and Luis Corvalán, *Gespräche mit Margot Honecker über das andere Deutschland* (Berlin: Das Neue Berlin, 2001).

20. Jürgen Osterhammel and Niels Petersson, *Geschichte der Globalisierung: Dimensionen, Prozesse, Epochen* (Munich: Beck, 2003), 46.

21. Shmuel N. Eisenstadt, *Die Vielfalt der Moderne: Heidelberger Max-Weber-Vorlesungen 1997* (Weilerswist: Velbrück Wissenschaft, 2000), 49, 55; Davis, *The Rise and Fall of the Confederate Government*, 1:131.

22. Monika Maron, quoted in Brigitte Zimmermann and Hans-Dieter Schütt, *Ohn-Macht: DDR-Funktionäre sagen aus* (Berlin: Neues Leben, 1992), 5.

23. Wolfgang Schivelbusch, *Die Kultur der Niederlage: Der amerikanische Süden 1865, Frankreich 1871, Deutschland 1918* (Berlin: Fest, 2001), 48–49. Laurence Shore argues that American national identity was shaped by southern culture up to the 1880s (*Southern Capitalists: The Ideological Leadership of an Elite, 1832–1885* [Chapel Hill: University of North Carolina Press, 1986], 188–89).

24. Jens Reich, *Abschied von den Lebenslügen* (Berlin: Rowohlt, 1992), 163.

25. Meticulous research on the almost forgotten crimes of the Stasi can be found in Hubertus Knabe, *Die Täter sind unter uns: Über das Schönreden der SED-Diktatur* (Berlin: Propyläen, 2007).

26. Jana Hensel, *Zonenkinder* (Reinbek: Rowohlt, 2002); for discussion, see Tom Kraushaar, *Die Zonenkinder und Wir: Die Geschichte eines Phänomens* (Reinbek: Rowohlt, 2004).

27. Bernhard Giesen, *Die Intellektuellen und die Nation: Eine deutsche Achsenzeit* (Frankfurt am Main: Suhrkamp, 1993), 236–56.

PART 5

The Middle East, Asia, and Africa

PETER SLUGLETT

Common Sense, or A Step Pregnant with Enormous Consequences

Some Thoughts on the Possible Secession of Iraqi Kurdistan

A t the time of the U.S. invasion of Iraq in 2003, the Kurdish parts of north-ern Iraq had enjoyed autonomy from Baghdad for some eleven years. In consequence, the possible secession of the Kurdish provinces (Dohuk, Arbil, Sulaymaniyya, and perhaps Taʾmim, which includes Kirkuk) to form an inde-pendent "Iraqi Kurdistan" was and still is very much on the political agenda, encouraged by the Kurdish provinces' de facto separation from the rest of the country, the fact that the younger generation of Iraqi Kurds knows English bet-ter than Arabic, and of course the seemingly endless chaos in the rest of the country.[1] The state of Iraq was created in 1920; as I show, the incorporation of the Kurdish areas into Iraq on the same footing as other parts of the state (that is, without providing for special treatment of the Kurdish population) generally passed off without major incident between the early 1930s and the 1960s and early 1970s. Noises made regarding a "Grand Kurdistan"—which would include the Kurdish parts of Iran, Iraq, and Turkey—have generally been rhetorical ges-tures rather than calls to arms, not least because of the very different aims of the various Kurdish political parties and groupings within the three states.

Let me try to set the topic into some sort of comparative framework. First, although the map of much of the Middle East was redrawn after the collapse of the Ottoman Empire at the end of the First World War, and although many of the states that were created at that time are not exactly "natural" political entities, their boundaries have generally remained fairly stable since then.[2] Apart from the various trajectories of Israeli expansion, the creation of Saudi Arabia, the boundary changes made after the British withdrawal from South Yemen in 1967, and the unification of "the two Yemens" in 1990, the only significant border change in the area was the transfer (by the French mandatory authorities) of the *sanjak* of Alexandretta (now the Turkish province of Hatay) from Syria to Turkey in 1938.[3]

Besides the Iraqi Kurds, the only other significant separatist/autonomist groups in the region (involving military operations that have incurred considerable loss of life) are the Kurds of Turkey, whose separatist sentiments have been largely inspired by the Turkish government's blanket insistence that, to simplify a more complex reality, all Muslims within the borders of the Turkish Republic must be Turks, thus denying the Kurds' identity as an ethnolinguistic minority.[4] However, current thinking on Turkish politics considers that the process of "traveling towards" European Union (EU) membership (which would entail "addressing civil-military relations, expanding human rights, promoting economic stability, and realizing the rule of law") will inevitably have positive results for the Kurds: the Adalet ve Kalkınma Partisi, which looks set to remain a major player in Turkish politics, has explicitly adopted the Copenhagen criteria for EU membership.[5] Incidentally, there is no evidence of collusion or coordination of policy between Ankara and Baghdad vis-à-vis the two countries' Kurdish populations, and even under Saddam Hussein, Iraqi regimes did not exhibit systematic political or other discrimination against Kurds living *outside* northern Iraq (for example, the sizable Kurdish population of Baghdad).

For these and other reasons I allude to below, it is a little difficult to relate the Kurds to many of the apparently more straightforward secessionist movements with which this book is concerned. However, using the kinds of criteria justifying secession put forward by Christopher Wellman (in particular), it is not difficult to argue that the ill treatment meted out to the Kurds by the governments of both Turkey and Iraq could serve as the moral basis for secession in each case. As already noted, the idea of a Kurdish state is complicated by the fact that the various Kurdish movements have developed separate trajectories within Iraq and Turkey (and to a lesser extent within Iran) and that movements within each host state are often hostile to each other—for example, the Patriotic Union of (Iraqi) Kurdistan, founded in 1976, was essentially a breakaway state created by those fed up with the tactics of the (Iraqi) Kurdistan Democratic Party. In addition, not all Iraqi Kurds speak the same Kurdish dialect; some

Iraqi Kurds speak the same dialect as some Turkish Kurds, while other Iraqi Kurds speak the same dialect as some Iranian Kurds, and so on.

To many Iraqi Kurds, the present situation in Iraq seems to present the opportunity to realize the dream of a Kurdish state first outlined in the unratified Treaty of Sèvres of 1920. To others (perhaps less romantic and more practical), moving in that direction seems foolhardy in the extreme. Of course, the longer the crisis continues in the "rest of Iraq," the more likely it is that the proponents of secession will gain a sympathetic hearing, and while a number of influential Americans *officially* advocate a federal constitution for Iraq in the form that it now exists, they are less adamantly opposed to secession than they were several years ago.[6]

THE KURDS OF THE OTTOMAN EMPIRE IN THE NINETEENTH AND EARLY TWENTIETH CENTURIES

With the exception of the five million Kurds now living in Iran (who form about 7 percent of its population), most Kurds today live in the various successor states of the former Ottoman Empire (Iraq, Syria, Turkey). The Ottoman Empire was one of the most long-lived political-administrative entities in history, lasting from about 1280 to 1918, although it did not extend over the same amount of territory for the whole of that period. In the course of the nineteenth century, or more accurately between 1830 and 1912, most of the empire's European provinces gradually either seceded or became detached from it, as a result of war or annexation or as part of treaties ending other conflicts.[7] This process was assisted by the rise of nationalism in nineteenth-century Europe and by the fact that while there were substantial Muslim populations in some parts of the Balkans (especially in Albania and Bosnia/Herzegovina), some two-thirds of the population of the Ottoman Balkans was Christian in the mid-nineteenth century.[8] Of course all the inhabitants of the Ottoman Empire, whether Muslim or Christian, spoke their own language (Arabic, Bulgarian, Greek, Serbian, etc.); Turkish was only *spoken* in Anatolia, although Ottoman Turkish was the official administrative language of the whole empire.

If the historical record is dissected from nationalist mythology, it becomes clear that the notion of "centuries of Ottoman Muslim oppression" is rather fanciful, since much of the local administration in the Balkans was carried out by the hierarchy of the Orthodox Church. In addition, the Ottoman government "did not concern itself with the daily life or the beliefs of its Christian population."[9] Nevertheless, for a variety of reasons, the ideology of ethnolinguistic nationalism proved persuasive when it appeared in the late nineteenth century (or, in the case of Greece, in the first quarter of the century). One of the consequences of the appearance of nationalism was the sudden decline (through a combination of casualties in war, attacks on the civilian population, "state terror," and eviction) in the numbers of the Muslim population. Thus in the course of the 1870s, the Muslim population of Bosnia declined by 35 percent and that of Bulgaria by about 55 percent.[10] By 1914, with the exception of Eastern Thrace, which remains part of the Turkish Republic, the Ottomans had lost all the territory that they had ever controlled in southeastern Europe.

There is a very great contrast between what happened in Ottoman Europe and what happened over the same period in the empire's Arab and Kurdish provinces. Here the population was overwhelmingly (at least 75 percent) Sunni Muslim, and although there were some Arab nationalist stirrings at the beginning of the twentieth century (especially between 1908 and 1914), these generally took the form of agitation for greater decentralization rather than for independence. Further, although the Ottomans had successfully reduced the powers of the Kurdish amirs in the first half of the nineteenth century, the process had not encountered much opposition, since, along with a degree of "social leveling" that was often also involved, such curbs were very much in the spirit of the *tanzimat* reforms, one of whose main professed aims was to strip overmighty subjects of their powers.[11] In any case, the implementation of the reforms in Kurdistan, as in other Muslim majority areas (for instance, in Syria or southern Iraq), did not evoke an immediate *nationalist* response.[12] In general, all but a tiny handful of Muslims and Christians in the Arab provinces remained committed to the ideal of Ottomanism, or *Osmanlılık*, which extolled the virtues of membership in a multiethnic and multinational state, and it was only the empire's collapse in 1918 that brought this ideal to a sudden and irreversible end.

The ideas of nationalism and national identity that had resonated in the nineteenth-century Balkans fell on stony ground in the Arab and Kurdish provinces largely because they had continued to be an integral part (as one might say) of an Ottoman moral universe in which religion, rather than ethnicity, constituted the basic marker of identity. Thus, in the late nineteenth and early twentieth century, "the empire, for most Muslims and even some Christians, was simply seen as the only remaining political force capable of forestalling European colonial ambitions."[13] Of course they were right, both in view of what had already happened (the loss of Tunis to France in 1881, Egypt to Britain in 1882, and Libya to Italy in 1911) and what would happen after the First World War (the division of the remaining Arab provinces between Britain and France under the mandate system).

Hence, for almost as long as the Ottoman Empire remained in existence, few Arabs or Kurds ever expressed a coherent desire or formulated a coherent plan to secede from it. On the contrary, many, if not most, felt proud to be members of it or associated with it. At the beginning of the twentieth century, "ethnic awareness" for Arabs and Kurds was still some years away. This simple fact should also put paid to the notion that ethnic hatreds between Arabs and Turks, or Kurds and Turks, or Arabs and Kurds (let alone Jews and Muslims) have existed "from time immemorial"; their roots are almost always much more recent. Most Kurds and Arabs regarded the empire as a politico-religious institution (headed by the sultan-caliph, as 'Abd al-Hamid II (1876–1909) always styled himself), which, however imperfect, remained perfectly adequate for their political needs until the last decade of the empire. In addition, when nationalism (both Arab and Kurdish) began to spread more widely in this region, it came first to the cities. It took some time to percolate through to the countryside, where the preeminent lifestyle continued to be a mixture of sedentary agriculture or (particularly in the case of the Kurds) transhumant pastoralism and where the preeminent form of social organization remained the tribe.

It is perhaps not surprising, then, that most of the early proponents of Kurdish nationalism, most of whom emerged after 1908, were Kurdish aristocrats who were either living voluntarily in or had been exiled to Istanbul or Paris and whose writings were (of course) in Turkish. However, it is certainly the case that in the years between 1908 and the First World War, the Committee of Union and Progress, which had taken power after the restoration of the constitution, had, for a variety of reasons, succeeded in alienating many leading figures in Ottoman Kurdistan (and in the Arab provinces as well). But the growing distance between the Kurds and the imperial center did not so much reflect anything that could be accurately labeled "Kurdish nationalism" as it did the Kurdish leadership's hostility toward both what it saw as the "new atheism" of Istanbul and Istanbul's attempt to assert its authority more vigorously over the region. Hence in common with the Shi'is of Iraq (and indeed in common with most Arabs), almost all Kurds rallied to the Ottoman standard when the empire declared war on Britain, France, and Russia in 1914.

POSTWAR DEVELOPMENTS: THE NEW STATE OF IRAQ

In brief, when the empire collapsed in 1918, and through the long period of uncertainty that lasted until and beyond the emergence of the Turkish Republic
at the end of 1922, the Kurds found themselves at something of a crossroads
as well as faced with several new sets of political realities. The situation was
further complicated by the fact that at the very end of the Mesopotamia campaign, British forces had seized Mosul some three days *after* the Allied/Otto-
man Armistice of Mudros of October 30, 1918, and were thus in de facto occupation of the Mosul *wilaya*, whose inclusion in the new state would become a
central plank of Britain's policy toward Iraq. In addition, seeking to capitalize
on the abrupt termination of Ottoman rule, Britain tried to "regularize its relations with the Kurdish tribes on the fringes of Mesopotamia."[14] This process
was entered into with greater vigor early in 1919, after the French had formally
abandoned their claim to Mosul (which had been assigned to them under the
Sykes-Picot Agreement). The new circumstances required at least a vague de-
marcation of the boundary between "Iraq," as it had now become, and what
eventually became the Turkish Republic. It also required lending support to
a local figure with some claim to authority in the region, and in the summer
of 1919, Shaykh Mahmud Barzinji, head of the Qadiri order in Sulaymaniyya,
a figure whom the British believed to be acceptable to a significant number of
tribal chiefs in the region, was appointed governor of Sulaymaniyya (and was
subsidized handsomely by the British for assuming the post), in the hope that
he would be able to preside over a "South Kurdish Confederation."

However, the unity that the Ottoman defeat first seemed to have produced
among the Kurds was short lived. The geography of the region, which is not
dissimilar to that of Afghanistan (mountainous terrain with fertile valleys), together with traditional tribal rivalries, made the preservation of "order" on British Indian lines virtually impossible. Kurdish politics were complicated enough,
but the effort to create a "Kurdistan" was further hampered by the well-known
British predilection for tidy administrative units, governed by "reliable" (in
other words, subsidized) local leaders. And of course, the whole concept of
"self-determination," however appealing it may have sounded, required a mod-
icum of agreement on who might be considered suitable representatives of the
"Kurdish people."[15] The other Kurdish leaders of northern Iraq did not accept
that Shaykh Mahmud's governorship of Sulaymaniya entitled him to be recognized as "king of Kurdistan," and he was in fact unable to exercise any au-

thority over Halabja and Panjwin, both only twenty miles from his capital. For these and other reasons, the desire for Kurdish autonomy did not produce any coherent movement toward Kurdish unity.[16] Both in southern Kurdistan (i.e., northern Iraq) and in northern Kurdistan (i.e., southeastern Anatolia), extreme uncertainty about the future (would the British stay in Iraq? would the Turks return?) caused an entirely comprehensible flurry of bet hedging, which was all the more encouraged by the Greek landings at Smyrna in May 1919.

Briefly, the possible outcome of the renewal of fighting in Anatolia—the "Christian foreigners" carving up Anatolia among themselves and imposing an Armenian state that would surely seek retribution for the massacres of 1915 (in which many Kurds had been implicated)—became the catalyst that drove the Kurds back into the arms of the Turks. This would eventually lead to the emergence, in the late summer of 1919, of what became the Turkish national movement headed by Mustafa Kemal, which called for a Turkish republic in an undivided Anatolia free of foreign occupation. Meanwhile, British attempts to seduce the Kurds of southeastern Anatolia (as well as their attempts to create loyal policemen among the Kurdish warlords of the Mosul *wilaya*) in 1919 triggered accusations of collusion and disloyalty, and opposition to British influence in the region began to grow. In January 1920, Kemal called for the election of a national assembly; by June it had become clear that the United States was not going to take the mandate for the future Armenia, and Britain was evidently having second thoughts about any involvement in "Turkish Kurdistan."

In August 1920, the Allies obliged the tottering Ottoman government to sign the Treaty of Sèvres, which, as well as providing for the partitioning of Anatolia between Britain, France, Greece, and Italy, also created the already obsolescent states of Armenia and Kurdistan (the latter, incidentally, excluded the Kurds of Iran, British-controlled Iraq, and French-controlled Syria). Sèvres was immediately disavowed by the Kemalists—and the subsequent creation of the Turkish Republic meant that it was never ratified—but the terms of articles 62 and 64 gave impetus to what had hitherto been the almost entirely embryonic notion of "Kurdistan."[17] Significantly, there was considerable disagreement between the various Kurdish supporters of "independent Kurdistan" as to where its boundaries should be.[18] Atatürk's call to arms was given greater urgency against the background of the impending dismemberment of Turkey outlined in the Treaty of Sèvres. This had the effect of rallying most of the Kurdish tribes in Anatolia, and in the spring of 1922 a Kemalist emissary was attracting support among tribal leaders in northern Iraq; perhaps this area too would fall to the Kemalists.[19] By the time of the signature of the Treaty of Lausanne in July 1923, Atatürk had succeeded in driving all foreign forces out of Anatolia and had established a new state with himself at its head. The future of Mosul was found too contentious to form part of the negotiations at Lausanne; British policy makers had decided that Iraq would not be viable without it, while the Turks wanted it included in the territory of the Turkish Republic. Eventually the dispute was referred to the League of Nations, which sent three boundary commissioners to determine the issue early in 1924.

The commissioners' reports are of considerable interest; they form the subject of a 2006 unpublished paper by Sarah Shields. Her findings are of particular interest because they show that the ethnicity of those interviewed by the commissioners was not always sufficient to be able to predict whether they would opt for "Iraq" or "Turkey." Thus some Arabs opted for the inclusion of the Mosul *wilaya* in Turkey, some Kurds for its inclusion in "Iraq," others for its inclusion in Turkey; yet others wanted to know whether Britain would be staying in Iraq and opted for or against the inclusion of the area within Iraq according to the reply. As we know, the commission decided that Mosul should be included in Iraq, and that, until fairly recently, was that.

THE KURDS IN IRAQ AND TURKEY

By the mid-1920s the political geography of the Kurdish areas had begun to assume much of the shape that it has today, the Kurds being divided between Iran and the new states of Iraq, Syria, and Turkey. In general terms, a succession of secular governments, particularly under Atatürk but also under his successors until the end of the 1980s, adopted consistently repressive policies toward the Turkish Kurds, which amounted to a virtual denial of their separate ethnic and linguistic identity, in a generally successful attempt to erase the hopes that had been raised by the Treaty of Sèvres.[20] The few Christians and Jews remaining in Turkey were not much interfered with, but all Muslims within the boundaries of the republic were declared to be Turks, and drastic reprisals—executions, massacres, and mass deportations—were launched against any attempts to assert Kurdish nationalism, identity, or independence. The Shaikh Sa'id rebellion (1925), the Khoybun revolt (1929–30), and the Dersim rebellion (1937), as well as more recent guerrilla activities in Anatolia following the foundation of the Parti Karkerani Kurdistan PKK in the mid-1970s, were all put down with great ferocity: in the earlier episodes, perhaps a quarter of a million Kurds were killed and over a million deported from their homes in the east and southeast to other parts of Turkey. [21] Such were the resoluteness and relentlessness (over a long historical period) of the official Turkish response to any suggestion of regional autonomy, let alone independence, for the Kurds. Thus:

> The habitual language of "unity and integrity" (*birlik ve bütünlük*), a popular parlance in politics, evokes this memory. David McDowall captures this sentiment when he says that "it [Turkey] has an emotional and ideological view that its frontiers cannot be changed without threatening the foundations of the Republic. . . . The integrity of Turkey within its present frontiers has acquired an almost mystical quality for those faithful to the legacy of . . . Mustafa Kemal Atatürk. [Hence the] Kurdish question contests the most critical assumptions of Turkish national identity, especially the core principle that there are no identities in Turkey other than the one covered by Turkish national identity." [22]

Two recent developments have put all this back on the table and made it a matter of more or less permitted debate. First, there has been a gradual change of mood in Turkey, which seems to have begun with a major survey commissioned by the Union of Turkish Chambers of Commerce in 1995, in which respondents thought that the "Kurdish question" in Turkey stemmed directly from government repression and considered that a sensible solution would be some form of limited federalism. [23] Second, Turkey's effort to enter the European Union has been a bumpy ride, obliging successive governments to rethink their policies towards the Kurds.

In Iraq, the situation of the Kurds was more complex. After several months' deliberation in 1924, the League of Nations commissioners decided that Mosul should be part of Iraq, a recommendation that, by and large, generally found favor in the Mosul *wilaya*. Early in 1926, the prime minister of Iraq declared that civil servants in the Kurdish area should be Kurds, that Kurdish and Arabic should be the official languages of the area, and that Kurdish children should be educated in Kurdish. Although these provisions were only half-heartedly carried out, it is fair to say that the Kurds' separate ethnic identity has generally been recognized to a greater or lesser extent by all Iraqi governments since then, and token Kurds served as ministers in virtually all the governments under the monarchy. Whatever repressive policies were adopted toward the Kurds (and of course whatever happened before the 1980s pales in comparison with what would happen then), there was no systematic attempt on the part of any Iraqi government to deny the existence of the Kurds or to claim that they were "really" Arabs, and so on.

Much of the Kurds' original enthusiasm for the state of Iraq in the 1920s derived from their belief that their status would in some sense be underwritten by a continuing British presence. Hence Britain's announcement that it would support Iraq's application for independence in 1932 caused serious misgivings, especially when it became known that the treaty would contain no minority guarantees. After serious rioting in Sulaymaniyya in September 1930, Shaikh Mahmud Barzinji indicated that he was once more prepared to go on the offensive, and fighting broke out in the spring of 1931. The revolt was decisively defeated, but almost simultaneously, a new and generally more effective nucleus of Kurdish opposition was developing, in the Barzani tribal lands in the subdistrict of Baradost. Mulla Mustafa Barzani, the younger brother of the Barzani religious and tribal leader Shaikh Ahmad, emerged in the early 1930s as the principal figure in Iraqi Kurdish politics, a position he was to retain until his death in exile in 1979. Mulla Mustafa and his tribal forces were important figures in the short-lived (Iranian Kurdish) Republic of Mahabad, a significant episode that may or may not qualify as "secession."[24] As a result, Mulla Mustafa went into exile in the Soviet Union and only returned after the overthrow of the ancien régime in Iraq in 1958.

IRAQ SINCE 1958

In spite of the unwillingness of successive Iraqi governments to render more than lip service to the principle, the Iraqi Kurds enjoyed certain basic freedoms denied to their fellows in Iran and Turkey, perhaps most importantly the recognition, tacit and grudging though it may often have been, of their separate ethnic status. This attitude only changed significantly in the wake of the bombing of Halabja with chemical weapons in 1988, the terrible events of 1988–89, and of course the failure of the Kurdish rising against Saddam Hussein in the spring of 1991.

Those who came to power in Iraq after the revolution of July 1958 had no special commitment to resolving the Kurdish question—none of them was Kurdish—but their general attitude toward the Kurds was positive. Barzani was invited back from the Soviet Union and returned to Iraq toward the end of the year. In the conflict that ensued in 1958–59 over whether Iraq should join the United Arab Republic, the Kurds' attitude was generally negative, the pan-Arab-inspired organization striking them as a most unlikely vehicle for the furthering of their aspirations, however defined. In January 1960 the Kurdistan Democratic Party (KDP), which had been founded in the 1940s, was legalized. Gradually, however, it emerged that many of the more conservative free officers were opposed to making any real concessions to the Kurds and also that Qasim's own commitment was limited. Eventually it became clear that Qasim was not willing to grant real autonomy, and by the beginning of 1961 he began to turn against Barzani. By September 1961 fighting had broken out in earnest and continued intermittently until 1975.

After the Ba'th came to power in 1968, the tide seemed to turn in the Kurds' favor; in 1970 a delegation of Ba'thists approached Barzani with a view to opening negotiations, which ultimately resulted in what became known as the "March Manifesto." This agreement would have recognized "the legitimacy of Kurdish nationality" and promised that Kurdish linguistic rights would be acknowledged, that Kurds would be permitted to participate in government, that Kurdish administrators would be appointed to oversee the Kurdish area, and that a new province based in Dohuk would be established. It also envisaged the implementation of the Agrarian Reform Law in the north, and, perhaps most controversially, as future events were to show, stated that "necessary steps shall be taken . . . to unify the governorates and administrative units populated by a Kurdish majority as shown by the official census to be carried out." The most contentious area—and here history is currently repeating itself—was the town of Kirkuk and the oil wells that surrounded it.

As events were to show, the manifesto was essentially a device that the Ba'th used to buy time in order to recast its Kurdish policy to its own advantage. The government's bad faith became apparent soon after the publication of the manifesto. Large numbers of families were forcibly removed from their homes to change the ethnic balance of particular areas, especially in and around Kirkuk, which the Kurdish leadership had insisted should form part of the Kurdish area and which the government wanted to retain within "Iraq proper." In September 1971, some forty thousand Fayli (Shi'i) Kurds were expelled to Iran from the border area near Khaniqin on the absurd grounds that they were not really Iraqis. These and other measures showed that the Ba'th were intent on limiting the extent of Kurdistan as far as possible. In September 1971 the Ba'th attempted to assassinate Barzani, and attacks on him and his sons also took place during

1972 and 1973. Tensions grew, and clashes erupted between government forces and Kurds in Sulaymaniyya and Jabal Sinjar, where several thousand Yazidi Kurds were forced to leave their homes in February–March 1973.

Although a major breakdown seemed inevitable, negotiations between the parties continued throughout the end of 1973 and the beginning of 1974. Most Kurds stood solidly behind Barzani and the KDP; in April 1974 fighting broke out once again, during which the Iraqi air force bombed several Kurdish villages. A mass exodus of refugees to Iran followed: over 110,000 arrived in the autumn of 1974, and in the spring of 1975 another 275,000 fled Iraq. For a few months, the Kurds had the upper hand; in spite of their numerical superiority, the government forces had as usual become seriously bogged down, and no end seemed in sight. At this point help for the Iraqi government arrived from an unexpected quarter; Iraq's desire to get the better of the Kurds coincided with the shah of Iran's interest in ending a series of frontier disputes and other hostilities with Iraq that had inflamed relations between the two countries since the mid-1960s. In March 1975, in the course of the OPEC conference in Algiers, Saddam Hussein and the shah came to an agreement, which, on the Iraqi side, effectively abrogated the Sa'dabad Pact of 1937, giving the Iranians free rights of navigation in the Shatt al-'Arab, and, on the Iranian side, closed the Iran-Iraq frontier in the north, thus preventing aid from reaching the Kurds and equally preventing the Kurds themselves from regrouping and rearming in and from Iran. The Iranian artillery (which had been supporting the Kurds) withdrew immediately, and the Kurdish resistance collapsed. Barzani left for Iran and died in the United States in 1979. An important by-product of this was the fracturing of the KDP and the formation in 1976 of the Patriotic Union of Kurdistan (PUK) under Ibrahim Ahmad and his son-in-law Jalal Talabani (the present president of Iraq).

In the months that followed, most of the refugees trickled back to Iraq under a series of amnesties. By 1979 an estimated two hundred thousand Kurds had been deported from the frontier area and some seven hundred villages burned down as part of a scorched earth policy that aimed to clear a strip along the border with Iran and Turkey some twenty kilometers deep and eight hundred kilometers long. During the war between Iran and Iraq, all the main Kurdish groups formed an alliance against Baghdad and stated that they would press together for autonomy within Iraq. Simultaneously, the PUK dropped its opposition to cooperation with Iranian forces, and by the spring of 1987, Iranian and PUK forces were fighting side by side against the Iraqi regime inside Iraqi Kurdistan. All this took place against a background of the most terrible brutality on the part of the Iraqi government. Eight thousand members of the Barzani clan were arrested in 1983 and have not been seen since. A further two thousand hamlets were stripped of their population, and as many as half a million Kurds were deported to lowland Kurdistan or southern Iraq.

In March 1988 Iranian troops captured Halabja; the day after, the town was attacked with chemical weapons, and over six thousand civilians, including large numbers of women and children, were killed. Even after the cease-fire on August 20, the Iraqis persisted in this policy, and in the face of further chemical attacks some sixty thousand Kurdish civilians fled to Turkey and a similar number to Iran. As a result of these attacks, and the relocation of much of the rural population, armed Kurdish opposition virtually ceased. Evidence that has come to light from secret police files captured in northern Iraq in the autumn of 1991 has revealed that it was the express policy of the Iraqi government to depopulate and destroy all Kurdish villages over an extremely wide area; as part of this policy, known as *al-Anfal*, about one hundred thousand Kurds were taken in trucks to southern Iraq in 1988 and 1989, executed, and then buried in preprepared mass graves in the desert west of Samawa.

After the traumatic events of *al-Anfal* neither the PUK nor the KDP could take on the Iraqi army. The invasion of Kuwait in August 1990 posed a considerable dilemma for the Kurdish leadership, some believing that they should force concessions out of Saddam Hussein while he was weak, others not wishing to side too openly with external forces against him. In December 1990 most Kurdish organizations joined the rest of the opposition in declaring their hostility to the Ba'th government, calling for an end to human rights abuses and for the introduction of democracy and the rule of law. For their part, the other opposition groups all accepted the notion of Kurdish autonomy, although not, of course, Kurdish secession, which had not yet appeared on the agenda.

After the defeat of the Iraqi ground forces in February 1991 two spontaneous and uncoordinated uprisings broke out in Iraq, one in the south and the other in the Kurdish area. For two weeks it appeared that the opposition had taken charge, and then the tables turned. Kurdish guerrilla forces were driven out of the northern cities, and by the beginning of April massive numbers of Kurdish refugees were camped out on the Iranian and Turkish borders. This human tragedy, enacted daily in front of millions of television viewers throughout the world, brought the desperate plight of the Kurds to a wide audience for the first time. In April 1991 "safe havens" (a military exclusion and no-fly zone north of latitude thirty-six degrees north) were set up in the Kurdish areas, enforced by Britain and the United States.

The safe havens led to the gradual withdrawal of the Iraqi civil and military authorities from the region and to the creation of a de facto autonomous region. For a time, the expectation that unity would be produced by adversity was partially realized. Elections were held in May 1992; the closeness of the vote resulted in Mas'ud Barzani and Jalal Talabani being asked to act as joint leaders of the political entity that emerged, the Kurdistan Regional Government. In fact, neither of the leaders ever participated personally in the government, and the international relief agencies took some time to give it de facto recognition, on the general grounds that they felt bound to deal with what might be misleadingly described as the legitimate government in Baghdad. For its part the Iraqi regime continued its economic blockade, assisted by the greed or fear of local strong men and others.

The Kurdish Regional Government's difficulties were compounded by a series of problems, personal, regional, national, and international. In broad terms, Barzani and Talabani presided over groups that were largely defined by region, and in addition the two leaders had been brought up in very different ideological schools. Support for Mas'ud Barzani (b. 1946) and the KDP came mostly from the Kurmanji-speaking northwest, the area bounded by the Tigris, the Great Zab, and the Turkish border, which includes Amadiyya, Aqra, Dohuk, and Zakho, while support for Jalal Talabani (b. 1933) came mostly from the Surani-speaking northeast, the area between the Great Zab and the Iranian border, which includes Arbil, Halabja, Rawanduz, and Sulaymaniyya. Barzani had inherited the leadership from his father Mulla Mustafa, who had symbolized an old-fashioned Kurdish identity that was more "tribal" than "political" and whose overreliance on Iran and the United States could be said to have been largely responsible for the Kurds' disastrous defeat in 1975.

In contrast, Talabani and his father-in-law Ibrahim Ahmad had generally adopted what they claimed to be a more progressive political line. Ahmad in his time had always been critical, as Talabani has been subsequently, of Mulla Mustafa Barzani's political judgment. Both tried to find common ground with the Ba'th in the late 1960s and early 1970s and remained extremely wary of Barzani's close ties with the United States and the Shah. Thus Ahmad and Talabani broke away from the KDP to found the PUK in Damascus in 1976; in 1945, Ahmad had been one of the cofounders of the original KDP in Mahabad, which had been envisaged as a pan-Kurdish political organization. Again, while Mas'ud Barzani inherited his father's tribal supporters (who showed little interest in changing or reforming the archaic social structures persisting in much of the region), Talabani's followers tend to come from more educationally sophisticated and socially aware strata in the larger cities of the east and south of the area.

The fact that there are substantial Kurdish populations in both Iran and Turkey has meant that both Mas'ud Barzani and Jalal Talabani have long been beholden to foreign masters, Barzani originally to Iran (with negative consequences for the KDP-Iran), and Talabani (although less consistently) to Syria. Both have had a complex relationship with Turkey, with whom they have sided against the PKK.[25] This has so far proved a shrewd calculation, in that in return for military cooperation against the PKK, Ankara has afforded a degree of de facto support to the Iraqi Kurdish autonomous region, which has been crucial in enabling it to survive. The capture of Abdullah Öcalan and the subsequent virtual cessation of PKK activity have enabled Ankara to be even more forthcoming, although it has continued to send troops into Iraqi Kurdistan to hunt down PKK fighters taking refuge there.

The bitter rivalry between Barzani and Talabani and their followers has more than once seriously threatened the survival of the autonomous region. Continuous infighting lost the Iraqi Kurds a great deal of the international support they had accumulated over the years, and the fighting also caused major interruptions in the relief effort. In the summer of 1996, at Talabani's invitation, Iranian troops entered the area controlled by the PUK; in response, Barzani called for assistance from Baghdad to remove them. Forty thousand Iraqi troops were sent to Arbil, which they captured from the PUK with the assistance of the KDP. In the ensuing weeks, Iraqi intelligence sought out and executed opponents of the regime who had taken refuge in Arbil, together with some of those attached to a rather rudimentary organization funded by the CIA, which, it had been hoped, would overthrow the regime in Baghdad. Some five thousand of those fortunate enough to survive were subsequently settled in the United States. Iraqi forces retreated, but the message, at least for the time being, was clear; no independent entity could survive in Kurdistan as long as Saddam Hussein remained in power, given the intense and apparently endemic factionalism in the region.

THE SITUATION SINCE 2003

As the preparations for the U.S.-led war against Iraq grew apace, many Kurds feared that the overthrow of Saddam Hussein would mean the end of U.S. protection. Whatever the outcome, Barzani and Talabani had little choice but to remain on the U.S. side. The overthrow of the regime presented the Kurdish politicians with new choices, pushing them, as time went on, toward the idea of a federal regime, in which they would manage their own oil and have their own control over their police and army. In many ways, this was understandable since "the Iraqi Army was the only enemy the Kurds had ever known."[26] The Bremer administration did not want to concede these powers and also did not want to give the Kurds control over the Kirkuk oilfields. The Kurds were supposed to give up their militias and let Baghdad control their oil and their borders with Iran and Turkey, but they refused to do either of these things. In January 2005, unofficial referendum booths were set up next door to the polling stations for the Iraqi elections. Two million Kurds voted in the "referendum"; 98 percent chose independence. "The outcome put Kurdish and Iraqi Arab leaders on notice that Kurdistan's voters would reject a permanent constitution that required any significant reintegration of the region into Iraq."[27] Another consequence of the election was that Jalal Talabani became president of Iraq. In June 2005 the Kurdish National Assembly prohibited the Iraqi military from entering Kurdistan without the assembly's approval.

Of course, the longer the crisis continues in the rest of Iraq, the more likely it is that the proponents of secession will gain the upper hand. Whatever may happen, it is as well to remember that the circumstances of "Iraqi Kurdistan" are very different from those of, say, the landlocked states of Austria, Luxembourg, and Switzerland, surrounded by friendly neighbors associated with the EU, which have every interest in the free movement of goods and individuals (or at least individuals holding the appropriate passports) across their borders. On the one hand, Kurdish secession may well be a hard row to hoe; on the other, there may never be a better time. Quite evidently, given the Iraqi Kurds' recent history, it is a morally defensible objective.

A recent article suggests that there are many alternatives to secession in various parts of the world, including power sharing, federalism, autonomy, cantonal arrangements, and so on.[28] The authors consider that integration is probably the best solution for "disgruntled minorities" but also acknowledge that the offer of autonomy may provide the disgruntled with opportunities for separatism that might otherwise have eluded them. Of course, the choice now facing the Kurds of Iraq is of a somewhat different kind; they have been able to seize the initiative and function as a sort of light in the darkness, as a beacon of stability in a region racked by sectarian violence, on the edge of civil war, and so on (although the extent to which they have been able to do so should not be exaggerated). Being above, or at least mostly quite far away from, the fray has been an enormous advantage for the Iraqi Kurds, but it is difficult to see how independence or secession from Iraq would benefit them in the long run and even more difficult to imagine how a new, fragile, and landlocked state might survive in the contemporary regional environment. Neither the Turks, the Iranians, nor the Syrians will wish an independent Iraqi Kurdistan well; while there is no doubt that the Iraqi Kurds are entitled to their autonomy, I very much doubt the wisdom of their seceding from Iraq, however tempting such a prospect may seem.

Notes

1. This possibility of an Iraqi Kurdistan has been aired before but should not be confused with the plan put forward in October 2006 by Senator Joseph Biden for a tripartite division of Iraq (about which little, mercifully, has been heard since the senator's promotion). Given the communal mosaic of the rest of the country (and particularly the deep divisions between the various Shi'i factions on a variety of crucial issues), it does not constitute a realistic solution to Iraq's problems on a broader level. See www .planforiraq.com.

2. Contrary to much current received wisdom, Iraq, certainly the area south of Mosul to the Persian Gulf, was a more or less unified political entity under the authority of whoever controlled Baghdad for most of the period between the 'Abbasids and the First World War, so the notion that it is "artificial" is not quite accurate. "[In the 1880s] Mosul and Basra were separated, and for 30 years—*and for the first time in its history— Iraq assumed the tripartite structure that has become entrenched in Western historiography as the basic administrative pattern of 400 years of Ottoman rule*" (Reidar Visser, "Historical Myths of a Divided Iraq," *Survival* 50, no. 2 [2008]: 99, [my emphasis]).

3. Neither the Saudi nor the Yemeni boundaries had been delineated at the time of the post–World War One peace settlement.

4. David McDowall, *A Modern History of the Kurds* (New York: I. B. Tauris, 1996); Martin Van Bruinessen, *Agha, Shaikh, and State: The Social and Political Structures of Kurdistan* (London: Zed Books, 1992); Susan Meiselas, *Kurdistan: In the Shadow of History*, 2nd ed. (Chicago: University of Chicago Press, 2008).

5. M. Hakan Yavuz, *Secularism and Muslim Democracy in Turkey* (Cambridge: Cambridge University Press, 2009).

6. Peter S. Galbraith, *The End of Iraq: How American Incompetence Created a War without End* (New York: Simon and Schuster, 2006).

7. Thus Greece (1828–29), Romania (1878), Montenegro (1878), and Albania (1912) became independent; Bessarabia was annexed by Russia in 1878, Serbia and Bosnia/

Herzegovina were annexed by Austria-Hungary in 1908, and what is now the Republic of Macedonia and northern Greece had become part of Bulgaria, Greece, or Serbia by 1914.

8. Nikolai Todorov, *The Balkan City, 1400–1900* (Seattle: University of Washington Press, 1983), 309–26.

9. Barbara Jelavich, *History of the Balkans* (Cambridge: Cambridge University Press, 1983), 48.

10. Justin McCarthy, *Population History of the Middle East and Balkans* (Istanbul: Isis Press, 2002), 48.

11. McDowall, *A Modern History of the Kurds*, 38–48. In some cases, the former hereditary rulers (and/or their sons) were sent into exile in Istanbul.

12. In fact, what happened in the Kurdish areas was that shaykhs of the various Sufi orders—particularly of the Mujaddi (revivalist) faction of the Naqshbandiyya, whose founder, Shaykh Khalid, had strong ties with the Ottoman court—gained power (McDowall, *A Modern History of the Kurds*, 50–51).

13. Bruce Masters, *Christians and Jews in the Ottoman Arab World: The Roots of Sectarianism* (New York: Cambridge University Press, 2001), 176.

14. McDowall, *A Modern History of the Kurds*, 108.

15. The idea of Kurdish self-determination was greatly encouraged by Woodrow Wilson's Fourteen Points (January 8, 1918), the twelfth of which states that in the event of an Allied victory "the nationalities now under Turkish rule should be assured an undoubted security of life and an absolutely unmolested opportunity of autonomous development."

16. By May 1919 the British authorities were obliged to remove Shaykh Mahmud, who had succeeded in alienating almost all those on whom he had relied to maintain his position in Sulaymaniya. Britain's Kurdish policy is described in detail in Peter Sluglett, *Britain in Iraq: Contriving King and Country* (London: I. B. Tauris, 2007), chap. 3.

17. "A Commission . . . shall draft within six months from the coming into force of the present Treaty a scheme of local autonomy for the predominantly Kurdish areas lying east of the Euphrates, south of the southern boundary of Armenia as it may be hereafter determined, and north of the frontier of Turkey with Syria and Mesopotamia" (art. 62); "If within one year from the coming into force of the present Treaty the Kurdish peoples within the areas defined in Article 62 shall address themselves to the Council of the League of Nations in such a manner as to show that a majority of the population of these areas desires independence from Turkey, and if the Council . . . recommends that it should be granted to them, Turkey hereby agrees to execute such a recommendation, and to renounce all rights and title over these areas" (art. 64).

18. Hakan Özoğlu, *Kurdish Notables and the Ottoman State: Evolving Identities, Com-*

peting Loyalties, and Shifting Boundaries (Albany: State University of New York Press, 2004), 38–40.

19. McDowall, *A Modern History of the Kurds*, 141.

20. I cannot elaborate on this here, but the abolition of the caliphate in 1924 and other indications of the early republic's determination to marginalize Islam were important factors in the growth of Kurdish hostility to the new regime from the late 1920s onward.

21. In 2000 it was estimated that some fifty thousand people (at least half of whom were Kurdish civilians) had been killed in the conflict between Turkish government forces and the PKK over the previous sixteen years.

22. Ümit Cizre, "Turkey's Kurdish Problem," in *Right-sizing the State: The Politics of Moving Borders*, ed. Brendan O'Leary, Ian S. Lustick, and Thomas M. Callaghy (Oxford: Oxford University Press, 2001), 226, 228.

23. Its Turkish acronym is TOBB. The organization was (and is) very close to the Turkish government, which made the criticisms of government policy that it contained especially shocking (Cizre, "Turkey's Kurdish Problem," 222–24).

24. Archie Roosevelt, "The Kurdish Republic of Mahabad," *Middle East Journal* 1, no. 3 (1947): 247–69.

25. McDowall, *A Modern History of the Kurds*.

26. Galbraith, *The End of Iraq*, 161.

27. Galbraith, *The End of Iraq*, 171.

28. Ian S. Lustick, Dan Miodownik, Roy J. Eidelson, "Secessionism in Multicultural States: Does Sharing Power Prevent or Encourage It?" *American Political Science Review* 98, no. 2 (2004): 209–30.

RAPHAEL CHIJIOKE NJOKU

Nationalism, Separatism, and Neoliberal Globalism

A Review of Africa and the Quest for Self-Determination since the 1940s

Since the end of colonial rule, sub-Saharan Africa has been troubled by civil wars and other forms of organized violence. While these conflicts together suggest Africa is a continent in retreat, those particularly connected with secessionist demands have raised doubts about the nature and viability of the emergent postcolonial states. At present more than a dozen active secessionist movements are underway in Africa in Algeria, Angola, Benin, Cameroon, Comoros, the Congo, Côte d' Ivoire, Equatorial Guinea, Ethiopia, and Somalia. Another flash spot of separatism is Nigeria, currently manifested in the Movement for the Emancipation of the Niger Delta. There is also the lingering ghost of the Biafran war in Nigeria in the form of the Movement for the Actualization of Biafra reactivated by Chief Ralph Uwazuruike in 1999.[1] The Sudan question, which first emerged in the 1950s, remains a serious problem, as the recent orgies of bloodletting in Darfur suggest. The less well known but virulent Casamance struggle in Senegal and the nascent Berber cries for "self-determination" in Morocco are examples of other independence struggles in Africa.[2]

Africanist scholars and politicians are polarized as to whether the right to self-determination means the freedom of every self-identified ethnocultural group to secede from a state, whether or not it constitutes a viable political and economic entity. The choice theory of secession, which Christopher Wellman defends in this book, argues that every nationality that demands statehood and is able to discharge its responsibilities is entitled to an independent existence as a nation-state.[3] Conceptually, this view is shaped by the ethnonationalist para-

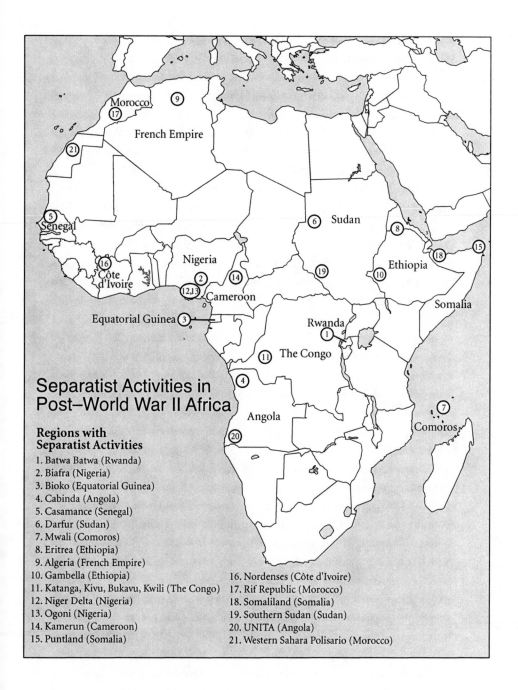

Separatist Activities in
Post–World War II Africa

**Regions with
Separatist Activities**

1. Batwa Batwa (Rwanda)
2. Biafra (Nigeria)
3. Bioko (Equatorial Guinea)
4. Cabinda (Angola)
5. Casamance (Senegal)
6. Darfur (Sudan)
7. Mwali (Comoros)
8. Eritrea (Ethiopia)
9. Algeria (French Empire)
10. Gambella (Ethiopia)
11. Katanga, Kivu, Bukavu, Kwili (The Congo)
12. Niger Delta (Nigeria)
13. Ogoni (Nigeria)
14. Kamerun (Cameroon)
15. Puntland (Somalia)
16. Nordenses (Côte d'Ivoire)
17. Rif Republic (Morocco)
18. Somaliland (Somalia)
19. Southern Sudan (Sudan)
20. UNITA (Angola)
21. Western Sahara Polisario (Morocco)

digm, which posits that ethnicity is the root of nationalism and that true nations are ethnic nations.[4] The proponents argue that a nation-state ought to
align with a homogenous group; the merging of diverse groups or nationalities
has created the foundation for separatist struggles along ethnic lines. This perspective, shared by some African scholars, has informed the resilient call for the
boundaries of the postcolonial state to be adjusted in order to create homogenous national communities that can live in peace.[5] One major problem with
the ethnonationalist paradigm in regard to Africa is the assumption that ethnic
conflict is a peculiar problem of multiethnic states; it therefore fails to offer an
explanation for intraethnic conflicts within a homogenous group. Just as in het-
erogenous societies, ethnic and political conflicts have troubled homogenous
groups. The spate of communal wars between the Egba and the Ijebu and the Ife
and the Modakeke that claimed thousands of lives among the Yoruba of Nigeria
in 2004 and 2005, respectively, teaches that ethnic identities are fluid and that
sharp differences can materialize at every level of societal organization—within
the family and among kinship, ethnic, or national communities.

Another view rules out any secessionist movement from independent states
under any circumstances. This accords with the official position of the Organization of African Unity (OAU), also known as the African Union (AU), which
is its new name. The OAU believes that political divorce undermines the legitimacy and territorial integrity of multinational states. Writing in 1975, five years
after the prolonged and devastating civil war in his country, Nigeria, Peter Ekeh
argued that "ethnic groups" like the Katanga in the Congo and the Igbo in Nigeria "are not nations in the 'modern' sense and cannot be treated as such."[6] Ekeh
was writing in an era of intense African nationalism, and yet his antisecession
doctrine was widely accepted by African nationalists and postcolonial leaders.
Even the most sensible among his peers, Julius Nyerere, the former president
of Tanzania, whose country was one of the first to recognize Biafra's secession
from Nigeria in 1967, shared this antisecession view. In declaring his support for
Biafra, Nyerere expressed agony over his pro-Biafra stand as "a setback to our
goal of national unity."[7] It is important to emphasize that the modern boundaries of the postcolonial state defended by African leaders were the accidental
and arbitrary product of European conquest and administration rather than expressions of African popular national identities. It is ironic that since the 1960s,
the OAU has been averse to changing colonial borders even though they are
widely considered to be one of the most humiliating legacies of colonialism and
have engendered disunity among diverse groups. The fight for Africa's inde-

pendence was waged in the idiom of rights to self-determination; yet, the post-colonial state is hostile to ethnic citizens fighting for self-determination. Like the OAU, the UN espouses antisecessionist doctrine in Africa on the grounds of respect for the principle of sovereignty and respect for the geographical status quo. The rule abhors boundary adjustments of existing states, the prohibition of the use of force, and intervention in the internal affairs of member nations.[8] One clause in article 3 of the OAU "Charter and Rules of Procedure" for conflict prevention, management, and resolution states the importance of "respect for the sovereignty and territorial integrity of each state."[9]

In upholding such rigid principles, the OAU invites conflicts in a region whose historical evolution and structures of state system are wired with ethnonation-alist thinking. Describing the characteristic "storm and stress" associated with new nations, Leonard Binder and coauthors have aptly summarized these challenges as determining who belongs to the nation (identity); ensuring the permeation of this idea of common nationhood (penetration); developing a clear understanding of who should participate in the political process (participation) and who has the right to govern (legitimacy); and arriving at an agreed-on formula for sharing common resources (distribution).[10] Time is crucial to resolving these issues; the roots of conflict and secession in postcolonial Africa lie in the fact that colonialism did not permit these processes to play out.

The problem of conflict is even more daunting in polities with meager resources and where politics understood as the survival of the postcolonial state (or rather its emergent leaders) is contingent on the power to claim territory and exploit the available resources. Attempts to change the status quo by groups claiming the right to self-determination thus naturally elicits hostility from the postcolonial state. African leaders and nationalist historians, therefore, preach centralization rather than decentralization of power. So one finds Kwame Nkrumah declaring at the summit of all heads of state in 1963 that the border problem is not a cause for secession but rather an argument for a political union on a continental scale. "Only African unity can heal this festering sore of boundary disputes between our various states."[11] President Modibo Keita of Mali added that "we must take Africa as it is, and must renounce any territorial claims, if we do not wish to introduce what we might call black imperialism. . . . African unity demands of each one of us complete respect for the legacy that we have received from the colonial system, that is to say: maintenance of the present frontiers of our respective states."[12]

More eloquent but naïve was the demonstrated readiness of the president of Guinea, Sékou Touré, in 1958 to merge his country with neighboring Mali.[13] The paternalistic position of the OAU on the question of self-determination for ethnic citizens legitimized not only the existing colonial borders but also the involuntary and criminal confining of peoples in states that they never gave their consent to be bound to. The African leaders openly betrayed their inexperience in supporting the UN's antisecessionist mandate in the Congo in 1961, which aimed to deny Katanga secession from Congo.[14] In condemning the UN resolution, René Lemarchand argued that the UN denied "the provincial authorities of Katanga the right to self determination" while empowering the Republic of Congo with the exclusive right to conduct external affairs.[15]

The logic of "modern" nationhood, deriving from the European concept of statehood, that was invoked in 1961 in support of the new Congo state had served until the end of World War II in advancing the goals of imperialism. Thereafter, decolonization implied equality of races, civil liberties for all citizens, and the ultimate end to empires. Decolonization resonated with neoliberalism—employed here to denote the global movement toward economic deregulation and greater political decentralization. The exponents of the so-called Washington Consensus (including the International Monetary Fund, the World Bank, and the Paris Club) represented these values as crucial to sustaining development in the Western world as well as to securing the elusive socioeconomic and political advancement of the developing world. On this view, what the African postcolonial state needs in order to moderate its ethnic conflicts is a unique form of highly decentralized political structure in harmony with the people's nationalisms and political consciousness. Onyeonoro Kamanu, a student of African politics, has analyzed the paradox of self-determination understood as a de jure force by which Africa's freedom from alien rule would be secured but considered by the OAU as inapplicable to the ethnic minorities on the continent.[16]

The OAU's stand on local self-determination movements disregards two critical issues. First, it ignores the precolonial nature of most African states, which were highly decentralized and democratic. Viewing the development of the postcolonial state only through western lenses makes it seem as if there was no political life in the continent until the coming of the Europeans. Second, it fails to take into account the fate of those precolonial states like the Oyo and Benin kingdoms that were constituted by "homegrown" imperial force. These empires could neither sustain the minorities' loyalties nor successfully assimilate them into the majority culture. Precolonial boundaries of states in Africa shifted as often as they did because local loyalties to hegemonic powers changed. These political realignments were a part of the dynamism integral to idioms of territorial sovereignty and decentralization. In other words, where ethnic feelings are strong, political decentralization must reign or else hegemonic powers fish in troubled waters.

Even if this aspect of Africa's political heritage was not documented in libraries and archives, we can say in retrospect that the tendency to resist assimilation was a clear indication of the people's unbending spirit to be free from any form of political domination—alien or homegrown. Ex-colonial powers have continued to deny the right of Africans to choose the forms of state structures most appropriate to the people's temperament and sensibilities, despite the fact that they have come to recognize their mistake in this regard on their own continent. As Juan Enrique has observed, European sovereign states multiplied from twenty-three in 1920 to forty-four in 1994. In other places where secession has relentlessly threatened national unity, such as Belgium, the political elite are "now considering the benefits of granting more autonomy to provinces and regions, rather than having a strong central government. When one considers that Europe had approximately 500 political entities in 1500, it appears that the unwinding of the continent's existing countries could continue for a long time."[17] As globalization expands and endures, the more attractive the idea of splitting from their states becomes to ethnonationalist agitators. Secession, therefore, is facilitated by integration on a supranational level.

SECESSION AND THE AFRICAN EXPERIENCE

Given that the political friction in Africa in part derives from a long tradition of shifting allegiance, one might argue that the record of riots, rebellions, ethnic conflicts, civil strife, and secessionist movements since the 1950s across the continent is another manifestation of that tradition, an expression of the people's disillusionment, in this case, with the postcolonial state. Such disillusionment resonates today in the persistent cries of aggrieved groups for national conferences on sovereignty. Aggrieved groups in Nigeria, Sudan, Somaliland, Senegal, and Morocco see these conferences as an opportunity to renegotiate terms for national union.[18]

The question arises as to whether the aggrieved groups have justified grounds for secession. Allen Buchanan has outlined a number of secessionist arguments and has made the case that self-determination and consent—perhaps the two reasons most often appealed to in attempts to legitimate separatist mobilizations across the world—are not sufficient alone to justify secession. But he also adds that arguments founded on rectification of past injustices, discriminatory redistribution, and self-defense under extreme conditions could combine with the others to fulfill conditions for secession.[19] Africans have a legitimate right to accept or reject the structure of the postcolonial state, a right that can be framed in terms of the argument regarding rectification of past injustices by the colonial system. To dismiss that right is to endorse the imperial law of "might is right" under which the postcolonial state was constituted, and it should come as no surprise that that right having been dismissed, the pains of military coups and civil wars quickly stifled the celebrations of independence in places like the Sudan, the Congo, Nigeria, and Somalia.

Indeed the recurrent conflict in the Sudan illustrates the need for African states to seek the consent of their minorities in forming a common union. The Sudan has been trapped in a genocidal spiral of ethnic conflicts, which have claimed more than two million lives, since its independence in 1956. The roots of the unending crises in the Sudan go back to 1955, when soldiers of northern origin used excessive force in quelling a local riot in the southern province.[20] This incident, interpreted by the separatists as having had a religious undertone, polarized the country along religious and geographical lines, pitting Muslims against non-Muslims and north against south. In the wake of increased military activities in the south by soldiers of northern/Muslim origins in 1955–56, the dominant Christian Dinka and Nuer southerners led a campaign for a separate statehood under the banner of Anya Nay.[21] Although the first civil war ended in 1972, the Anya Nay was subsequently converted into the Southern Sudan People's Liberation Army, which endures today as one of the dominant factions in the Sudan's fractionated and unending struggle for secession.

Douglas Johnson, who has studied the root causes of the Sudanese civil war, has argued inter alia that ethnic and religious rivalries, combined with precolonial authority asserting itself, account for the lingering conflicts in the Sudan. This historical approach to the intractable civil war takes us back to the fourteenth century when the Arabs first arrived in the Sudan. The Arab presence marked a turning point in the sense that by the 1550s, when Islam had taken roots, especially in the northern part of the country, it created a deep cleavage between the Muslims and the non-Muslims, who were living in the southern part of the Sudan and who were mostly adherents of either the indigenous religion or Christianity. In relation to politics, the Islamic religion makes a distinction between "those who [can] claim the protection of the law, and those without legal rights." As Johnson further notes, Islam also established the idea of free and subjugated peoples. Since then, inhabitants of certain sections of the north, especially in established settlements in the area bordering the Nile River confluence in Khartoum, have seen themselves as having a "personal stake" in the subjugation of the south.[22]

In June 1983, for example, President Gaafar El Nimeiry, a Muslim northerner, passed his notorious decree no. 1, which among other things authorized the use of flogging, amputation, stoning, and execution (including crucifixion) for capital punishments, as enshrined in the Sharia code of jurisprudence. The chances of reconciliation between the rival groups were drastically narrowed by the adoption of these measures. The ensuing second civil war ended following a brokered peace agreement that was signed in 1985, which allowed for a certain degree of self-autonomy for the groups in the south.

One of the prevailing theories of secession suggests that a group's quest to secede may be justified on the grounds that it upholds the value of liberty, which stresses freedom of choice, including in matters connected with political union in a multiethnic state. The theory understands secession to be a morally justified way of preventing the establishment of a Taliban-like state that suppresses, inter alia, the right to social life, freedom of speech, association, and legitimate economic pursuits.[23] One may better appreciate why the secessionists in the Sudan have refused to drop their struggle if one sees it in terms of an attempt to prevent the formation of a Taliban-like state. Amid the latest conflicts in the Darfur region, which started in 2003, the former unity among the various groups in the south has given way to factional demands for secession from Khartoum, Sudan's capital.

While the international community had, in 1955, waved aside the Sudanese conflict along with other incidents of ethnonationalism in the former French colonies of Algeria, Chad, and Comoros, regarding them as normal "tribal" conflicts in Africa, secessionist movements in the Congo (1960–64) and Nigeria (1967–70) were to confront the world community with the need for a clear policy stand on the legal rights or otherwise of ethnic separatism in Africa. In the Congo, Katanga's quest for independence from the former Belgian colony materialized in 1960, a few weeks after Joseph Kasavubu was sworn in as the country's new president.[24] Patrice Lumumba, a socialist ideologue whom Kasavubu had appointed prime minister, quickly attempted to consolidate power by uniting all regions of the mammoth country after the Soviet model. This move, coupled with competition for control of mineral-rich Katanga, caused the province's leader, Moise Tshombe, to declare it, with the support of Belgium, an independent sovereign state.[25] Here, we see the dynamics of neocapitalist struggles and the tensions it generates. The civil war resulting from all this proved too much for the new African leaders to handle. The ultimate resolution in 1964 came after a UN military mission, authorized by the secretary general, Dag Hammarskjöld.[26] The Congo was eventually reunited, but the country now known as the Democratic Republic of Congo (DRC) has been plagued by unending civil wars despite the attempts, motivated by self-interest, of UN and Western arbitrators to bring peace to it.[27] Presently the DRC is at the mercy of local warlords, multinationals, and foreign governments who have vested economic interests in the mineral rich country.

Similarly diverse actors with vested economic and political interests have played determinant roles in the secessionist movements in Nigeria and other places. In Nigeria, the Igbo-led struggle in the oil-rich eastern region to secede from the former British colony was met with firm British and Nigerian federal government opposition resulting in a bloody civil war that lasted from 1967 to 1970.[28] The Biafran war marked the height of an attempt by the force of British maxim guns between 1900 and 1914 to manage an amalgam of different nationalities. Before the Igbo rebellion, there had been, for example, the Hausa-Fulani-led Arewa movement (in the northern region) and the Yoruba-led Omo Oduduwa movement (in the western region). The Biafran episode was doomed even before it got underway. Among other things, the manner with which some middle-ranked Igbo officers in the Nigerian army carried out the January 1966 coup that toppled the northern-led Alhaji Tafawa Belewa government left a bitter feeling among the northerners, who complained that "the Igbo regime had at last came out into the open, its aim was to take over the country, exploiting and colonizing the backward north."[29] A *revanchist* countercoup of July 1966 left 43 Igbo officers, including the commander-in-chief of the armed forces, and 171 other soldiers dead. For a couple of months mutinies against Igbo officers continued in the northern and western regions.[30] Additionally, civilian massacres claimed the lives of about thirty to fifty thousand people of eastern Nigerian origin—most of them Igbo.[31] Other targets of the second round of killings included the minorities in the east—the Ijo, Efik, Ibibio, Ogoja, and so on. An official newspaper of the northern Nigerian government, the *New Nigerian*, in its October 19, 1966, issue carried an extract from the speech of the country's leader, Lieutenant Colonel Gowon, to northerners: "I receive complaints daily that up till now Easterners living in the North are being killed and molested and their property looted. . . . It appears that it is now going beyond reason and is now at the point of recklessness and irresponsibility."[32] The pogrom formed a rallying point for the easterners in the Biafran secessionist movement. The Igbo political elite, who argued that their people were no longer accepted anywhere outside of their eastern Nigerian homeland, declared the sovereignty of the Republic of Biafra on May 30, 1967.[33]

Like the Belgians with respect to the Congo conflict, Britain faced a difficult foreign policy decision in regard to the civil war in Nigeria, its former colony.[34] Some irrefutable evidence now shows that Britain would have had no serious regrets if the eastern region had seceded from Nigeria—especially given the practice of ethnic cleansing in the north. The primary consideration for Britain, however, was economic. As David Hunt (the British high commissioner to Nigeria) explained in his memoirs, the overriding interest of Britain was to protect its economic interests.

> HMG (Her Majesty's Government) would recognise Biafra if it seemed likely to endure as a country. But H. M. G. did not want to be among the first to recognise and would hope to have avoided recognition should the F.M.G. [Federal Military Government] be ultimately victorious. In fact our policy would be determined not by principle but by the practical ends of defending our oil and other interests in Nigeria (of these we agreed oil was much the most important).[35]

Britain's self-interested motivations were not known to the ordinary people in Europe and North America who sympathized with the dominant Christian Igbos and offered their support to Biafra's struggle through private efforts, a development that troubled the Nigerian government.[36] The primacy of British economic interests was again apparent—thus underscoring the dynamics of neocapitalist struggles and the clash of interests it generates. As Harold Wilson, then British prime minister, graphically explained in his personal memoir in 1971, Britain was in a dire economic situation during the Biafran war. His calculation was that Nigeria's oil wealth was vital to Britain's economic recovery.[37]

While Britain's position on the Nigerian crisis was clearly self-serving, the French government's policy was altogether dubious and ambiguous. France encouraged Biafra because it wanted to see Nigeria's influence as a regional power in West Africa weakened. The region harbors more Francophone speakers than Anglophone speakers. But France also supplied arms to the federal government

for over eleven months. It was only on July 31, 1968, weeks after the UN imposition of an arms embargo on the Nigerian federal authorities, that the French
Parliament made public its support of Biafra's claim to self-determination.[38]

It would be naïve not to expect Europeans to be primarily concerned with
their own economic interests in African conflicts considering the degree of Western dependence on Africa's natural resources. This dependence is a function of
the several centuries of contact between Africa and Europe that have permanently joined the fate of the two continents. In the wake of the rhetoric of decolonization in the 1950s, and the physical separation between the former colonies
and the European metropoles, Euro-African interdependence has found expression in neocolonialism, mutual military and economic cooperation, cultural exchanges (like the commonwealth), humanitarian missions, and other platforms
of diplomatic exchange. These networks have not, however, helped in addressing the problem of self-determination and sovereignty created by colonialism.

In a November 11, 1968, interview with Charles Kenyatta, a former aide to
Malcolm X, Colonel Ojukwu, the ex–Biafran leader, made a prophetic statement on the future of separatist movements in Africa. "If this Biafra is stifled,
then perhaps in twenty years another will emerge."[39] After the demise of Biafra
in 1970, there was no major secessionist war until the Eritrea/Ethiopia struggle
flared up in 1991. The interlude between 1970 and 1991 may be attributed to
a number of factors, among them UN/OAU antisecessionist policies in Africa,
which successfully isolated both Katanga and Biafra and frustrated their goals.
The international politics of the Cold War era also discouraged other secessionist agitations, although it did not make Africa less volatile. Secessionist bids
returned on the heels of the disintegration of the Union of Soviet Socialist Republics in 1990–91.

In May 1991, Eritrea proclaimed its independence after a plebiscite was held
whose result showed that Eritreans favored secession from Ethiopia.[40] In 1992,
the UN validated the result of the plebiscite as a means of punishing Ethiopia for
its former alliance with the Communist Bloc. The formal declaration of Eritrea's
independence was signed in 1993.[41] The journey to Eritrean secession started in
the 1940s, when Gebremeskel Weldu, a Christian, founded the Unionist Party
(UP) as an umbrella organization for those demanding the unification of Eritrea with its motherland, Ethiopia.[42] Even though the UP's goals fit into the British Military Administration's plans to restructure the boundaries of the former
Italian colonial territories along ethnic lines, Britain secretly worked out a plan
in 1943 for the merger of parts of Eritrea, including the plateau region, a strong-

hold of the UP, with Ethiopia without due consideration of what the people (particularly the minority Muslim and prosecessionist elements) wanted.[43] The remaining part of Eritrea was to be merged with Anglo-Egyptian Sudan. This was in line with a plan drafted by Britain in 1947 on the grounds that unless Eritrean Muslims (the separatists) were "prepared to think for themselves, the Plateau Christians" would have to "do the thinking for them."[44] Although Ethiopia would later cash in on the claim that Eritrea was formerly part of its territory and with the support of the UN reclaim the former Italian colony, the seed of separatism that was sowed at this time would germinate and grow in the 1980s.[45] Among other issues that brought about Eritrea's separatist agitation was the fluttering of the Ethiopian state under economic hardship of the late 1970s, the drought of 1983–86, and the totalitarian and bloody leadership of Colonel Mengistu (r. 1974–91).[46] This view of Mengistu as a brutal dictator is supported by the emergence of the Oromo (Galla) Liberation Front in the mid-1970s after Emperor Haile Selassie was toppled from power in a military coup in 1974. The Oromo, who boast about seventy-five hundred secessionist fighters, constitute 40 percent of the country's 50 million people.[47] The Amhara, although fewer in number than the Oromo, have enjoyed political and economic control of Ethiopia for the last century. The conflict between the two groups led to the adoption of the federal constitution in 1994. The preamble of the constitution captures the mood at the time:

> We, the Nations, Nationalities and Peoples of Ethiopia: Strongly committed, in full and free exercise of our right to self-determination, to building a political community founded on the rule of law and capable of ensuring a lasting peace, guaranteeing a democratic order, and advancing our economic and social development. Firmly convinced that the fulfillment of this objective requires full respect of individual and people's fundamental freedoms and rights, to live together on the basis of equality and without any sexual, religious or cultural discrimination.[48]

However, the most important part of the constitution is article 39, which states that "every Nation, Nationality and People in Ethiopia has an unconditional right to self-determination, including the right to secession."[49] As with the USSR constitution, this clause has helped to moderate separatist demands or at least brought the question of secession to a stalemate. It is possible that the situation might explode anytime, but the freedom of choice with respect to membership as enshrined in the 1994 federal constitution serves to reassure the component parts that their right to secede from a tyrannical state is sacrosanct and that political union is not a matter of life and death.[50]

In other states where neither political devolution nor the right to secession is constitutionally guaranteed, as is the case in Somalia, political violence and instability have remained a problem. The state of Somalia, which has no visible central government at present, may best represent the African tendency toward shifting loyalties and separatism that were long a part of the precolonial order. As Ibrahim Igal, the head of the Somaliland Administration in Hargeisa, puts it, "The history of the Somali people is that they have never had a central authority. We were independent tribes and we lived together in equality. We fought over water and over grazing now and then, but nobody ruled over anybody else."[51] Somalia has traveled the same route to secession as Eritrea/Ethiopia in the sense that its merger with British-ruled Somaliland in the context of decolonization failed to create the unity envisaged by the country's nationalists.[52] In May 1991, four months after the fall of Mohamed Siad Barre, Somalia's former dictator, the people of what used to be British Somaliland declared their independence from the rest of Somalia, thus bringing to successful conclusion a struggle that had begun in 1988. This proclamation was made through the elders' congress. By 1992, the Somali National Movement, the main northwest secessionist group that started the revolt against Barre, began to split into factions in the course of fighting for control of Berbera, the only modern port in the country. During fighting in 1988, President Mohamed Barre had ordered his fighters to bomb Hargeisa, Somaliland's capital and a separatist stronghold, an attack that resulted in the deaths of up to fifty thousand people.[53] In Somaliland today, public sentiment points to this episode as the reason why the idea of reconciliation with Mogadishu is absurd.

Yet, Somaliland has failed to secure the crucial international recognition of its contested status as a sovereign state. An OAU mission that visited the territory in 2006 raised the hope of recognition of Somaliland, but the favorable report of that mission was not followed through on by the OAU's governing heads of states. The OAU "refused to recognize Somaliland's independence citing the maxim that there would be chaos if colonial boundaries were not observed."[54] This episode is typical; with the exception of Eritrea, the international community has consistently expressed hostility toward all shades of separatism in Africa. Because the success of Eritrea in the early 1990s coincided with the disintegration of the Soviet Union, Yugoslavia, and Czechoslovakia, one might begin to wonder whether there is a double standard in play, considering the positive manner in which the UN and the Western powers have welcomed separatist movements in the former Soviet Union bloc and their former satellite countries. No such ease of acceptance has been demonstrated in relation to the conflicts in other places, especially in Africa.

However, unlike the conflicts witnessed in the immediate postcolonial era, those arising since the 1990s seem to be receiving more sympathetic ears from nonstate actors within the international community. This development is, of course, linked to the emergent system of supranational bodies and to the ways nonstateside actors have approached human rights, genocide, dictatorships, and minority rights, especially in the past two decades. From Sudan, Katanga (Congo), Eritrea (Ethiopia), and Biafra (Nigeria) to Angola, Somaliland (Somalia), Rwanda, Burundi, Liberia, and Sierra Leone, the world community has been summoned to deal with humanitarian problems, human rights abuses, refugee problems, poverty, and diseases and to assist in postconflict reconstruction, peace building, and, since the 1990s, instituting democratic reforms.

UNDERSTANDING THE COMPLEXITIES OF AFRICAN CONFLICTS

The argument has been made here that the inherited structures of the postcolonial state in Africa breeds conflict and that the tendency for one group to dominate others makes conflict nearly inevitable and secession even more desirable. It is imperative to understand that all of Africa's numerous ethnic groups are so politically conscious that no one powerful group can successfully dictate terms of political cooperation for others. The right way to go is for the various states to embrace nonmajoritarian governmental systems because all of the politically conscious ethnic groups are determined to control their separate destinies. Highly decentralized forms of federalism, a multiparty system, a grand coalition cabinet, and autonomy are some of the possible ways to political harmony in Africa. This political wisdom has been tragically ignored by Africa's political elites, and only a handful of scholars engaged in the analysis of African politics have shown commitment to the idea. As a result, ever more complex secessionist movements and civil wars have materialized. Today, it is difficult to discern which wars are being waged for self-determination and which are being waged for private interests like access to power and political spoils.

To properly understand the intransigence of these conflicts, they and their motivations (other than the quest for self-determination) must be assessed. It is also imperative to underscore why ethnonationalism and secessionist movements will persist into the indefinite future. Some of these wars were driven by a modest demand for autonomy, but because of the manner in which the dominant political elite went about handling them, these struggles ended up as agitations for self-determination or secession. Three models of civil wars and secessionist movements can be identified, although some case studies may fit into two or more models.

The first of the three models of African wars involve a number of cases better described as "mass-phobia ruptures." This category of wars is often triggered by fierce interethnic competitions for access to power and control of very limited available resources. Of course, in all nations, citizens and leaders vie for power and resources, but most do not plunge into the kind of horrible violence, characterized by widespread killings, that has been witnessed in Africa in recent decades. Genocide and ethnic cleansing might be understood as another approach to secession, a solution to the problem of heterogeneity within an existing state or subnational territory, where the majority group dominates and where meager resources are not equally and fairly distributed. The conflicts between northern and southern Sudan, Congo and Katanga, Ethiopia and Eritrea, and Nigeria and Biafra and the recurrent Hutu/Tutsi civil genocidal conflicts in Rwanda and Burundi reflect this approach to the problem of heterogeneity within a state. Many of these wars were preceded by an emotive period of speculation and by the rise of xenophobia that emerged out of a stereotype of the enemy built on fear, hatred, and demonization of the "other." The cases of Rwanda and Burundi vindicate this model. In this context, one may postulate that one reason we have no plausible and dispassionate theory of secession is because scholars of secession are assuming that secessionist movements must be aligned with a clearly defined ethnic group occupying an unbroken territory.[55] That the brand of ethnonationalism the conflict in Rwanda and Burundi inspires has not involved territorial claims or secessionist demands may be due to the fact that the various ethnic groups in Rwanda and Burundi are widely dispersed. What we see here is the practice of genocide as a way of solving the problem of heterogeneity and secession in the Great Lakes region since the period of decolonization. Therefore ethnic movements leading to secession are a special species of ethnonationalism rather than the norm.[56] In other words, ethnic mobilization may manifest itself in other forms, in, for example, economic and/or ideological struggles, and might not necessarily be about seceding from an existing state, particularly for groups that are territorially dispersed. Dominique Jacquin-Berdal contends that the Eritrea/Ethiopia and Somaliland/

Somalia wars of secession were more directly connected with economic issues than ethnicity.

In some of the places where mass-phobia ruptures have been witnessed—Nigeria, Ethiopia, Rwanda/Burundi, and Uganda—political devolution via federalism, quota systems, zoning systems, and affirmative action, among other strategies, has been attempted as a means of moderating the conflicts. While these strategies have been useful to an extent, they have not altogether eliminated the conflicts, and that is because a new but similar dynamics of political and economic competition accompanies each new political constituency.

Ideological struggles inform a second model of African conflicts. Such struggles are mirrored in those conflicts caused by both individual and group differences in cultural and ideological beliefs, including religious beliefs. Conflicts of this sort are the most intractable and most seemingly irreconcilable because of their complex nature. Although on different planes, the Katanga/Congo and Ethiopia/Eritrea conflicts reflect certain attributes of ideological struggle in the form of an East/West divide. Patrice Lumumba of the Congo was a self-confessed Marxist. Colonel Mengistu of Ethiopia embraced Marxist-Leninist ideology. Both ideologues fought proxy wars with the Western world. The conflicts in Somalia and Sudan, however, are more typical of the wars associated with this model. The Somali and Sudanese cases, as the evidence shows, have roots in religious and ethnic sectionalism. The recent Darfur crisis is more a religious than interethnic conflict, although it is difficult to separate one from the other. The northern-based Muslim group, the Janjaweed (militant herders from the Arab Baggara of the northern Rizeiget), has brutally assaulted the more Christian-dominant Fur, Massaleit, and Zaghawa groups in the southwest who are opposed to their presence in the region.

The Janjaweed are backed by the northern-controlled Sudanese government's army. The parties are tied together by their opposition to religions other than Islam. Their aim is to eliminate the secessionists who are made of an amalgam of groups that include the Sudan People's Liberation Movement and the Justice and Equality Movement. The secessionist foot soldiers are recruited primarily from the non-Arab Fur, Zaghawa, and Massaleit groups. The government of Sudan has consistently denied supporting the Janjaweed, but the facts on the ground prove the contrary. The UN Commission on Darfur excoriated the Sudan government's August 24, 2004, helicopter assault on the Darfur villages of Yassin, Hashaba and Gallab.[57] The conflict in Darfur has been complicated by successive dictatorships, drought, desertification, and overpopulation in the area.

The Darfur conflict has caused terrible human rights and humanitarian havoc. In January 2005, the UN set up a commission of inquiry, which issued a report estimating internally displaced persons from Darfur at about 1.6 million people, with approximately 200,000 refugees living in Chad alone. The report was the result of the September 18, 2004, UN Security Council resolution 1564.[58] Overall, the conflict has claimed about 400,000 lives. Yet a resolution to the conflict appears a long way off because there are internal and external forces with vested interests fueling the conflict.

China, Malaysia, and India are in Sudan to exploit oil resources. Oil was first discovered in the Sudan in 1979; this discovery helped fuel the second civil war (1983–85).[59] The Asian countries have invested heavily in Sudan oil and as such, China, a member of the UN Security Council, has used its veto power to frustrate UN efforts to intervene militarily in Darfur. Combinations of all these rainbow interests have resulted in a seemingly intractable crisis in Darfur and indeed the whole of Sudan.

Scholars, among them Jeffrey Haynes, have argued that such civil wars in Africa as witnessed in the Sudan are the result of developmental failures. Haynes adds that democratization and equitable distribution of developmental gains will moderate such conflicts.[60] One can agree with Haynes that "developmental failure" is one of the major causes of conflicts in Africa with one important caveat—namely, that religious ideologues of a fanatical bent are highly unlikely to accept any deal suggesting accommodation for rival groups. Competing ideologists are equally driven by domination and exploitation rather than by a desire to please heaven, as they claim. As the Cold War warriors prosecuted their struggles within the bipolar world order while thinking locally, so have religious extremists in Somalia and Sudan turned their respective local struggles into global concerns by forging alliances with other Islamic groups engaged in conflicts and with terror networks around the globe. Libyan president Muammar Gaddafi, for example, has found a partner in the Islamic government of Sudan for his plan to expand the sphere of Arab/Islam influence across Africa. Both countries now aim to achieve the complete Arabization of the Sudan. Additionally, Osama Bin Laden, the terrorist kingpin of Al Qaeda, was the privileged guest of the Sudanese government until his expulsion from the country in 1996 as a result of pressure from the West. It may sound pessimistic, but *ideological* civil wars are intractable, and they often defy any peaceful solution. This explains why an enduring peace has eluded both Sudan and Somalia for decades.

Entrepreneurial wars describes a third genre of secessionist war fought in Africa. These wars are ruthlessly waged for profit making through resource control by a group of professional warlords. Discussions with some individual actors in the Liberian and Sierra Leone conflicts reveal that soldiers engaged in wars of this kind do not care about secession in the traditional sense of an ethnically aligned quest to carve out a territory from an existing state.[61] Given the underlying personal agenda, these wars are often waged with all weapons of combat, and banditry and rebellion are widespread. History has shown that personal rulers are more reluctant to relinquish or share power than are military or party dictatorships; so it is with war entrepreneur gangsters in Africa.[62] As demonstrated by Jonas Savimbi in Angola, Charles Taylor in Liberia, and Forday Sankah in Sierra Leone, the entrepreneur warriors will never accept any peace deals except those that grant them total control of the ultimate "prize."[63] These warlords show how successful "war entrepreneurs think globally but act locally, using violence to exploit marketable natural resources without necessarily controlling the entire state."[64]

The phenomenon of warlords in Africa fits into the perspective on nationalism and separatist movements that claims, in the popular "tribal" idiom, that ethnic groups are givens; a sort of an "archaic reality underlying modernity, resurfacing when modernization fails or cracks."[65] If indeed ethnic groups are problems that arise where modernity fails, then that means that westernization and the postcolonial state structures modeled after the European state system have failed in Africa. The legitimacy of the modern state resides in its ability to adequately manage common resources (human, natural, and technological); to ensure protection of life and property; and to exercise redistributive justice. Failure on the part of the state to live up to these expectations, according to the Enlightenment theory, renders its position as a national arbiter illegitimate.[66] For the state to expect continued loyalty, it must perform at the level of the people's expectations.

For various reasons, the African postcolonial state has not been able to fulfill most of its responsibilities toward the masses. It is therefore both theoretically and normatively conceivable that the entrepreneurial wars represent the emergence of a nonconventional form of separatism. This possibility is buttressed by the inability of both regional and international mediators (including the OAU and UN) in both Angola and Sierra Leone to get the principal combatants to agree to deal because they failed to secure a booty proportionate to that enjoyed by their Liberian counterpart in the 1990s. It is very instructive to observe that in these three countries—Angola, Sierra Leone, and Liberia—territorial claims are not the bone of contention yet, that territory changed hands between the governments and the rebels until the concerted intervention of the international community to get rid of the various warlords proved to be the turning point for peace. Savimbi, for instance, ruled his central province of Bie together with Huambo for almost four decades with the support of major Western powers, including the United States. The war in Angola ended only when government forces gunned down Savimbi in 2002.

The purpose of this chapter has been to explain why Africa has become a hotbed of separatist movements and how this relates to the nationalist movements of the post-1945 era. The spate of crises besieging the postcolonial state is a manifestation of the masses' disaffection with the performance of the state as a protector of human life and freedom. Poor leadership has been identified by other studies as a major cause. The leadership problem, however, is connected to the enormous challenges of nation building created by colonialism. The challenge has been, therefore, to construct an argument that shows how Africa's crisis stems from the peculiar history of the continent. Decentralization should have been promoted as a strategy for peace, but centralization has instead been considered the avenue for national survival. In this policy endorsed and upheld by the UN after 1945, and accepted by the OAU from 1963 on, are found the roots of social discontent and the motor of ethnonationalism and secessionism.

While supranationalism and national consciousness helped build new states in the Western world, the record of contemporary experience indicates that across the world, particularly in Eastern Europe and Africa, localization and separatism are increasingly challenging the entrenched structures of nation-states. Some observers think the tendency toward ethnonationalism is a problem of underdevelopment. But the direction of the world over the past four decades has been increasingly toward decentralization and deregulation. Our practice as scholars cannot divorce the history and culture of the continent from the economic and political situation and from the varied identities the economic and political situation reflects. Secessionist movements will continue to trouble the African postcolonial state so long as civil, political, and groups' rights are not properly recognized as necessary to protecting individual liberties and to preserving human dignity in one's relations with others and the state. Elsewhere I have argued that primordial sentiments are legitimate social capital that could be harnessed for developmental needs, including politics.[67] Ethnic nations are true nations and ethnic citizens deserve their due right to self-determination. Understanding this peculiarity of the African continent will open the way for a better prognosis of ethnonationalism and secessionist movements in Africa.

Notes

1. *Guardian* (Lagos), Aug. 28, 2008; *Daily Sun* (Port Harcourt), Sept. 20, 2008.

2. For a commentary on the Berber question, see *Middle East Analysis*, Nov. 21, 2007.

3. See Jack Forbes, "Do Tribes Have Rights? The Question of Self-Determination for Small Nations," *Journal of Human Relations* 18, no. 1 (1970): 670–9.

4. See Anthony D. Smith, *The Ethnic Revival in the Modern World* (Cambridge: Cambridge University Press, 1981).

5. See Colin Legum, *Pan Africanism: A Short Political Guide* (London: Pall Mall Press, 1962), 229–32, and Emmanuel N. Amadife and James W. Warhola, "Africa's Political Boundaries: Colonial Cartography, the OAU, and the Advisability of Ethno-National Adjustment," *International Journal of Politics, Culture and Society* 6, no. 4 (1993): 533–54.

6. Peter P. Ekeh, "Colonialism and the Two Publics in Africa: A Theoretical Statement," *Comparative Studies in Society and History* 17, no. 1 (1975): 91–112.

7. Julius Nyerere, address, second meeting of the OAU, Cairo, July 20, 1964. See also Foreign and Commonwealth Office (hereafter FCO) 38/249, recognition of Biafra by countries outside of the UK, 1968, National Archives, Kew, U.K. (hereafter NAK).

8. *UN Charter*, art. 2.4, June 26, 1945.

9. OAU doc. AHG/Res. 16.1.

10. Leonard Binder et al., *Crisis and Sequences in Political Development* (Princeton: Princeton University Press, 1971).

11. Proceedings of the Summit Conference of Independent African States (hereafter PSCIAS), Addis Ababa, May 1963, vol. 1, sec. 2, doc. CIAS/GEN/INF/36, p. 7.

12. PSCIAS, doc. CIAS/GEN/INF/33, p. 2.

13. Sékou Touré, broadcast, Nov. 30, 1958, published in *République de Guinée: L'action politique du PDG-RDA* (Conakry: Imprimerie Nationale, 1959), 149–50.

14. See UN doc. S/5002 (S/4985/Rev. 1, as amended), and *UN Charter*, arts. 1 and 55.

15. René Lemarchand, "The Limits of Self-Determination: The Case of the Katanga Secession," *American Political Science Review* 56, no. 2 (1962): 404; Foreign Office (hereafter FO) 371167213, criticism of UN role in Katanga, 1963, NAK.

16. Onyeonoro Kamanu, "Secession and the Right of Self-Determination: An OAU Dilemma," *Journal of Modern African Studies* 12, no. 3 (1974): 355–76.

17. Juan Enriquez, "Too Many Flags?" *Foreign Policy* 116 (Fall 1999): 30.

18. See, for instance, *Nigerian Tribune* (Ibadan), Sept. 2, 2008.

19. Allen Buchanan, *Secession: The Morality of Political Divorce from Fort Sumter to Lithuania and Quebec* (Boulder, Colo.: Westview Press, 1991), 74.

20. FO 371/113697, mutiny in southern Sudan, 1955, NAK.

21. FO 371/113697, mutiny in southern Sudan, 1955, and 371/113581–5, political development in the Sudan during 1955, NAK.

22. Douglas H. Johnson, *The Root Cause of Sudanese Civil Wars* (Bloomington: Indiana University Press, 2003), 3–5. See also Robert B. Edgerton, *Africa's Armies: From Honor to Infamy* (Boulder, Colo.: Westview Press, 2002), 115–20.

23. Buchanan, *Secession*, 29–32, 34–35.

24. FCO 371/14663, Joseph Kasavubu activities, 1960, NAK.

25. FCO 371/146640, Belgian troops in Congo, Katanga, and the bases, 1960, NAK; FCO 371/324, Moise Tshombe, 1969, NAK; FO 371/154915, negotiations on the future of province between Moise Tshombe of Katanga Province and central government of Belgian Congo, 1961, NAK.

26. FCO 371/155004–9, UN military operations in Katanga and ceasefire, 1961, NAK; FCO 371/154885, fighting between UN and Katanga armed forces, 1961, NAK.

27. FCO 371/154915, negotiations on the future of province between Moise Tshombe of Katanga Province and central government of Belgian Congo, 1961, NAK.

28. FCO 25/232, secession of eastern region from Nigeria, Biafra, 1967–68, NAK.

29. Walter Schwarz, *Nigeria* (London: Pall Mall Press, 1968), 229–30.

30. See a recent discussion of this in the *Nigerian Tribune* (Ibadan), Feb. 11, 2008.

31. *Crisis Series*, vol. 3, *Pogrom* (Enugu: Government Printer, 1966), 2–10.

32. *New Nigeria* (Kaduna), Sept. 30, 1966.

33. FCO 25/232, secession of eastern region from Nigeria, Biafra, 1967–68, NAK. See also Emeka Odumegwu Ojukwu, "The Ahiara Declaration: The Principles of the Biafran Revolution," Ahiara Village, Biafra, June 1, 1969.

34. FCO 65/231, reports of internal situation in Biafra, 1969, NAK.

35. FCO 95/223, Nigeria, brief for talk with Sir David Hunt, high commissioner designate, 1967, NAK; Ministry of Power, 63/238, note for the records, Nigeria, June 5, 1967, NAK; report on an interdepartmental meeting, June 2, 1967, NAK.

36. FCO 65/246, question of recognition of Biafra and Nigerian fears of African countries doing so, 1969, NAK.

37. Harold Wilson, *The Labour Government, 1964–1970: A Personal Record* (London: Weidenfeld and Nicholson, 1971), 26, 400.

38. FCO 65/246, question of recognition of Biafra and Nigerian fears of African countries doing so, 1969, NAK.

39. Emeka Odumegwu Ojukwu, interview with Charles Kenyatta, Umuahia, Nov. 11, 1968.

40. "Ethiopia: Rebels Take Charge," *Time Magazine*, June 10, 1991.

41. "Eritreans Vote in a Plebiscite to Separate from Ethiopia," *Washington Post*, Apr. 28, 1993.

42. FO 371/96719, review of principal events in Ethiopia in 1951, NAK; Tekeste Negash, *Eritrea and Ethiopia: The Federal Experience* (Uppsala: Nordiska Afrikainstitutet, 1997), 37.

43. FO 371/41531, overseas planning committee, propaganda plan for Eritrea, 1944, NAK.

44. FO 371/63212, Eritrea, monthly political report, no. 13, Jan. 1947, NAK.

45. FO 371/63156, appeal for return of Eritrea and Somaliland to Ethiopia, 1947, NAK; FO 371/96726, federation of Ethiopia and Eritrea, 1952, NAK.

46. Kourosh Farrokhzad, "The IMF: The International Manipulation of Funds," *Peace Magazine*, Jan.–Feb. 1996, 6.

47. "Ethiopia: Rebels Take Charge."

48. Preamble, *The Constitution of the Federal Republic of Ethiopia*, Addis Ababa, 1994.

49. *The Constitution of the Federal Republic of Ethiopia*, 18.

50. Farrokhzad, "The IMF," 6.

51. Ibrahim Igal, interview with the Integrated Regional Information Networks, UN Office for the Coordination of Humanitarian Affairs, Hargeisa, May 28, 2007.

52. FO 371/108162, movement for united Somalia, 1955, NAK. See also John G. Drysdale, *The Somali Dispute* (London: Pall Mall Press, 1963).

53. Jeffrey Gettleman, "Somaliland Is an Overlooked African Success Story," *International Herald Tribune* (Paris), Mar. 2, 2007.

54. Jean-Jacques Cornish, "AU Supports Somali Split," *Mail and Guardian* (London), Feb. 10, 2006.

55. Dominique Jacquin-Berdal, *Nationalism and Ethnicity in the Horn of Africa: A Critique of the Ethnic Interpretation* (Lewiston, N.Y.: Edwin Mellen Press, 2002), 2.

56. Donald Horowitz, *Ethnic Groups in Conflict* (Berkeley: University of California Press, 1985), 20.

57. UN Security Council, res. 1564, Sept. 18, 2004, 2.

58. UN Security Council, res. 1564.

59. Peter Tesch, "Oil Issues Threaten to Derail Sudan," *Sunday Business Post* (Dublin), Apr. 3, 2005.

60. Jeffrey Haynes, "Religion, Ethnicity and Civil War in Africa: The Cases of Uganda and Sudan," *Round Table* 96, no. 390 (2007): 375.

61. Interview with an anonymous victim of the civil conflict in Sierra Leone, Nov. 20, 2007.

62. See Samuel P. Huntington, *The Third Wave: Democratization in the Late Twentieth Century* (Norman: University of Oklahoma Press, 1991), 109, 315.

63. See David Keen, *The Privatization of War: A Political Economy of Conflict in Sierra Leone* (London: James Currey, 1997); Mark Bradbury, *Rebels Without a Cause* (London: CARE, 1995); Mats Berdal and David M. Malone, eds., *Greed and Grievance: Economic Agendas in Civil Wars* (Boulder, Colo.: Lynne Rienner, 2000); and Stephen J. Stedman, "Spoilers Problems in Peace Processes," *International Security* 22, no. 2 (Fall 1997): 5–53.

64. See Robin Luckham et al., "Conflict and Poverty in Sub-Saharan Africa: An Assessment of the Issues and Evidence," *IDS Working Paper* 128 (2001).

65. Jan Nederveen Pieterse, "Varieties of Ethnic Politics and Ethnic Discourse," in *The Politics of Difference: Ethnic Premises in a World of Power*, ed. Edwin N. Wilmsen and Patrick McAllister (Chicago: University of Chicago Press, 1996), 27.

66. Jean-Jacques Rousseau, *Discourse on Political Economy and the Social Contract*, trans. Christopher Betts (Oxford: Oxford University Press, 1994).

67. See Raphael Chijioke Njoku, "Ethnicity, Modernity and the African Postcolonial State in Theoretical Perspective," in *Power and Nationalism in Modern Africa*, ed. Toyin Falola and Salah M. Hassan (Trenton, N.J.: African World Press, 2008), 67–86.

ALAN M. WACHMAN

Did Abraham Lincoln Oppose Taiwan's Secession from China?

In the People's Republic of China (PRC), Abraham Lincoln's stance on national unity during the U.S. Civil War has been summoned up by PRC officials, media, and elites in an effort to explain and legitimate their own response to those they disparage as "separatists" in Tibet and Taiwan.[1] The most prominent use of the U.S. Civil War trope, though, has emerged in PRC rhetoric about Taiwan—the subject of this chapter.

Beijing has framed its dispute about sovereignty over Taiwan as a battle between a small number of separatists on the island who seek to secede from China and an otherwise unified Chinese nation determined to preserve its territorial integrity—by force, if necessary. To Beijing, vigorously opposing separatism and preserving Chinese territorial integrity is a cause no less noble than was Abraham Lincoln's resort to war as a way of preventing the secession of southern states.

In its quest for moral authority, Beijing has recalled the rhetoric and posture of Abraham Lincoln toward the Confederacy, apparently unaware that it has misconstrued Lincoln's sentiments by citing his words out of context and that it has drawn erroneous lessons from the example of the U.S. Civil War. Nationalists in the PRC are not alone in wielding Lincoln's legacy in an attempt to justify the forceful suppression of secessionist movements. Other nationalists in other states have done the same. Yet, a close reading of what Lincoln wrote, coupled with a reconsideration of the history of China's relationship with Taiwan, leaves one to wonder whether Lincoln would, indeed, have sympathized with Beijing's approach to Taiwan's autonomy.

Beijing's claim that its opposition to Taiwan "independence" is analogous to that of Lincoln's opposition to the secession of southern states is not simply an affront to historical veracity. By inculcating its populace with a view that Taiwan seeks to secede from China and, therefore, that force is warranted if all other means to assert sovereignty are resisted, Beijing has propagated a perspective that has deleterious implications for the prospect of a negotiated settlement of the cross–Taiwan Strait controversy. Moreover, the PRC's misconstruction of U.S. Civil War history and of Lincoln's views about the use of force in defense of the Union has legitimated an uncompromising and occasionally bellicose approach by Beijing to interactions with Taiwan that may have had the unintended consequence of pushing Taiwan further away from the PRC.

TAIWAN AND CHINA

As late as the Ming Dynasty (1368–1644), Taiwan—a large island about one hundred miles off the southeast coast of China—was not under the effective control of the Chinese court or claimed by it as imperial territory. Indeed, it seems that Chinese elites of the time were only vaguely aware of Taiwan's existence and, for the most part, saw it as beyond the frontier.[2] Taiwan's relationship to China changed considerably after Ming China was overrun by Manchu conquerors, who established the Qing Dynasty (1644–1911). The Manchus, a tribal confederacy that saw itself and was seen as distinct from the Chinese, established an empire in Asia with China at its core. After its conquest of China in 1644 until the middle of the eighteenth century, the Manchus expanded their control over Asian territory, stretching the empire's boundaries beyond that of Ming China to encompass—among other lands—Mongolia, what is now the Xinjiang region in western China, Tibet, and—in 1684—Taiwan.

From the middle of the eighteenth century until the collapse of the Qing Dynasty in 1911, the Manchus lost control over much of the territory they had conquered. In 1895, following a war with Japan prompted by competition for influence over the Korean peninsula, the Qing court was compelled by Japan to sign the Treaty of Shimonoseki, whereby the Qing ceded the island of Taiwan. Hence, from 1895 until 1945, when Japan was defeated at the end of World War II, Taiwan was a part of the Japanese Empire.

By the time the Qing court acquiesced in the cession of Taiwan, it was a power in rapid decline. In 1911, the Manchu-ruled Qing Dynasty ended, and, in 1912, Chinese nationalists and military figures established the Republic of China (ROC), marking the end to millennia of imperial rule. The ROC government, although the only government recognized abroad as legitimate in China, did not then control all the territory that it claimed as China's. Taiwan was still a Japanese colony and the newly established ROC government evinced no interest in recovering it. By the time Japan was defeated and the war ended in 1945, the ROC had come to see strategic value in establishing Chinese control over Taiwan. The governments of the United States and Great Britain agreed with the ROC that territories Japan had taken from China since the end of the nineteenth century should be returned to the ROC. Consequently, ever since Japan surrendered in 1945, Taiwan has been governed by the ROC and by no other state.

However, shortly after the ROC government established control of Taiwan, it lost control over much of China's territory in a civil war with the Chinese Communist Party (CCP) and, in 1949, the ROC ruling elite and what was left of its military was impelled by CCP advances to take refuge on Taiwan. From October 1, 1949, until the present, the PRC government has exercised effective control over most of the territory that the ROC had claimed as China's, and the PRC is now recognized nearly universally as the legitimate government of China.

By contrast, since 1949 the ROC government has only exercised effective control over Taiwan and a number of smaller island appurtenances, and it is no longer recognized as the legitimate government of China. Indeed, once the ROC underwent the transformation to democracy in the early 1990s, it abandoned its claim to be the government of all China, acknowledging that it currently has jurisdiction over Taiwan and other smaller islands but not over the mainland territories it once claimed.

Notwithstanding the division of Chinese territory, the government of the PRC has been adamant that it is the sole, legal government of all China, of which it asserts Taiwan is a part. Until 1991, the ROC government concurred in the view that Taiwan is a part of China, but it has since embraced the reality of division. Nevertheless, the PRC claims sovereignty over Taiwan and has castigated the "ruling authorities" on Taiwan, particularly those who advocate that Taiwan have de jure independence from China, as traitorous "separatists," seeking to divide one China into "two Chinas" or to make permanent a division between one China and one Taiwan.

Beijing was particularly peeved by the rhetoric of ROC presidents Lee Teng-hui (1988–2000) of the Nationalist Party (KMT) and Chen Shui-bian (2000–2008) of the Democratic Progressive Party (DPP)—both of whom were born and raised on Taiwan and seen by the PRC as working for de jure independence. Beijing became more conciliatory and less bombastic when Ma Ying-jeou of the KMT—born in Hong Kong of parents who associated with the mainland—was elected president in 2008. Ma entered office with the notion that the PRC and the ROC should adopt a stance of "mutual nondenial" by which they would interact with one another as best they could without seeking to resolve the dispute about sovereignty.[3]

From 1949 until 1979, the official position of the PRC government was that it sought to "liberate" Taiwan (by force, if necessary) from what it saw as the "reactionary clique" that then governed it. After the start of the Korean War in June 1950, the United States greatly complicated this intra-Chinese dispute by sweeping Taiwan into its defensive alliance system in the Pacific region, which emerged as a response to cold war. From 1954 until 1979, the United States and the ROC maintained a mutual defense treaty, which assured Taiwan of American support in the event of an attack on it by the PRC.

In 1979, when the United States and the PRC normalized diplomatic relations, the PRC also adjusted its policy toward Taiwan. Ever since, Beijing has asserted that its aim is the "peaceful unification" of China, an outcome it expected would lead Taiwan to abandon any claim to sovereignty and to coexist with the mainland as part of China. Beijing has proposed allowing Taiwan to retain a "high degree of autonomy" within a framework that the PRC eventually dubbed "one country, two systems." To most people in Taiwan, who believe the ROC is a sovereign state, this offer is not very appealing.

Until the early 1990s, the PRC pursued unambiguously the path of "peaceful unification." On Taiwan, the democratization of the late 1980s brought with it increasingly vocal calls from emerging political elites, who had previously been suppressed by the ruling party of the ROC from active political participation. These new elites called for a permanent separation of Taiwan and China. In their view, the ROC government itself was an alien colonizer that had simply replaced the Japanese colonizers. Their hostility toward unification and assertion of Taiwanese—not Chinese—nationalism was viewed with great alarm in Beijing, which viewed the efforts of these new elites as a threat to the sovereignty and territorial integrity of China.

Consequently, the PRC began to shift its emphasis from encouraging peaceful unification to discouraging "independence." Doing so entailed an adjustment in the tactics of the PRC, a change that involved an increased reliance on threats of force. These threats were rendered plausible by the rapid modernization and development of the PRC's military capabilities. Batteries of missiles were emplaced on the shores of Fujian, opposite Taiwan. Military exercises were undertaken to simulate assaults on Taiwan. This public saber rattling by Beijing complicated the PRC's message of "peaceful reunification."

In 1996, responding to what Beijing perceived as a sequence of provocations from Taiwan and the United States, the PRC conducted a test of missiles in the waters immediately northeast and southwest of Taiwan. This "missile crisis" made those who saw the PRC's threats of force as a harbinger of destabilization in Asia by an emerging Chinese power even more nervous.

In a period when there was much chatter about the "rise of China" and the potential for the emergence of a "China threat," it is not surprising that Beijing felt the need to frame its threats and use of force against Taiwan in a way that it hoped would garner sympathy. Among the thematic strategies it employed is the valorization of Abraham Lincoln's use of force in defense of the Union during the U.S. Civil War.

The resort to Lincoln was not new. Prominent Chinese leaders have manifested a touch of Lincolnophilia since the start of the twentieth century. Sun Yat-sen, the Abrahamic forebear of both the KMT of Chiang Kai-shek that was long the ruling party of the ROC and the CCP of Mao Zedong that established the PRC, explicitly called up Lincoln as a model for his own nationalist creed, "the three principles of the people." Sun reportedly wrote that his own three principles "correspond with the principles stated by President Lincoln—'government of the people, by the people, for the people.' I translated them into . . . the people to have[,] . . . the people to govern[,] and . . . the people to enjoy."[4]

Sun's admiring effort to emulate the bold simplicity and cadence of Lincoln's Gettysburg Address became embedded in the hagiographic record of Sun's contributions to China's revolution, even though the three principles of the people only vaguely reflect the ideals Lincoln championed. The apparent link between Sun and Lincoln was enshrined in the first article of the 1947 constitution of the ROC—a document that remains in effect on Taiwan. It reads, "The Republic of China, founded on the Three Principles of the People, shall be a democratic republic of the people, to be governed by the people and for the people."[5]

Chinese Communists also associated themselves with Lincoln, among other American political icons. Mao Zedong reportedly told a Reuters correspondent in 1945 that "a free, democratic China would . . . realize the 'of the people, by the people, and for the people' concept of Abraham Lincoln and the 'four freedoms' proposed by Franklin Roosevelt."[6]

OF SUCCESSION AND SECESSION

To be sure, Beijing and Taipei both seek leverage, validation, and support from abroad. Beijing's appropriation of Lincoln is only one facet of this rivalry for legitimacy in the eyes of the international community. To make its case, each disputant has done what it can to propagate a history of the cross-Taiwan Strait controversy that corresponds to its own policy preferences.

Masterful diplomatic prowess, economic influence, and a selectively ruthless use of power have enabled Beijing to dominate the discussion of Taiwan's status. Beijing presents itself as the only aggrieved party and depicts international actors sympathetic to Taiwan as maliciously meddling in China's internal affairs or as wantonly ignorant of historical truths about the cross-strait controversy.

The PRC has largely succeeded in propagating its preferred rhetorical and conceptual parameters for framing the matter of Taiwan's status. Evidence of this success is the unquestioning acceptance by many foreign observers of the idea that Taiwan is a "renegade province." Even though the PRC denies it has ever used the phrase, the moniker "renegade province" and the hierarchy it implies has come to represent the relationship between the PRC and Taiwan. After all, just as the PRC is big on almost every index, Taiwan is small. In contests of sovereignty, bigness apparently confers a degree of legitimacy that eludes the small.

However, Beijing's claim to Taiwan and its depiction of Taiwanese nationalists as threatening to secede from China depends on a *particular* view of China's civil war. Beijing believes that when the PRC was established in 1949, it succeeded the ROC, which was, consequently, extinguished. The ROC rejects the notion that it was eliminated and contends it survives in one corner of its formerly vast domain. It had long viewed the Communists as having staged an insurrection and considered the central government's war to have been a legitimate means of suppressing rebellion and protecting the territorial integrity of China. The ROC faulted the CCP for dividing the state and rejected Beijing's view that taking most of China's territory by force entitled it to rule all of China's territory. These views appear irreconcilable.

That the PRC's case is contestable has not impeded its assumption of an unimpaired right to present itself as the successor state. It draws encouragement from its membership in the UN—where it displaced the ROC in 1971—and the stark imbalance between the many states that recognize it and the plucky few that recognize the ROC. From its perspective, Taiwan's assertions of sovereignty amount to incipient secession, which it refuses to abide.

SINCEREST FORM OF FLATTERY?

The interest in Lincoln waxes and wanes in the PRC. Former president Jiang Zemin, who attended an American missionary school near Shanghai, apparently takes pride in his capacity to recite the Gettysburg Address from memory, in English. He frequently cited Lincoln to reinforce his view that Beijing has an obligation to defend the unity of China—as he understands it—by force, if necessary.[7] Former premier Zhu Rongji drew his arrow from the same quiver. Standing beside President Clinton in 1999, Zhu said, "Abraham Lincoln, in order to maintain the unity of the United States and oppose independence of the southern part . . . resorted to the use of force and fought a war. . . . So I think Abraham Lincoln . . . is a model."[8]

Railing against Washington's defense of Taiwan, which Beijing sees as supporting "two Chinas," an editorial in *Renmin Ribao* (*People's Daily*) states:

> President Abraham Lincoln . . . waged a resolute struggle politically, militarily and diplomatically against conspirators who tried to create "two Americas." In this struggle, he made the following famous remark: "This piece of land the American people are occupying and living on can only be 'home to the big family of one nation' and cannot be home to the big family of two or more nations." . . . Some people think that they are making an ingenious move in obstructing China's reunification when it is a stupid move that would not even be approved by their forefather.[9]

One senses that Beijing's apprehension of Lincoln is flawed. The *Renmin Ribao* editorialist either missed or dismissed Lincoln's point. The passage cited comes from a speech that, today, would be labeled a state of the union address.[10] In it, Lincoln wrote:

> A nation may be said to consist of its territory, its people, and its laws. The territory is the only part which is of certain durability. . . . That portion of the earth's surface which is owned and inhabited by the people of the United States, is well adapted to be the home of one national family; and it is not well adapted for two, or more. Its vast extent, and its variety of climate and pro-

ductions, are of advantage, in this age, for one people, whatever they might have been in former ages. Steam, telegraphs, and intelligence have brought these to be an advantageous combination, for one united people.[11]

Lincoln was not writing abstractly about the merits of union, as the editorial implies. Rather, his point was that dividing American territory would undermine economic efficacy from which all would otherwise benefit. He expanded, quoting his own inaugural address: "Physically speaking, we cannot separate. We cannot remove our respective sections from each other, nor build an impassable wall between them. . . . There is no line, straight or crooked, suitable for a national boundary, upon which to divide. Trace through, from east to west, upon the line between the free and slave country, and we shall find a little more than one-third of its length are rivers, easy to be crossed, and populated, or soon to be populated, thickly upon both sides; while nearly all its remaining length, are merely surveyor's lines, over which people may walk back and forth without any consciousness of their presence. No part of this line can be made any more difficult to pass, by writing it down on paper, or parchment, as a national boundary."[12]

This is not the case for China and Taiwan. The physical separation is manifest in Taiwan's essence as an island, distanced from the continent by a strait one hundred miles in breadth. While Lincoln argued—perhaps hyperbolically—that no line could be found that would adequately ensure the separation of the Confederate States, nature has endowed Taiwan with permanent division from the continent. Indeed, considering the physical separation of Taiwan and the mainland territory, what is it that makes the island immutably a part of China (as Beijing would have it) rather than benignly apart?

Lincoln continued. "Our strife pertains to ourselves—to the passing generations of men; and it can, without convulsion, be hushed forever with the passing of one generation."[13] This humbling insight applies as well to China's civil war; it can be seen as a preoccupation of a generation that is now aged or passed. Those generations following in its wake were neither directly involved in the chaos that war created nor committed to the ideology that drove men to battle. Their relationship to the struggles of the 1930s and 1940s is remote and inherited, if it is felt at all.

That the populations of the island and the mainland have little animus between them makes plain that the "Taiwan problem" is not analogous to the strife dividing Turks and Greeks on Cyprus, Serbs and Albanians in the former

Yugoslavia, Hutus and Tutsis in Rwanda, Israelis and Palestinians, or northern Irish Protestants and Catholics. It is hard to make sense of the idea that the Taiwan situation is gravely volatile, as many observers suggest, given the robust interdependent economic relationship between Taiwan and the PRC as well as the flourishing cross-strait exchange of information and people. While the experiences, values, and habits of the people living on each side of the strait may be distinct, they are not incompatible. The yawning chasm in attitudes and developmental sophistication that divides the peoples of North and South Korea is certainly not present in the relationship between the PRC and Taiwan. Indeed, a greater variance in social values and worldview may be detected between urban and rural China than between the urban and commercial hubs of the PRC and most of Taiwan.

The pitiful paradox of the cross-strait conflict is that war could erupt between people who have little hatred for one another. Indeed, residual bitterness directed by PRC elites toward Japan outstrips any hostility they feel about the people of Taiwan. At a popular level, the cross-strait conflict is virtual. It is filtered through abstractions and slogans that have little to do with the daily commercial and other interactions encouraged or tolerated by both sides. The "Taiwan problem" is unlike the American Civil War, in which interaction between combatants was strained by the very issues in dispute.

CCP: TELLING NORTH FROM SOUTH

To be sure, historical analogies are often difficult to employ with the desired effect. Unless there is a preexisting sympathy on the part of the reader or audience to the views of the one who proposes the juxtaposition, one can always find flaws in the details that undermine the merit of the intended similitude. In this instance, though, it is not the analogy per se that is flawed, but the presumption of the PRC that it should be seen as the analogue of the Union defending the territorial integrity of the state against a secessionist force in Taiwan. That view depends on an acceptance of Beijing's reading of the history of China's civil war.

Wen Jiabao, the PRC premier, told the *Washington Post* on the eve of his departure for the United States in November 2003 that "the Chinese people will pay any price to safeguard the unity of the motherland. I assume that you are familiar with the words of President Lincoln, who once said, 'a house divided against itself will not stand.'"[14] While Lincoln did indeed speak these words, he was quoting the Bible (Matthew 12:25), as was his wont.[15] Lincoln used the phrase often, but it is most closely associated with a speech he gave in Springfield, Illinois, on June 16, 1858, after receiving the Republican nomination for senator. Lincoln then invoked the passage repeatedly during his debates with Stephen Douglas, in the late summer and fall of that year. He also said "the Union (composed of States) is perpetual."[16]

One wonders what Premier Wen makes of Lincoln's remarks elsewhere in the speech he cited. First, Lincoln describes the Union as emerging from a voluntary compact: "We find the proposition that, in legal contemplation, the Union is perpetual, confirmed by the history of the Union itself. The Union is much older than the Constitution. It was formed in fact, by the Articles of Association in 1774. It was matured and continued by the Declaration of Independence in 1776. It was further matured and expressly declared and pledged, to be perpetual, by the Articles of Confederation in 1778. And finally, in 1787, one of the declared objects for ordaining and establishing the Constitution, was 'to form a more perfect union.'"[17]

While they oppose the idea of unification with China, the people of Taiwan are certainly not withdrawing from any compact they ever made.[18] Beyond that, Wen Jiabao perpetuates the view of the PRC as the analogue of the Union defending its territorial integrity. This deserves scrutiny.

Beginning in the 1920s, the CCP established autonomous soviets on Chinese territory. By 1945, when Japan was defeated, the CCP had gained control of large tracts of territory over which the ROC government was the legitimate authority, recognized as such by a majority of the world's states and, paradoxically, by the CCP itself. At war's end, the CCP contravened the directives of the central government and took territory surrendered by Japanese troops, expanding the Communist scope of control at the expense of China's unity. From the vantage of the ROC government, among others, these acts by the CCP were rebellious challenges to the authority of the state. When the CCP established a new state, the PRC, without first eliminating the government of the ROC, it—not the KMT-led government of the ROC that fled to Taiwan—created a second state, dividing China. Thus, the CCP had more in common with the U.S. Confederacy in the South than with the defenders of the Union in the North. That is not how the PRC tells the story, but history is the victor's spoils.

It is worth noting that the ROC was not alone in viewing the CCP's relationship to the Chinese central government as analogous to the Confederacy's relationship to the Union. In 1944, the United States sent a military observer mission to the Communist redoubt in Yenan where the leadership of the CCP was holed up, a delegation Washington dubbed the "Dixie Mission." The connotation was then clear: "DIXIE for the rebel side."[19]

Odd though it may now seem, the CCP itself acknowledged its rebellious role. In August 1944, following the arrival of a "Press Party to the Northwest" and the Dixie Mission, the CCP issued a statement concerning the centrality of diplomacy to its competition with the KMT-led government. The dispatch of eight foreign journalists to Yenan was approved, reluctantly, by Chiang Kai-shek, giving the Communist Party direct contact with foreign journalists for the first time since Edgar Snow had visited Mao in 1939.[20] The announcement by the CCP starkly characterizes the condition the party had fostered as one in which there existed "two Chinas." It states: "Thanks to the great efforts by our party, government, army, and people, and owing to the increasing reactionary [nature] and incompetence of some in the [KMT], the contrast between the two Chinas (the new democratic China and the fascist China) is becoming more obvious in the anti-Japanese camp."[21]

The CCP leadership viewed with excitement the visit by foreign journalists and members of the Dixie Mission. However, it acknowledged that it was not the legitimate government of China and would need to surmount restrictions imposed by that government to engage in diplomatic endeavors. The directive states, "On the one hand, the Chongqing Nationalist government is still the central government recognized by the Chinese people (including us) and the allied countries. . . . On the other hand, the [KMT] does not want us to conduct independent diplomatic activities. Only by breaking through all kinds of prohibitions and restrictions set by the [KMT] can we further our diplomatic activities with the allied countries and gain direct international support."[22]

This suggests that Beijing's wish to be seen today as the Union defending the territorial integrity of the state can only be justified if one ignores how there came to be a People's Republic of China in the first place.

LINCOLN: REVOLUTIONARY OR COUNTERREVOLUTIONARY?

Lincoln did, indeed, valorize the perpetual character of political union as Jiang Zemin, Zhu Rongji, and Wen Jiabao have stated. Lincoln's views on revolution evolved. He did voice support for revolution in the 1840s and 1850s. As president, though, confronting the secession of southern states from the Union that he was elected to preserve, Lincoln took a more restrained view. In his First

Inaugural Address Lincoln noted that "this country, with its institutions, belongs to the people who inhabit it. Whenever they shall grow weary of the existing government, they can exercise their constitutional right of amending it,
or their revolutionary right to dismember, or overthrow it."[23]

Later that year, in a July 4 address to Congress, Lincoln took up the matter
again, stating: "Plainly, the central idea of secession, is the essence of anarchy. A
majority, held in restraint by constitutional checks, and limitation, and always
changing easily, with deliberate changes of popular opinions and sentiments, is
the only true sovereign of a free people. Whoever rejects it, does, of necessity,
fly to anarchy or to despotism. Unanimity is impossible; the rule of a minority,
as a permanent arrangement, is wholly inadmissible; so that, rejecting the majority principle, anarchy, or despotism in some form, is all that is left."[24]

By the time fighting broke out between the Union and the Confederacy, Lincoln had greatly qualified his earlier support for revolution: "The right of revolution, is never a legal right. The very term implies the breaking, and not the
abiding by, organic law. At most, it is but a moral right, when exercised for a
morally justifiable cause. When exercised without such a cause revolution is no
right, but simply a wicked exercise of physical power."[25]

So, Lincoln might well have found the challenge to the central government
of China by the CCP to be repugnant. Admittedly, his moral threshold for justifying revolution is not well articulated, and one knows that the CCP made
ample efforts to demonstrate the moral bankruptcy of the KMT-led government. Lincoln is clear, though, that sovereignty resides in the people, and this is
a view of sovereignty that the CCP has yet to embrace, despite rhetorical assertions to the contrary. Lincoln's fervent support for constitutional government
by the elected representatives of the populace and all the attendant values associated with American constitutional democracy also undermine the efforts
by the PRC to claim the mantle of Lincoln to cloak its rationale for extending
sovereignty over Taiwan.

In addition, if battling secession is the obligation of the executive of a state,
Lincoln also demonstrated his determination to avoid firing the first shot. Lincoln addressed his opponents in the Confederacy by entreating them to refrain
from war. "In *your* hands, my dissatisfied fellow countrymen, and not in *mine*,
is the momentous issue of civil war. The government will not assail *you*. You can
have no conflict, without being yourselves the aggressors."[26] The government of
the PRC has not made a comparable pledge to the people of Taiwan. Indeed, it
has trumpeted its right to use force while demurring that "Chinese do not fight

Chinese." In what may be a rhetorical dodge, Beijing says its expanding military capabilities are intended to combat foreign forces that might interfere in the cross-strait controversy. Even in the year after Ma Ying-jeou was inaugurated—a time when cross-strait tensions appeared to have diminished—the buildup of missiles across from Taiwan and military exercises simulating an assault on the island persisted.[27]

Lincoln's reluctance to fight is misconstrued in PRC pronouncements. For instance, in an article published by the PRC's *Zhongguo Xinwen She* (China news agency) before Wen Jiabao's 2003 trip to the United States, Xu Shiquan, formerly the director of the Institute of Taiwan Studies at the Chinese Academy of Social Sciences and then the vice president of the All-China Taiwan Studies Society, cited Lincoln's brief Second Inaugural Address to highlight the justice of fighting to preserve the Union. According to the report, Xu quoted Lincoln as having said that "both parties deprecated war; but one of them would make war rather than let the nation survive; and the other would accept war rather than let it perish. And the war came."[28] Xu presumably wishes to associate the PRC with Lincoln and the Union, resigned to fight only to ensure that the nation does not perish. However, the crux of Lincoln's address was not a claim that the Union alone was righteous in its willingness to fight for the preservation of the Union and the Confederacy unjust for making war. Lincoln's doleful address pivots on the citation of another Biblical verse, "Woe unto the world because of offences! for it must needs be that offences come; but woe to that man by whom the offence cometh!"[29] The verse originates in an account of Jesus warning of the ill consequences that will befall anyone who would "offend" those who believe in him. Lincoln employs the passage to undergird his humility in the face of a war that he depicts as divine retribution for both the North and South having tolerated slavery on American soil. Lincoln states: "If we shall suppose that American Slavery is one of those offences which, in the providence of God, must needs come, but which, having continued through His appointed time, He now wills to remove, and that He gives to both North and South, this terrible war, as the woe due to those by whom the offence came, shall we discern therein any departure from those divine attributes which the believers in a Living God always ascribe to Him?"[30]

This was no boastful claim to moral superiority over a wanton and reckless adversary who had driven him to do what he preferred not to do. It was the resignation of a man who had witnessed the ravage of war and acquiesced in an understanding that the North was in some measure as culpable as the South and was being held to account by a just god whose punishment was the war itself.[31]

Finally, PRC leaders who sense a commonality between their own opposition to Taiwan's autonomy and Lincoln's defense of national unity ought to consider that they are not able to claim, as Lincoln did, that they are acting to preserve the territorial integrity of a state over which they once exercised, but then lost, sovereignty and effective control. Beijing invokes the concept of territorial integrity to posit a unity that only existed before the PRC was established. Beyond others, this point underscores how the efforts by political leaders in Beijing to be seen as Chinese Lincolns defending the sovereignty and territorial integrity of their nation rest on a misapprehension of Lincoln and the U.S. Civil War.

IMPLICATIONS

Highlighting the PRC's misconstruction of the American Civil War and the words of Abraham Lincoln is more than mere academic pedantry. All nationalists and many statesmen butcher history. Leaders of states are not empowered because of their mastery of history, nor does infidelity to it frequently prove politically fatal. That the PRC leadership miscasts itself as the Union or misrepresents what Lincoln meant is neither exceptional nor noteworthy.

However, by perpetuating a view of Taiwan as seeking to secede from China and denouncing the leaders of Taiwan as separatists—secessionists—the PRC may fuel the very division it claims it is determined to avoid. Secession should not be viewed as the foreordained outgrowth of political discontentment and actions taken by the malcontented party only. Secession, like union, is the product of interaction between communities that may—under certain conditions— be configured to constitute a single state. In instances where secession is on the minds of political elites who have come to see themselves as representing the grievances of a particular community in its interaction with the metropolitan state, the response of that metropolitan state to expressions of difference and grievance by the incipient separatist may allay or aggravate the inclination to be separate. Secession is only one possible by-product of the dialogue and interactions that occur when a community that has existed as part of a greater unity becomes disaffected from that union and seeks to establish or recover an autonomous status.

Properly speaking, Taiwan cannot secede from the PRC because the island has never been governed by the PRC. However, if Taiwan chooses to renounce its ties to China and declare that it is and will remain a Taiwanese state, those who view China as an entity in which both the territories governed by the PRC and the territory of Taiwan comprise a unified polity will see reason to assert that Taiwan has seceded. For a time, the PRC feared that the government headed by president Chen Shui-bian of the DPP would renounce its ties to China. With the election of Ma Ying-jeou in 2008, those fears have subsided, even though Ma is no less committed to the sovereignty and autonomy of the ROC than was Chen. Indeed, President Ma has been accused by Major General Luo Yuan of the People's Liberation Army of promoting "peaceful separation."[32]

The establishment of a new, non-Chinese state, if it occurs, will not be simply the outgrowth of separatist inclinations in Taiwan. This contingency, if it comes to pass, will flow from dialogue and interactions between Beijing and Taipei. In other words, how Beijing reacts to Taiwan's aversion to unification with the PRC will have as much to do with the outcome as will the urge by people on Taiwan to sustain their autonomous status. How Beijing "hears" Taiwan's disinclination to unify and how Beijing reacts—whether with inducements or penalties—are factors that affect the process.

Secession is one possible conclusion of the elaborate dance of political de-sire and defiance. Both the metropolitan state that values unity and the separate community that prefers division play a role in constructing a path to that out-come. A reflexively harsh response by the metropolitan state to the early flick-ers of defiance may drive the disaffected community to see no possibility of co-existence under one flag and leave its elites to feel that division is the only way of preserving distinction. An overly rigid, punitive, and unyielding reaction by the metropolitan state to the emanations of division may hasten the wish of the disaffected to be or remain separate.

Unity seems always to demand compromise. If one party to a prospective union is unwilling to live with less than what it perceives as ideal, conflict is sure to arise. Beijing may have made a tactical error in the 1990s by deciding to step up efforts to prevent Taiwan from declaring independence instead of per-sisting in efforts to encourage Taiwan to see merit in unification. Confronted with Beijing's "two-handed" approach since the mid-1990s—the "soft" hand of-fering economic and political incentives and the "hard" hand wielding military threats—Taiwan's electorate is too distracted by the belligerent ways in which Beijing has sought to quash independence to view with equanimity all the PRC may have put on the table to encourage unification. Even with Ma Ying-jeou as president and Hu Jintao emphasizing mutual benefit in cross-strait ties, Taiwan was sufficiently concerned about the true intentions of the PRC that it sought advanced armaments from the United States.

Against this backdrop, Beijing's appropriation of the U.S. Civil War narrative plays in Taiwan as an assertion by the PRC that it is the Union to which Taiwan must remain subordinate. Beijing's invocation of Lincoln's use of force and the invective that is so often directed by PRC statesmen, media, and academic analysts toward those in Taiwan who wish to remain autonomous leaves them to discount as a ploy any goodwill extended by Beijing. In sum, the insecurity that may drive the PRC civilian and military leadership to hail Lincoln's use of force as the virtuous defense of unity has the unintended effect of deepening the chasm between Beijing and Taipei, giving Taiwan even more reason to seek separation. For it to be otherwise, Beijing would have to appeal to the populace of Taiwan to make manifest benefits—other than the expectation that it would no longer need to fear attack by the PRC—that might accrue to Taiwan, were the island community prepared to give up a degree of the autonomy and independence it has long enjoyed. To date, Beijing has been far more successful demonstrating its capacity to do harm to an independent Taiwan than it has been in making evident the benefits that would flow from the unification of Taiwan and the mainland territory of China.

Another consequence of the PRC's misconstruction of the U.S. Civil War and of Lincoln's attitude toward force is the entrenchment of sentiments in the PRC—as well as in Taiwan—that undermine the possibility of compromise by Beijing. Where territorial disputes are at stake, the risk of escalation to armed conflict is great.[33] To avoid that path, parties to the dispute must either be prepared to compromise or delay resolution until one has amassed such a preponderance of power that the other capitulates. With the apparently equanimous Hu Jintao leading the PRC and Ma Ying-jeou seeking a "diplomatic truce" in cross-strait relations, the temperature in relations between Beijing and Taipei has dropped greatly from the days when Lee Teng-hui and Chen Shui-bian incited Beijing's ire. Lincoln's resort to force is less often cited with reference to Taiwan than it was—although the March 2008 demonstrations in Tibet provoked Beijing to do so in a different context.[34] Yet despite the improvement in cross-strait dialogue, the architecture of the underlying controversy remains unchanged.

A survey of attitudes in the PRC conducted by the Zogby polling organization for the New York–based Committee of 100 suggests that "the majority in China believe that the Taiwan issue will eventually be resolved through peaceful unification as a result of expanded cross-strait exchange and communication. A majority or plurality of the Chinese public and elites are optimistic about the future of the Taiwan problem and believe that the issue is evolving toward a peaceful resolution."[35] The PRC seems less receptive to other outcomes, including protracted division. Beijing certainly evinces no intention to compromise on the matter of China's sovereignty over Taiwan.

Where attitudes about a territorial dispute have become entrenched—as is certainly the case in the cross-strait dispute—"factors contributing to dispute resolution must run counter to the institutionalizing tendencies of these disputes"; otherwise they persist indefinitely and the longer they persist, the more likely it is that armed conflict will result.[36]

Such disputes have been and can be resolved without resort to arms. Doing so, though, demands that the disputants adjust their ways of thinking about the nature of their dispute or the territory at issue. Such a change may emerge "when systemic shock, technological shock, or regime change alters the power parity [between disputants], value of territory, or identity of the parties to the dispute."[37] Naturally, such changes cannot be anticipated, nor can one be certain what effect they will have.

Entrenched disputes may also be resolved when a national leader emerges as an "idea entrepreneur." For leaders to succeed in redirecting their people from the habits of thought that have entrenched a dispute over territory they must "succeed in reconfiguring perceptions of the disputed territory among their constituencies."[38] The longer and harder Beijing works to institutionalize a fixed view of Taiwan as seeking to divide China the deeper the PRC leadership digs itself into a rhetorical hole out of which it will be ever more difficult to climb.

In one sense, history really does not matter at the negotiating table. Resolution of outstanding territorial disputes occurs in spite of irreconcilable historical narratives. Disputants do not sit down to negotiate, compare historical accounts, and then agree to settle their territorial dispute when one side persuades the other of the superiority of its historical claim. Differences about the past and the grievances to which they give rise remain.

Yet historical narratives and the associations that are made between a given account of history and justice do matter in conditioning a population to see reason—or no reason—to compromise. If the leadership of the PRC is powerful enough to effect a solution to the cross–Taiwan Strait controversy by fiat and without concern for public reaction, then this issue is moot. However, there are many indications in the PRC press and from the PRC leadership itself that

Beijing has become increasingly aware of and responsive to "public opinion" where the question of Taiwan—among other sensitive matters touching on China's national pride—is concerned.

Thus, the nature of the PRC argument about its sovereignty over Taiwan, the invocation of Abraham Lincoln as a model of a national leader prepared to use force to preserve the Union, and the way that the PRC leadership has framed the question of Taiwan's status as a matter of secession are all factors that encourage the PRC policy and intellectual elites to resist compromise. This makes the prospect of a peaceful resolution to the cross-strait controversy still seem remote and the prospect of armed conflict still seem possible.

Notes

1. "Full Text: Fifty Years of Democratic Reform in Tibet," *Xinhua* (Beijing), Mar. 2, 2009, http://news.xinhuanet.com/english/2009-03/02/content_10928003.htm, accessed Jan. 29, 2010.

2. Emma Jinhua Teng, *Taiwan's Imagined Geography: Chinese Colonial Travel Writing and Pictures, 1683–1895, Harvard East Asian Monographs* 230 (Cambridge: Harvard University Asia Center and Harvard University Press, 2004).

3. "Taiwan Pursues 'Mutual non-denial' with China," *China Post* (Taipei), Sept. 5, 2008, http://www.chinapost.com.tw/taiwan/china-taiwan%20relations/2008/09/05/173277/ Taiwan-pursues.htm, accessed Dec. 23, 2009.

4. Quoted in Lyon Sharman, *Sun Yat-sen: His Life and Its Meaning* (Stanford: Stanford University Press, 1934), 271. The passage attributed to Abraham Lincoln is taken from Abraham Lincoln, "Address Delivered at the Dedication of the Cemetery at Gettysburg," in *The Collected Works of Abraham Lincoln*, 11 vols., ed. Roy Basler (New Brunswick: Rutgers University Press, 1953–55), 7:18–23.

5. The constitution of the ROC was adopted by the national assembly on December 25, 1946, promulgated on January 1, 1947, and effective as of December 25, 1947 (*Republic of China Yearbook, 1998* [Taipei: Government Information Office, 1998], 669).

6. Ruan Ming, "From Mao to Jiang: The Saga of China," *Taipei Times*, Oct. 1, 1999, http://www.taipeitimes.com/News/insight/archives/1999/10/01/4722, accessed Jan. 29, 2010.

7. Steve Mufson, "China's Deng Xiaoping Is Dead at 92; Party Chief Jiang Zemin, 70, Holds Reins but Faces Tests," *Washington Post*, Feb. 20, 1997, A01.

8. "Text of Press Conference of President Clinton and Chinese Premier Zhu Rongji in the Old Executive Office Building, Transcribed by the Federal Document Clearing House," *AP Newswire*, Apr. 8, 1999.

9. Gu Ping, "Analysis of Sino-U.S. Relations: In Friendship Both Benefit; If Friendship Breaks Both Suffer," *Renmin Ribao,* May 31, 2001.

10. David Herbert Donald, *Lincoln* (New York: Simon and Schuster, 1995), 395.

11. Abraham Lincoln, "Second Annual Message to Congress," Dec. 1, 1862, in *Collected Works,* 5:527.

12. Lincoln, "Second Annual Message to Congress," 5:528.

13. Lincoln, "Second Annual Message to Congress," 5:529.

14. Donald, *Lincoln,* 206–9.

15. The biblical passage reads: "And Jesus knew their thoughts, and said unto them, every kingdom divided against itself is brought to desolation; and every city or house divided against itself shall not stand."

16. "*Washington Post* interview with Premier Wen Jiabao," *People's Daily Online,* Nov. 24, 2003, http://english.peopledaily.com.cn/200311/23/eng20031123_128838.shtml, accessed Dec. 23, 2009.

17. Abraham Lincoln, "First Inaugural Address," Mar. 4, 1861, in *Collected Works,* 4:253.

18. I am indebted to Steven M. Goldstein for elucidating this point.

19. Barbara W. Tuchman, *Stilwell and the American Experience in China: 1911–1945* (New York: Macmillan, 1970), 463.

20. Kenneth E. Shewmaker, *Americans and Chinese Communists: 1927–1945, A Persuading Encounter* (Ithaca: Cornell University Press, 1971), 158–79.

21. "Directive of the CCP on Diplomatic Work (18 August 1944)" in *The Rise to Power of the Chinese Communist Party,* ed. Tony Saich (Armonk, N.Y.: M. E. Sharpe, 1996), 1212.

22. "Directive of the CCP on Diplomatic Work (18 August 1944)," 1212.

23. Lincoln, "First Inaugural Address." 4:260.

24. Abraham Lincoln, "Message to Congress," July 4, 1861, quoted in Thomas J. Pressly, "Bullets and Ballots: Lincoln and the 'Right of Revolution,'" *American Historical Review* 67:3 (1962): 658.

25. Pressly, "Bullets and Ballots," 659; Donald, *Lincoln,* 268–69.

26. Lincoln, "First Inaugural Address," 4:261.

27. Richard C. Bush III, "Cross-strait Relations Improve; China Still Deploys Missiles," *China Times* (Taipei), June 27, 2009.

28. Zeng Jia, "An Expert Points Out That the United States Should Not Underestimate the Danger of Chen Shui-bian's 'Taiwan Independence' Provocation," *Zhongguo Xinwen She* (Beijing), Nov. 21, 2003; "Cong Meiguo Nanbei zhanzheng kan Zhongguo tongyi" [View the unification of China from the perspective of the U.S. Civil War], CCTV, Dec. 21, 2003, http://www.cctv.com/program/hxla/20031222/102109.shtml, accessed Dec. 23, 2009; Lincoln, "Second Inaugural Address," 8:332.

29. Matthew 18:7.

30. Lincoln, "Second Inaugural Address," 8:332.

31. Donald, *Lincoln*, 567.

32. Lu I-ming, "The Aggression in China's Goodwill," *Taipei Times*, Dec. 1, 2009, 8, http://www.taipeitimes.com/News/editorials/archives/2009/12/01/2003459841, accessed Jan. 29. 2010.

33. John Vasquez and Marie T. Henehan, "Territorial Disputes and the Probability of War, 1816–1992," *Journal of Peace Research* 38:2 (2001): 123–138.

34. The spokesman for the PRC Ministry of Foreign Affairs responded in a press conference to a comment by an American official about abuses of human rights in Tibet. The spokesman cited Lincoln's inaugural address of 1861 in which he noted that "in view of the Constitution and the laws the Union is unbroken." The spokesman concluded, "If the official can take a closer look at what President Lincoln said in this address, he will be able to better understand the resolve and efforts of the Chinese Government and people to maintain national unity, sovereignty and territorial integrity. Please stop applying double standards here," http://www.fmprc.gov.cn/eng/xwfw/s2510/t469115.htm, accessed Dec. 23, 2009.

35. Committee of 100, "Hope and Fear: American and Chinese Attitudes Toward Each Other Parallel Survey on Issues Concerning U.S.-China Relations," Dec. 2007, 7.

36. Ron E. Hassner, "The Path to Intractability: Time and Entrenchment of Territorial Disputes," *International Security* 31:3 (Winter 2006–7): 137.

37. Hassner, "The Path to Intractability," 137.

38. Hassner, "The Path to Intractability," 138.

CONTRIBUTORS

DAVID ARMITAGE is the Lloyd C. Blankfein Professor of History at Harvard University. Among his eleven books to date are *The Ideological Origins of the British Empire* (2000), *The Declaration of Independence: A Global History* (2007), and *The Age of Revolutions in Global Context, c. 1760–1840* (coeditor, 2010). He is currently working on a study of ideas of civil war from Rome to Iraq.

ROBERT E. BONNER teaches history at Dartmouth College. His major publications include *Colors and Blood: Flag Passions of the Confederate South* (2002), *The Soldier's Pen: Firsthand Impressions of the Civil War* (2006), and *Mastering America: Southern Slaveholders and the Crisis of American Nationhood* (2009). He is currently researching the geopolitics of American slavery and writing a biography of Alexander H. Stephens, the Georgia politician who identified slavery as the "cornerstone" of the Confederate States of America.

BRUNO COPPIETERS is professor of political science at the Vrije Universiteit Brussel (Free University of Brussels). His published works deal mainly with federalism and conflicts over sovereignty in the Caucasus and the Balkans. He has coedited the following books: *Contextualizing Secession: Normative Studies in Comparative Perspective* (2003), *Statehood and Security: Georgia After the Rose Revolution* (2005), *Moral Constraints on War: Principles and Cases* (2nd ed., 2008).

CHARLES B. DEW teaches the history of the American South at Williams College, where he is Ephraim Williams Professor of American History. He is the author of *Ironmaker to the Confederacy: Joseph R. Anderson and the Tredegar Iron Works* (rev. ed., 1999), *Bond of Iron: Master and Slave at Buffalo Forge* (1994), and *Apostles of Disunion: Southern Secession Commissioners and the Causes of the Civil War* (2001).

DON H. DOYLE is the McCausland Professor of History at the University of South Carolina. Among his publications are *Nations Divided: America, Italy and the South-*

ern Question (2002) and *Nationalism in the New World* (2006). He is currently writing a book on the international dimensions of the American Civil War.

SUSAN-MARY GRANT is professor of American history at Newcastle University in England. She is the author of *North over South: Northern Nationalism and American Identity in the Antebellum Era* (2000) and *The War for a Nation: The American Civil War* (2006) and editor of *Legacy of Disunion: The Enduring Significance of the American Civil War* (2003) and *Themes of the American Civil War: The War Between the States* (2009). She is the current editor of the journal *American Nineteenth Century History*.

PAUL KUBICEK is professor and chair of the Department of Political Science at Oakland University. He has written numerous articles and book chapters on postcommunist states. His most recent books are *Organized Labor in Postcommunist States* (2004) and *A History of Ukraine* (2008). He is currently working on a project on processes of decolonization in Central Asia.

MARGARET MOORE is professor in the Political Studies Department at Queen's University, Kingston, Canada. Among her publications are *Foundations of Liberalism* (1993) and *Ethics of Nationalism* (2001).

RAPHAEL CHIJIOKE NJOKU is associate professor of African history at the University of Louisville, Kentucky. He is the author of *Culture and Customs of Morocco* (2005) and *African Cultural Values: Igbo Political Leadership in Colonial Nigeria 1900–1966* (2006) and coeditor of *Missions, States, and European Expansion in Africa* (2007), *War and Peace in Africa* (2010), and *Africa and the Wider World* (2010). Njoku is currently writing a book on African masquerades and carnival of the African diaspora.

ALEKSANDAR PAVKOVIĆ teaches political theory and comparative politics at the University of Macau in China and Macquarie University in Sydney. His main research interests are the theory and practice of secession and the uses of political violence. His publications include *The Ashgate Research Companion on Secession* (with Peter Radan, forthcoming), *Creating New States* (2007, with Peter Radan), *Patriotism: Philosophical and Political Perspectives* (2007, coedited with Igor Primoratz), and *The Fragmentation of Yugoslavia* (2000).

PAUL QUIGLEY is lecturer in American history at the University of Edinburgh. He received his PhD from the University of North Carolina at Chapel Hill and is currently completing a book on nationalism in the Civil War–era American South for Oxford University Press.

PETER RADAN is professor of law at Macquarie University. Among his publications are *The Break-up of Yugoslavia in International Law* (2002), and (with Aleksandar Pavković) *Creating New States, Theory and Practice of Secession* (2007). He is currently coediting (with Aleksandar Pavković) *The Ashgate Research Companion on Secession*.

ANDRÉS RESÉNDEZ is a professor in the History Department at the University of California, Davis. Among his publications are *Changing National Identities at the Frontier: Texas and New Mexico, 1800–1850* (2005) and *A Land So Strange: The Epic Journey of Cabeza de Vaca* (2007).

TERRY RUGELEY is professor of Mexican and Latin American history at the University of Oklahoma. He is the author of *Yucatán's Maya Peasantry and the Origins of the Caste War* (1996), *Of Wonders and Wise Men: Religion and Popular Cultures in Southeast Mexico* (2001), *Maya Wars* (2001), *Alone in Mexico: The Astonishing Travels of Karl Heller, 1845–1848* (2007), and *Rebellion Now and Forever: Mayas, Hispanics, and Caste War Violence, 1800–1880* (2009).

PETER SLUGLETT is professor of Middle Eastern history at the University of Utah, Salt Lake City. Among his publications are *Britain in Iraq: Contriving King and Country* (2007) and (with Marion Farouk-Sluglett), *Iraq since 1958: From Revolution to Dictatorship* (3rd ed., 2001).

FRANK TOWERS teaches U.S. history at the University of Calgary in Alberta, Canada. He is the author of *The Urban South and the Coming of the Civil War* (2004) and coeditor of *New Histories of the Old South: Slavery, Sectionalism, and the Nineteenth-Century's Modern World* (2010). He has also published several essays on politics, labor, and race in the U.S. South.

ALAN M. WACHMAN is on the faculty of the Fletcher School of Law and Diplomacy at Tufts University. Prominent among his publications about China and Taiwan are

Why Taiwan? Geostrategic Rationales for China's Territorial Integrity (2007) and *Taiwan: National Identity and Democratization* (1994). He is currently finishing a book on Mongolia's foreign policy and national security in the context of great power rivalries in Asia.

CHRISTOPHER WELLMAN is professor of philosophy at Washington University in Saint Louis and professorial fellow at the Centre for Philosophy and Public Ethics, Charles Sturt University. Among his books is *A Theory of Secession: The Case for Political Self-Determination* (2005).

STEFAN ZAHLMANN teaches German history, comparative history, and media history at the University of Konstanz in Germany. He has recently published a book on the Confederacy and the German Democratic Republic, *Autobiographische Verarbeitungen gesellschaftlichen Scheiterns* (2009), and is currently working on a book about Americans and Germans during the American Civil War and World War I.

INDEX

LaVergne, TN USA
06 October 2010

199698LV00003B/2/P